South East Asia: A Guide to Reference Material

Regional Reference Guides

General Editor:
John McIlwaine
School of Library, Archive and Information Studies

No.1: Africa: A Guide to Reference Material
JOHN MCILWAINE

No.2: South East Asia: A Guide to Reference Material
ANDREW DALBY

South East Asia: A Guide to Reference Material

Andrew Dalby

Librarian
The London Goodenough Trust
for Overseas Graduates

HANS ZELL PUBLISHERS

London • Melbourne • Munich • New York • 1993

Hans Zell Publishers
is an imprint of Bowker-Saur Ltd, a division of Reed Reference Publishing.
60 Grosvenor Street, London W1X 9DA, United Kingdom.

British Library Cataloguing in Publication Data

Dalby, Andrew
    South East Asia : Guide to Reference Material -
    (Regional Reference Guides: Vol. 2)
    I. Title II. Series
    016.959

    ISBN 1-873836-00-7

Library of Congress Cataloging-in-Publication Data

Dalby, A. K. (Andrew Kenneth)
    South East Asia : a guide to reference material / Andrew Dalby
    316p. 240cm. -- (Regional reference guides : no. 2)
    Includes bibliographical references.
    ISBN 1-873836-00-7
    1. Asia, Southeastern--Bibliography   I. Title.   II. Series.
23221.D35   1993
[DS521]
016.959--dc20   93-7674
                                                                              CIP

Cover design by Robin Caira

Printed on acid-free paper.

Printed and bound in Great Britain
by Antony Rowe Ltd., Chippenham, Wiltshire.

Contents

Introduction   vii

Scope and arrangement; Some other bibliographies; The format;
Acknowledgements

General and national surveys   1

*Within each country section, general narrative surveys are followed by annual
reports, statistics, and official and commercial almanacs and directories*

SOUTH EAST ASIA   1
BURMA   5
THAILAND   14
INDOCHINA   21
CAMBODIA   26
LAOS   28
VIETNAM   32
MALAYSIA   39
SINGAPORE   46
BRUNEI   50
INDONESIA   51
PHILIPPINES   59

Biography   66

*In this and the following subject sections, entries are sub-arranged
geographically in the sequence that is set out above*

Historical materials   83

Topography   105

ATLASES   105
INDEX-GAZETTEERS   112
GUIDE BOOKS, DESCRIPTIVE GAZETTEERS   113
NAVIGATION GUIDES   139
FRONTIERS   142

Fauna, flora, natural resources 143

GENERAL 143
FAUNA 145
Mammals 145; Birds 147; Fish, fisheries 149; Other animals 152
FLORA 154
Major floras 154; Local and specialized lists of plants 159; Trees,
forestry 167; Useful plants, food plants 171; Materia medica 175
MINERAL RESOURCES 178

Languages and peoples 180

GENERAL SURVEYS AND LANGUAGE ATLASES 180
NATIONAL LANGUAGES 190
*Within each language section, monolingual dictionaries and encyclopaedias are
followed by bilingual dictionaries; specialized dictionaries; idioms and phrases;
language and script*
Burmese 191; Khmer 196; Lao 200; Malay 203; Pilipino 212; Thai 214;
Vietnamese 217
MINORITY LANGUAGES OF LITERATURE 227
Achehnese 227; Balinese 228; Batak 229; Buginese and Makasarese
230; Cham 231; Javanese 231; Madurese 233; Minangkabau 233; Mon
234; Shan 235; Sundanese 235; White Tai 236; Tai Yuan 237
EXTERNAL LANGUAGES OF RELIGION AND POLITICS 238
Arabic 238; Chinese, Pali, Sanskrit 238; English 239
SOME LANGUAGES OF ORAL CULTURE 240

Index of authors, titles and subjects 253

NOTE. Index entries and all cross-references throughout this work relate to
entry numbers, not to page numbers. Entries **1-30** are to be found in the
introduction; entries **31-853** form the main sequence.

Introduction

This is a selective guide to sources of reference about south east Asia. I hope that by bringing works of this kind together in one list it will help researchers, librarians and others to find information quickly.

Books listed here are reasonably comprehensive within their terms of reference; they contain facts rather than opinions; and their facts are arranged systematically or alphabetically or in the form of tables, charts or maps. Such an arrangement promotes quick reference. The aim of this book is to promote it further by identifying works that can help a range of users-- sometimes a wider range than the authors and publishers foresaw -- and by clarifying, where necessary, the principles on which these works are organized and indexed.

Those working in depth in a single subject field, or on a single south east Asian country, will naturally also look further, to the local and specialized bibliographies that lead to the wealth of books and papers on many aspects of south east Asian studies. But even specialists will find guidance here: keys to reference books on neighbouring countries and in related subjects, sources of sometimes vital comparative material and background information.

The countries of south east Asia have much in common in ecology and civilization, but they are sharply divided by history. Politics and language have erected boundaries that continue to confine research and restrict comparative study. I hope this book will contribute to the lowering of the boundaries.

SCOPE AND ARRANGEMENT

The languages of reference books

Reference works on south east Asia are to be found in Burmese, Chinese, Dutch, English, French, German, Japanese, Khmer, Lao, Malay (including Bahasa Indonesia and Bahasa Malaysia), Pilipino (including Tagalog), Russian, Spanish, Thai, Vietnamese -- and of course in many other languages. This book cites and analyses books in all these languages on occasion: but it is aimed at users who can read English, the world's most widely used second language, and I have weighted the selection in favour of works in English, as more likely to be useful to the greater number. When citing works in other languages I have usually given a rough translation of the title and I have tried to give very practical guidance on contents and arrangement. Reference works not in English, and likely because of their opaque arrangement or lack of indexing to be wholly unapproachable to those unfamiliar with the language in which they are written, are rather less likely to be included.

The main divisions and their scope

The list begins with a selection of general country surveys, a publishing genre that has been growing ever since the European explorations: and Vietnam exemplifies an east Asian tradition of such works independent of European influence. In the age of global strategy, country surveys are published by national governments, by foreign governments for diplomatic or military purposes, and by commercial publishers. Their emphases differ, from the cultural and historical to the political and economic.

This general chapter is subdivided by countries, as set out in the table of contents; and **the same sequence of countries is followed within each subject division throughout the rest of the book.** But here, in each country section, the general country surveys (typically intended to retain their currency for more than a single year) are followed by a selection of official reports, statistics, and government and commercial almanacs and directories, all these often being annual publications. These materials are all brought together in the first chapter because of the considerable overlaps among them: where the almanacs and statistical yearbooks fail, the general country surveys may help to fill the gap.

Biographical sources (current and historical) and some historical materials follow; then topographical sources, which include guide books, the descriptive gazetteers on which some colonial governments spent so much effort, atlases and navigation guides.

The remaining chapters deal with information that falls less readily into national divisions. The first covers natural resources (fauna, flora, minerals) and their uses. As elsewhere, the list is confined to a selection of works which are most comprehensive and most likely to be convenient for quick reference to a range of readers. For further information on floras the user will probably consult (1) D. G. Frodin: *Guide to standard floras of the world.* Cambridge: Cambridge University Press, 1984. 619 pp.

The last chapter covers ethnography, and the languages of the region. Major dictionaries and some more specialized reference books have been selected for listing under each national language and under each local language that has a literary culture. There are hundreds of languages in south east Asia which have no tradition of written literature; when I found a comprehensive, reasonably definitive dictionary for such languages, I listed it, but, beyond this, users seeking information on local languages will be able to look to several specialized bibliographies: (2) Franklin E. Huffman: *Bibliography and index of mainland Southeast Asian languages and linguistics.* New Haven: Yale University Press, 1986. 640 pp. 0-300-03679-5, alphabetical by author with detailed subject index; (3) Yu. Ya. Plam, editor: *Bibliografiya lingvisticheskikh rabot po yazykam Yugo-Vostochnoi Azii.* Moscow: Nauka, 1988. 2 v. [Bibliography of linguistic research on the languages of south east Asia] in a subject arrangement with interspersed sectional indexes of names; and also Sebeok [607], Parkin [608] on Austroasiatic languages, and a series of surveys of research on languages of Indonesia, 631, 712.

The selection of official serials

In certain fields this list is especially selective. Only the major statistical yearbooks for each country, and some historical collections of statistics, will be found. As for the great range of more detailed statistical publications, there was no need to list them here because a recent guide has appeared, (4) Jennifer Brewster, Anne Booth: *Bibliography of statistical sources on Southeast Asia, c. 1750-1990.* Canberra: Australian National University, Research School of Pacific Studies, Economic History of Southeast Asia Project, 1990. 120 pp. (Sources of the economic history of Southeast Asia, Data paper series, 1.) There is some useful information to be found also in (5) Gloria Westfall: *Bibliography of official statistical yearbooks and bulletins.* Alexandria, Virginia: Chadwyck-Healey, 1986. 247 pp. 0-85964-124-4, and in (6) Joan M. Harvey: *Statistics Asia and Australasia.* Beckenham: CBD Research, 1983. 440 pp. 0-900246-41-3. Second edition: first published 1974.

The annual reports of colonial territories, nowadays sometimes still published in the form of official yearbooks, are also listed selectively. Brewster and Booth give more details on some of these: occasionally useful, to, is (7) Thomas F. Willer: *Southeast Asian references in the British parliamentary papers, 1801-1972/73: an index.* Athens, Ohio: Ohio University Center for International Studies, Southeast Asia Program, 1978. 88 pp. (Papers in international studies, Southeast Asia series, 48.)

The publications of national censuses (often to be found summarized in the statistical yearbooks and the country surveys) are not included here. For guidance on them, the user can look to: (8) Eliane Domschke, Doreen S. Goyer: *The handbook of national population censuses: Africa and Asia.* New York: Greenwood, 1986. 1032 pp. 0-313-25361-7.

Among the directories a few government organization manuals have been included. For more, readers will probably consult (9) Vladimir M. Palic: *Government publications ... Government organization manuals.* Oxford:

Pergamon Press [1977]. 553 pp.; **(10)** Richard I. Korman: *Checklist of government directories, lists and rosters.* Westport: Meckler; Cambridge: Chadwyck-Healey, 1982. 51 pp. 0-930466-38-1.

World reference books

Reference books covering a very wide geographical area -- the whole world, or the whole of Asia, or the whole Third World -- are generally excluded from this list. South east Asia inevitably makes up only a small part of their contents, and they are usually easily found on library reference shelves.

Examples are:
(11) *The Times atlas of the world: comprehensive edition.* London: Times Books, 1992. 221 pp. 0-7230-0492-7. (Maps by Bartholomew.) 9th edition. This gives better topographical coverage, for most countries of the region, than any regional atlas;
(12) *Asia yearbook.* Hong Kong: Far Eastern Economic Review, 1972- . Earlier title: *Far eastern economic review yearbook.* 1960-1971;
(13) *Statistical yearbook for Asia and the Pacific.* Bangkok: United Nations Economic and Social Commission for Asia and the Pacific, 1973-. This superseded: *Statistical yearbook for Asia and the Far East.* Bangkok: United Nations Economic and Social Commission for Asia and the Far East;
(14) Ainslie T. Embree, editor: *Encyclopedia of Asian history.* New York: Scribner; London: Collier Macmillan, 1988. 4 v.;
(14a) *Bowker-Saur who's who in Asian and Australasian politics.* London: Bowker-Saur, 1991. 475 pp. 0-86291-593-7.

Reference books on activities and facilities elsewhere in the world relating to south east Asia have also been excluded. As an example of such sources, usually easily found in reference libraries, one may cite:
(15) J. D. Pearson: *A guide to manuscripts and documents in the British Isles relating to South and South-East Asia.* London: Mansell, 1989-90. 2 v. This supplements: M. D. Wainwright, N. Matthews: *A guide to Western manuscripts and documents in the British Isles relating to south and south east Asia.* Oxford: Oxford University Press, 1965. 432 pp;
(15a) Brenda E. Moon: *Survey of library resources.* Hull: Brynmor Jones Library, University of Hull, 1973. 162 pp. (South-East Asia Library Group). This includes relatively few collections from south east Asia itself.
(15b) Geoffrey Roper, editor: *World survey of Islamic manuscripts.* London: Al-Furqan Islamic Heritage Foundation, 1992- . Vol. 1. 1-873992-04-1 (Distributed by Brill, Leiden). 3 volumes are planned of this survey, arranged in alphabetical order of countries. Vol. 1 includes Brunei (pp. 115-120: 5 collections). Unfortunately little information was forthcoming from

Indonesia (pp. 443-454: 9 collections). The chapter on Malaysia, to appear in vol. 2, will cover 19 collections. Finally, no user should overlook the *South East Asia Library Group newsletter*, an indispensable source of information on activities and publications on all aspects of south east Asia.

Exploration reports

Since country surveys are included here, one might look here too for reports of exploration: these are in a sense antecedent to reference books. But they are almost by definition not definitive descriptions of the countries explored: the need for exploration demonstrated that definitive descriptions could not yet be written. The literature of exploration in south east Asia is vast: see, for example, the relevant sections of Cordier's bibliography [242]. Yet some of the later publications in this genre include so much in the way of maps, illustrations, tabulated information and appendices that they begin to be of reference use. They include (16) Francis Garnier and others: *Voyage d'exploration en Indo-Chine effectué pendant les années 1866, 1867 et 1868 par une commission française présidée par M. le capitaine de frégate Doudart de Lagrée*. Paris: Hachette, 1873. 2 v. and atlas. [Exploration in Indo-China carried out in 1866-8 by a French team led by Capt. Doudart de Lagrée]; (17) Auguste Pavie and others: *Mission Pavie: Indo-Chine 1879-1895*. Paris: Leroux, 1898-1911. 9 v. and atlas. [The Pavie expedition in Indo-China, 1879-95]], which superseded: Auguste Pavie and others: *Mission Pavie: exploration de l'Indo-Chine. Mémoires et documents*. Paris: Leroux, 1894. 2 v. in 3. Vol. 2 part 2 of this set, not republished, was: M. Massie: *Dictionnaire laotien*. Paris: Leroux, 1894. 127 pp. [Laotian dictionary.] On the explorer see: J.-L. Gheerbrandt: *Pavie*. Paris, 1948. 154 pp.; (18) Nelson Annandale, Herbert C. Robinson and others: *Fasciculi Malayenses: anthropological and zoological results of an expedition to Perak and the Siamese Malay states, 1901-1902*. London: Longmans, Green; Williams & Norgate, 1903-6. 5 parts and supplement. Published for the University Press of Liverpool. [Malay pamphlets.]

Some subjects, in the south east Asian context, have not lent themselves to setting out in reference books. Where quick-reference materials appeared to me not to exist, I have not pretended that they do. Thus literature and religion, for example, though they do figure in the index, get relatively small space in this list. For such subjects, however, the more general surveys and encyclopaedias that are listed here are not without their use. I look forward to the bibliography of Buddhism now in preparation by Craig Jamieson of Cambridge University Library.

SOME OTHER BIBLIOGRAPHIES

The guidelines for the series 'Regional Reference Guides' exclude bibliographies (though, naturally, many of the works listed here do include bibliographies among other materials). But it will be useful in this introduction to list one or two recent bibliographical works to which readers can go when hunting for information beyond what can be found in the reference sources dealt with here. These bibliographies have all been helpful in the initial preparation of the present work: so has Cordier's *Bibliotheca indosinica* [242], indispensable for its coverage of older publications.

South east Asia as a whole

(19) G. Raymond Nunn: *Asia: reference works, a select annotated guide*. London: Mansell, 1980. 365 pp. Annotated bibliography arranged under headings for regions and countries. This will be found especially useful for its listing of selected bibliographies; (20) G. Raymond Nunn: *Southeast Asian periodicals: an international union list*. London: Mansell, 1977. 456 pp. This is useful for its inclusiveness, listing directories and official publications such as annual reports of government departments. There are also some examples of such reference works as telephone directories and railway timetables. The arrangement, under librarians' conventional names of issuing bodies rather than under titles in many cases, may be found difficult to work with.

The countries of south east Asia

These are the most recent general bibliographies for the study of each south east Asian country:
(21) Sylvia C. Engelen Krausse, Gerald H. Krausse: *Brunei*. Oxford: Clio Press, 1988. 251 pp. (World bibliographical series, 93);
(22) Patricia M. Herbert: *Burma*. Oxford: Clio Press, 1991. 329 pp. 1-85109-088-6. (World bibliographical series, 132);
(23) Walter Aschmoneit: *Kampuchea: sozialhistorische Bibliographie zu Kampuchea von der Vorgeschichte bis 1954*. Münster: SZD-Verlag, 1981. 184 pp.;
(24) Herman C. Kemp: *Annotated bibliography of bibliographies on Indonesia*. Leiden: KITLV Press, 1990. 433 pp. (Koninklijk Instituut voor Taal-, Land- en Volkenkunde. Bibliographical series, 17); and on Timor see Rowland [209]; sometimes useful for West Irian is Fraiser McConnell: *Papua New Guinea*. Oxford: Clio, 1988. 379 pp. 1-85109-030-4. (World bibliographical series, 90);
(25) Helen Cordell: *Laos*. Oxford: Clio Press, 1991. 217 pp. (World bibliographical series, 133.); see also: Pierre-Bernard Lafont: *Bibliographie du*

Laos. Paris: Ecole Française d'Extrême-Orient, 1964-78. 2 v. (Publications de l'Ecole Française d'Extrême-Orient, 50);

(26) Ian Brown, Rajeswary Ampalavanar: *Malaysia*. Oxford: Clio Press, 1986. 308 pp. (World bibliographical series, 12); see also Heussler **[278]**;

(27) Jim Richardson: *Philippines*. Oxford: Clio Press, 1989. 373 pp. (World bibliographical series, 106); for older material see: A. P. C. Griffin, T. H. Pardo de Tavera and others: *Bibliography of the Philippine Islands*. Washington: Government Printing Office, 1903. 397 + 439 pp.; see also *Philippine studies* **[361]**;

(28) Stella R. Quah, Jon S. T. Quah: *Singapore*. Oxford: Clio Press, 1988. 258 pp. (World bibliographical series, 95);

(29) Michael Watts: *Thailand*. Oxford: Clio Press, 1986. 275 pp. (World bibliographical series, 65);

(30) Michael Cotter: *Vietnam: a guide to reference sources*. Boston: Hall, 1977. 272 pp.

I have found all these bibliographies useful, and I have cited them on occasion as sources for further information on works that I could not examine or did not have room to analyse in detail. But the different purpose of the present list is sufficiently signalled by the relatively small overlap between it and them.

THE FORMAT

A single numerical sequence of entries -- the bold numerals -- runs throughout the book and is used in cross references and in the index.

Bibliographical descriptions are brief, but sub-titles are often given very fully if they form a list of contents or a statement of the scope and arrangement of the work. For works that have titles in several languages, all titles in Roman script are given fully, to assist searching in other bibliographies and library catalogues, but alternative titles in non-Roman scripts may be omitted. An ISBN is given where available: but only one for each title, and this will tend to be the ISBN for the hardback issue in the country of first publication. Unchanged and facsimile reprints have been mentioned where noted, but no attempt has been made to list them comprehensively.

Early reference books retain their uses for those working in a historical context: thus, in describing them as 'superseded', I am taking the publisher's viewpoint and not the potential user's. This said, however, many users will certainly be looking for the latest material and not the earliest. Therefore, within each subject division and geographical subdivision, entries in this list will normally begin with the latest relevant work and end with the earliest.

Likewise, within each entry, the fullest description is usually allotted to the **latest** substantive edition. The extent of updating between editions (an important piece of information for users of both earlier and latest editions!) is stated quite fully when possible. As will be seen, I have indicated explicitly when I have some doubt whether a publication that I have seen described as a 'new edition' has undergone much substantive renewal.

Periodicals librarians know that the time spent on cataloguing a title is normally in inverse proportion to its usefulness. The priorities of government departments (as publishers of reports and statistics) and of the producers of commercial directories are quite different from those of bibliographers: and those of bibliographers are themselves rather different from those of users! I decided to put a firm limit on the time (and ink) to be expended on the tracing and listing of publication dates and changes of title. I believe that by concentrating on the selection and listing of serials of most general usefulness, and by giving a reliable indication of their relationships and succession, I have done something of value.

In the descriptions of works, contents are listed selectively. Pagination is given sometimes as an indication of the general emphasis of the work, sometimes to highlight a particularly detailed or useful section of it. Quotations (from texts, editors' prefaces, or blurbs) are sometimes given when they specify usefully the aims or limitations of a work: such quotations have been freely rearranged and abridged. In describing supplements and superseded editions, the imprint (publisher and place) is omitted when identical with that of the preceding work. If the evidence suggests that the author (whether an individual or an organization) acted as publisher, the place of publication alone is given as imprint.

ACKNOWLEDGEMENTS

I am grateful to friends at Cambridge University Library and the School of Oriental and African Studies, where much of this work was done, for their hospitality; to Maureen, Elizabeth and Rachel, for patience; to John McIlwaine, the series editor, and to Hans Zell, for persisting in publishing; to WordPerfect, used throughout; and to the London Goodenough Trust for Overseas Graduates, which provides, for its librarian as it has for generations of scholars from many parts of the world, an unrivalled environment for study.

And I will be grateful to users of this bibliography who make suggestions for improvements which could be adopted in a second edition.

General and national surveys

Within each country section, general narrative surveys are followed by annual reports, statistics, and official and commercial almanacs and directories.

31

Harald Uhlig: *Südostasien*. Frankfurt am Main: Fischer Taschenbuch Verlag, 1988. 719 pp. 3-596-26379-4.
(Fischer Länderkunde, 4.)

[South east Asia.] In a paperback series of regional geographies. Sections: The cultural region, pp. 13-231; the states of south east Asia, pp. 232-618. Very brief on Laos (pp. 323-337) but a well-balanced and very solid survey in narrative form, with keywords usefully picked out in italics. Special interest in the relationship of ethnicity to land use; note e.g. diagrams on this topic relevant to Thailand and Borneo (pp. 74, 156). Indexes of names and subjects. 37 maps and charts include forest clearance in Thailand (p. 187); oil and gas (p. 212).

Superseded: Harald Uhlig, editor: *Südostasien, austral-pazifischer Raum.* 1975. 491 pp. 3-436-0196-3. South east Asia takes up pp. 19-358 of this work.

32

Cyclopedia of South-East Asia. Tokyo: Heibonsha, 1986. 511 pp. 4-582-12604-9.

A small-format encyclopaedia in Japanese (headwords also in English or romanized, but no English index). Covers history, current affairs, culture, literature. Brief, factual articles, none exceeding 1 page. Statistical tables pp. 462-8; time charts and chronological table pp. 470-479; hypsometric maps (Japanese and Roman scripts) on endpapers.

33

Southeast Asian regional transport survey. Singapore: Straits Times Press, 1972-3. 3 v. in 5.
Asian Development Bank. Prepared by Arthur D. Little Inc. and associated consultants.

Report of a survey undertaken just before 1970, principally concerned with planning for the 1970s and 1980s. Covers Indonesia, Laos, Malaysia, Philippines, Singapore, South Vietnam, Thailand. The viewpoint is professedly supranational. Much statistical, tabular and map information throughout. Contents:

Book 1: overview. Economic potential of the region; Opportunities and needs; Improvements to seaports, inland transport, air transport, tourism facilities; Regional cooperation opportunities; Recommendations. Appendices include case studies of port, airport and inland transport projects.

Book 2 part 1: Economic potential of the region in detail; Analysis of the inland transport system. Book 2 part 2: Analysis of ports, sea transport and air transport systems.

Book 3 (2 parts): appendices. These include: (Part 1) Population outlook; Sub-national profiles (statistics for major sub-regions of the seven countries); National resource, production and export maps; Agriculture; Fisheries; Vegetable oils; Rubber production; Forestry; Metals; Petroleum; Manufacturing; Tourism. (Part 2): National highway suystems; Rail systems; Rail abandonment on Java; Survey of major ports; Ocean freight rates; Air traffic forecasts.

34

Charles A. Fisher: *South-East Asia: a social, economic and political geography*. London: Methuen, 1964. 831 pp.

Second edition. A general survey followed by chapters on individual countries. Rich in maps and statistical tables.

35

Frederick V. Field, editor: *Economic handbook of the Pacific area*. Garden City, N. Y.: Doubleday, Doran, 1934. 649 pp.
For the Institute of Pacific Relations.

Useful for its generous statistical tables. Covers Malaysia, Indochina, Indonesia, Philippines, Thailand among other countries. Weights and measures, pp. 598-610. Contents: Population; Land utilization; Food production and consumption; Transportation; Public finance (pp. 187-318); Capital movements; Trade; International mineral products; International agricultural and textile products.

36

John Crawfurd: *A descriptive dictionary of the Indian islands and adjacent countries*. London, 1856. 459 pp.

'The first encyclopedia of what is now Indonesia, focused upon the Javanese, includes a great deal of material on the Malay Peninsula, the Philippine Archipelago, and mainland South-East Asia, particularly Thailand' (Ricklefs). An alphabetical encyclopedia, partly based on Crawfurd's own earlier works, but citing fresh information from correspondents from as late as 1850. Covers natural history, anthropology, history, government, commerce. 'Siam', 15 pp.; 'Tamarind', 12 lines. Excludes Burma.

Reprinted with introduction by M. C. Ricklefs: Kuala Lumpur: Oxford University Press, 1971. (Oxford in Asia historical reprints.)

See the anonymous review: 'Notice of Mr Crawfurd's Descriptive dictionary' in *Journal of the Indian Archipelago* n. s. vol. 1 (1856) pp. 291-5.

37

William Milburn: *Oriental commerce, or the East India trader's complete guide: containing a geographical and nautical description of the maritime ports of India, China, Japan and neighbouring countries, including the Eastern Islands, and the trading stations on the passage from Europe, with an account of their respective commerce, productions, coins, weights and measures, their port regulations, duties, rates, charges &c., and a description of the commodities imported from thence into Great-Britain and the duties payable thereon, together with a mass of miscellaneous information collected during many years' employment in the East India Service and in the course of seven voyages to India and China.* London: Kingsbury, Parbury and Allen, 1825. 586 pp.

New edition by Thomas Thornton.

First edition, with a different subtitle: London: Black, Parry, 1813. 2 v. This claimed to cover also 'the coasting or country trade from port to port; also the rise and progress of the trade of the various European nations with the eastern world, particularly that of the English East India Company from the discovery of the passage round the Cape of Good Hope to the present period; with an account of the Company's establishments, revenues, debts, assets &c. at home and abroad'. Cited from Cordier [242].

Annuals

38

Southeast Asian affairs. Singapore: Institute of Southeast Asian Studies.

Regional political survey followed by a survey of each country's politics for the preceding year, with additional articles on topical issues: e.g. in the 1991 edition (the 18th annual volume: 320 pp.) Richard P. Cronin, 'Changing dynamics of Japan's interaction with Southeast Asia', pp. 49-68. A few statistical tables.

Almanacs and directories

39

The Far East and Australasia: a survey and reference book of Asia, Australasia and the Pacific. London: Europa Publications.

Annual reference volume, first published 1969. long factual monographs for each country. Sub-sections include: physical and social geography, history, economy, statistics, directory. '23rd edition, 1992.'

40

Major companies of the Far East and Australasia. London: Graham and Trotman.
Edited by Jennifer L. Carr.

Annual: first published under this title 1990. Vol. 1 of each year is devoted to south east Asia. Last seen: 1991/92 ('eighth edition'), published 1991. 1-85333-604-1.

Before 1990 the title was *Major companies of the Far East.* Contents of vol. 1 of the 1987 edition (309 pp.): Brunei; Indonesia, pp. 11-50; Malaysia, pp. 51-111; Philippines, pp. 115-166; Singapore, pp. 169-224; Thailand, pp. 227-272. Each chapter arranged alphabetically by company name; address, executives, activities, financial information, shareholders, number of employees. Alphabetical and activity indexes.

41

The chronicle & directory for China, Japan, Corea, Indo-China, Straits Settlements, Malay States, Siam, Netherlands India, Borneo, the Philippines, &c. Hong Kong: Daily Press Office.

Known under varying titles between 1863 and 1900.

Specialized directories

42

Handbook: Southeast Asian institutions of higher learning, 1989-1991. [Bangkok?] ASAIHL [1989?]. 1350 pp.
Association of Southeast Asian Institutions of Higher Learning. Lee Foundation.

8th edition. A detailed self-description by member institutions, largely universities, in Brunei, Hong Kong, Malaysia, Philippines, Singapore, Thailand, Australia and some more distant countries. Some information on libraries. Many maps of campuses. First edition: 1965.

BURMA

43

Guide to foreign investment in Myanmar. Rangoon: Union of Myanmar
Foreign Investment Commission, 1990.

'Part 2'. A revision of 'part 1' which appeared in 1989. An official general
and economic survey, including practical information and contact addresses.
Map showing new official romanizations of place names. Cited from
Herbert [22].

44

Frederica M. Bunge, editor: *Burma: a country study.* Washington:
United States Government Printing Office, 1983. 326 pp.
American University, Foreign Area Studies. (DA pam, 550-61.)

Contents: Historical setting; The society and its environment; The economy;
Government and politics; National security, including an interesting survey
of 'insurgency', by Melinda W. Cook.

Superseded: John W. Henderson and others, *Area handbook for Burma.* 1971.
341 pp.

T. D. Roberts and others, *Area handbook for Burma.* 1968. 375 pp.

Ancestral to this series is: *Burma.* New Haven: Human Relations Area Files,
1965. 1579 pp. (Subcontractor's monograph, HRAF-37, NYU-2.) An
unpublished, officially inspired anthropological and political survey,
available on microfilm from Cornell University Library according to the
National Union catalog 1968-1972.

45

Burma. [Rangoon, 1975.] 82 pp.

An official outline survey with some statistics. Contents: The land; The
people; The state; The economy, pp. 26-39; Social services; Cultural life, pp.
42-65; Social life; Places of interest.

Note also: *A handbook on Burma.* Rangoon: Directorate of Information, 1968.
179 pp. 'Revised edition.' This was a similar work on a larger scale. List of
banks nationalized in 1963, pp. 101-3. Achievements in international sport,
1948-68, pp. 160-168. Score of national anthem, p. 179.

46

Hans-Ulrich Storz: *Birma: Land, Geschichte, Wirtschaft*. Wiesbaden: Harrassowitz, 1967. 302 pp.
(Schriften des Instituts für Asienkunde, 21.)

An economic and general survey of impressive range and objectivity. Contents: Geography; Ethnography (brief); History; Economic and development policy; Infrastructure; Energy; Agriculture; Forestry; Mining; Industry. Numerous maps, charts and statistical tables.

47

Burma handbook. Simla: Government of India, 1943. 126 pp., 11 maps. Government of Burma [i.e. British administration in exile].

Packed with statistical tables ending 1939/40. A description of the country as if under British rule: little or no mention of Japanese occupation until the section 'Relations with Japan', pp. 112-4. Contents: The country; Population (and ethnology) pp. 4-22; Production, pp. 22-47; Communications (with detailed routes and list of railway stations) pp. 48-80; Gazetteer, forming an index to preceding section, pp. 80-100; The British connection and the constitution of 1937; Relations with India, China, Japan; Health notes. Note especially 'Who's who in Burma', pp. 114-123, tracing current positions of politicians who remained in Japanese-occupied Burma.

48

Sir J. G. Scott: *Burma: a handbook of practical information*. London: O'Connor, 1921. 536 pp.

3rd edition. Contents: The country and climate; Government; Industries; Archaeology, architecture, art, music; Religion; Language and literature; Hints to visitors or new residents; brief geographical survey with statistics; list of districts; lists of commoner fauna, flora, minerals (English, Burmese, scientific names) pp. 499-518. Many photographs. Certain sections separately credited: fauna, Eugene W. Oates; flora, A. T. Gage; forests, C. W. Bruce; transport, H. J. Richard; music, P. A. Mariano. 'An endeavour has been made to bring this new edition up to date. Unfortunately, this has not been possible in the specialists' chapters. All of them, except Capt. Gage, are dead.'

[Second] revised edition: London: Moring, 1911. 520 pp. This includes musical scores, omitted from the 3rd ed.

First edition: 1906. See the review by J. R. Hobday in *Geographical journal* (October 1907) pp. 431-3.

Scott was at least as well known for a highly perceptive work published under a pseudonym: Shway Yoe: *The Burman: his life and notions*. London: Macmillan, 1882. 2 v. See the review of this by E. B. Tylor in *Nature* vol. 26 (1882) pp. 593-5 and correspondence in vol. 27 pp. 5-6.

49

Joseph Dautremer: *Burma under British rule*. London: T. Fisher Unwin, 1913. 391 pp.
Translated and with an introduction by Sir George Scott.

A systematic survey, 'much more like a consular report of the ideal kind. Mr Dautremer holds up the energy of the Briton to the admiration and emulation of his countrymen in Indo-China, but there is a sort of polite sarcasm in the way in which he chronicles roads which start with the idea of going somewhere and end nowhere' (Scott). Administrative divisions and towns, pp. 144-169; What to see in the Province (with road and rail information) pp. 199-239; Products; Trade; Industries. Brief sections on the 'tributary states' and the Andaman Islands.

Cheap edition: 1916.

The original French edition was: Joseph Dautremer: *Une colonie modèle: la Birmanie sous le régime britannique*. Paris: Guilmoto, 1912. 300 pp. [A model colony: Burma under British rule.]

Note also: John Nisbet: *Burma under British rule and before*. London: Constable, 1901. 2 v. The fullest of the unofficial surveys, useful as dealing with the kingdom before British annexation. Note Vol. 2 pp. 1-46: Britain and France in further India; Railways in Burma and their proposed extension across Yunnan. See the review in *Nature* vol. 65 (1902) pp. 243-4.

On the older survey by Father Sangermano see Herbert [22] p. 7.

50

Alleyne Ireland: *The province of Burma*. Boston: Houghton, Mifflin, 1907. 2 v. (1023 pp.).
(Colonial administration in the Far East.)

The completed part of a grandiose plan to compare administrative methods, their cost and efficiency, in European colonies. Vol. 1: General description; Acquisition of Burma by the British; People, Government, General administration, Civil service, Justice, Police, Prisons, 'Public instruction' [state education]. Vol. 2: Finance, Land revenue, Forestry, Public works, Local administration, Trade and shipping.

Appendices: vol. 1: population (from the census of 1901), climate, social statistics. Vol. 2: medical and vital statistics, financial and economic statistics, statistics on trade and shipping.

51

Henry Yule: 'On the geography of Burma and its tributary states, in illustration of a new map of those regions' in *Journal of the Royal Geographical Society* vol. 27 (1857) pp. 54-108.

Contains (pp. 95-108) a list and brief description of the 'Twelve Shan States' as then enumerated which were subject to the Burmese superintendent at Moné (Möngnai), and of some more distant states.

Reports

52

Report to the Pyithu Hluttaw on the financial, economic and social conditions of the Socialist Republic of the Union of Burma. Rangoon.

The latest official annual report, first published under this title for 1972/3: last seen 1988/9.

Earlier title: *Report to the people by the Government of the Union of Burma on the financial, economic and social conditions for 1971-72.* Rangoon: Central Press, 1972.

53

Burma: administrative and social affairs. Rangoon: Department of Information, 1964-9.

The first, published 1964, surveyed progress in 1962-3; the second covers 1963-4. Contents: autonomous states, pp. 1-20; central departments and boards, pp. 21-76. Some statistical information.

Companions to: *Burma: national economy.* Rangoon: Director of Information, 1964-6. 'A record in broad outline of the work and progress of the various Government departments concerned with national economy,' issued by the new Revolutionary Government of the Union of Burma. The first, undated, volume, covered 2 March 1962 to 1 March 1963; the second was dated 1963-64 and records the nationalisation of many privately owned industries. Some statistical tables.

54

Is trust vindicated? A chronicle of the various accomplishments of the Government headed by General Ne Win during the period of tenure from November 1958 to February 6 1960. Rangoon: Department of Information, 1960. 567 pp.

A narrative of progress made by Ne Win's Caretaker Government arranged under headings for ministries and boards. Very brief chapters on the autonomous states, pp. 503-530. Appendix 9: List of Defence Services Officers attached to or serving on a part-time basis in civil departments. Many statistical tables.

Superseded: *Government in the Union of Burma: GUB 1958 Nov.-1959 Feb..* Rangoon: Department of Information, 1959. 161 pp. A similar, briefer survey. The Cabinet (with photographs), pp. i-iv.

55

Financial and economic annual of Burma, July 1943. Rangoon: Bureau of State Printing Presses, 1943.
[Compiled by Myanaung U Tin and Maung Maung Gyi.]

Includes cabinet lists, 1942 and 1943, chart of government departments, administrative map. Incorporates provisional data from the 1941 census. 'The task was none too easy as important official records had been destroyed in accordance with the British scorched earth policy.'

Contents: General conditions of finance and economy in 1942-3; Reports of government ministries; Finance; Agriculture, mines, forests, commerce and industry; Foreign trade; Banking; Transport and communication. Much statistical information.

56

Report on the administration of Burma. Rangoon: Superintendent, Government Printing Office.

The official government report on Burma as a British territory, published annually under varying titles between 1861/2 and 1941.

Statistics

57

Statistical year book. Rangoon: Central Statistics and Economics Department, New Secretariat; Central Statistical Organization.

Published, probably biennially or irregularly, from 1961: issues also recorded for 1963 (published 1966), 1965, 1967, 1975 (published 1976).

Contents of 1963 edition: Climate; Population (including origin and number of resident foreigners by district); Migration; Vital and health statistics; Education; Labour; Crime; Social statistics; Agriculture; Forestry; Industry, mines and power; Construction; Foreign trade; Coastal and internal trade (including prices of foods etc. at selected towns); Transportation; National income; Fiscal; Monetary; Household expenditure. The 1961 edition covers the period from 1950.

Note also: *The national income of Burma.* Rangoon: Ministry of National Planning; Superintendent, Government Printing and Stationery, 1951-63. Annual collection of statistics. 1951 volume (44 pp.) covers 1938/9 and 1946-51: contents: National product, income and expenditure; Balance of payments; Current and capital accounts of public authorities; Combined capital accounts; Social accounts of Burma.

Louis J. Walinsky: *Economic development in Burma 1951-60.* New York: Twentieth Century Fund, 1962. 680 pp. Particularly useful for its documentary appendix and its statistical tables.

58

U Khin Maung Lwin, M. Mya-tu: *Handbook of biological data on Burma.* Rangoon: Burma Medical Research Institute, 1967. 291 pp.

A collection of statistical information. Contents include: Environment (rainfall, temperature, atmospheric pressure). Population, 1872-1967; table of 73 ethnic groups (English and Burmese names); 1967 population by State, District, Sub-district and Township. Human morphology. Nutrition: food composition tables for 178 Burmese foods; vitamin A content of Burmese vegetables (with Burmese names) and banana species; list of edible plants, Latin, English and transliterated Burmese. Metabolism; Blood and cardiovascular system; Digestive system; Urinary system; Disease; Vital statistics. List of rural health centres and maternity centres.

Note also: *Physical fitness of the Burmese.* Rangoon: Burma Medical Research Institute, 1968. 71 pp. (Special report series, 5.) Includes 32 tables.

An earlier work of related interest: *Anthropometric data from Burma.* Calcutta: Office of the Superintendent, Government Printing, 1906. 235 pp. (Ethnographic Survey of India.) Cited from Cordier [242].

59

J. J. Bennison: *Report of an enquiry into the standard and cost of living of the working classes in Rangoon.* Rangoon: Superintendent, Government Printing and Stationery, 1928. 221 pp.

A pioneering survey. Much statistical information on population, employment, family budgets and cost of living, divided by district, by occupation (e.g. rickshaw pullers; Corporation coolies) and by ethnic origin. Graphs (8 pp.) showing changes in cost of living, 1913-28. Statistical tables (pp. 96-205) include average cost and quantity of foods consumed per person and per family in great detail. Appendices include: nutritive value of foods in calories; daily rations for Asiatic prisoners; migration between

India and Burma derived from number of 'deck passengers' in both directions, 1921-5.

60

Census tables only. Rangoon: Superintendent, Government Printing, 1925. 4 v.
(Nos 36, 41, 42, 43.)

Under this curious 'title' appeared volumes of statistics for the hill states, a continuation of the *Burma gazetteer: volume B* series. The most informative are nos. 41 and 42 for the Northern and Southern Shan States, giving population of every village, subdivided by religion. No. 36: Chin Hills. No. 43: Karenni States.

Almanacs and directories

61

Trade directory of Myanmar. Rangoon: Ministry of Trade, 1992. 854 pp.
Earlier edition: 1989. 157 pp.

Export list of Myanmar. Rangoon: U Soe Myint, 1990. 99 pp. List of products available for export, stating the standards which they meet. Directory of exporting organizations, pp. 88-99.

62

Yangon directory 92-93. 315 pp. + indexes.
Yangon City Development Committee.

A large format trade directory in English and Burmese.

63

Rangoon guide book. Rangoon: Directorate of Information [1969]. 222 pp., plates.

Official publication with many poor quality photographs and some statistical and directory information. Lists and tables include: Local administrative units, pp. 68-78; Air services and fares, pp. 114-126; posting days for overseas mail, pp. 129-131; lists of cinemas, schools, fire stations, post offices, hospitals, police stations, government departments and corporations, law courts, etc., pp. 164-202; old and new street names, pp. 204-211.

For a newer list of street name changes see: Tin Maung Latt, editor: *City of Yangon modernization record.* Rangoon: Public Relations Information Division, 1990. 67 pp. Cited from Herbert [22].

64

Burma trade directory. Rangoon: Burma Commerce.

Annual with some years missed. Nunn [19, 20] reports editions between 1952 and 1963/4. The fourth (1956 [pasted over '1955/56']. 810 + 92 pp.) has a first part giving firms in alphabetical order, a who's who of businessmen, a listing of government and diplomatic personnel; then a classified list of trades; then general information on Burma.

Note also: *Burma yearbook and directory.* Rangoon: Student Press. Nunn [19, 20] reports editions between 1952 and 1957/8.

Burma business directory and national trade register. Rangoon. Annual from 1956 to 1958.

65

The directory of social welfare agencies and organizations, Burma. Rangoon: Superintendent, Government Printing, 1959. 105 pp.

Second edition. Two parts: in Rangoon, outside Rangoon. In questionnaire format: gives address, telephone number, principal officers, aims and activities. Includes some international agencies.

First edition: 1956. This contained a subject index to the organizations' chief aims and activities.

66

The quarterly civil list for Burma: list of officers in civil employ in Burma with full particulars. Rangoon.
Compiled by the Government of Burma. Home Department.

Cited from Cordier [242] and Nunn [20]: issues recorded between 1894 and 1948. Each fourth quarter this was replaced by the more biographically informative *History of services* [249].

Nunn also refers to a later title: *Annual list of Government gazetted officers.* Rangoon, 1950-56 or later.

67

Burma parliamentary companion. Rangoon: British Burma Press, 1940. 688 pp.

A general reference book. Selected contents: members of Burma Government, p. v; Departments and subjects under their control; Rice production by district; List of administrative divisions and population; Telephone map; List of police stations; texts of selected laws and regulations, pp. 29-325, 371-543; List of polling booths 1936, pp. 326-340;

Election results 1936, pp. 341-367; Municipalities and representation, pp. 544-557; List of hospitals and dispensaries; Road map and list of dak-bungalows on each route, pp. 560-596; List of unparliamentary expressions ('hateful foreigners' [when applied to Government]; 'murderous ruffian'); World parliamentary survey.

68

The Burma handbook and directory 1895: a compendium of useful information on matters relating to, or connected with, the Province of Burma. Rangoon: Rangoon Times Press, 1895. 319 pp.

Contents: General information relating to Burma (official regulations etc.) pp. 1-27; The official directory, a directory of the Home, the Supreme, and local Governments, with the establishments of the departments of the Government of Burma, pp. 29-83; General addresses directory, being an alphabetical list of the principal European, Eurasian, Indian and Burman residents in Lower and Upper Burma, pp. 85-307; Rules for mineral and mining leases, pp. 311-319.

69

Notes and statistics in four parts. Rangoon: Superintendent, Government Printing.
Running title: Notes and statistics, Burma. 'Compiled in the Office of the Chief Secretary to the Chief Commissioner.'

1893 ('third edition for the combined provinces'). 274 pp.

1891 ('second edition for the combined provinces'). 252 pp. Contents of 1891 edition: Part 1, General: outline of the administrative and military establishment (no names), revenue and expenditure statistics, list of newspapers. Parts 2-3 (pp. 15-229), Lower Burma, Upper Burma: Lists of districts, subdivisions, townships and circles; revenue and expenditure; local establishments (no names). Part 4: Lists of post offices, mail routes (with means of transport), telegraph offices, railway stations.

70

Burma pocket almanac and directory. Rangoon: G. W. D'Vauz.

First published 1886. 1889 and 1890 editions recorded in Cordier [242] col. 83. Not seen.

THAILAND

71

Barbara Leitch LePoer, editor: *Thailand: a country study.* Washington: United States Government Printing Office, 1989. 366 pp.
Library of Congress, Foreign Research Division. (DA pam 550-53.)

Sixth edition. Contents: Historical setting; The society and its environment; The economy; Government and politics; National security (including police). Appendix of statistics, pp. 289-311: note especially three detailed tables of major military equipment.

Fifth edition: Frederica M. Bunge, editor: *Thailand: a country study.* 1981. 352 pp. (American University, Foreign Area Studies.) Note p. 305: Thai military awards and decorations in accepted order of precedence.

'Third revision' [fourth edition]: John W. Henderson and others: *Area handbook for Thailand.* 1971. 413 pp. Sections: Social pp. 1-165; Political pp. 167-229; Economic pp. 231-301; National security pp. 303-328.

'Second revision' [third edition]: Harvey H. Smith and others: *Area handbook for Thailand.* 1968. 558 pp.

'Reprinting with minor revision' [of the second edition]: 1966. 555 pp. The main change here was the inclusion of a 'preface to the second printing', pp. vii-xii, noting major recent events.

'Revision' [second edition]: George L. Harris and others: *Area handbook for Thailand.* 1963. This contains some maps, charts and statistical tables eliminated from later editions.

'Incomplete edition': Wendell Blanchard, editor: *Area handbook for Thailand.* Washington: Human Relations Area Files, Washington Branch, 1957. 865 pp. Mimeographed. Not seen: cited from the *National Union catalog.* This work was also ancestral to HRAF Press's series *Thailand* [73].

72

L. Sternstein: *Thailand: the environment of modernisation.* Sydney: McGraw-Hill, 1976. 200 pp. 0-07-093321-9.

Noted here for its generous statistical tables, charts and maps; useful too for bibliographical references to specialised reports and statistical publications. Forest vegetation schemata, pp. 37-8; rural settlement patterns, pp. 68-9; 'Bangkok, past, present and future', pp. 94-120 with 15 maps; 'Agriculture and fisheries', pp. 143-160 with 16 maps; map of oil exploration concessions, p. 177.

73

Frank J. Moore: *Thailand: its people, its society, its culture.* New Haven: HRAF Press, 1974. 607 pp. 0 87536 929 4.
Human Relations Area Files. (Survey of world cultures.)

Completed 1971 except for the political chapters 14-17, which were written by Clark D. Neher in early 1974.

Superseded: Wendell Blanchard: *Thailand: its people, its society, its culture.* 1966. 528 pp. 'Revised edition.'

First edition: Wendell Blanchard and others: *Thailand: its people, its society, its culture.* 1958. 528 pp. (Human Relations Area Files, Washington Branch. Country survey series, 8.)

Blanchard's 1958 compilation, which was a reworking of his *Area handbook for Thailand* [71], also superseded: Lauriston Sharp, Walter F. Vella, Frank J. Moore, editors: *Thailand.* Ithaca, 1956. (Cornell University, Southeast Asia Program. HRAF subcontractor's monograph, 42.)

74

Thailand official yearbook 1964. Bangkok: Government House, 1965. 706 pp.
Phya Srivisar, Chairman of the Editorial Board.

An official survey, 'the first of its kind: it is intended to appear once in a while without any definite period of issue.' Contents: Government; Foreign affairs; National defence; Social welfare and health services; Justice, pp. 239-326; National economy; Trade and finance; Mass media; Education, pp. 428-495; Religion; Arts and culture, pp. 525-627; Sports; Tourism. Statistics, lists of organizations and persons.

A second edition: 1968.

Thailand facts and figures [80] is in essence an abridged form of this work, published in intervening years.

75

Siam: basic handbook. London, 1945. 147 pp.

'Restricted' and thus not widely available: I used the copy at SOAS. A survey compiled for British wartime use, giving up-to-date information on Japanese-dominated Thailand so far as known. The name 'Thailand' is rejected by the compilers for its association with 'chauvinistic tendencies'. Contents: Introduction, pp. 1-17. Political, pp. 19-81, including surveys of recent events. Appendices: Transliteration of names; Personalities (a brief alphabetical who's who), pp. 84-94; Weights and measures. Economic, pp.

97-147. Maps of minerals, agriculture, administrative divisions; statistics of rice production by province.

76

Siam: general and medical. Bangkok: Ministry of Commerce and Communications, 1930. 315 pp.

Accompanied by: *Siam: nature and industry*. 1930. 315 pp. The two works together form an official country survey.

77

W. A. Graham: *Siam*. London: Moring, 1924. 2 v.

Third edition. A systematic survey. Vol. 1: Geography, Flora, Fauna, Geology, Races, History, Social organization, education, Language and literature, Survey of earlier works on Thailand; Government (full outline of ministries and their activities), pp. 308-384. Vol. 2: Industries, Commerce and trade, Communications and transport, Arts, Religion. Appendices: Lists of fauna (pp. 295-302) and flora with Latin, English and romanized Thai terms, and of minerals in English and Thai; tables of currency, weights and measures. Separate index to each volume.

First edition: W. A. Graham: *Siam: a handbook of practical, commercial and political information*. London: Moring, 1912. 637 pp. See the review of this by: C. O. Blagden in *Journal of the Royal Asiatic Society* (April 1913) pp. 464-5.

Note also: G. E. Gerini: *Siam and its productions, arts and manufactures: a descriptive catalogue of the Siamese section at the International Exhibition of Industry and Labour held in Turin April 29-November 19, 1911; supplemented with historical, technical, commercial and statistical summaries on each subject*. [Turin] 1912. 339 pp. 'English edition, revised and brought up to date.' Cited from Cordier [242].

78

Sir John Bowring: *The kingdom and people of Siam, with a narrative of a mission to that country in 1855*. London, 1857. 2 v.

Partly indebted to Pallegoix [79] but also the result of observation and enquiry by Bowring, who was there to negotiate a trade agreement with Great Britain. Contents: vol. 1: geography, population and customs, natural resources, manufactures, commerce, taxation, language and literature, religion, foreign religious missions. Vol. 2: dependencies (Laos, Cambodia, the Karens, northern Malay states, states of northern Thailand), foreign diplomatic and commercial relations. Bowring's narrative is in vol. 2, pp. 248-340.

Reprinted: Kuala Lumpur: Oxford University Press, 1969. 2 v. (Oxford in Asia historical reprints.) New introduction by David K. Wyatt, in essence a biography of Bowring, pp. v-xiii.

79

[Jean-Baptiste] Pallegoix: *Description du Royaume Thai ou Siam, comprenant la topographie, histoire naturelle, moeurs et coutumes, legislation, commerce, industrie, langue, littérature, religion, annales des Thai et précis historique de la Mission.* Paris: Mission de Siam, 1854. 2 v.

[Decription of the Thai Kingdom or Siam, comprising its topography, natural history, life and customs, law, commerce, industry, language, literature, religion, the annals of the Thai and an outline history of the Mission.] Opens with a geographical description of the country and a survey of tributary states. The section on religions is also extensive.

Reprinted: Farnborough: Gregg, 1969. 0-576-03302-1.

I have seen a reference to an English translation (Shanghai, 1877) but have been unable to confirm it.

Reports

80

Thailand facts and figures. Bangkok.
Ministry of National Development. Department of Technical and Industrial Cooperation.

A brief narrative and statistical survey, recorded for 1965-7 and for some years after 1969, thus published in the years in which *Thailand official yearbook* [74] was not. Last seen: 1974 (97 pp.).

Statistics

81

Statistical yearbook, Thailand. Bangkok.
Ministry of Finance, Department of General Statistics; Central Service of Statistics, later National Statistical Office.

First edition covered 1915/16 (some have said 1909, but I have not been able to confirm it). Annual, but sometimes two or more years are combined. In English and Thai. The title has varied: early volumes, published 1916-35, were called *Statistical yearbook of the Kingdom of Siam*.

Contents of the 1991 edition (429 pp.): Climte; Population; Health, vital statistics; Immigration; Tourism; Education; Public justics; Agriculture, fisheries, forestry, mining; Transport and communications; Foreign trade; Currency and banking; Prices; Public finance; National income; Labour; Energy; State employment and pensions.

For further sources of statistics on Thailand see: *Annotated statistical bibliography.* (National Statistical Office.) First recorded 1961: last seen 1987/8. Earlier editions called *Statistical bibliography.*

82

Thailand in figures. Bangkok: Tera International, 1990. 772 pp.

Contents: General and business information; General and social statistics; Economic statistics (pp. 219-452); Provincial statistics (pp. 463-761). Very brief indexes but a big, useful, well-presented collection of statistics.

83

Constance M. Wilson: *Thailand: a handbook of historical statistics.* Boston: Hall, 1983. 360 pp.

Covers the period 1850-1979.

84

Climatological data of Thailand, 20 year period (1951-1970). Bangkok: Meteorological Department, 1972.

Note also: 'Rainfall records of the Kingdom of Siam' in *Journal of the Siam Society* vol. 4 part 2 (1907) pp. 47-106.

Almanacs and directories

85

The organizational directory of Thailand. Bangkok: Office of the Prime Minister, Public Relations Department.

1982 edition seen (332 pp.). In Thai and English. Arranged by department, with organizational charts and a map of government offices.

Apparently a successor to: *Organizational directory of the Government of Thailand.* Bangkok. (U. S. Operations Mission to Thailand, Public Administrative Division.) In Thai and English. Nunn [19] recorded editions of about 1960 and 1969. 1966 (138 + 51 pp.) was the seventh edition: the second part listed provincial administrations.

86

Gordon H. Allison, Auratai Smarnond: *Thailand's government (including dictionary-locator)*. [Bangkok:] Siam Security Brokers, 1972. 155 pp.

Part 1: Thai government structure, pp. 1-21; Provincial administration; Buddhist era; Terms of respect. Part 2: Dictionary-locator, an English-Thai glossary of names of government bodies, with many cross-references. Includes quasi-governmental organizations such as research institutes; also includes names of higher-level administrative divisions. Thai forms are given in script and in Allison's non-standard transcription.

87

Thailand yearbook. Bangkok: Temple.

Annual from the 1964/5 issue. Includes: the Government; banking, social services, taxation, population; list of diplomats and international organizations; list of temples; directory of individuals. Occasional articles on cultural and historical topics: Watts [29] notes the article on the history of Thai printing fonts in the 1985 volume.

88

The Siam directory: the book of facts and figures. Bangkok: Tawanna.

Claims to have been 'founded 1955' but Nunn [20] records holdings from 1947. Last seen 1991/2. Recent editions list Royal Family, National Assembly, Government, diplomatic corps; Trade associations, marketing, tourism; Finance; Business firms (864 pp.); Hospitals; Higher education. No table of contents.

89

Kompass Thailand: register of industry and commerce of Thailand. Bangkok: Kompass Publications (Thailand).

An alphabetical and classified trade directory. Last seen 1990/91 (1058 pp.).

Note also: *Million baht business information Thailand*. Bangkok: International Business Research (Thailand). 1992 edition: 112 + 960 pp.

The Thai Chamber of Commerce business directory, 1979/80. Bangkok: Marketing Media, 1979. Classified arrangement: Chambers of Commerce with their members, pp. A1-A60; Air cargo services; Airlines; Consuls and Diplomats; Hospitals; Hotels; Immigration Office; Tourist organizations; Law offices; Banking, finance and insurance firms, pp. C1-C62; classified trade index, pp. D1-D296; alphabetical catalogue of selected firms, pp. E1-E130. Earlier title:

Bangkok Chamber of Commerce directory.

Thailand investment July 1987: directory of BOI promoted companies. Bangkok, 1987. 199 pp. (Published for the Office of the Board of Investment.) General information on foreign investment in Thailand, pp. 1-75; Classified directory of Thai companies indicating assets and main areas of business, pp. 79-185; index; statistics of key economic indicators.

90

Commercial directory for Thailand. Bangkok.
Ministry of Commerce.

Last known: 1969; fifth edition: 1941; third edition: 1929. Titles have varied: *Commercial directory of Thailand: Commercial directory of Siam: Commercial directory for Siam; Importers and exporters directory for Siam.*

91

The directory for Bangkok and Siam; a handy and perfectly reliable book of reference for all classes. Bangkok: Bangkok Times Office.

Annual from 1890 to 1937.

1932 edition. 454 pp. An almanac with general information on Siam, texts of laws and treaties, calendar, administrative survey. Official directory, pp. 211-315: listing of royal family, government, civil service, diplomatic and consular officials. General directory: classified listing of officials of missions, secular societies of various kinds, newspapers, banks, pp. 317-344; of 'merchants, professions, etc.' i.e. personnel of trade and professional concerns in alphabetical order of name of firm, pp. 344-405; firms 'in the Peninsula' and 'Tin Companies'. Alphabetical directory of foreign residents, pp. 415-454.

Note also: *The Siam directory.* Bangkolem: S. J. Smith. Annual, 1878 to 1892.

92

Directory of scientific and technological institutions in Thailand. 1976. 231 pp.
Compiled by Office of the National Research Council, Research Registration Division.

A survey in questionnaire format, with diagrams of administrative structure. No lists of personnel. Arranged hierarchically under government ministries (thus universities, pp. 88-187, under 'Office of State Universities'). A separate grouping of nationally owned business enterprises, pp. 188-229.

INDOCHINA

93

Indo-China. [London, 1944.] 536 pp.

Admiralty, Naval Intelligence Division. (Geographical handbook series. B.R., 510.) Compiled in Cambridge and edited by H. C. Darby.

An official wartime survey, based on French sources including the *Bulletin économique de l'Indochine*, illustrated with photographs, many sketch maps and tables. Contents: Geology and physical geography; coasts; vegetation; fauna; medical services and health; people; history; government; demography; agriculture, forestry, fisheries, pp. 256-315; industry; labour; commerce; finance; ports, roads, railways, waterways. An appendix adds further statistics, and summarizes what was known of political and economic conditions since 1939.

Note also: *French Indo-China.* London: Her Majesty's Stationery Office, 1919. 78 pp. (Handbooks prepared under the direction of the Historical Section of the Foreign Office, 78.)

94

A. Agard: *L'Union Indochinoise Française ou Indochine Orientale: régions naturelles et géographie économique.* Hanoi: Imprimerie d'Extrême-Orient, 1935. 370 pp.

[The French Indochinese Union or Eastern Indochina: ecological regions and economic geography.] Illustrated with photographs from the Aéronautique Militaire de l'Indochine and from the Gouvernement Général de l'Indochine. Not seen.

95

Guide du français arrivant en Indochine. Hanoi: Taupin, 1935. 72 pp.

[Guide for the French migrant newly arrived in Indochina.]

Note also: Paul d'Enjoy: *La colonisation de la Cochin-Chine: manuel du colon.* Paris: Société d'Editions Scientifiques, 1898. 390 pp. [The colonization of Cochinchina: colonist's manual.]

96

Eugène Teston, Maurice Percheron: *L'Indochine moderne: encyclopédie administrative, touristique, artistique et économique.* Paris: Librairie de France [1932]. 1028 pp.

'Publié avec le concours de la Compagnie Financière et Commerciale pour la France et l'Etranger sous les auspices du Gouvernement Général de l'Indochine ...'

[Modern Indochina: an administrative, touristic, artistic and economic encyclopaedia.] Under official patronage.

97

J. de Galembert: *Les administrations et les services publics indochinois.* Hanoi: Mac-Dinh-Tu, 1931. 1023 pp.
Revised by E. Erard.

[Administration and public services of Indochina.] Second edition. Detailed description of the administrative system of French Indochina.

98

Sylvain Lévi, editor: *Indochine.* Paris: Société d'Editions Géographiques, Maritimes et Coloniales, 1931. 2 v.
Exposition Coloniale Internationale, Paris, 1931. Commissariat Général.

[Indochina.] Produced for the International Colonial Exhibition. Vol. 1: Chapters on population, history, religion, literature, art and archaeology, each dealing separately with the primary divisions of French Indochina. Vol. 2: Survey of the French Government of Indochina: civil and military administrations, law, taxation, postal service, education, economy, surveying, culture. Appendix of population statistics.

99

Georges Maspero, editor: *L'Indochine, un empire colonial français.* Paris: Van Oest, 1929-30. 2 v. (356 pp., 58 plates, 12 maps).

[Indochina: a French colonial empire.] A lavishly illustrated coffee-table variety of the country survey genre. Vol. 1: The country, the people, history, social life, religion, literature. Vol. 2: French administration: history, organization, education ('the socializing and civilizing mission of France'), archaeology, science; agriculture, economy; public works; tourism.

100

Etat actuel du Tunkin, de la Cochinchine et des royaumes de Camboge, Laos et Lac-Tho. Paris: Galignani, 1812. 2 v.
'Par M. de la Bissachère; traduit d'après les relations originales de ce voyageur.'

[The present state of Tongking, Cochinchina and the kingdoms of Cambodia, Laos and Lac-Tho.] Revised edition of an early country survey, compiled by Antoine Jean-Baptiste Auget de Montyon from the papers of Pierre Jacques Lemonnier de la Bissachère, a missionary in Tongking.

Relatively detailed outlines of agriculture, vol. 1 pp. 105-147, and internal trade, pp. 196-220.

Reprinted: Farnborough: Gregg, 1971. 2 v. in 1. 0-576-03476-2.

Also available in a German translation: *Gegenwärtiger Zustand von Tunkin, Cochinchina und der Königreiche Camboja, Laos und Lac-Tho, von de la Bissachère.* Weimar: Landes-Industrie-Comptoir, 1813. 446 pp. Translated by E. A. W. von Zimmermann.

The first edition had borne a different title: *Exposé statistique du Tunkin, de la Cochinchine, du Camboge, du Tsiampa, du Laos, du Lac-Tho.* London: Dulau, 1811. 2 v. 'Par M. M[ontyo]n, sur la relation de M. de la Bissachère, missionaire dans le Tunkin.' [Statistical survey of Tongking, Cochinchina, Cambodia, Champa, Laos, Lac-Tho.]

The text of la Bissachère's manuscript, completed in 1807, has since been published in its unamended form: Pierre Jacques de la Bissachère: *La relation sur le Tonkin et la Cochinchine, publiée d'après le manuscrit des Archives des Affaires Etrangères.* Paris: Champion, 1920. 185 pp.

On the author see the anonymous obituary: 'Notice sur la vie et les travaux de M. de la Bissachère, missionaire' in *Annales maritimes et coloniales* (1830) pp. 451-2 [Ouline of the life and achievements of M. de la Bissachère, missionary], and the introduction to the 1920 edition.

Reports

101

Rapport au Conseil de Gouvernement. Hanoi.

The regular administrative reports on French Indochina, issued under this or a similar title from 1913 to the late 1920s. Two parts: *Situation générale de l'Indochine; Fonctionnement des divers services indochinois.*

Previous title: *Situation de l'Indochine.* 1897-1907.

Separate reports were afterwards issued for administrative divisions, notably: *Rapport sur l'exercice du protectorat.* Phnom Penh. Recorded for 1929-39; *Rapport sur la situation administrative, économique et financière du Laos.* Vientiane. From 1928 to 1944; *Rapport d'ensemble sur la situation du Protectorat d'Annam.* Hue. From 1929; *Rapport sur la situation administrative, économique et financière du Tonkin.* Hanoi. From 1929/30; *Rapport au Conseil Colonial ... sur l'état de la Cochinchine.* Saigon. From 1928/9.

There is in general no regularity in titles, and no attempt is made here to trace changes from year to year. Some more information on these reports will be found in Cordier [242] and Brewster [4].

Statistics

102
Annuaire statistique de l'Indochine. Hanoi, Saigon: Imprimerie d'Extrême-Orient.
Direction des Affaires Economiques; Service de la Statistique Générale.

[Statistical annual of Indochina.] 12 editions appeared, published 1927-1949 and covering 1913/22 to 1947/48. Vol. 1, called *Recueil de statistiques*, was accompanied by a supplement.

Note also: *Histoire budgétaire de l'Indochine.* Hanoi: Imprimerie d'Extrême-Orient, 1930. 105 pp. (Exposition coloniale internationale, Paris, 1931. Indochine Française, Section d'Administration Générale, Direction des Finances.) [Budgetary history of Indochina.]

103
E. Bruzon: *Atlas [du Service Météorologique de l'Indochine].* 1931. 42 plates.
Exposition Coloniale Internationale, Indochine Française, Section des Sciences. Service Météorologique.

A total of 69 maps, including: Meteorological stations 1926, 1930; Monthly isobar maps; Typhoon trajectories (Indochina, South China Sea, Philippines and West Pacific) month by month, 1911-29; Monthly isotherm maps; Monthly rainfall maps (average rainfall, number of rainy days).

Note also: Khiou Bonthonn: *Le climat du Cambodge.* Phnom-Penh: Ministère des Travaux Publics, 1965. 240 pp. [The climate of Cambodia.]

Almanacs and directories

104
Annuaire des Etats-Associés: Cambodge, Laos, Vietnam. Paris.

[Annual of the Associated States, Cambodia, Laos, Vietnam.] This (known for 1953) was the latest incarnation of the official administrative annual of French Indochina, formerly published in Saigon and Hanoi.

Previous titles: *Annuaire administratif des services communs: Annuaire de l'administration française en Indochine,* both of the late 1940s.

Until 1943 the title was: *Annuaire administratif de l'Indochine,* the successor to: *Annuaire administratif, commercial et industriel de l'Indo-Chine* [Administrative, commercial and industrial annual of Indochina], published from 1912. The more recent editions arranged thus: part 1, lists of French and local government departments and their functions; part 2, list of officials in order of seniority; part 3, name and subject indexes.

Previous titles: *Annuaire général, administratif, commercial et industriel, de l'Indo-Chine.* 1905-11: *Annuaire général de l'Indo-Chine.* 1903-4: *Annuaire général, commercial, administratif & industriel de l'Indo-Chine.* 1901-2: *Annuaire général, commercial et administratif de l'Indo-Chine Française.* 1900: *Annuaire général de l'Indo-Chine Française.* 1899: *Annuaire commercial et administratif de l'Indo-Chine Française.* 1898.

Before 1898 there were separate annuals for the subdivisions of French Indochina.

For Annam and Tongking: *Annuaire de l'Indo-Chine Française: IIe partie, Annam et Tonkin.* Hanoi: Schneider, 1891-7: *Annuaire de l'Indo-Chine: IIe partie, An-Nam et Tonkin.* 1889-90: *Annuaire de l'Annam et du Tonkin.* 1887. 280 pp.

For Cochinchina: *Annuaire de l'Indo-Chine Française: première partie, Cochinchine.* Saigon: Imprimerie Coloniale, 1891-7: *Annuaire de l'Indochine Française: première partie, Cochinchine et Cambodge.* 1889-90: *Annuaire de la Cochinchine Française.* Saigon: Imprimerie Impériale, etc., 1866-88.

For Cambodia: *Annuaire du Cambodge.* Phnom-Penh: Imprimerie du Protectorat, 1887-97, 1905.

105

Kuo Shou-hua: *Directory of Viet-Nam, Laos and Cambodia.* Taipei: Central Cultural Supply Agency [1966]. 320 pp.

106

Indochine adresses 1938-39: annuaire complet de l'Indochine: officiel, commerce, industrie, plantations, mines, adresses particulières. Saigon: Portail, 1939.

[Indochina addresses. Complete yearbook of Indochina: officialdom, trade, industry, plantations, mines. Private addresses.] An earlier edition under a different title: *Annuaire de l'Indochine complet (européen et indigène) de toute l'Indochine, commerciale, industrielle, des plantations, des mines. Adresses particulières.* 1933/4. Saigon, 1934. 1012 pp.

107

L. Barthès: *Les 10,000 adresses: publication trimestrielle comprenant les adresses exactes de tous les colons et fonctionnaires de la Colonie.* Hanoi: Gallois, February 1908. 302 pp.

[The 10,000 addresses: quarterly publication listing the exact addresses of all the colonists and officials of the Colony.] First edition: May 1907. 160 pp.

CAMBODIA

108

Russell R. Ross, editor: *Cambodia: a country study*. Washington: United States Government Printing Office, 1990. 362 pp.
Library of Congress, Foreign Research Division. (DA pam 550-50.)

Contents: Historical setting, by Donald M. Seekins; The society and its environment, by Robert K. Headley, jr; The economy, by Tuyet L. Cosslett; Government and politics, by Rinn-Sup Shinn; National security, by Frank Tatu, the longest section with much historical background. Appendix A: Tables includes 'Major weapons of the Khmer People's Revolutionary Armed Forces 1987'; Appendix B: 'Major political and military organizations' (list of acronyms). 'It should be noted that, as a result of the Khmer Rouge policy of eradicating the traces of its predecessor and of establishing an anti-modernistic regime, after mid-1975, statistical and quantitative data are contradictory and virtually nonexistent.'

Superseded: Donald P. Whitaker and others: *Area handbook for the Khmer Republic (Cambodia)*. 1973. 389 pp. (American University, Foreign Area Studies.)

Frederick P. Munson: *Area handbook for Cambodia*. 1968. 365 pp. In this the economic section is strongest (pp. 211-293, many tables).

Area handbook for Cambodia. 1963. 415 pp. (United States Army.) Not seen; there was also an earlier version issued in 1956.

109

Michael Vickery: *Kampuchea: politics, economics and society*. London: Frances Pinter; Boulder: Lynne Rienner, 1986. 220 pp. 0-86187-422-6. (Marxist regimes series.)

A survey of history, politics and government, economic system, and current policy, based on fieldwork up to 1984.

110

Cambodia. Phnom Penh: Royal Cambodian Government, 1962. (Ministry of Information.)

Not seen: cited from Ross [108].

111

David J. Steinberg and others: *Cambodia: its people, its society, its culture*. New Haven: HRAF Press, 1959. 351 pp.
Human Relations Area Files. (Survey of world cultures.)

Revised by Herbert H. Vreeland. A general survey. Longer chapters: Historical setting; Ethnic groups and languages; Dynamics of political behaviour; Theory and structure of government; Foreign relations; Agricultural development; Domestic and foreign trade.

Earlier edition: 1957. 345 pp. (Country survey series.)

112
Etienne Aymonier: *Le Cambodge.* Paris: Leroux, 1900-1904. 3 v.

[Cambodia.] A general and archaeological survey including some adjacent regions. V. 1: Country; People; Institutions; Law. Detailed survey of Cambodia (except Angkor Wat) and Lower Cochinchina. V. 2, 'The Siamese provinces': Siam and the Siamese; Institutions; Archaeology; Mènam epigraphy. Detailed survey of eastern Thailand. V. 3, 'Le groupe d'Angkor' (survey, pp. 1-324) 'et l'histoire' (general history of Cambodia and neighbours, pp. 325-807). Maps throughout, though sometimes inaccurate, help to identify sites described.

See the review by: A. Cabaton in *Revue de l'histoire des religions* (1906) pp. 74-82. Cordier [242] col. 2656 refers to other reviews.

The need for an index was filled by: G. Coedès: 'Index alphabétique pour *Le Cambodge* de M. Aymonier' in *Bulletin de la Commission Archéologique de 'Indochine* (1911) pp. 85-169, also issued as an offprint: Paris: Imprimerie Nationale, 1911.

Statistics

113
Annuaire statistique du Cambodge. Phnom Penh.
Ministère du Plan, Institut National de la Statistique et des Recherches Economiques.

Successive editions covered 1949/51, 1937/57, 1958/60, 1958/61 and subsequent periods to 1971. The last was called simply *Annuaire statistique.* The volumes for 1937/57 and 1958/61 (published 1958, 1962) were called *Annuaire statistique retrospectif du Cambodge.*

Note also: *Economic data book, Khmer Republic.* Phnom Penh: United States Embassy, 1975. 311 pp. Roneoed.

Almanacs and directories

114
Annuaire diplomatique et consulaire. Phnom Penh.

Ministère des Affaires Etrangères.

[Diplomatic and consular yearbook.] Editions recorded between 1959 and 1965. Cited from Nunn [20], who also notes: *Liste des membres des missions diplomatiques et consulaires accréditées auprès du Cambodge*. Phnom Penh, 1956 [List of members of diplomatic and consular missions accredited to Cambodia]; *Missions diplomatiques et consulaires accréditées auprès du Cambodge* .... Phnom Penh, 1957-8; and: *Liste des membres du corps diplomatique et consulaire et des organismes internationaux*. Phnom Penh, 1967.

115

Emile Faraut: *Guide-annuaire de la ville de Pnom-Penh et des environs; excursion à Angkor*. Phnom-Penh: Coudurier et Montégout, n.d. 76 pp.

[Yearbook and guide to Phnom-Penh and environs; excursion to Angkor.] Includes plans of Phnom-Penh and Angkor. The author was secretary-archivist to the Chambre de Commerce et d'Agriculture du Cambodge.

Note also: *Annuaire illustré du Cambodge*. Saigon: Claude, 1904. 317 pp. [Illustrated yearbook of Cambodia.] Both cited from Cordier [242].

LAOS

116

Martin Stuart-Fox: *Laos: politics, economics and society*. London: Frances Pinter; Boulder: Lynne Rienner, 1986. 220 pp. 0-86187-427-7.
(Marxist regimes series.)

A country survey with a fairly standard format, though emphasising the effect of the local application of Marxist ideology. Contents: Political history of the Lao state; Social structure (including ethnic divisions); Political system; Economic system; Transport and communications; Domestic policies; Foreign policy. Charts of government structure; tables of 1985 population by province, financial data, etc.

There is much useful information in: Joseph T. Zasloff, Leonard Unger, editors: *Laos: beyond the revolution*. London: Macmillan, 1991. 348 pp. 0-333-51330-4. Outcome of a 1988 conference, incorporating more recent data. See the full summary in Cordell [25] p. 9.

117

Joseph T. Zasloff: *Pathet Lao: leadership and organization*. Santa Monica: Rand, 1973. 176 pp.
A report prepared for Defense Advanced Research Projects Agency.

Contents: The Pathet Lao leadership; The People's Party of Laos; Politics and administration; The Pathet Lao fighting forces; Background and profiles of Pathet Lao leaders. Appendices: Central Committee of the Neo Lao Hok Sat in 1950, 1956, 1964; Programs; Peace proposals; Front groups and mass organizations.

Reprinted: Joseph T. Zasloff: *The Pathet Lao: leadership and organization.* Lexington: Heath, 1973.

118

Donald P. Whitaker and others: *Area handbook for Laos.* Washington: United States Government Printing Office, 1972. 337 pp.
American University, Foreign Area Studies. (DA pam 550-58.)

The 1972 edition is an improvement on its predecessors: 'new information and source materials have become available on the area of Laos controlled by the Lao Patriotic Front (Neo Lao Hak Set) ... The country [is] in fact a divided one, with ... two de facto administrations.' Chapters: Social; Political; Economic; National security. Each chapter is in two parts for the two administrations. Appendix: Geneva Agreement, 1962. Reprinted as: Donald P. Whitaker and others, *Laos: a country study.* 1979 [not seen]; 1985.

Superseded: T. D. Roberts and others, *Area handbook for Laos.* 1967. 349 pp., which admitted: 'Recent information for the Pathet Lao area is either not available or is extremely biased and unreliable ... some parts of the total picture are missing.'

Earlier edition: Wendell Blanchard and others, *Area handbook for Laos.* 1958. Based on Ginsburg [122].

119

Facts on foreign aid to Laos. Vientiane: USAID Mission to Laos, 1971. 202 pp.
United States Embassy in Vientiane.

A political and statistical survey of the country. Includes lists of the government and its ministries.

Followed by: *Facts on foreign aid to Laos, supplement no. 1: Refugees.* 1971.

Note also: *Background notes: Kingdom of Laos.* Washington: United States Government Printing Office, 1970. (Department of State, Bureau of Public Affairs, Office of Media Services.)

Briefing notes on the Royal Kingdom of Laos. Vientiane: USIS, 1959. 100 pp. This includes biographical notes on main personalities.

120

Frank M. Lebar, Adrienne Suddard, editors: *Laos: its people, its society,*

its culture. New Haven: HRAF Press, 1960. 294 pp.
Human Relations Area Files. (Survey of world cultures [8].)

Based on Blanchard [118] and Ginsburg [122]. Longer sections: Historical setting; Religion; Social structure; Theory and structure of government; Foreign relations; Domestic and foreign trade. Tables include: Population estimates by province, 1958; Wages paid in the construction industry in Vientiane, 1956; US aid to Laos, 1959. See the review by: P. B. Lafont in *Bulletin de l'Ecole Française d'Extrême-Orient* vol. 51 no. 1 (1961) pp. 208-215.

Followed by a 'revised' edition: 1967. 294 pp. I have not seen this: somehow it 'took into account the major events which had taken place in Laos during the period 1960 to 1967' (Cordell [25]) within the same page span. It claims to be the 'third edition', counting Ginsburg [122] as the first.

121

René de Berval, editor: *Kingdom of Laos: the land of the million elephants and of the white parasol*. Saigon: France-Asie, 1959. 506 pp.

Covers geography, history, calendar, music, arts, Buddhism, religious festivals, rites and ceremonies, cookery, traditional medicine, script, language, literature, proverbs, legends, education, economy, international relations. Numerous maps.

Among individual articles note: A. R. Mathieu: 'Chronological table of the history of Laos', pp. 32-49: Tiao Maha Upahat Phetsarath: 'The Laotian calendar', pp. 97-125; Thao Nhouy Abhay: 'People's names', pp. 190-193; id.: 'Versification', pp. 345-358; B. Fall, 'The international relations of Laos': Fall's article had first appeared in *Pacific affairs* vol. 30 (1957) pp. 22-34.

Previously published in French: René de Berval, editor: *Présence du royaume lao*. 1956. 451 pp. (*France-Asie* nos 118-120 [March 1956].) [Reality of the Kingdom of Laos.] This edition did not contain the article by B. Fall.

122

G. C. Hickey and others; Norton S. Ginsburg, editor: *Area handbook on Laos*. Chicago: University of Chicago, 1955. 328 pp.
Human Relations Area Files.

A compilation ancestral to those of Lebar [120] and Blanchard [118]. Not seen.

123

Le Royaume du Laos: ses institutions et son organisation générale. [Vientiane] 1950. 154 pp.

[The Kingdom of Laos: its institutions and general organization.] An official manual.

Note also: Dominique Guerrini: *Organisation administrative au Laos.* Vientiane: IRDA, 1967. 79 pp. A textbook: cited from Cordell [25].

124

Lucien de Reinach; P. Chemin Dupontès, editor: *Le Laos.* Paris: Guilmoto, Librairie Orientale et Américaine [1911]. 392 pp.

Posthumous edition revised by Paul Doumer. Contents: France's involvement in Laos [with text of treaties]; Geography; Population, ethnography, languages; Religion, calendar, festivals; Life and customs; Politics and administration; Economic resources; Weights, measures, currency; Industry, arts, crafts; Trade; Transport, with list of routes.

First edition: L. de Reinach: *Le Laos.* Paris: A. Charles [1901]. 2 v. (707 pp.) Includes six maps: vol. 2 consists of appendices. See the review signed: R. C. in *Bulletin de la Comité de l'Asie Française* (December 1901) pp. 410-412.

125

Notice sur le Laos français. Hanoi: Schneider, 1900. 191 pp.
By the administrative personnel of Laos; edited by Lieutenant-Colonel Tournier.

I have not seen this and quote Cordell's summary [25]: 'geography; the peoples of Laos (pp. 10-124), a description of the ethnic groups including the Lao and their customs, religion and way of life; French administration; fauna; flora; agriculture; forest resources; industries; mines; communications; and commerce. The tone is one of optimism for a prosperous economic future.'

Statistics

126

Annuaire statistique du Laos. Saigon, Vientiane.
Direction de la Statistique, Service de la Statistique du Laos, Service National de la Statistique, Comité du Plan.

[Statistical annual of Laos.] First published in 1951 for 1949/50; at first very irregular, up to 1953/57 which was published 1961. Series resumed in 1970 (with title *Annuaire statistique*): thereafter annual until 1973, the last. Contents: climate, territory, population, agriculture, forestry, industry, transport, communications, finance, trade, public health, education, religion, crime, civil service, revenue, domestic consumption, prices.

Note also: *Laos: annual statistical report*. Vientiane. (USAID Mission to Laos.) Nunn [20] records annual editions from 1960 to 1967.

10 years of socio-economic development in the Lao People's Democratic Republic. Vientiane: State Statistical Centre, 1985. Includes statistics for 1976-85.

Directories

127
Vientiane guide 1991. Vientiane, 1990. 66 pp.
Compiled and edited by the Women's International Group.

Intended chiefly for expatriates: health, education, shopping, services, leisure. Street atlas with index.

128
Liste de mm. les membres du corps diplomatique et consulaire. Vientiane. Ministère des Affaires Etrangères. Direction du Protocole.

[List of members of the diplomatic and consular corps.] Cited from Nunn [20], who records issues between 1955 and 1972.

129
Almanach lao. Vientiane.

[Lao almanac.] Cited from Nunn [20], who records issues for 1943 and 1944.

VIETNAM

130
Ronald J. Cima, editor: *Vietnam: a country study*. Washington: U. S. Government Printing Office, 1989. 386 pp.
(Library of Congress, Federal Research Division.)

Contents: Historical setting; The society and its environment; The economy; Government and politics; National security. Chronology of important events, pp. xv-xxi. 14 maps (including Military regions, 1986); charts of party and government structure. Tables include: population by province; Ethnic composition (Name of group, alternative names, locations, population: pp. 313-8). Note especially Appendix B: Party leaders in the 1980s (31 biographies of current or recent members of the Politburo and the Central Committee Secretariat, emphasizing political experience and views).

Replaces separate volumes for North and South Vietnam, 136, 137.

131

Melanie Beresford: *Vietnam: politics, economics and society.* London: Frances Pinter; Boulder: Lynne Rienner, 1988. 242 pp. 0-86187-448-X. (Marxist regimes series.)

The series is in the 'area handbook' genre. Contents: History and political traditions; The social system; The political system; The economy; The régime's policies. Practically nothing is said of ethnic minorities.

Note also: Nguyễn Văn Chien: 'Compiling the national atlas' in *Vietnam courier* (1983 no. 12) pp. 19-21.

132

Vietnamese studies. Hanoi: Xunhasaba, 1964-.

Edited by Nguyen Khac Vien. A North Vietnamese periodical many of whose issues are devoted to single topics and are of some reference value. See 621. Also published in French: *Etudes vietnamiennes.* Hanoi: Xunhasaba, 1964-.

133

George L. Harris and others: *Area handbook for Vietnam.* Washington: United States Government Printing Office, 1962. 513 pp.
American University, Foreign Area Studies.

Reprinted: 1964. Superseded by 136, 137.

First edition: *Area handbook for Vietnam.* 1957. (Human Relations Area Files, Washington Branch.)

Note also: *Viet Nam documents and research notes.* Saigon: United States Mission in Vietnam, 1967- . (United States Mission in Viet Nam, Joint U. S. Pacific Affairs Office, North Viet Nam Affairs Division.) A series containing several compilations of quick-reference type concerning North Vietnam and the war in the South: see 150.

134

Pierre Huard, Maurice Durand: *Connaissance du Viêt-Nam.* Paris: Imprimerie Nationale; Hanoi: Ecole Française d'Extrême-Orient, 1954. 357 pp.

[The study of Vietnam.] A cultural survey, with many line drawings. Contents: Geography, history, anthropology, material culture, social life, etc. Indexes of Vietnamese words used in the text, pp. 307-324; of personal names, pp. 325-334; of place-names, pp. 335-8. The indexes give Chinese characters as well as quoc-ngu forms.

Subdivisions of Vietnam

135

Nguyễn Ngọc-Bích: *An annotated atlas of the Republic of Viet-Nam.* Washington: Embassy of Viet-Nam, 1972. 62 pp.

A rather scrappy factual survey of South Vietnam accompanied by very poor maps.

136

Harvey H. Smith and others: *Area handbook for North Vietnam.* Washington: United States Government Printing Office, 1967. 494 pp. American University, Foreign Area Studies. (DA pam, 550-57.)

'Third edition' but the first dealing with North Vietnam alone. (For the first two editions see 133.) Contents: Social, including 'Ethnic groups and languages' pp. 67-83; 'Living conditions' pp. 115-136. Political, including 'Foreign relations pp. 195-220; 'Public information and propaganda' pp. 221-244. Economic, including 'Agriculture' pp. 267-296. National security. Diagram of formal government structure and of its actual functioning; table of Politburo members. Some sections identical with the *Area handbook for South Vietnam* [137]. Now superseded by Cima [130].

137

Harvey H. Smith and others: *Area handbook for South Vietnam.* Washington: United States Government Printing Office, 1967. 510 pp. American University, Foreign Area Studies. (DA pam 550-55.)

'3rd edition' but the first dealing with South Vietnam alone. (For the first two editions see 133.) Contents: Social, including 'Religion' pp. 169-190. Political, including 'Foreign relations' pp. 257-280. Economic, including 'Agriculture' pp. 313-336. National security. Tables include: Changes in leadership 1954-66; Budget, subdivided by minstry, 1959-65. Diagrams of military ranks and insignia, government departments, military command. Some sections identical with the *Area handbook for North Vietnam* [136]. Now superseded by Cima [130].

138

Handbook for U. S. forces in Vietnam. Washington: United States Government Printing Office, 1966. 171 pp.

Includes information on the government and armed forces of the Republic of Vietnam and on the Viet Cong; on tactics, techniques, combat support.

Note also: *A pocket guide to Vietnam.* Washington: United States Government

Printing Office, 1962. 130 pp. (Office of Armed Forces Information and Education.)

139

L'Annam. Hanoi, 1931. 221 pp.
Prepared by a group of officials of the Protectorate of Annam under the direction of the Association des Amis du Vieux Hué. Published for the Exposition Coloniale Internationale.

Note also: J. Silvestre: *L'Empire d'Annam et le peuple annamite: aperçu sur la géographie, les productions, l'industrie, les moeurs et les coutumes de l'Annam.* Paris: Alcan, 1889. 380 pp. (Publié sous les auspices de l'Administration des Colonies.) [The Empire of Annam and its people: survey of the geography, products, industry, life and customs of Annam.]

140

G. Garros: *Les usages de Cochinchine.* Saigon: Condurier et Montegout, 1905. 476 pp.

[Customs of Cochinchina.] Manual of custom and business practice, especially relating to buildings, land ownership, trade and sea transport.

141

Variétés tonkinoises: philologie, enseignement, littérature, concours littéraires, caractères chinois, histoire, organisation communale, contribuable, contributions, propriété foncière, impôt foncier, calendrier, paganisme, Boudhisme, Confucianisme, mariage légal, jurisprudence pratique, rites, funérailles, hiérarchie mandarinale, flore, faune, ornithologie, ichtyologie, minéralogie, bois et bambous, abaque, poids et mesures, guide du métreur. Hanoi, 1903. 583 pp.
'Par A+B.' [By E. Souvignet.]

[Tongking miscellanies: philology, education, literature, literary competitions, Chinese script, history, social organization, taxation, land ownership, calendar, religions, marriage, jurisprudence, rituals, funerals, mandarinate, flora, fauna, birds, fish, minerals, timber and bamboo, the abacus, weights and measures, assessor's guide.] Information on traditional Vietnamese life, useful although idiosyncratically arranged.

142

Alfred Schreiner: *Les institutions annamites en Basse-Cochinchine avant la conquête française.* Saigon: Claude, 1900-1902. 3 v.

Chapters: Historical survey; Annamite society; Government; Provincial administration; Canton; Commune; Education and religion; Family; Coins and measures (and calendar); Land ownership; Taxation; Army and navy; Justice and punishment; Civil law. 47 pp. of addenda conclude vol. 3.

Reprinted: Farnborough: Gregg, 1969. 0-576-03995-0.

143

Savigny, Bischoff: *Les richesses du Tong-kin, les produits à y importer et l'exploitation française: guide administratif, commercial, industriel, agricole, etc.* Paris: Oudin, 1885. 203 pp.

[Riches of Tongking; products suitable for import; French development. An administrative, commercial, industrial and agricultural guide.] Includes a glossary and an alphabetical survey of needed industries. See the review in: *Annales de l'Extrême-Orient* vol. 7 (1884-5) pp. 351-2.

144

Trang-hoï-duc; G. Aubaret, translator: *Histoire et description de la Basse Cochinchine (pays de Gia-Dinh).* Paris: Imprimerie Nationale, 1863. 359 pp.

Compiled by Trang-hoï-duc, Lieutenant of the Viceroy of Gia-Dinh, about 1810; the translator has added copious annotations and rearranged the text, in which the geographical survey had come first. Contents: The conquest of Lower Cochinchina (formerly Cambodian) by Annam; Wars with Siam; Revolt of the Tay-s'on; Life and customs; Geography and climate; Geographical survey (pp. 133-286); Agriculture and fisheries. Appendices by G. Aubaret: Government and civil service of the Kingdom of Annam; Administration of Lower Cochinchina [status in 1863 when the territory was shared between Annam and France].

Reprinted: Farnborough: Gregg, 1969. 0-576-03301-4.

Original publication: Trang Hội Đức: *Gia Định thông chí.* [Hanoi, 1820?]

Reports

145

Thành tích tám năm hoạt động của chánh phủ 1954-1962. Saigon, 1962. 1072 pp.

[Report on activities of the Government during eight years 1954-1962.] An official South Vietnamese publication. Superseded: editions with dates 1954-58, 1954-60, 1954-61.

Statistics

146
Niên giám thống kê = Statistical yearbook. Hanoi, Saigon.
National Economy Department, Ministry of National Planning and Statistics, National Institute of Statistics.

The current series is known from 1985, though it is said to have been issued for internal circulation from 1976. The preceding series, issued by the South Vietnamese government in Saigon, covered the years 1949/50 to 1972. Its title varied: sometimes *Viet-Nam statistical yearbook, Annuaire statistique du Viet-Nam, Việt-Nam niên-giám thống-kê* or *Niên-giám thống-kê Việt-Nam.*

Contents of the 1972 edition (published 1973: 415 pp.): Climate, communications, education and culture, public health, justice, trade, industry, public finance, money and banking, national income, labour, agriculture, forestry, fisheries, prices, population, social welfare, foreign aid. In Vietnamese and English.

147
Sơ liệu thống kê = Statistical data of the Socialist Republic of Vietnam. Hanoi: General Statistical Office.

Published annually (perhaps with some irregularity) from the 1961 edition, with a preceding volume covering 1955/60. In Vietnamese and English. Brief (around 100 pages).

A companion historical compilation: *Sơ liệu thống kê, 1930-1984.* Hanoi, 1985. [Statistical data, 1930-1984.] Not seen: cited from unclear references in Cima [130].

148 cancelled

Directories

149
Directory of officials of Vietnam: a reference aid. Springfield, Virginia: NTIS, 1992. 119 pp.
Central Intelligence Agency. Directorate of Intelligence.

'Identifies personalities who hold key positions in the Communist Party, national government, legislative bodies, military organizations, the diplomatic service, and selected mass organizations.' Based on the official Vietnamese media. A simple list of names, without biographical information, arranged by organization. Alphabetical index of persons, pp. 109-119. Adds 'telegraphic spellings' (as used by the Vietnam News Agency), a substitute for diacritical marks -- which are not included.

Previous edition: 1988. 71 pp.

Earlier edition: 1985. 140 pp. This covered a wider range of 'cultural organizations' and included an index of organizations.

Earlier edition: 1983. 133 pp.

150

Viet Nam government organization manual, 1957/58. Saigon, 1958. 275 pp.
National Institute of Administration, Research and Documentation Division.

An outline and a list of names for the South Vietnamese government. A supplement (174 pp.) was published in 1960.

Note also: *VWP-DRV leadership, 1960 to 1973.* Saigon: United States Mission in Vietnam, 1973. 2 parts (138 pp.). (Viet Nam documents and research notes, 114.) Lists of leaders of North Vietnam. Part 1: The Party; Part 2: The Government.

151

Trade directory of the Socialist Republic of Vietnam, 1990. Colchester: Seatrade Organisation, 1990. 47 pp.
Edited by the Commercial Section of the Embassy of the S R Vietnam, London.

Contents: National corporations; Local corporations; Production and export-import enterprises; Trade representation abroad. In each case gives address, telephone number, etc., and specifies major activities.

152

Industrial and commercial directory = Annuaire industriel et commercial = Công-thương Việt-Nam. Saigon: Trinh Húng, 1962.
Association of Vietnamese Engineers and Technicians.

Editions also recorded for 1960 and 1952/3, the latter under a different title: *General directory of Vietnam = Annuaire général du Vietnam = Tông niên giám Việt-Nam.*

153

Annuaire commercial du Tonkin. Hanoi: Dang-Long, 1939. 112 pp.

[Commercial yearbook of Tongking.]

154

A. Coquerel: *Vade mecum commercial de la Cochinchine.* Saigon: Claude, 1905. 695 pp.

[Commercial companion to Cochinchina.] The compiler was secretary-archivist to the Saigon Chamber of Commerce.

Note also: *Annuaire illustré de la Cochinchine.* Saigon: Claude, 1904. 391 pp. [Illustrated yearbook of Cochinchina.] Sixth annual edition (Nunn [20] records a seventh, published in 1905). Previous or alternative title: *Guide-annuaire illustré de la Cochinchine.*

L. Tabouillot, F. Faure: *Guide commercial: livre d'or des négociants de Cochinchine.* Saigon: Legros, 1904. 119 pp. (Chambre de Commerce de Saigon.) [Commercial guide: Saigon merchants' golden book.] All cited from Cordier [242].

155

Niên-giám văn-nghệ-sĩ và hiệp-hội văn-hóa Việt-Nam 1969-70. Saigon, 1970. 815 pp.
Nha Văn-Hóa.

[Yearbook of South Vietnamese artists, writers and cultural associations.] Not seen.

MALAYSIA

156

Frederica M. Bunge, editor: *Malaysia: a country study.* Washington: United States Government Printing Office, 1984. 366 pp.
American University, Foreign Area Studies. (Area handbook series. DA pam, 550-45.)

Fourth edition.

Superseded: John W. Henderson and others: *Area handbook for Malaysia.* 1970. 639 pp.

Bela C. Maday and others: *Area handbook for Malaysia and Singapore.* Washington: United States Government Printing Office, 1965. (American University, Foreign Area Studies.) Maday's work superseded the *Area handbook for North Borneo* [165] and *Malaya* [160] and was in turn superseded, as regards Singapore, by Vreeland [181].

157

E. K. Fisk, H. Osman-Rani: *The political economy of Malaysia.* Kuala Lumpur: Oxford University Press, 1982. 364 pp.

A survey of the twenty-five years since independence. Contents include: Geographical setting; Infrastructure; Demography; Political, social and economic structure; Development planning; Trade and external relations; Agriculture; Minerals; Manufacturing; Money and banking; Public finance.

158

John Gullick: *Malaysia: economic expansion and national unity.* London: Benn; Boulder: Westview Press, 1981. 290 pp.

A country survey by a former member of the Malayan Civil Service. Contents: History; Ethnic communities; Politics and government; Economic policy; Agriculture; Mining; Industry; Trade; Defence and foreign policy; Education; Language; Culture. Little on Sabah and Sarawak.

Supersedes: J. M. Gullick: *Malaysia.* London: Benn, 1969. 304 pp.

159

Wang Gungwu: *Malaysia: a survey.* Singapore: Donald Moore, 1964. 466 pp.

Compiled as Malaysia came into existence in 1963. A country survey, including Singapore. Contents: Physical and human geography; History; Society and culture; Economy; Politics and government.

Subdivisions of Malaysia

160

Norton Ginsburg, Chester F. Roberts and others: *Malaya.* Seattle: University of Washington Press, 1958. 533 pp.
'Based on a research project performed in 1955-56 under contract to the Human Relations Area Files at the University of Chicago.' (Publications of the American Ethnological Society.)

161

R. L. German: *Handbook to British Malaya.* London: Malay States Information Agency.

An official survey, published annually, with numerous photographs and statistical tables. Recorded for 1926 to 1935, with a final undated issue probably of late 1937. The latter (201 pp.) contains: Geography and population; Geology (with coloured map); History of British rule; Administration; the Malay regiment; Finance; Land and labour; Trade and economy; Education; Communications; Hygiene and sanitation; Game; Fisheries; Native industries.

Note also: H. Conway Belfield: *Handbook of the Federated Malay States*. London: Stanford [1907]. 184 pp. Third edition. The author was British resident of Selangor. Second edition: [1904]. 174 pp. First edition: [1903]. 170 pp.

Federated Malay States with a chapter on the Straits Settlements: general information for intending settlers. London: His Majesty's Stationery Office, 1912. 52 pp. (Issued by the Emigrants' Information Office.)

162

R. O. Winstedt, editor: *The Straits Settlements and the Federated and Unfederated Malay States*. London: Constable, 1923. 280 pp.

A country survey, each chapter by a named author. Geography, geology; Flora, fauna; Population, language, literature; Religion; Arts and crafts; History; Archaeology and antiquities; Administration, finance, economy; then a chapter each on the Straits Settlements, the Federated States, the Unfederated States. Some statistics; many photographs.

Note also: *Papers on Malay subjects*. Kuala Lumpur, Singapore, 1907-29. (Committee for Malay Studies.) Not strictly a reference work: a series of papers which, however, built up into a fairly comprehensive cultural survey of the country, with particularly useful monographs on some of the individual Malay states.

163

Précis of information concerning the Straits Settlements and the native states of the Malay Peninsula. London: Her Majesty's Stationery Office, n.d.
War Office, Horse Guards, Intelligence Division.

164

N. B. Dennys: *A descriptive dictionary of British Malaya*. London: London and China Telegraph Office, 1894. 423 pp.

The work was originally intended as a revision of Crawfurd's *Descriptive dictionary* [36] but finally remained restricted to the Malay Peninsula, including Singapore. 3000 entries.

165

George L. Harris and others: *North Borneo, Brunei, Sarawak (British Borneo)*. New Haven: HRAF Press, 1956. 287 pp.
Human Relations Area Files. (Country survey series [2].)

Treats the region as a whole, making little difference between e.g. Brunei and the rest. Covers history and geography, religion, social life, trade and agriculture.

This may be regarded as a shorter version of the material previously published as: Norton S. Ginsburg, editor: *Area handbook on British Borneo*. Chicago: University of Chicago, 1955. 443 pp. (For Human Relations Area Files.) The latter compilation was also the immediate source of:

George L. Harris, editor: *Area handbook for British Borneo*. Washington: United States Government Printing Office, 1956. 278 pp. (American University, Foreign Area Studies.) Not seen: cited from Krausse [21]. This was to be superseded by Maday's *Area handbook for Malaysia* [156].

166

Owen Rutter: *British North Borneo: an account of its history, resources and native tribes*. London: Constable, 1922. 404 pp.

Contents: Geography; Ethnography; Early history; Administration by the British North Borneo Company; Agriculture; Mineral resources; 'Native affairs'.

167

B. A. St J. Hepburn: *The handbook of Sarawak, comprising historical, statistical and general information concerning the colony*. Singapore, 1949.

Reports

168

Malaysia. Kuala Lumpur.
Department of Information.

An official annual survey. Contents: National economy; Banking and currency; Public finance; Trade and industry; Agriculture; Foreign relations; Mass media; Development; Social services; Labour; Transport and communications.

Previous title: *Malaysia: official year book*. Kuala Lumpur. The first under this title was 'Volume 3', 1964. First published (without the information on Sabah and Sarawak, see below) as: *Federation of Malaya: official year book*. 1961-2. 'Nos 1-2'.

This may be regarded as a replacement of the British publication: *Annual report on the Federation of Malaya*. London. Published for 1948 to 1957; preceded by: *Annual report on the Malayan Union*. For 1946 and 1947.

Pre-war titles: *Annual report on the social and economic progress of the people of the Federated Malay States*. 1931-8: *Annual reports on the Federated Malay States*. 1899-1930, consisting as the title suggests of separate reports for each state.

An accompanying title: *Annual reports on the Unfederated Malay States* was issued from 1919 to 1927 (and separate reports for each unfederated state continued to appear until 1938). Previous title: *Annual reports on the states of Kedah, Kelantan, Perlis and Trengganu* (title varies) 1910-1918.

There was concurrently an *Annual report on the Straits Settlements* going back, under varying titles, to 1861.

The *Colony of North Borneo annual report*, earlier called *Report on North Borneo* and *Administration report*, is reported for 1908 to 1940 and 1947 to 1962, after which some information appears in the Malaysian official year book (above).

An *Annual report on Sarawak*, earlier *Administration report*, also appeared in pre-war years and for 1947-62.

For some further details of all these reports, and of those on individual Malay states, see Brewster [4] and Willer [7].

Statistics

169
Buku tahunan perangkaan Malaysia = Yearbook of statistics, Malaysia. Kuala Lumpur.
Department of Statistics.

The series begins with the 1984 volume, published 1985. In English and Bahasa Malaysia. Contents of the 1990 volume, published 1991 (340 pp.): Detailed contents, pp. xxiii-xxxv; Key indicators, pp. v-xxii; Climate; Population and vital statistics; Agriculture; Manufacturing and industry; Services; External trade and balance of payments; Prices; Employment; Finance; Transport and communications; Education; Health and crime; Miscellaneous.

Earlier titles: *Annual statistical bulletin, Malaysia = Siaran perangkaan tahunan Malaysia*. From 1972: *Annual bulletin of statistics, Malaysia = Buletin perangkaan tahunan*. 1964-71.

Some statistics appeared in the pre-war *Malayan year book* [175], published by the Statistics Department in Singapore. This ran from 1935 to about 1939 and incorporated: *Malayan statistics*. London, 1932-4.

170
Siaran perangkaan tahunan = Annual bulletin of statistics. Kota Kinabalu. Department of Statistics Malaysia, Sabah Branch.

Annual statistical bulletin for Sabah, published for 1964 to 1982. In English. Printed from typescript.

171
Siaran perangkaan tahunan = Annual statistical bulletin Sarawak. [Kuching.]
Department of Statistics Malaysia, Sarawak Branch.

In English and Bahasa Malaysia. Last seen 1987 (published 1988: 294 pp.). Editions for 1964-71 were entitled *Annual bulletin of statistics.*

172
V. V. Bhanoji Rao: *National accounts of West Malaysia 1947-1971.* Singapore: Heinemann Educational Books, 1976. 100 pp.

Derives national accounts data 'by demand aggregates at current and constant prices, and gross domestic product data at constant factor cost by industry of origin'. Statistical appendix.

173
Manual of statistics relating to the Federated Malay States. Kuala Lumpur: F. M. S. Government Printing Office.

Recorded for dates between 1904 (91 pp.) and 1933.

174
Rainfall statistics of the British Borneo Territories (Sarawak, Brunei, North Borneo), period 1896-1957. N.p., 1961. 174 pp.
Compiled by the Department of Civil Aviation and Meteorological Services, British Borneo Territories.

Statistical tables and some maps. There is some useful information on West Malaysia in a collection of reprints:

Ooi Jin Bei, Chia Lin Sen: *The climate of West Malaysia and Singapore.* Singapore: Oxford University Press, 1974. 262 pp. (Oxford in Asia university readings.)

Almanacs and directories

175

Information Malaysia: yearbook. Kuala Lumpur: Berita.

A commercial almanac and handbook of impressive range. 1990/91 edition: 1990. 726 pp. Main sections: Background (Calendar; Diplomatic representation; Environment; History, immigration; National symbols; Places of interest; Population; Relioion). Culture (Religious festivals; Social life; Arts and crafts). The economy (Natural resources; Infrastructure; Industry; Commerce; Finance; National plan and current budget). Political (Constitution; Legislature and executive with list of ministries). Social (Education and welfare; Media; Sports). The States (detailed survey: about 15 pp. each, with maps of administrative subdivisions, communications, etc.). Many other tables, figures and maps. Coloured geological maps in preliminary pages.

Biennial publication. Earlier editions are more difficult to use as they lack contents pages.

Incorporated: *Malaysia yearbook*. Kuala Lumpur: Straits Times Press. A similar but briefer compilation. First published under this title 1963. Previous titles: *Federation of Malaya year book* (from about 1956): *Malayan year book*. Singapore, 1935 to about 1939: *Federated Malay States year book*. Kuala Lumpur: Government Printing Office, 1924 to about 1932.

176

Organisation of the Government of Malaysia. Kuala Lumpur: Di-chetak Di-jabatan Chetak Karajaan.

Published from about 1967.

177

Kompass Malaysia. Kuala Lumpur: Kompass.

An alphabetical and classified trade directory. 1991 and 1988 editions seen. Earlier title: *Kompass buku merah*. This was perhaps the successor to: *The new Straits times directory (buku merah) of Malaysia*. Published from 1977/8 to 1981/2. This in turn succeeded, as regards Malaysia, the long-established *Straits times directory*, see 190.

178

Ch'ng Kin See, Ahmad Bakeri bin Abu Bakar: *Panduan perpustakaan di Malaysia = Directory of libraries in Malaysia*. Kuala Lumpur: National Library of Malaysia, 1978. 324 pp.

Covers 177 libraries, academic, public and special. Includes a subject index to special collections.

Note also: Edward Lim Huck Tee: *Libraries in West Malaysia and Singapore: a short history*. Kuala Lumpur: University of Malaya Library, 1970. 161 pp. This includes a chapter on books and libraries in Malaya before the beginning of Western influence.

179
Malaya: a guide for businessmen and visitors. Singapore: Public Relations Office; Kuala Lumpur: Information Service.

First published 1953: last noted 1962. A semi-official directory and handbook in magazine format. No table of contents. Numerous statistics. Advertisements.

180
Prince of Wales' Island register and directory.

1820 and 1829 issues recorded by Cordier [242].

SINGAPORE

181
Barbara Leitch LePoer: *Singapore: a country study*. Washington: United States Government Printing Office, 1991. 328 pp.
Library of Congress, Federal Research Division. (Area handbook series. DA pam, 550-184.)

Second edition. Contents: Historical setting; The society and its environment; The economy; Government and politics; National security. Appendix of tables, including: Population by ethnic group and language, 1980; Chinese speech groups and their alternate names; Major equipment of the Armed Forces, 1988. Charts include: Organization of the Armed Forces, Police Force and Civil Defence Force; Military rank insignia. Schematic maps of expressways, p. 168; of the Mass Rapid Transit system, p. 170.

First edition: Nena Vreeland and others: *Area handbook for Singapore*. Washington: United States Government Printing Office, 1977. 210 pp. Chart of educational system, p. 37; List of international organizations of which Singapore was a member, pp. 172-4; Sources of imports and direction of exports, pp. 179-182. Several other charts and tables based on the 1975/6 edition of *Yearbook of statistics* [187].

For an earlier relevant work in the same series see Maday's *Area handbook for Malaysia* [156].

182

Background notes: Singapore. Washington: United States Government Printing Office, 1987.
Department of State, Bureau of Public Affairs. Office of Public Communication. (Department of State publication, 8240.)

Earlier edition: 1975.

183

You Poh Seng, Lim Chong-Yah, editors: *Singapore: twenty-five years of development.* Singapore: Nan Yang Xing Zhou Lianhe Zaobao, 1984.

Summary of economic development between 1959 and 1984 by academics from the National University of Singapore. Includes: Linda Low, 'Public enterprises in Singapore', pp. 253-287; Jon S. T. Quah, 'The public bureaucracy in Singapore', pp. 288-314.

Note the same editors' earlier survey: You Poh Seng, Lim Chong-Yah: *The Singapore economy.* Singapore: Eastern Universities Press, 1971. 421 pp. The final chapter is a collection of statistics.

184

John Cameron: *Our tropical possessions in Malayan India: being a descriptive account of Singapore, Penang, Province Wellesley and Malacca, their peoples, products, commerce and government.* London, 1865. 408 pp.

By the then editor of the Singapore *Straits times.* Appendices: List of the fruits to be found in the bazaars of the Straits Settlements, pp. 397-402; List of the chief fruit and forest trees indigenous to the Straits Settlements, pp. 403-8.

Reprinted with an introduction by Wang Gungwu: Kuala Lumpur: Oxford University Press, 1965. 408 pp.

Reports

185

Singapore. Singapore.
Ministry of Culture, Information Division; later Ministry of Communications and Information, Information Division.

First published under this title for 1969. (The 1969 volume was called *Singapore year book '69* on the half-title page.) An official survey and annual report with selected statistical information. Contents of 1989 volume: The people; History; Natural history; Government and politics; Law;

International relations; Trade, industry and tourism; Primary production; Finance and banking; Employment; Transport and communications; Mass media; Housing and utilities; Defence; Internal security; Education; Health and the environment; Community development; Culture and recreation. Statistical appendix, pp. 227-309.

Earlier title: *Singapore year book, 1964-1968*. 1965-9.

Successor to: *Annual report on Singapore, 1946-1963*. Published 1947-65: The title varied: *Report on Singapore: Colony of Singapore annual report*. For the pre-war series see *Annual report on the Straits Settlements* [168].

186

Singapore facts and pictures. Singapore: Ministry of Culture, Ministry of Communications and Information.

Annual, beginning 1969. A brief official survey, pictorial yet with some solid text and statistics. Previous title: *Singapore facts and figures*. 1966-8.

Statistics

187

Yearbook of statistics, Singapore. Singapore: Chief Statistician. Department of Statistics.

Annual, first published for 1967. Contents of the 1984/5 edition (299 pp.): Key indicators; Demography; Labour; National income; Production and industry; Trade and services; Transport and communication; Finance and insurance; Prices; Education; Health; Culture and recreation.

188

Economic and social statistics, Singapore, 1960-1982. Singapore: Department of Statistics, 1983. 270 pp.

Contents: Climate; Land use; Demography, employment; National income; Balance of payments; Agriculture, fisheries; Industry; Energy; Building; External trade; Transport, communication; Finance; Prices; Education; Health; Culture and recreation.

For further sources of Singapore statistics see: *An annotated bibliography of statistical publications*. Singapore: Department of Statistics. Annual publication from 1972, with a subject index.

Directories

189

Singapore Government directory. Singapore: Ministry of Information and the Arts; Ministry of Communications and Information, Information Division.

Last seen: 1991 (818 pp.). List of departments and chief officers; then an alphabetical index of names. 1988 edition: 514 pp.

190

Times business directory of Singapore (buku merah). Singapore: Times Periodicals.

Last seen: 1991/92. '111th edition.' 414 + 208 pp.

1984 edition: 302 pp. White pages: Indexes of local and foreign companies; Personnel; Products and brand names; Directory of officials and public bodies; Postal codes; Geographical index. Pink pages: Classified index of products.

Previous titles: *The Straits times directory of Singapore.* Singapore: Times Publishing. From 1976/7: *The Straits times directory of Singapore and Malaysia: The Straits times directory of Malaysia.* About 1965: *The Straits times directory of Singapore and Malaya.* From 1949 to 1964.

This was the successor to a pre-war series: *The Singapore and Malayan directory.* Singapore: Fraser and Neave, Printers Ltd., 1922-40; *The Singapore and Straits directory.* Singapore: Singapore and Straits Printing Office, 1880-1921; T. J. Keaughran: *Singapore directory for the Straits Settlements.* Singapore, 1877-8 (cover title: The Straits Settlements directory); previously in two series, (1) *Straits calendar and directory.* Singapore, 1861-76 (1875 according to Cordier); (2) *Penang almanac and directory.* 1861-76; *Singapore almanac and directory.* Singapore, 1846-60; *Penang, Singapore and Malacca almanac and directory.* 1843-5 (1846 according to Cordier).

191

Tradelink 1987/88 SMA directory. Singapore: Singapore Manufacturers' Association.

1987 edition: 470 pp. Sections on specific industries; products and services index; trade name index; addresses.

The directory has been published under varying titles since 1957, when it was called *Directory of Singapore manufacturers.*

Note also: *Singapore Indian Chamber of Commerce trade directory.* Singapore.

The 1986 edition was entitled *Trading with Singapore*. Review and statistics; list of addresses; list of products and services; list of members. Cited from Quah [28].

192

Shipping guide of Singapore. Singapore: USAHA Advertising Corporation.

Eighth edition: 1980; second edition: 1970. Includes list of associations, list of registered vessels, guide to legislation.

Note also: *Singapore tide tables and port facilities*. Singapore: Port of Singapore Authority. (Hydrographic Department.)

193

The Singapore and Straits bazaar book. Singapore: Singapore and Straits Printing Office, 1889. 136 pp.
Edited by David Chalmers Neave.

Cited from Cordier [242].

BRUNEI

194

D. E. Brown: *Brunei: the structure and history of a Bornean Malay Sultanate*. Brunei: Brunei Museum, 1970. 237 pp.
(Monograph of the Brunei Museum journal.)

The text of a doctoral thesis: included here for its useful appendices, which include: Malay names and titles in Brunei; The first, second and third persons [etiquette of court speech]; District tenure; List of officials; Glossary and note on spelling.

195

M. S. H. McArthur, A. V. M. Horton, editor: *Report on Brunei in 1904*. Athens, Ohio: Ohio University, Center for Southeast Asian Studies, 1987. 283 pp.
(Monographs in international studies.)

Report of an official of the Malayan Civil Service despatched to Brunei in 1904 to analyse the country's problems. History, geography, constitution, economic and social conditions.

Republication, with commentary, of two reports: M. S. H. McArthur: *Notes on a visit to the rivers Belait and Tutong*. 1904; M. S. H. McArthur: *Report on*

Brunei in 1904. 1904. Subsections of the latter include: Constitution; Districts; Population; Trade; Government and ruling class; Resources; Revenue.

In 1906 McArthur, as Resident, was to commence publication of the *Annual report* of the Government of Brunei [196].

Reports and statistics

196
Brunei. Bandar Seri Bagawan: Media Publishing.

The official annual survey and report, published under this title from 1978. Includes some statistics and an appendix setting out the organization of the government.

Previously issued under varying titles by the State Secretariat and, earlier, Her Majesty's Stationery Office in London: *State of Brunei annual report*, etc. First published 1906.

197
Brunei statistical yearbook. Bandar Seri Begawan: State Secretariat. Economic Planning Unit, Statistics Section.

Annual, probably beginning 1973/4 (but sources differ. At any rate, 1974/5 was the second edition). Contents of 1983/4 volume (214 pp.): Area, population and vital statistics, pp. 6-27; Labour and places of employment, pp. 28-40; Agriculture, forestry and fishery; Mining; Power; External trade; Transport and communication; Finance; Prices and wages; Education, pp. 86-110; Health; National accounts statistics (and statistics of businesses), pp. 117-206; Press, broadcasting, books; Climate; Public security. The arrangement has remained constant for some years.

Almanacs and directories

198
Buku panduan badan-badan perusahaan perniagaan Negara Brunei Darussalam. Bandar Seri Begawan: Unit Perancang Ekonomi Kementerian Kewangan, 1985. 89 pp.

[Directory of businesses in the State of Brunei Darussalam.]

INDONESIA

199
Frederica M. Bunge, editor: *Indonesia: a country study*. Washington:

United States Government Printing Office, 1983. 343 pp.
American University, Foreign Area Studies. Department of the Army,
Headquarters. (Area handbook series. DA pam 550-39.)

4th edition. Contents: Historical setting; The society and its environment;
The economy; Government and politics; National security. Military
organization chart, p. 245; Map of armed forces defence areas, p. 247;
Diagrams of officer insignia with US equivalents, p. 259. Tabular
information includes: Structure of gross domestic product, 1960, 1967, 1971,
1980; Crop, forestry, fishery production and trends; Order of battle for army,
navy, air force.

Superseded: Nena Vreeland and others: *Area handbook for Indonesia.* 1975.

John W. Henderson and others: *Area handbook for Indonesia.* 1970. 569 pp.

Area handbook for Indonesia. 1964. 737 pp.

John Cookson, editor: *Area handbook for Indonesia.* 1959. 2 v. (Special
warfare.)

200

Ruth T. McVey, editor: *Indonesia.* New Haven: Yale University,
Southeast Asia Studies, 1963. 600 pp.
Human Relations Area Files. (Area and country survey series.) By
arrangement with HRAF Press. Developed pursuant to a contract between
Yale University and the U. S. Department of Health, Education and Welfare,
Office of Education.

Contents: Physical and human resource patterns; Cultures and communities
(pp. 24-96); The Chinese minority; The agricultural foundation; From
colonial to guided economy (pp. 155-247); Labor in transition; The course of
Indonesian history; Dynamics of guided democracy (pp. 309-409); Genesis
of a modern literature; Music and theatre in Java and Bali. Includes map of
'Forest and sawah in Java and Madura 1:3,800,000'.

This compilation draws on a 3-volume monograph compiled in 1956 by Yale
for the Human Relations Area Files; and on John Cookson's *Area handbook*
of 1959 [199].

201

Netherlands East Indies. [London, 1944.] 2 v.
Admiralty, Naval Intelligence Division. (Geographical handbook series. B.R.,
518.) Compiled in Cambridge and edited by H. C. Darby. Gwen Raverat
drew some of the maps.

A wartime country survey illustrated with photographs, many sketch maps and tables; initially for official use only. Vol. 1: Geology and physiography; geographical description (Sumatra, islands adjacent to Sumatra, Java and Madoera, Borneo, Celebes, Lesser Soenda Islands, Moluccas, Dutch New Guinea); climate, soils, vegetation, medical services and health conditions. Note appendix 3: maps and charts (pp. 439-488). Vol. 2: The people; history; government and law; demography; agriculture, forestry, manufacturing, labour, commerce, finance; ports (pp. 339-398), roads, railways, sea transport. Appendices 6-10: Sarawak, Brunei, Labuan, British North Borneo, Portuguese Timor.

Earlier publication: *A manual of Netherlands India (Dutch East Indies)*. 1918. 548 pp. (Naval Staff, Intelligence Department. I.D., 1209.) Initially for official use only. Geography; Inhabitants (pp. 124-244); Government; Economy; Products (pp. 303-374); Communications; History.

202

G. F. E. Gonggryp and others: *Geillustreerde encyclopaedie van Nederlandsch-Indië*. Leiden: Leidsche Uitgeversmaatschappij, 1934. 1583 cols.

[Illustrated encyclopaedia of the Dutch East Indies.] A concise alphabetical encyclopaedia with some halftone illustrations. Most entries are brief: the majority are for place names. Note, under 'Java', a lengthy table of administrative subdivisions, cols 530-594.

203

Handbook of the Netherlands East-Indies. Buitenzorg, 1930.
Department of Agriculture, Industry and Commerce, Division of Commerce.

The purpose of this official handbook was 'to provide a synopsis of Netherlands performances in these parts, an illustration of Government interference on various spheres, a sketch of the economical character and power of the Netherlands East Indian Archipelago'. Contents: climate, flora, fauna, history, population, immigration, health, education, government, 'judicature,' finance and banking, agriculture, labour, trade, transport, tourism. Many photographs and statistical tables.

Previous edition: 1924.

Successor to an earlier title: *Yearbook of the Netherlands East Indies*. Batavia, 1920. Included a detailed survey of the development of harbours, pp. 215-251, with many plans and photographs. This edition was also published in Dutch as: *Jaarboek van Nederlandsch-Indië*.

First English and Dutch editions: 1916. In this the chapters included more historical background.

204

J. Paulus, D. G. Stibbe, editors: *Encyclopaedie van Nederlandsch-Indië.*
The Hague: Nijhoff; Leiden: Brill, 1917-21. 4 v.
Cover title: Encyclopaedie van Nederlandsch Oost-Indie.

[Encyclopaedia of the Dutch East Indies.] Second edition. A massive work
of semi-official inspiration. Alphabetically arranged, and containing all the
kinds of information to be looked for in, e.g., a British colonial gazetteer
(administration, statistics, resources, local administrative units and
topography) combined with entries under scientific names for flora and
fauna, and with historical biography. The alphabetical sequence includes
many cross-references, e.g. for Malay and other vernacular names for flora
and fauna.

Longer entries for major subdivisions, e.g. the entry for Celebes (vol. 1 pp.
443-467) deal with: the place name, exploration, geology, physiography,
topography (pp. 449-461), climate, population, administrative boundaries,
economy, and conclude with a bibliography.

At end of vol. 4: List of articles, many of them for minor place names,
printed in the first edition (see below) and not repeated in the second (pp.
875-890); Corrigenda; Index of personal names, pp. 897-922.

Supplements were published as a series of 62 fascicles, 1922-1940, edited by
Stibbe and others. Fascs 1-60 make up vols 5-8 of the set: entries in them are
in no overall order, but each volume includes an index of personal names
and each includes a cumulating index of supplementary articles.

First edition: 1896-1905. 4 v. Edited by P. A. van der Lith, Joh. F. Snelleman.

Abridged edition: T. J. Bezemer, editor: *Beknopte encyclopaedie van
Nederlandsch-Indië.* 1921. 632 pp. An excellent concise reference work which
also forms a dictionary of local names for flora, fauna, etc.

205

Handboek voor Cultuur- en Handelsondernemingen in Nederlandsch-Indië.
Amsterdam, 1917.

[Handbook for agricultural and commercial enterprises in the Dutch East
Indies.]

206

D. van Hinloopen Labberton: *Geillustreerd handboek van Insulinde,
zijnde een synthetische catalogus van den oeconomischen staat van den
Nederlandsch-Indischen Archipel, naar de gegevens van de Regeerings-
Bureaux en bevoegde deskundigen op ieder gebied.* Amsterdam: Vivat,

1910. 380 pp.

[Illustrated handbook of the East Indies: a comprehensive manual of the economic condition of the Dutch East Indian Archipelago, based on data from official sources and from experts in each area.] A development survey: Land and people; Administration and public services (pp. 115-269); the Indies in the world economy; European economic development and humanitarian work in the Indies. Many illustrations.

207
C. J. Temminck: *Coup d'oeil général sur les possessions néerlandaises dans l'Inde archipélagique.* Leiden: Arnz, 1846-9. 3 v.

[General survey of the Dutch possessions in the East Indian archipelago.]

Subdivisions of Indonesia

208
Java and Madura. London: Her Majesty's Stationery Office, 1920. 97 pp.
(Handbooks prepared under the direction of the Historical Section of the Foreign Office, 82.)

Contents: Geography; political history; social and political conditions; economic conditions, pp. 43-89, including means of communication, industry, commerce, finance.

The Historical Section was established in 1917 to provide background information on countries which British diplomats might need to know about at the prospective Peace Conference. The resulting brief geographical and political surveys were published when the Conference's work was largely over. Several are relevant to Indonesia:

No. 80: *Portuguese Timor.* 1920. 26 pp.

No. 75: *Dutch Timor and the lesser Sunda islands.* 1919. 38 pp.

No. 72: *Sumatra.* 1919. 72 pp.

No. 87: *Dutch New Guinea and the Molucca Islands.* 1920. 54 pp.

No. 84: *Dutch Borneo.* 1920. 45 pp.

No. 74: *Celebes.* 1919. 34 pp.

209
Ian Rowland: *Timor, including the islands of Roti and Ndao.* Oxford: Clio Press, 1992. 119 pp. 1-85109-159-9.

(World bibliographical series, 142.)

Covers both halves of the island, thus differing from most other books in the series, which are devoted to obvious political units. Largely a bibliography, and very useful as such, but also containing a worthwhile introductory outline: Geology, geography, flora and fauna, ethnology and history. Indonesian annexation of east Timor and its aftermath, pp. xxxi-xxxv.

210

Hélio Augusto Esteves Felgas: *Timor português*. Lisbon: Agência Geral do Ultramar, 1956. 570 pp.

[Portuguese Timor.] A standard survey: geography, flora and fauna, ethnology and linguistics, administration (with history), development.

211

W. C. Klein, editor: *Nieuw Guinea: de ontwikkeling op economisch, sociaal en cultureel gebied in Nederlands en Australisch Nieuw Guinea*. The Hague: Staatsdrukkerij- en Uitgeverijbedrief, 1953-4. 3 v. with 4 loose maps.

[New Guinea: the economic, social and cultural development of Dutch and Australian New Guinea.] Impressive scope: each chapter by a named author. Vol. 1: History; Languages; Religious missions (pp. 82-229); Geology and resources; Aviation; Public works; Posts, telephones, telegraphs; The labour problem ('The training of the native as a labourer in the modern sense'). Vol. 2: Mapping; Climate; Soil; Subsistence agriculture, non-native settlement (pp. 106-190); Fauna; Vegetation and flora; Forestry; Fisheries; Shipping. Vol. 3: Exploration (pp. 1-120); Health; Government, police, justice; Finance; Plantation agriculture (list of plantations, p. 301); Enlightenment of natives; Second World War; Strategy; Industrial opportunities; Trade. In Dutch, with English summaries.

Also: *Vademecum voor Nederlands-Nieuw-Guinea*. Rotterdam: Nieuw-Guinea Instituut, 1956. 216 pp. Aimed at settlers. Survey of towns, pp. 134-209.

Reports

212

Indonesia: an official handbook. Jakarta.
Department of Information, Directorate of Foreign Information Services.

The official annual survey, with some statistical information: first published under this title for 1978. Contents include: Land and people; History;

Government; Development; Defence; Security; Mass media.

Previous title: *Indonesia handbook*. First published for 1970. The 1975 edition contained a lengthy survey of provincial development under the current five-year plan, pp. 89-271; and a supplement of statistics, pp. 273-358.

213
Indisch verslag. The Hague.

[Indian report.] The official annual report on the Dutch East Indies, published under this title for 1920-1939.

Previous titles: *Koloniaal verslag*. 1866-1919: *Verslag van bestuur en staat van Nederlandsch-Indië, Suriname en Curacao*. The series goes back to 1847.

Statistics

214
Statistik Indonesia = Statistical yearbook of Indonesia. Jakarta.
Central Bureau of Statistics.

First published for 1975. In English and Bahasa Indonesia. Contents of 1983 edition (709 pp.): List of conventional signs, p. xlviii; Narrative summary, pp. lvii-cxxviii; Geography; Population, labour; Social affairs; Agriculture; Industry, foreign trade; Communications, transport; Finance, prices.

Pre-war editions: *Statistisch jaaroverzicht van Nederlandsch-Indië = Statistical abstract*. 1922/3 to 1940. (Centraal Kantoor voor de Statistiek. After 1930 this was considered vol. 2 of the *Indisch verslag* [213]). Before 1922, statistics for the East Indies formed a section of: *Jaarcijfers voor het Koninkrijk der Nederlanden = Statistical annual for the Netherlands*, going back to 1887.

Note also: Nugroho: *Indonesia facts and figures*. Jakarta, 1967. 608 pp. Largely statistical, with appendix on the Central Bureau of Statistics.

Demographic factbook of Indonesia. Jakarta: Lembaga Demografi FEUI, 1974. 404 pp. 'Revised edition,' slightly updated from the first (1972).

For further sources of current Indonesian statistics see: *Daftar buku terbitan Biro Pusat Statistik = List of publications issued by Central Bureau of Statistics*. Irregular; 1988 edition seen.

215
Buku saku statistik Indonesia = Statistical pocket book of Indonesia. Jakarta.

An annual or biennial publication more concise than the above. Begun 1957 to continue: *Statistisch zakboekje voor Nederlandsch Indië*. 1934-40. Title varies.

216

W. M. F. Mansvelt and others: *Changing economy in Indonesia: a selection of statistical source material from the early 19th century up to 1940.* The Hague: Nijhoff, 1975- .

Vol. 1: Export crops, 1816-1940; vol. 2: Public finance, 1876-1939; vol. 3: expenditures on fixed assets; vol. 4: Rice prices. The series continues.

Brewster [4] p. 5 records an earlier series of a similar kind: *Mededeelingen van het Centraal Kantoor voor de Statistiek Indies.* In this series nos 160-168, edited by Mansvelt and published by the C. K. S., 1936-9, consist of historical statistics.

Almanacs and directories

217

Buku alamat pejabat negara R. I. = *Book of addresses of state functionaries of the Republic of Indonesia.* Jakarta: Alda, Dharma Bakti, 1984. 680 pp.

English table of contents, pp. 6-8. Includes 'non-departmental government institutions (many concerned with research and development), pp. 441-486; provincial governors, regents and mayors, pp. 489-523; Indonesian representatives abroad, pp. 527-554; Members of House of representatives, pp. 566-634. Many photographs of departmental heads (but none at State Secrets Institute).

Similar lists have appeared under various titles: *Daftar nama dan alamat pejabat-pejabat negara Republik Indonesia.* (Departemen Penerangan.) About 1976: *Daftar alamat dan nomor telepon pedjabat-pedjabat negara.* 1971: *Personalia van staatkundige eenheden (regeering en volksvertegenwordiging) in Indonesiä.* 1949.

218

Regeerings-almanak voor Nederlandsch-Indië. Weltevreden etc.

[Government almanac for the Dutch East Indies.] An official handbook and directory, published about 1820 to 1940. Contents of the 1930 edition (2 v.) include: Vol. 1: General index; Narrative outline of the government, its departments and local administrations, pp. 1-515; Army and navy, pp. 516-603 (including lists of vessels, harbours, etc.); Banks, pp. 666-676; Appendix of laws and regulations, pp. 1*-872* including lists of former Governors-General and of local administrative divisions. Vol. 2: Calendar; Personnel of government departments, Army and Navy, pp. 43-799; Orders of knighthood; Bank and steamship company personnel; Index of names (selective) pp. 850-919.

219

Standard trade and industry directory of Indonesia. Jakarta: Kompass Indonesia.

Annual since 1979: the 10th edition, 1989/90, is in two big volumes, comprising an alphabetical and a classified guide. Early editions, called *Standard trade directory of Indonesia*, were published by the Indonesian Chamber of Commerce and Industry, and included a government directory.

PHILIPPINES

220

Frederica M. Bunge, editor: *Philippines: a country study.* Washington: United States Government Printing Office, 1984. 368 pp.
American University, Foreign Area Studies. (Area handbook series. DA pam, 550-72.)

Third edition. Contents: Historical setting; The society and its environment; The economy; Government and politics; National security. Map and list of cultural-linguistic groups, pp. 68-9; Annual household income by region, p. 125; Land use map, p. 147; Map of guerrilla activity, p. 240; Military insignia, p. 273. Some tabular information, notably: Crop, forestry, fishery production, 1964/6, 1971, 1980; Major weapons of army, navy, air force, 1983. Appendix: Mutual defense treaty between the U. S. A. and the Republic of the Philippines, 1952.

Second edition: Nena Vreeland and others: *Area handbook for the Philippines.* Washington: United States Government Printing Office, 1976. 458 pp. American University, Foreign Area Studies. (DA pam 550-72.) Tabular data in this edition include: unemployment rates; protein and calorie deficiencies; chronology of agrarian reform measures; military ranks and pay scales; incidence of major crimes before and during martial law.

First edition: Frederic H. Chaffee and others: *Area handbook for the Philippines.* 1969. 413 pp. Partly a condensation of Eggan [221].

221

Fred Eggan and others: *Area handbook on the Philippines.* New Haven: Human Relations Area Files, 1956. 4 v. (1832 pp.).
University of Chicago, Philippine Studies Program. (Subcontractor's monograph, HRAF-16 Chicago-5.) Also cited as published by the University of Chicago.

This work formed the basis of Chaffee's compilation [220]. Not seen.

222

Zoilo M. Galang: *Encyclopedia of the Philippines*. Manila: Exequiel Floro, 1950-58. 20 v.

Third edition. A compilation arranged thematically: vols 1-2 literature, vols 3-4 biography (to about 1920), vols 5-6 commerce and industry, vols 7-8 art, vols 9-10 education, vols 11-12 government and politics, vols 13-14 science, vols 15-16 history, vols 17-18 'builders' (more biographies from the more recent period), vols 19-20 general information. No index, but there is an outline of contents at the end of vol. 20. Much too long. 'Cast our faults on the sands of Oblivion and write our virtues in the pages of Eternity' (Galang).

First edition: Manila: P. Vera, 1935-6. 10 v. Most copies of this were destroyed in the Second World War, and the whole second edition was burnt before it could be distributed.

223

Albert Kolb: *Die Philippinen*. Leipzig: Koehler, 1942. 503 pp.
(Geographische Handbücher.)

[The Philippines.] Contents: The country; The people and way of life; Economic survey (Agriculture, pp. 165-314; fishery; forestry; mining; industry; trade); Markets and towns; Demography; The political future. 13 folding and loose maps; many statistical tables, charts and small maps; many photographs. Appendix of statistics, pp. 438-457.

224

W. Cameron Forbes: *The Philippine Islands*. Boston: Houghton Mifflin, 1928. 2 v.

An exhaustive country survey, though desultorily arranged. Vol. 1: Geography; History; Governmemt; Public order; Finance; Justice; Health; Public works; Education; Prisons; Development of Baguio; Tribal peoples. Vol. 2: 'Moros' (Islamic peoples); Church and state; Attitude of Filipinos [to U. S. suzerainty]; Political parties; Assembly; recent political history; The independence movement. Appendices of statistics and documents.

Note also: L. P. Hammond: *A survey of economic conditions in the Philippine Islands*. Boston, 1928.

C. H. Forbes-Lindsay: *The Philippines under Spanish and American rules*. Philadelphia: Winston, 1906. 566 pp. A chatty country survey with a fairly substantial section of regional descriptions. Emphasizes the benefits of American rule.

Francisco Javier de Moya y Jiménez: *Las Islas Filipinas en 1882: estudios históricos, geográficos, estadísticos y descriptivos.* Madrid: El Correo, 1883. 363 pp. [The Philippines in 1882: historical, geographical, statistical and topographical studies.] A reprint of articles from *Revista de Espana.*

[Sinibaldo de Mas y Sans:] *Informe sobre el estado de las Islas Filipinas en 1842.* Madrid, 1843. [Report on the state of the Philippines in 1842.] Only a few copies issued, and those with some missing pages owing to censorship.

225

J. Mallat: *Les Philippines: histoire, géographie, moeurs, agriculture, industrie et commerce des colonies espagnoles dans l'Océanie.* Paris: Bertrand, 1846. 2 v.

[The Philippines: history, geography, way of life, agriculture, industry and commerce of the Spanish possessions in Oceania.] The second, 'atlas' volume contains miscellaneous plates, a general map and a plan of Manila.

Reports

226

Philippine yearbook. Manila.
National Economic and Development Authority, National Census and Statistics Office.

A fat official survey, published every two years since 1975. Contents of the 1989 edition (1348 pp.): History, geograaphy, government, defence, crime, demography, education, culture, health and welfare, science, resources and development, power, industry, labour, income, trade and prices, tourism, transport and communications, public finance, banking and insurance, national accounts and balance of payments. Narrative treatment but with generous statistics.

Note appendix A: List of provinces, cities and municipalities; B: Directory of government agencies; D: directory of public and private colleges and universities.

227

Annual report of the President of the Philippines to the President and Congress of the United States. Washington: United States Government Printing Office.

The official annual report, published under this title for 1936 to 1939. Previous titles: *Annual report of the Governor General of the Philippine Islands*: *Annual report of the United States of America Philippines Commission.* Recorded from 1900.

Statistics

228

Philippine statistical yearbook. Manila.
National Economic and Development Authority, National Census and Statistics Office, National Statistical Coordination Board.

Published under this title for 1977 onwards. In English. Contents of the 1990 edition (various paginations): Overview (15 pp.); Population and housing; INcome and prices; Economic accounts; Natural resources; Agriculture; Industrial establishment; Foreign trade; Tourism; Vital, health, nutritional statistics; Education, labour and employment; Social services; Transport and communications; Energy and water resources; Public finance; Money and banking; Public order and justice; Science and technology.

Previous titles: *NEDA statistical yearbook of the Philippines*. 1974-6: *Philippine statistics yearbook*. 1969: *Yearbook of Philippine statistics*. 1940, 1946, 1957, 1958, 1966.

229

25 years of economic and financial statistics in the Philippines, 1949-1973. Manila: Central Bank of the Philippines, n.d. 5 v.

Contents: Money and banking; Loans and investment; Foreign exchange and trade; Public finance and prices; Production and labour.

Note also: *Philippine statistics, 1903-1959: handbook*. Manila, 1960. 144 pp. (Bureau of the Census and Statistics.)

Almanacs and directories

230

Republic of the Philippines official directory. Manila, etc.

1967 edition examined (280 pp.): fairly inclusive, listing many minor and local boards and committees for which government departments are responsible, with their addresses and chief officers. Includes hospitals and colleges.

First published in English (as *Official directory of the Republic of the Philippines*) 1946.

This succeeds the pre-war *Directorio oficial* of the Philippines Assembly, and the *Official roster of officers and employees in the civil service of the Philippine Islands*, first published 1902, for which see Doeppers [296].

For the wartime government see: *Personnel of the Philippine puppet government*. Washington: Office of Strategic Services, Research and Analysis Branch, 1944. 29 pp.

231

Kompass Philippines: registry of industry and commerce of the Republic of the Philippines. Manila: Kompass.

Second edition, 1989/90 (1990 on cover): 1179 pp. An alphabetical and classified business directory.

Note also: *Philippine company profile*. Manila: Mahal Kong Pilipinas Foundation. Editions for 1993 and 1988 (1575 pp.) seen: first published 1987? Details of major companies.

Top-1000: Philippines best 1000 corporations. Manila: Mahal Kong. A more select compilation. 1988 edition seen: perhaps a successor to: *Business day's 1000 top corporations in the Philippines*. Manila: Business Day, 1981.

Directory of TNCs in the Philippines. Manila: IBON Databank Philippines, 1988. 144 pp. The result of a research survey on the influence of transnational corporations on Philippine life. The 'directory' (311 entries) is in tabular format on pp. 34-68, followed by indexes and statistical information.

232

Cockatoo's handbook: Philippines. Manila: Cockatoo Press, 1990. 799 pp. Author: Daniel Ludszuweit. Editor: Bill Jeffries.

A very informative handbook and directory, but difficult for quick reference becaue of its quirky arrangement. Contents, interspersed with general and cultural information, include: Ethnic groups, pp. 39-49; Chronology, pp. 51-74; Art and culture with useful addresses; Education with list of colleges; Health, hospitals; Travel, with lists of companies and routes, pp. 168-200; Post and telephone costs; Immigration and residence, pp. 233-256. Metro Manila (history, travel, places of interest and useful addresses), pp. 257-415, including elaborate guide to food, restaurants and cuisines, pp. 313-382. Other regions, pp. 416-674. Languages: glossary of Philippine English, p. 678; brief English-Tagalog, English-Cebuano and English-Ilonggo dictionaries. Very small scale Metro Manila street atlas with index, pp. 749-796. Many specialised maps throughout.

Earlier edition(s?) not seen.

233

Fookien times Philippines yearbook. Manila: Fookien Times.

An annual survey. Last seen 1987/8: in a series that began 1926.

Note also: *Philippine yearbook*. Manila: Philippine Herald. Published about 1933 to 1952.

234

Efren Yambot, editor: *Philippine almanac and handbook of facts*. Quezon City.

Recorded for 1973, 1975, 1977 (240 pp.). History (including chronology), statistics, business guide, regional survey.

235

Ravenstock's Manila city directory, containing alphabetical and classified lists of firms, a directory of residents, a directory of United States, Insular, Povincial and Municipal officers, a directory of religious institutions, masonic bodies, public and private schools, clubs, etc., and other miscellaneous information pertaining to the Philippine Islands. Manila: Philippine Education Co.

The 1927/8 edition (1026 pp.) was 'vol. 33: 25th year. Founded in 1903.' It listed about 20,000 Manila residents and about 10,000 firms, as well as about 18,000 names from the remainder of the Philippines.

236

Guía oficial de las Islas Filipinas. Manila.

[Official guide to the Philippines.] A directory, annual but with many missing years, published under this title 1893-8. Previous titles: *Guía oficial de Filipinas*. 1879-92: *Guía de forasteros en Filipinas*. 1858-65: *Almanaque filipina i guía de forasteros*. 1834.

237

Catholic directory of the Philippines. Manila: Catholic Bishops Conference of the Philippines, 1983. 857 pp.
Edited by Pedro S. de Achutegui.

Alphabetical listing of the ecclesiastical jurisdictions, with a list under each of parishes and priests, congregations, religious institutions (including church schools and hospitals).

238

Research institutes and researchers of Asian studies in the Philippines. Tokyo: Centre for East Asian Cultural Studies, 1966. 133 pp.
(Directories, 5.)

Universities, pp. 1-80; governmental organizations; learned societies; researchers belonging to other organizations. Addenda, pp. 119-126; index of persons.

Note also: Andrew Gonzalez, Arlene Matocinos: *A directory of linguists and language education specialists in the Philippines*. Manila: Linguistic Society of the Philippines, 1981. 133 pp. Roneoed. Alphabetical list of names and addresses (no other details) followed by geographical and specialism lists.

Biography

239

Directory of selected scholars and researchers in Southeast Asia. Singapore: Regional Institute of Higher Education and Development, 1974. 1214 pp.

Lists over 5000 scholars, the majority from Indonesia, Philippines, Thailand: excludes Burma. Biographical information and lists of publications. Very elaborate indexing: age, origin, qualifications, subject area, level of post.

Note also: *Research institutes and researchers of Asian studies in Cambodia, Laos, Malaysia, Singapore and the Republic of Vietnam.* [Tokyo] 1970. 183 pp. (Centre for East Asian Cultural Studies. Directories, 8.) Individuals are listed (with brief biographical information) under the names of their institutions.

Marina G. Dayrit, editor: *Directory of librarians in Southeast Asia.* Quezon City: University of the Philippines Library, 1980. 140 pp. (Published for the Congress of Southeast Asian Librarians.) 982 qualified librarians are included. Factual biographies, full of abbreviations (list, pp. v-viii), in alphabetical order. Index by nationality, pp. 131-140.

240

Ch'en Wei-lung: *Tung-nan-ya hua-ch'iao wen-jen chuan-lüeh.* Singapore: South Seas Society [1977]. 118 pp.

[Biographies of eminent Chinese of south east Asia.] A sequence of 36 biographical sketches, the earliest Ku Hung Ming (1856-1927), the latest S. Y. Liu (1901-75). Entirely in Chinese, but contents page includes Roman transliteration of names.

241

W. Wijnaendts van Resandt: *De gezaghebbers der Oost-Indische Compagnie op hare buiten-comptoiren in Azië.* Amsterdam: Liebaert, 1944. 316 pp.
Centrale Dienst voor Sibbekunde. (Genealogische bibliotheek, 2.)

[The Dutch East India Company's governors at its trading stations in Asia.] Each chapter is organised chronologically, giving brief biographies of successive governors. Not confined to south east Asia. Contents include: Gouvernement van Malacca, pp. 200-231 (covers 1641-1795); Siam and Ligor, pp. 259-271 (covers 1622-1762); Tonkin, pp. 297-303 (covers 1637-1700). Index of personal names, pp. 304-316.

242

Henri Cordier: *Bibliotheca indosinica: dictionnaire bibliographique des ouvrages relatifs à la péninsule indochinoise.* Paris: Leroux, 1912-32. 5 v. (Publications de l'Ecole Française d'Extrême-Orient, 15-18, 18 bis.)

[Indochinese library: a bibliographical dictionary of works relating to the south east Asian peninsula.] Vols 1-4 are paginated in a single sequence; there is an addendum towards the end of vol. 4. Arrangement: Burma, cols 1-515, 2833-2858; Assam, cols 516-710, 2861-2870; Thailand, cols 712-995, 2873-2900; Laos, cols 996-1083, 2789-2806; Malaya including Singapore, cols 1105-1504, 2901-2914; Indochina, and Vietnam in particular, cols 1511-2646, 2917-2984; Cambodia, cols 2649-2786; Champa, cols 2809-2826. The main work was completed in 1915 and covers publications up to mid-1914. Vol. 5, published much later, is an author and subject index compiled by M.-A. Roland-Cabaton.

An exhaustive bibliography, included here because each country section contains a sub-section 'Vie des missionaires catholiques' which gives brief biographical details as well as bibliographical references: Burma, cols 289-296, 2847-8; Assam, cols 665-6, 2867-8; Thailand, cols 831-840, 2889-90; Laos, cols 1047-1050, 2797-2800; Malaya, cols 1330-1336, 2907-8; Indochina, particularly Vietnam, cols 2043-2126, 2943-8; Cambodia, cols 2731-6. There are also sub-sections on protestant missionaries: Burma, cols 299-308; Thailand, cols 841-2; Malaya, cols 1349-1352.

Reprinted: New York: Burt Franklin, 1967. I have not seen the reprint.

BURMA

243

Chao Tzang Yawnghwe alias Eugene Thaik: *The Shan of Burma: memoirs of a Shan exile.* Singapore: Institute of Southeast Asian Studies, 1987. 276 pp.

Included here for its substantial Part 3: Who's who in Shan State: historical and political personalities, a personal perspective (pp. 155-252: about 3200 entries). An alphabetical compendium of twentieth century notables (including current rebel leaders and warlords) relying largely on the author's extensive memory -- and hence not infallible.

Compare: Bertil Lintner: 'The Shans and the Shan States of Burma' in *Contemporary Southeast Asia* vol. 5 (1984) pp. 403-450, which also ends with a 'Who's who in the Shan States'.

244

R. E. McGuire, editor: *Burma: register of European deaths and burials.* London: British Association for Cemeteries in South Asia, 1983.

Second edition. A list of deaths of Europeans in Burma with a record of tomb inscriptions: covers the period 1682 to 1947. Arranged in order of districts, with a name index.

Note also: Maurice H. Rossington, editor: *Burma: supplement to register of European deaths and burials.* 1987. Cited from Herbert [22], who also gives references (p. 88) to lists of Allied war deaths in Burma.

245

Gustaaf Houtman: *Burmese personal names.* Rangoon: Department of Religious Affairs, 1982. 89 pp.

Explains the logic behind the choice of names; also provides information on titles and terms of address.

246

Bohmu Ba Thaung: *Sahsodawmya atthappatti.* Rangoon: Zwe, 1971. 642 pp.

[Biographies of authors.] 172 authors are covered: the arrangement is chronological by date of death. Entirely in Burmese: the contents list gives names and dates (Culasakkaraja era). Alphabetical index of entries, pp. 613-8.

247

Who's who in Burma 1961. Rangoon: People's Literature Committee and House, 1961. 220 pp.

'It is proposed to publish the *Who's who in Burma* triennially ... The publishers regret the omission of other well known persons: their sense of modesty has been a great handicap in making this publication more complete.' Filed in alphabetical order of last name. Terse, objective entries, giving current position and address. About 500 entries.

248

Who's who in Burma: a biographical record of prominent residents of Burma with photographs and illustrations. Calcutta, Rangoon: Indo-Burma Publishing Agency [1927]. 262 pp.

An early example of an illustrated who's who.

249

History of services of gazetted and other officers in Burma. Rangoon: Superintendent, Government Printing.
Compiled by the Government of Burma.

An annual who's who of the British establishment in Burma. Issued in two volumes. Vol. 1: Services of gazetted officers. Vol. 2: Services of other officers. Nunn [20] gives locations for editions betwen 1899 and 1912. See also *Quarterly civil list* and the continuation *List of government gazetted officers* [66].

Note also: *India Office and Burma Office list.* Annual, 1938-1947.

250

Khin Thet Htar: *Who's who in medicine in Burma.* Rangoon: Ministry of Health, Department of Medical Research, 1973. 203 pp.
Burma Medical Research Council. Special report series, 9.)

Part 1: Directory of institutions, naming principal staff; Part 2: Index of specialisms; Part 3 (pp. 47-203): biographies of 541 doctors and researchers, in alphabetical order of first name. Terse, objective entries: date of birth, education, employment record, current research, publications, address.

THAILAND

251

Who's who in Thailand. Bangkok: Advance Publications, 1973- .

A monthly biographical magazine, with about 20 to 30 biographies in each issue. Interesting but of very slight reference value: no cumulative indexes after vol. 1. Last seen 1982.

252

Khrai pen khrai nai prathet Thai. Bangkok, 1963. 2 v. (2451 pp.)
Thammasat Mahavitthalayai. Khana Rathaprasasanasat.

[Who's who in Thailand.] Produced from questionnaires by the National Institute of Development Administration. 'Mostly government employees: some quite prominent people are not included' (Nunn [19]).

253

Adrien Launay: *Histoire de la Mission de Siam.* Paris: Téqui, 1920. 2 v. in 3.

[History of the Siam mission.] Arranged chronologically under names of missionaries, with accompanying documents.

Also available in Thai translation: Adrien Launay: *Ruang chotmaihet khong khana Bat luang Farangset*. Bangkok, 2468-70 [1925-7]. Translated by Arun Amatyakul. (Prachum phongsawadan = A collection of chronicles.)

254

New list of missionaries in China, Korea and Siam; corrected to March 1889. Shanghai: American Presbyterian Mission Press, 1889.

For details of preceding lists under various titles, 1866 to 1886, see Cordier [242] col. 839.

255

Robert B. Jones: *Thai titles and ranks; including a translation of Traditions of royal lineage in Siam by King Chulalongkorn*. Ithaca: Department of Asian Studies, Cornell University, 1971. 147 pp. Southeast Asia Program. (Data paper, 81.)

Translation printed parallel to the Thai text (which the King had compiled in 1878), followed by Jones's article 'Development of royal titles' (pp. 115-140) and by 'Appendix: Royal Kin terminology' and 'Relationship terminology' (pp. 141-3).

Watts [29] usefully refers to a long review article by: M. Vickery in *Journal of the Siam Society* vol. 62 (1974) pp. 158-173.

INDOCHINA

256

Hommes et destins: dictionnaire biographique d'Outre-Mer. Paris: Académie des Sciences d'Outre-Mer, 1975- . 668 pp.
(Publications de l'Académie des Sciences d'Outre-Mer. Travaux et mémoires.)

[Men and destinies overseas: a biographical dictionary.] Signed biographies, 1 to 5 pages in length, of French and other persons linked with French activities abroad. Extends to 8 volumes, each with its own alphabetical order but each containing a cumulative index. Some volumes are of varied contents, some are concerned with particular regions or topics.

Note especially vol. 6: *Asie*. 1985. 2-900098-08-4, naturally concerned largely with French Indochina; vol. 8: *Gouverneurs, administrateurs, magistrats*. 1988. 467 pp. 2-900098-10-6.

257

9 mars 1945-9 mars 1948: à la mémoire de 23 administrateurs des services civils et des colonies. SILI, 1948. 68 pp.
Preface by Emile Bollaert, Bureau de la Presse et de l'Information du Haut-Commissariat de la France pour l'Indochine.

[9 March 1945 to 9 March 1948: in memory of 23 administrators of the civil and colonial services.] Biographies of French officials in Indochina killed during the war of 1945-8, with photographs.

258

Biographical information on prominent nationalist leaders in French Indochina. Washington: Department of State, 1945. 90 pp.
Department of State, Interim Research and Intelligence Service, Research Analysis Branch. (R & A, 3336.)

Some inaccuracies due to wartime information problems.

259

Souverains et notabilités d'Indochine. Hanoi: Imprimerie d'Extrême-Orient, 1943. 112 pp.
Gouvernement Général de l'Indochine.

[Rulers and notables of Indochina.]

260

A. Brébion; Antoine Cabaton, editor: *Dictionnaire de bio-bibliographie générale ancienne et moderne de l'Indochine Française.* Paris: Société d'Editions Géographiques, Maritimes et Coloniales, 1935. 446 pp.
(Annales de l'Académie des Sciences Coloniales, 8.)

[General biographical and bibliographical dictionary to early and modern French Indochina.] Brébion died in 1917. As completed by Cabaton the work contains 1600 biographies, including both indigenous notables and Europeans. 'Subject index' to their principal activities and interests, pp. 431-446.

Various chronological lists are scattered through the alphabetical sequence. Lists of Kings and Protectors of Cambodia, pp. 56-9; Kings of Champa, pp. 65-8; of Annam, pp. 74-80; of the Laotian kingdoms, pp. 80-83; Governors of Cochinchina, pp. 83-6; Residents of Laos, pp. 223-4; Residents of Tongking, pp. 409-410. List of chiefs of the French administration of justice, pp. 208-9. Lists of missionaries: Dominicans 1693-1910, pp. 122-130; Franciscans 1580-1822, pp. 161-4; Société des Missions-Etrangères 1660-1910, pp. 354-398; Jesuits 1615-1733, pp. 88-93.

Biography

For a fuller list of Jesuit missionaries see Manuel Teixeira, 'Missionários Jesuítas no Vietnão' in *Boletim eclesiástico do Diocese de Macau* vol. 62 (1964) pp. 815-907. [Jesuit missionaries in Vietnam.] (Cited from Cotter [30].) Note also the lists of missionaries in Cordier's *Bibliotheca indosinica* [242].

261

Antoine Brébion: *Bibliographie des voyages dans l'Indochine Française du IXe au XIXe siècle*. Paris, 1910. 299 + xliv pp.

[Bibliography of travels to French Indochina, 9th-19th centuries.] Included here because it is arranged chronologically, and thus provides a date list of travellers to Vietnam, Cambodia and Laos, at least of those who wrote of their activities. Indexes: Titles of anonymous works, pp. iii-vii; Authors, pp. ix-xliv.

Reprint: New York: Lenox Hill, 1970. 0-8337-0359-5. (Burt Franklin bibliography & reference series, 395. Geography and discovery, 8.)

Cordier [242] col. 2390 records a supplement, paginated 301-322 and dated 1911: this is not included in the reprint.

262

A. Brébion: *Livre d'or du Cambodge, de la Cochinchine et de l'Annam 1625-1910: biographie et bibliographie*. Saigon: Schneider, 1910. 79 pp.

[Golden book of Cambodia, Cochinchina and Annam 1625-1910: biography and bibliography.] List of French people who had lived in southern Indochina in chronological order of arrival. See the review by: Charles B. Maybon in *Bulletin de l'Ecole Française d'Extrême-Orient* vol. 10 (1910) pp. 618-9.

CAMBODIA

263

Who's who in Cambodia: a reference aid. Washington, 1985.
Central Intelligence Agency, Directorate of Intelligence. (CR85-10626.)

Cited from Ross [108].

Note also: *Personnalités du Cambodge*. Phnom Penh: Réalités Cambodgiennes, 1963. 303 pp. [Personalities of Cambodia.] From the publishers of a weekly news magazine.

Leading personalities in Cambodia. Phnom Penh: United States Embassy, 1961. 61 pp.

LAOS

264

Liste des personnalités laos. Vientiane.
Ministère des Affaires Etrangères. Direction du Protocole.

[List of Lao personalities.] Cited from Nunn [20], who records issues between 1958 and 1972.

265

Lao personal names. Washington, 1967. 65 pp.
Central Intelligence Agency.

Analysis of the structure of Lao names; transliteration tables; lists of family and personal names with popular romanizations; titles and forms of address. Not seen: cited from Cordell [25].

VIETNAM

265a

Merritt Clifton, editor: *Those who were there: eyewitness accounts of the war in Southeast Asia, 1956-1975 & aftermath.* Paradise, California: Dustbooks, 1984. 297 pp. 0-913218-97-9.

A bibliography of English language publications, included here because it provides a list of Americans (and a few others) who participated in the Vietnam war and have written or spoken on the subject.

266

Council of Ministers of the Socialist Republic of Vietnam: reference aid. 1977. 103 pp.
Central Intelligence Agency.

A list of the 38 ministers of newly unified Vietnam (in alphabetical order of *personal* name) giving current positions, previous positions and a photograph.

Note also: *Who's who in North Vietnam.* [Washington] 1972. 342 pp. [Department of State, Office of External Research. Prepared from Central Intelligence Agency files.] A typescript compilation on 207 North Vietnamese party, government and military leaders. The information is undigested, partly in questionnaire format, partly reprinted from earlier publications by others. Includes membership lists of political and military organizations, pp. xi-xxiv.

Who's who of the Republic of South Vietnam = *Chánh phu cach mang lam thoi Cộng Hòa mien nam Việt Nam.* N.p.: Giai Phóng, 1969. 54 pp. Biographies, with photographs, of 42 members of the Provisional Revolutionary Government of South Viet Nam and of its Advisory Council. An official publication of the resistance.

267

Who's who in Vietnam?. Saigon: Vietnam Press, 1974. 968 pp.

'Third edition.' Reproduced from typescript. Biographies are in c.v. format, including address, religion, family status, club memberships, publications, etc. Includes some North Vietnamese personalities.

Supersedes a cumulating series: *Who's who in Vietnam.* Saigon: Vietnam Press Agency, 1967-72. 5 v. Poorly reproduced from typescript in loose-leaf format. Each of these earlier volumes had a separate alphabetical order, but there was limited duplication between them. They were in questionnaire format with many wasted words, e.g. 'Mother's profession: deceased. Name of spouse's father: irrelevant.'

268

Trần Văn Giáp: *Lược truyện các tác giả Việt-Nam.* Hanoi: Khoa Học Xã Hội, 1971. 2 v.

[Short survey of Vietnamese authors.] Vol. 1 (521 pp.) covers 735 authors of the 11th to 20th centuries publishing in Chinese and in nôm. Pp. 517-520: publication statistics by reign, 1072-1925. Vol. 2 pp. 1-245: 19th-20th century authors publishing in roman script, ending with those born in 1917. Pp. 246-251: statistics of publication by language, 1930-35. Pp. 255-341: cumulative index of authors and titles for both volumes.

First edition of vol. 1, with its own name and title index: Hanoi: Su Hoc, 1962. 576 pp.

269

Maurice M. Durand, Nguyễn Trần-Huân: *Introduction à la littérature vietnamienne.* Paris: G.-P. Maisonneuve et Larose, 1969.
(Collection UNESCO. Introduction aux littératures orientales.)

[Introduction to Vietnamese literature.] A history in two parts: nôm literature, by Durand, pp. 1-108; quôc-ngu literature of the French and modern periods, by Huân, pp. 109-168. Of particular reference use is the 'Biographical dictionary of Vietnamese authors', pp. 181-225. The authors were both at the Ecole Pratique des Hautes Etudes, Paris. See the review by Nguyễn Dình Hòa in *Journal of the American Oriental Society* vol. 92 (1972) pp. 364-8.

270

Nguyễn Huyền Anh: *Việt-Nam danh-nhân từ-điển*. Saigon: Khai-Trí [1967]. 559 pp.

[Biographical dictionary of Vietnam.] Revised edition. Numerous, brief articles, covering the whole of Vietnamese history from the legendary reign of the second emperor, An-Duong-Vuong (succeeded 257 B.C.) but omitting his macrobiotic predecessor.

First edition: Saigon: Hội Văn-Hóa Bình Dân, 1960. 380 pp. See the review of this by Nicole Louis in *Bulletin de l'Ecole Française d'Extrême-Orient* vol. 52 (1965) pp. 562-7.

Note also the abridgement: Nguyễn Huyền Anh: *Tiêu-từ-điển nhân-vật lịch-sử Việt-Nam*. Saigon: Thùy-Phương, 1971. 344 pp. This includes a chronology of monarchs, beginning 2879 B.C., and an alphabetical list of battles and other historical incidents A.D. 40-1949.

271

Adrien Launay: *Histoire de la Mission de Cochinchine 1658-1823*. Paris: Dounion et Retaux, 1923-5. 3 v.
Société des Missions-Etrangères.

[History of the Cochinchina mission, 1658-1823.] Biographies of missionaries in chronological order, with texts of their reports and correspondence. Vol. 3 contains appendices: Christianity in Cochinchina; The persecutions of 1645 and 1663; Franciscans in Cochinchina 1583-1769.

Note also: Adrien Launay: *Histoire de la Mission du Tonkin*. Paris: Maisonneuve Frères, 1927. Vol. 1. (Société des Missions-Etrangères.) [History of the Tongking mission.] Biographies of missionaries in chronological order, with texts of their reports and correspondence. The work remained incomplete: volume 1 covers 1658-1717.

272

Phan-Kế-Bính: *Nam Hại di nhân liệt truyện*. Hanoi: Bach-Thái-Buoi, 1912. 170 pp.

[Biographies of great men of the South Sea, i.e. of Annam.] Entirely in Vietnamese. For further bibliographical details see Cotter [30] p. 54.

MALAYSIA, SINGAPORE AND BRUNEI

273

New Malaysian who's who. Kuala Lumpur: Kasuya, 1990. 2 pts in 3 v. 983-9624-00-8; 983-9624-01-6.

'Comes in three (3) prestigious volumes: part I on Sabah and Sarawak in one (1) volume and part II on West Malaysia in two (2) volumes. We also featured about 200 pages of brief notes on the Federation of Malaysia and its component states, the Malaysian economy, decorations and honours, political parties and general business laws and information' -- this is pp. xli-cxc, repeated in each part. Directories of accountants, lawyers, architects and engineers are on pp. cxci-cdlix, also repeated in each part. A spacious work in questionnaire format, with some photographs.

Kasuya also publish an *ASEAN who's who*, which I have not yet seen.

274

Mas Osman: *Biografi penulis Brunei*. Bandar Seri Begawan: Dewan Bahasa dan Pustaka Brunei, 1987. 164 pp.

[Biographical dictionary of Brunei authors.] In Malay. Biographies of about 70 Brunei authors, with photographs. Guide to pen names, pp. 156-164.

275

A biography of Malaysian writers. Kuala Lumpur: Dewan Bahasa dan Pustaka, 1985. 319 pp.

100 entries, mainly for living authors. Includes a few writers from Singapore and Indonesia who have influenced Malaysian literature, but generally confined to those writing in the 'national language'. Discursive biographies, with lists of works and photographs. List of pseudonyms, pp. 310-319.

276

Brunei forms of address, titles and government officials. Bandar Seri Begawan, 1984. 56 pp.

Elucidates the etiquette of address in government circles in Brunei. Cited from Krausse [21], where there is also a reference to a work on the historical dimension of Brunei ranks and titles: P. M. Yusuf: 'Adat istiadat diraja Brunei Darussalam' in *Brunei Museum journal* vol. 3 no. 3 (1975) pp. 43-108.

277

Who's who in Malaysia and Singapore 1983/1984. Petaling Jaya: Who's

Who, 1983. 2 v.

Concise biographies, with many photographs, arranged in alphabetical order after an initial section of rulers and cabinet ministers. This is the latest I have seen of a long series, begun in 1955. Earlier editions were edited by J. Victor Morais and were in one volume, with varying titles, e.g.: *Who's who in Malaysia, Singapore and Brunei 1978/1979*. Various paginations. 24 pages on Brunei: *The who's who in Malaya and guide to Singapore*. 1967. 384 + 128 pp. Kuala Lumpur: Morais, 1967: *The leaders of Malaya and who's who 1957/1958*. 450 pp.

278

Robert Heussler: *British Malaya: a bibliographical and biographical compendium*. New York: Garland, 1981. 193 pp.

The bibliographical section will be found very useful: 499 entries, covering the period 1867-1942. The work is included here, however, for the second section, which consists of brief biographies of British administrators in Malaya.

The author's biographical source material is studied in depth in two companion works: Robert Heussler: *British rule in Malaya: the Malayan Civil Service and its predecessors, 1867-1942*. Oxford: Clio Press, 1981. 356 pp.; Robert Heussler: *Completing a stewardship: the Malayan Civil Service, 1942-1957*. Westport: Greenwood Press, 1983. 240 pp.

279

Dictionary of Malaysian Chinese. Kuala Lumpur: Mace, 1980. 231 pp.

Very concise who's who of the Chinese community of Malaysia: about 1800 entries, with some photographs. Entirely in Chinese.

280

Ilias Zaidi: *Biografi penulis dan karya*. Kuala Lumpur: Fargoes, 1976. 304 pp.

Readable biographies, in Bahasa Malaysia, of about 100 Malaysian authors, with photographs and extracts from their works.

281

Thomas R. P. Dawson, editor: *Who's who in sports in Malaysia and Singapore*. Petaling Jaya, 1975. 724 pp.

No more published. Cited from Quah [28].

282

The Malayan civil list. Kuala Lumpur, Singapore: Government Printing Office.

Published from 1921 to at least 1939. An outline of the establishment followed by a list of personnel with their careers, seniority, pension rights, etc.

Took the place of two earlier publications: *The Straits Settlements civil service list shewing the civil establishments, names and designations of the civil servants of Government, &c. &c. &c*. Singapore: Government Printing Office. Published from 1893 (if not before) to 1920.

The Federated Malay States civil service list. Kuala Lumpur: Federated Malay States Government Printing Office.

INDONESIA

283

Apa & Siapa sejumlah orang Indonesia 1983-1984. Jakarta: Grafiti, 1984. 1170 pp.
Produced by the magazine *Tempo*.

In Bahasa Indonesia. Discursive biographies accompanied by factual information in a marginal column, and usually by a good photograph. An attractive, useful work.

Previous edition: 1981-1982. 905 pp.

284

O. G. Roeder, Mahiddin Mahmud: *Who's who in Indonesia: biographies of prominent Indonesian personalities in all fields*. Singapore: Gunung Agung, 1980. 428 pp.

Second edition. Factual biographies concentrating on education, career, visits abroad; includes addresses. Photographs of nearly all persons included. About 1000 entries. List of the Cabinet, pp. 392-3; Foreign diplomatic representatives; Military headquarters, hospitals, universities; Car license plate codes; calendar of holidays; List of acronyms, pp. 406-426.

First edition, by Roeder alone: Jakarta: Gunung Agung, 1971. 544 pp. Rather larger.

285

The Indonesian military leaders: biographical and other background data. Jakarta: Sritua Arief Associates, 1979. 422 pp.

Second edition.

First edition: *Who is who in Indonesian military*. 1977. Data on over 300 military leaders who occupy important positions in military and civil administration. Questionnaire format with some wasted space (e.g. 'educational background: ?').

286

Leo Suryadinata: *Eminent Indonesian Chinese: biographical sketches*. Singapore: Institute of Southeast Asian Studies, 1978. 230 pp.

Readable brief biographies of about 500 persons, in English (though names are also given in Chinese characters), with indication of sources. Some derive from personal interviews.

287

Sritua Arief: *Who's who in Indonesian business*. Jakarta, 1976. 938 pp.

A reprint of the first edition but with a long section of additional entries (pp. 771-935). No cumulative index. About 450 entries, with many photographs, in questionnaire format.

288

F. de Haan: *Priangan: de Prianger-Regentschappen onder het Nederlandsch Bestuur tot 1811*. Batavia: Bataviaasch Genootschap van Kunsten en Wetenschappen, 1910-12. 4 v.

[The Priangan Regency under Dutch rule to 1811.] The author was archivist at Batavia. A complicated, exhaustive work including some material useful for reference.

Vol. 1: Historical outline, followed by a separately paginated section of biographies (1. Superintendents in date order, 1686-1811: pp. 1-130; 2. Regents, in alphabetical order of provinces, pp. 131-180; 3. other personalities in alphabetical order, pp. 181-309).

Vol. 2: Documents; Appendices (including appendix 20, 'Portuguese words in Company Dutch', pp. 771-782).

Vols 3-4: Notes; Statistics and tables, including lists of Commandants and Inspectors with dates of office.

289

J. P. I. du Bois: *Vies des Gouverneurs Généraux, avec l'abrégé de l'histoire des établissemens hollandois aux Indes Orientales ... et en général tous les événemens publics ou particuliers dignes de remarque relatifs aux affaires des Indes ... rapportés, année par année, sous l'administration de chacun des chefs de la nation hollandoise en Asie; orné de leurs portraits ...* The Hague: Pierre De Hondt, 1763.

[Lives of the Governors General, with a short history of the Dutch colonies in the East Indies, and notable political and other events relevant to Eastern affairs in general, arranged year by year under the adminstrations of successive Dutch governors in Asia, illustrated with their portraits.] Included here as a chronology and because of its arrangement as a series of biographies.

PHILIPPINES

290

Florentino B. Valeros, Estrellita Valeros-Gruenberg: *Filipino writers in English: a biographical and bibliographical directory.* Quezon City: New Day, 1987. 236 pp. 971-10-0285-X.

About 600 entries, unillustrated, with detailed information on careers and publications.

Note also: Cesar T. Mella: *Directory of Filipino writers past and present.* Manila: CTM, 1974. 256 pp. Enthusiastic ('young, ravishing') compilation of brief biographies with photographs. Most of the 600 entries are for contemporary, or even future, authors.

291

Herminia M. Ancheta, Michaela Beltran-Gonzalez: *Filipino women in nation building: a compilation of brief biographies.* Quezon City: Phoenix, 1984. 337 pp.

Laudatory biographies of eminent Filipino women, about 2 pp. each, with dreadful photographs. Arranged under fields of activity, with index.

292

Victor J. Sevilla: *Justices of the Supreme Court of the Philippines.* Quezon City: New Day, 1984-5. 3 v.

Included here because of its arrangement as a series of biographical articles in chronological order. Covers 107 judges who were members of the Supreme Court between 1901 and 1985. Includes a selection of their decisions. Cited from Richardson [27].

293

Bicol biographical encyclopedia. Naga City: Bicol Research & Publication centre, 1968-9. 2 v.

A who's who of the region: two independent volumes of short, formal biographies, arranged by speciality (educators, professionals, elected officials, government employees, private employees, businessmen, barrio leaders). Vol. 2, which is reproduced from typescript, contains some photographs, an addendum section ('special mention', pp. 325-333) and (under 'special features') some remarkably fulsome biographies of future personalities, one of whom was at this stage still 'a popular coed in the campus'.

294

Isidro L. Retizos, D. H. Soriano: *Philippines who's who.* Quezon City: Capitol, 1957. 327 pp.

Discursive biographies of the living: many photographs interspersed with the text. An initial section of national heroes and figures of the past and of members of the Supreme Court (40 pages).

295

E. Arsenio Manuel: *Dictionary of Philippine biography.* Quezon City: Filipiniana Publications, 1955- .
Joint author for vol. 3: Magdalena Avenir Manuel. 'For the Filipiniana Publications Biography series.'

Three volumes have appeared (the third in 1986), each in its own alphabetical order. No overall order or indexing, but each volume has a name and subject index. Discursive biographies, some of great length ('J. C. De Veyra': vol. 3 pp. 161-224) of dead Filipinos, many of them literary figures, with extracts from their works.

Note also: *Eminent Filipinos.* Manila, 1965. 294 pp. (National Historical Commission. Publication, 1.) Signed, eulogistic biographies of historical figures with pictures. About 230 entries.

296

Franz J. Weissblatt, editor: *Who's who in the Philippines; a biographical dictionary of notable living men of the Philippine Islands.* Manila: McCullough, Roces, 1937-40. 2 v.

Vol. 1 consists of very expansive biographies of VIPs; vol. 2, commendably brief biographies of everybody else.

Biography

Note also: Rodrigo C. Lim: *Who's who in the Philippines*. Manila: Nera, 1929. 2 v.

Rosenstock's press reference library, Philippine edition. Manila: Rosenstock, 1913. 'A biographical dictionary published for the exclusive use of newspapermen' (Doeppers).

For the many briefer biographical sources on the Philippines, see: Daniel F. Doeppers, Michael Cullinane: *A union catalogue of Philippine biographical reference works*. Madison, 1983. 34 pp. (University of Wisconsin, Center for Southeast Asian Studies. Bibliographical series, 8.)

297 cancelled

Historical materials

298

Nicholas Tarling, editor: *The Cambridge history of Southeast Asia.* Cambridge: Cambridge University Press, 1992. 2 v. 0-521-35505-2; 0-521-35506-0.

A collaborative history, each chapter by a named author. Most of the contributors come from Australia, New Zealand and Singapore. Each chapter concludes with a bibliographical essay: there is also a bibliography of bibliographies, by Paul Kratoska, in vol. 2.

Vol. 1: *From early times to c. 1800.* Part 1: from prehistory to c. 1500 C.E. The writing of Southeast Asian history; Southeast Asia before history; The early kingdoms; Economic history (pp. 183-275); Religious and popular beliefs. Part 2: from c. 1500 to c. 1800. Interactions with the outside world and adaptations in Southeast Asian society; Political development; Economic and social change; Religious developments; The age of transition.

Vol. 2: *The nineteenth and twentieth centuries.* Part 1: from c. 1800 to the 1930s. The establishment of the colonial regimes; Political structures; International commerce, the state and society; Economic and social change; Religious and anti-colonial movements; Nationalism and modernist reform. Part 2: from World War II to the present. The end of European colonial empires; Political structures of the independent states; Economic and social change; Religious change; Regionalism and nationalism.

299

J. C. Eade: *Southeast Asian ephemeris: solar and planetary positions, A.D. 638-2000.* Ithaca: Cornell University, Southeast Asia Program, 1989. 175 pp.. 0-87727-704-4.

A tabulation of years (10 to a page) of the Culasakkaraja era, 638 AD to date. The introduction, pp. 9-35, explains the application of the solar and lunar data in the tables to the determination of precise day-to-day calendar equivalences.

300

Oey Hong Lee: *Power struggle in South-East Asia.* Zug: Inter Documentation, 1976. 614 pp. with 11 microfiches. 3 85750 018 2.

The microfiches are a reprint of 70 political documents: constitutions, party programmes, etc. There is a list of the documents on pp. 603-614 of the printed volume. The remainder of the volume forms a lengthy introduction to the collection, consisting largely of a country-by-country survey of political debate in the early 1970s.

Philippines: 4 documents, 1972-6; Indonesia: 21 documents, 1971-6; Malaya and Singapore: 6 documents, 1971-5; Laos: 10 documents, 1973-5; Vietnam: 13 documents, 1973-5; Cambodia: 8 documents, 1975-6; Thailand: 4 documents, 1974-6; Burma: 4 documents, 1974-5.

Almost half of the 70 documents are reprinted from: *Summary of world broadcasts. The Far East.* Caversham Park: BBC, 1949- . (Monitoring Service of the British Broadcasting Corporation.) Daily.

301

Jan M. Pluvier: *A handbook and chart of South East Asian history.* Kuala Lumpur: Oxford University Press, 1967. 58 pp.

Exclusively concerned with political power. Brief historical surveys of each state; lists of rulers and government leaders 1780-1967, giving only brief forms of names. Includes sultanates of Malaya, Sumatra, Java but avoids listing local rulers of Celebes, Sunda Islands, Moluccas, and never mentions Shan states. A fold-out chart tracks the progress of colonial domination.

302

History of the Second World War. London: Her Majesty's Stationery Office.

The official British history: a big series in which several volumes are relevant to south east Asia. These include: F. A. E. Crew: *The Army Medical Services campaigns: vol. 5, Burma.* 1966. 754 pp.; F. S. V. Donnison: *British military administration in the Far East 1943-1946.* 1956. 483 pp.: S. W. Kirby: *The war against Japan.* 1957-69. 5 v.

Note also: Charles Cruickshank: *SOE in the Far East.* Oxford: Oxford University Press, 1983. 285 pp. Official history of the involvement of the Special Operations Executive, the secret arm of the British armed forces, in the Second World War in the Far East from 1940 to 1945.

303

Bisheshwar Prasad, editor: *Official history of the Indian armed forces in the Second World War 1939-45.* Calcutta: Combined Inter-Services Historical Section.
Spine title: *Indian armed forces in World War II.*

Several volumes of this series are relevant to south-east Asia.

Those in the sub-series *Campaigns in the Eastern theatre* are: Bisheshwar Prasad: *The retreat from Burma 1941-42* (1954. 500 pp.); N. N. Madan: *The*

Arakan operations 1942-1945 (1954. 371 pp.) and S. N. Prasad and others: *The reconquest of Burma* (1958-9. 2 v.).

Also relevant: K. D. Bhargava, K. N. V. Sastri: *Campaigns in South-East Asia 1941-42* (1960. 424 pp.); Rajendra Singh: *Post-war occupation forces: Japan and South-East Asia* (1958. 317 pp.); B. L. Rainey, editor: *Medical services. Campaigns in the Eastern Theatre* (1964. 525 pp.).

304

Roger M. Smith, editor: *Southeast Asia: documents of political development and change.* Ithaca: Cornell University Press, 1974. 608 pp.

Documents are presented in English and often abridged; there is a linking commentary. Sections (with dates of earliest and latest documents): Thailand 1932-67, by Clark D. Neher; Burma 1947-69, by Josef Silverstein; Indonesia 1945-67, by Herbert Feith and Alan Smith; Malaysia and Singapore 1928-69, by J. Norman Parmer; Viet-Nam 1945-73, by Marjorie Weiner Normand, Roy Jumper; Laos 1954-70, by Roger M. Smith; Cambodia 1955-1970, by Roger M. Smith; the Philippines 1951-73, by David Wurfel.

305

Paul Wheatley: *The Golden Khersonese: studies in the historical geography of the Malay peninsula before A.D. 1500.* Kuala Lumpur: University of Malaya Press, 1961. 383 pp.

Of permanent reference value for its comprehensive extracts from early authors from beyond the region who said something of its geography: Chinese, Greek and Latin, original texts and translations; Indian and Arabic, translations only.

BURMA

306

Klaus Fleischmann, editor: *Documents on communism in Burma 1945-1977.* Hamburg: Institut für Asienkunde, 1989. 278 pp. 3-88910-057-0. (Mitteilungen des Instituts für Asienkunde, 172.)

Includes 42 documents and reports, all in English.

307

Than Tun, editor: *The royal orders of Burma, AD 1598-1885.* Kyoto: Kyoto University, Center for Southeast Asian Studies, 1983-90. 10 v.

Chronological sequence: each volume contains introduction, notes, English translation of orders, Burmese text. Vol. 10 includes glossary and subject index.

See: Than Tun: 'Observations on the translation and annotation of the royal orders of Burma' in *Crossroads* vol. 4 no. 1 (Special Burma studies issue) (1988), pp. 91-99.

308

Hugh Tinker, editor: *Burma: the struggle for independence 1944-1948.* London: Her Majesty's Stationery Office, 1983-4. 2 v.

An official compilation of about 1250 documents. Includes very useful biographies of their 'authors', both British and Burmese.

309

Michael Robinson, Lewis A. Shaw: *The coins and banknotes of Burma.* Manchester, 1980. 160 pp. 0-9507053-0-6.

Covers Arakan and Burma from 15th to 20th centuries, with some information on earlier times. Includes British and Japanese banknotes issued in Burma in the Second World War. Coins are illustrated with halftone photographs in the text: there are 14 coloured plates oif banknotes at the end.

Note also: M. Robinson: *The lead and tin coins of Pegu and Tenasserim.* Sale, Cheshire, 1986. 83 pp., 23 plates. 'Many more coins and sources of information have been discovered [since 1980].'

310

Albert D. Moscotti: *Burma's constitution and elections of 1974.* Singapore: Institute of Southeast Asian Studies, 1977. 184 pp. (Research notes and discussion series, 5.)

Collection of documents on the development of a new constitution during 1971-4. Includes a chronology and a list of members of the People's Assembly as elected in 1974.

311

Joel M. Maring, Ester G. Maring: *Historical and cultural dictionary of Burma.* Metuchen: Scarecrow, 1973. (Historical and cultural dictionaries of Asia, 4.)

Brief entries in simple English on Burmese history, culture, physical geography, natural history, economics, politics and demography -- but mainly on the first two.

Note also: Maung Zaniya: *Myanma-hmu abidan.* Rangoon: Padei-tha, 1969.

480 pp. [Dictionary of Burmese studies.] An alphabetical companion: entirely in Burmese.

312

Gerald Davis, Denys Martin: *Burma: postal history*. London: Robson Lowe, 1971. 204 pp.

A historical outline, useful for its lists and statistics. Covers 1824-1937. Informative on the history of rail and steamer services and the opening of overland routes. List of post offices with dates of activity, pp. 174-180.

313

Frank N. Trager, editor: *Burma: Japanese military administration: selected documents 1941-1945*. Philadelphia: University of Pennsylvania Press, 1971. 279 pp.
Translated by Won Zoon Yoon, Thomas T. Winant.

66 documents: 1-2 plans for conquest; 3-23 Japanese military administration; 24-5 Burma Defence Army; 26-34 Central executive administration; 35-46 Independence of Burma; 47-9 Judiciary system; 50-51 the Japanese Language School; 52-66 Shan States. Some documents abridged 'by the translator' for unspecified reasons. Appendix A: List of the Thirty Comrades (name, assumed name and wartime position, Japanese name); Appendix B: List of prominent Japanese in Burma; Appendix C: Glossary of terms and organizations in Burma; Appendix D: Organizational charts.

314

Charles Duroiselle: *Inventaire des inscriptions pâlies, sanskrites, môn et pyû de Birmanie*. Paris, 1912. 15 pp.
(Bulletin de l'Ecole Française d'Extrême-Orient, vol. 12 no. 8.)

[Inventory of the Pali, Sanskrit, Mon and Pyu inscriptions of Burma.]

Nunn [20] cites: *List of inscriptions found in Burma*. Rangoon: Archaeological Survey of Burma, 1921.

These lists are in many cases superseded by: Charles Duroiselle, C. O. Blagden: *Epigraphia Birmanica*. Rangoon, 1919-36. 5 v. [Burmese inscriptions.] Reprinted: Rangoon, 1960; and: G. H. Luce, Pe Maung Tin: *Inscriptions of Burma*. Rangoon: Rangoon University Press; Oxford: Oxford University Press, 1933-56. 5 portfolios. See also articles by Luce and Pe Maung Tin in *Bulletin of the Burma Historical Commission* vol. 1 (1960).

315

Mg May Oung: 'The chronology of Burma' in *Journal of the Burma*

Research Society vol. 2 (1912) pp. 8-29.

316

A. M. B. Irwin: *The Burmese and Arakanese calendars*. Rangoon, 1909. 92 pp.

A description of the two calendars, a suggestion for reforming them to eliminate errors, and tables for converting Burmese to and from European dates of the eighteenth and nineteenth centuries. See the review by: J. F. Fleet in *Indian antiquary* (September 1910) pp. 250-256.

The work was supplemented by: Sir Alfred Irwin: 'The elements of the Burmese calendar from A.D. 638 to 1752' in *Indian antiquary* (November 1910) pp. 289-315.

Superseded: A. M. B. Irwin: *The Burmese calendar*. London: Sampson Low, 1901. 68 pp.

Note also: Htoon Chan: *The Arakanese calendar with the corresponding dates in Burmese and English 1820-1918*. Akyab, 1905. 450 pp. The last work is cited from Cordier [242], where details of some other Burmese-Gregorian calendars will be found (cols 263-4).

317

Horace Hayman Wilson: *Documents illustrative of the Burmese war, with an introductory sketch of the events of the war*. Calcutta; Government Gazette Press, 1827. Various paginations.

Deals with the Anglo-Burmese war of 1824-6. The main section of documents extends to 248 pp. An appendix (93 pp.) included statistical tables.

THAILAND

318

Harold E. Smith: *Historical and cultural dictionary of Thailand*. Metuchen: Scarecrow, 1976. 213 pp. 0-8108-0926-5.
(Historical and cultural dictionaries of Asia, 6.)

Brief entries, about 5 per page, for places, people, religious and cultural concepts, and events in history, written in simple English. 'Kings of Thailand' (chronological table) pp. 81-2.

319

Larry Sternstein: 'An "historical atlas of Thailand"' in *Journal of the*

Siam Society vol. 52 no. 1 (April 1964) pp. 7-20, with 5 maps.

The five maps are taken from a Thai historical atlas published about 1935 by the Royal Survey Department (see Sternstein p. 7 for publication details) and are accompanied by an analytical and critical text.

320

Reginald Le May: *The coinage of Siam.* Bangkok: Siam Society, 1932. 134 pp., 32 plates.

A historical survey incorporating a catalogue of known types, keyed to the plates.

Note also: H. A. Ramsden: *Siamese porcelain and other tokens.* Yokohama: Jun Kobayagawa, 1911. 37 pp., 20 plates. A brief catalogue (including Burmese gambling counters, pp. 36-7) of 345 items, all of which are illustrated.

These works were reprinted together as the first and last sections in: *Siamese coins and tokens: an anthology by Le May, Ramsden, Guehler, and Harding Kneedler.* London: Andrew, 1977. 389 pp. 0-903681-09-9. This also includes five articles reprinted from the *Journal of the Siam Society*, 1937-49.

INDOCHINA

321

Claude Hesse d'Alzon: *La présence militaire française en Indochine 1940-1945.* Vincennes: Publications du Service Historique de l'Armée de Terre, 1988. 375 pp.

[The French military presence in Indochina, 1940-45.] Official history of the French Army in south east Asia during the Second World War. Appendices include: Chronology 1939-45; lists of military units and operations. Reference owed to Cordell [25].

322

Vietnam, Laos and Cambodia: chronology of events, 1945-68. London: British Information Services, 1968. [151 pp.]
Central Office of Information.

Cited from Ross [108] and Cordell [25].

323

Allan B. Cole, editor: *Conflict in Indo-China and international repercussions: a documentary history 1945-1955.* Ithaca: Cornell University Press, 1956. 265 pp.

A selection of 104 official documents originating from France, the United States, Cambodia, Laos and Vietnam. They cover early US involvement in the conflict as well as French and Japanese activities. Includes statistics on French expenditure in money and personnel; statistics on US aid to France and Vietnam. Chronology of the decade, pp. 245-257.

324

G. Coedès, H. Parmentier: *Listes générales des inscriptions et des monuments du Champa et du Cambodge.* Hanoi: Imprimerie d'Extrême-Orient, 1923. 301 pp.

[General lists of inscriptions and ancient monuments of Champa and Cambodia.] Tabular format. Part 1: inscriptions, by Coedès: Champa, pp. 4-37; Cambodia, pp. 38-154. Alphabetical and geographical indexes; references to museum collections and to publications. Note the addenda, pp. 298-9. Part 2: geographical lists of ancient monuments, by Parmentier. Champa, pp. 183-211; Cambodia, pp. 212-297.

An earlier work: G. Coedès: 'Inventaire des inscriptions du Champa et du Cambodge' in *Bulletin de l'Ecole Française d'Extrême-Orient* vol. 8 (Paris, 1908) pp. 37-92. [Inventory of inscriptions of Champa and Cambodia.]

These lists are in many cases superseded by: G. Coedès: *Inscriptions du Cambodge.* Hanoi: Ecole Française d'Extrême-Orient, 1937-66. 8 v. (Collection de textes et de documents sur l'Indochine, 3.) [Inscriptions of Cambodia.]

CAMBODIA

325

Serge Thion: 'Chronology of Khmer communism, 1940-82' in David P. Chandler, Ben Kiernan, editors: *Revolution and its aftermath in Kampuchea: eight essays.* New Haven: Yale University, Southeast Asia Studies, 1983, pp. 291-319.

Cited from Ross [108].

326

A. Leclère: *Cambodge: fêtes civiles et religieuses.* Paris: Hachette, 1917.

[Cambodia: secular and religious festivals.]

327

Georges Maspero: *L'Empire Khmèr: histoire et documents.* Phnom-Penh: Imprimerie du Protectorat, 1904. 115 pp.

[The Khmer Empire: history and documents.] Tabular information includes: list and chronology of kings; list of travellers to Cambodia. Indexes of authors and of inscriptions referred to in the text.

See the review article by: A. Raquez: 'A propos de *L'Empire Khmèr: histoire et documents*' in *Revue indo-chinoise* (30 April 1906) pp. 587-592.

328
Charles Lemire: *Etablissement du Protectorat Français au Cambodge: Exposé chronologique des relations du Cambodge avec le Siam, l'Annam et la France*. Paris: Challamel, 1879. 48 pp.

[Establishment of the French Protectorate in Cambodia: chronological outline of Cambodian relations with Thailand, Annam and France.] A chronological outline from A.D. 363-1877, ending with the 'reforms introduced in accordance with the wise counsel of the French administration'.

LAOS

329
Martin Stuart-Fox, Mary Kooyman: *Historical dictionary of Laos*. Metuchen: Scarecrow Press, 1992. 258 pp.
(Asian historical dictionaries, 6.)

A highly useful handbook. The main alphabetical section includes entries for persons, places, events and concepts ('Kip', 1 line; 'Opium', 1 page). Maps, pp. xv-xxiii; Chronology, pp. xxv-xliv; Long classified bibliography; Lists of kings, French 'Résidents', prime ministers, pp. 240-4; Lists of members of governments oand central committees, 1945-91; Population tables, 1921-85.

330
Sylvain Dupertuis: 'Le calcul du calendrier laotien' in *Péninsule* no. 2 (1981) pp. 24-118.

[The calculation of the Laotian calendar.] Based on a Lao text.

331
Pierre Somchine Nginn: *Les fêtes profanes et religieuses au Laos*. Vientiane: Comité Littéraire, 1967. 61 pp.

[Secular and religious festivals in Laos.] Second edition. A popular work, arranged according to the calendar.

First edition: Compiègne, 1961.

VIETNAM

332

William J. Duiker: *Historical dictionary of Vietnam*. Metuchen: Scarecrow, 1989. 269 pp. 0-8108-2164-8.
(Asian historical dictionaries, 1.)

There is a strong emphasis on modern political and economic history. Many headwords are in English; on the Vietnamese, no diacritical marks are given. Tabular information: Chronology (mostly modern) pp. 247-264; Population, pp. 265-7; Production and trade statistics, pp. 268-9.

333

James S. Olson: *Dictionary of the Vietnam war*. New York: Greenwood Press, 1988. 0 313 24923 1.

Alphabetical entries from 6 lines to 2 pages, always with brief lists of sources, which are entirely US publications. Articles seem objective but choice of topics reflects US interest almost exclusively: US involvement in the war, its military units, its personalities. Appendix A: 'The population and provinces of South Vietnam 1971'; Appendix C: 'Vietnam War acronyms and slang expressions' (21 pp.); Appendix E: 'A chronology of the Vietnam War 1945-1975'(14 pp.).

Note also: David Burns Sigler: *Vietnam battle chronology*. Jefferson, North Carolina: McFarland, 1992. 184 pp. 0-89950-683-6. Chronology, pp. 1-134, in essence a list of 'Operations' as named in the US military jargon, arranged chronologically with locations and units involved on both sides. Alphabetical index of Operations, pp. 135-146; index by Major Command Unit, pp. 156; name and subject index; index of military units, pp. 181-4.

Harry G. Summers, Jr: *Vietnam War almanac*. New York: Facts on File, 1985. 414 pp. Contents: Chronology 1959-75, pp. 29-52; The Vietnam War A-Z, pp. 63-365. Wholly devoted to US concerns and US personalities.

John S. Bowman, editor: *The Vietnam War: an almanac*. New York: World Almanac Publications, 1985. Not seen.

334

Shelby L. Stanton: *Vietnam order of battle*. Washington: US News Books, 1981. 396 pp. 0-89193-700-5.
Cover title: US Army and allied ground forces in Vietnam: order of battle.

A large format compendium of information on the activities of individual battalions of the United States Army and its allies in Vietnam, 1961-75. Many illustrations and maps: note especially the atlas of location maps of troop detachments on successive dates within the period, pp. 362-385.

335

The United States Air Force in Southeast Asia. Washington: United States Government Printing Office, 1981- .
Office of Air Force History.

Detailed official history. Four volumes published so far. The first is by R. F. Futrell and is subtitled *The advisory years to 1965.* 398 pp.

Until the series is complete the gaps are partly filled by: Carl Berger, editor: *The United States Air Force in Southeast Asia 1961-1973: an illustrated account.* Washington: United States Government Printing Office, 1984. (Office of Air Force History.) 2nd edition (first edition: 1976). This has an appendix: 'List of Air Force Medal of Honor winners'.

A companion work on the Army: *United States Army in Vietnam.* Washington: United States Government Printing Office, 1983- . United States Army, Center of Military History. An official history of great length.

The central section will consist of three volumes subtitled *Advice and support.* Two are already published: the first by Ronald H. Spector, with a second subtitle *The early years 1941-1960.* 1983. 391 pp. (also published: New York: Collier Macmillan, 1985); the third by Jeffrey J. Clarke, with a second subtitle *The final years 1965-1973.* 1988. 561 pp.

Additional special volumes include: John D. Bergen: *United States Army in Vietnam: Military communications: a test for technology.* 1986. 515 pp., with useful maps and a detailed index.

On the Navy: *The United States Navy and the Vietnam conflict.* Washington: United States Government Printing Office, 1976- . Department of the Navy, Naval History Division. I have seen only two volumes in the proposed series. The first is by Edwin Bickford Hooper, Dean C. Allard, Oscar P. Fitzgerald and subtitled *The setting of the stage to 1959.*

On the Marines: *The U.S. Marines in Vietnam.* Washington: U.S. Marine Corps, History and Museums Division, 1977- . Vol. 1- . Nine chronological volumes are planned, beginning with vol. 1 by Robert H. Whitlow, subtitled *The advisory and combat assistance era 1954-1964.* 1977. 190 pp. Includes Appendix A: USMC and VNMC Senior Officers; Appendix C; Glossary of acronyms; Appendix D: Chronology.

Subsequent volumes, each by a different author, contain similar tabulated information and cover shorter periods: '1965' published 1978; '1966' published 1982; '1967' published 1984; '1969' published 1988; '1970-1971' published 1986; '1973-1975' published 1990. Additional special volumes include one on chaplains, published 1985; one on military law, published 1989.

Finally there is a separate work on Special Forces: Francis J. Kelly: *U.S. Army Special Forces 1961-1971*. Washington: United States Government Printing Office, 1973. 227 pp. Department of the Army. (Vietnam studies.) Rich in organizational charts and tabulated information, e.g. 'Disposition, December 1962'; 'Camps, 1961-4'; 'Conversion of U.S. to Vietnam Army Ranger Camps, 1970-71'. Many maps, e.g. of deployment in 1962, 1963, 1964, 1967.

Reprinted: Francis J. Kelly: *The Green Berets in Vietnam 1961-71*. Washington: Brasseys (US), 1991. (An AUSA book. Published with the Institute of Land Warfare, Association of the U.S. Army.)

336

Indochina monographs. Washington: United States Army Center of Military History, 1980-82. 5 v.

Histories of the Republic of Viet Nam Armed Forces in the Vietnamese War. The individual titles are: Dong Van Khuyen: *The RVNAF*, 1980. 401 pp. Dong Van Khuyen: *RVNAF logistics*, 1980. Ngo Quang Truong: *RVNAF and US operational cooperation and coordination*, 1980. Ngo Quang Truong: *Territorial forces*, 1981. Hoang Ngoc Lung: *Intelligence*, 1982.

337

Gareth Porter, editor: *Vietnam: the definitive documentation of human decisions*. Stanfordville, NY: Earl Coleman Enterprises, 1979. 2 v. (1399 pp.).

Documents on Indochina 1941-1975 with introductions.

Abridged version: Gareth Porter, editor: *Vietnam: a history in documents*. New York: New American Library, 1981. 490 pp. Contains 275 documents with brief introductions, in chronological order 1941-1975: nearly all US and Vietnamese. Includes (pp. 453-472): Chronology 1940-1975.

Note also: Allan W. Cameron, editor: *Viet-Nam crisis: a documentary history 1940-1956*. Ithaca: Cornell University Press, 1971. 480 pp. A collection of 190 documents.

South Viet Nam National Front for Liberation: documents = Mat Tran Dan Toc Giải Phong Mien Nam Việt Nam. N.p., Giai Phóng, 1968. 150 pp. 1965 Programme, Manifesto, 1967 Political Programme, miscellaneous statements 1965-8.

For documents of the United States involvement see: *United States-Vietnam relations 1945-1967*. Washington: United States Government Printing Office, 1971. 12 parts. (Department of Defense, Office of the Secretary of Defense.) Prepared by the Department of Defense OSD Task Force: Leslie Gelb, chairman. Printed for the use of the House Committee of Armed Services.

This consists of excerpts, with commentary, from: *History of U.S. decision-making process of Vietnam policy*, a 47-volume compilation printed for internal circulation by the United States Government.

The same 12-part abridgement was also published as: *The Pentagon papers: secret history of the Vietnam War as published by the New York Times*. New York: Quadrangle Books, 1971. 810 pp.; New York: Bantam Books, 1971. 677 pp.; and as: *The Pentagon papers: the Senator Gravel edition: the Defense Department history of United States decision-making on Viet-Nam*. Boston: Beacon Press, 1971-2. 5 vols. Vol. 5 of this edition is 'Critical essays by Noam Chomsky and Howard Zinn' and index.

338

Danny J. Whitfield: *Historical and cultural dictionary of Vietnam*. Metuchen: Scarecrow, 1976. 369 pp. 0-8108-0887-0.
(Historical and cultural dictionaries of Asia, 7.)

Over 1300 articles, some fairly lengthy. The emphasis is on history, especially earlier periods, on topography and on the terminology of indigenous culture. Nearly all headwords are in Vietnamese (with diacritics). The emphasis is thus wholly different from that of Duiker's dictionary [332], produced by the same publisher. Includes (pp. 339-346) a chronology of dynasties and rulers by Chingho A. Chen (Chinese University of Hong Kong). Historical sketch maps, pp. 347-358.

339

Ðoàn-Them: *Việc từng ngày*. Saigon: Phạm Quang Khai, 1968-1971. 5 v.

[Daily annals.] Political, economic, financial, cultural, social and international events. Annual volumes covering the years 1965-1969: the 1968 volume, the fullest, extends to 481 pp.

Forms a continuation of: Ðoàn-Them: *Hai muoi nam qua: việc từng ngày 1945-1964*. [Saigon:] Nam-Chi Tung-Thu, 1966. 424 pp. Very detailed chronology of military and political events in Vietnam: entries day by day from 1 January 1945 to 31 December 1964.

340

Nha Khi Tuong: *Lich the ky 20, 1901-2000.* Hanoi: Pho Thong, 1968. 216 pp.

[20th century calendar.] Tables of dates for each year (6 months to a page) permitting conversion between Gregorian calendar and the Vietnamese names of years and days.

Note also: Raymond Deloustal: *Calendrier annamite-français de 1802 à 1916, avec une liste chronologique des rois d'Annam.* Hanoi: Imprimerie d'Extrême-Orient, 1908. 153 pp. The author was chief interpreter with the Service Judiciaire de l'Indo-Chine.

341

Văn kien Đảng. Hanoi: Ban Chap Hanh Trung Uong Đảng, 1964. 3 v. Đảng Lao Động Việt Nam, Ban Nghiên Cứu Lịch Sử Đảng.

[Documents of the Party. Viet Nam Workers' Party, Committee for the Study of Party History.] Three volumes, arranged chronologically: v. 1, 27-10-1929 to 7-4-1935; v. 2, 10-8-1935 to 1939; v. 3, 25-1-1939 to 2-9-1945. Also cited as *Văn kien lịch sử Đảng* [Documents of Party history].

Some documents also available in English: *Historic documents of the Lao Dong Party.* Hanoi: Foreign Languages Publishing House, 1970.

342

Political alignments of Vietnamese nationalists. Washington, 1949.
Department of State, Division of Research for the Far East Office of Intelligence Research. (O. I. R. report, 3708.) By I. Milton Sacks (according to Cotter [30]).

A history of the nationalist movement in Vietnam. Contents: The era of plots, 1884-1918; Nationalist movements, 1918-41; Vietnam during World War II; Nationalist alignments since the outbreak of the French-Vietnamese War. Charts of: International connections of the Indochinese Communist Party in 1930; Development of communist Organizations in Indochina, 1921-31; History of the Vietnamese Nationalist Party; Development of Communist organizations in Indochina, 1931-5. Index of names. Chronology 1931-1949, pp. 169-173.

343

Contribution à l'histoire des mouvements politiques de l'Indochine Française. Documents. Hanoi: Imprimerie d'Extrême-Orient, 1933-4. 7 v.

Gouvernement Générale de l'Indochine, Direction des Affaires Politiques et de la Sûreté Générale.

Unusually full publication, by the French colonial government, of documents of its nationalist opponents. Includes some portraits. Vol. 1: *Le "Tân-Việt Cach-Mệnh Đảng" ou Parti Révolutionnaire du Jeune Annam (1925-1930).* 63 pp. The party was disbanded in 1929 but its remnants formed the Đông-Dương Cộng-Sản Lien-Doan, Indochinese Communist Federation, which later merged with the Parti Communiste Indochinois of vol. 4. Vol. 2: *"Việt-Nam Quốc-Dân Đảng" ou Parti National Annamite au Tonkin 1927-1932.* 1933. 52 pp. Vol. 3: *Le "Việt-Nam Quốc-Dân Đảng" ou Parti National Annamite des émigrés en Chine (1930-1933).* 62 pp. Vol. 4: *Le "Đông-Dương Cộng-Sản Đảng" ou Parti Communiste Indochinois (1925-1933).* 1933. 138 pp. Vol. 5: *La Terreur Rouge en Annam (1930-1931).* 307 pp. The Nghe-Tinh Soviets. Vol. 6 never published. Vol. 7: *Le Caodaïsme (1926-1934).* 112 pp.

344
Nguyễn Bá Trác: *Hoàng-Việt giáp tý niên biểu.* Saigon: Bộ Quốc-Gia Giáo-Dục, 1963. 455 pp.
Edited by Trương-Bửu-Lâm and others. (Tủ sách Viện Khao Cô = Publications of the Institute of Historical Research = Publications de l'Institut de Recherches Historiques, 4.)

Quoc-ngu edition, with new introduction in English and French, of a chronological tabulation of Vietnamese history, 2879 B.C. to A.D. 1924. Includes, for each year, cyclical year name; Vietnamese monarch, regnal year, and events, headed VN; Chinese emperor, regnal year, and events, headed TQ; notes on Korean and Japanese rulers and events, headed NB; notes on events elsewhere, headed NK. Index of names, pp. 385-451. First published in Chinese characters in 1924.

345
Albert Schroeder: *Annam: études numismatiques = Đại Nam hóa tê đô lục.* Paris: Leroux, 1905. 2 v. (651 pp., 111 plates).

[Annam: numismatic studies.] Contents. Vol. 1: history of currency in independent and protected Annam (pp. 1-414) covering mining, minting (including relevant legislation), weights and measures; coin legends. Dynastic chronologies, pp. 19-42; numismatic chronology, pp. 43-74. Coin catalogue (614 entries) pp. 415-507. Survey of currency in French Indochina, pp. 508-637, including catalogue entries 615-653. Vol. 2: plates 1-45, illustrations of minting etc.; plates 46-111, 653 coin types. The dynastic chronologies were also issued separately: Albert Schroeder: *Chronologie des souverains de l'Annam.* 1905. 28 pp.

An English translation of the Annam part of the catalogue, with poor quality illustrations, has been published, misleadingly attributed to Bernard J. Permar (apparently the translator) and Walter Lozozki: *Catalog of Annam coins 968-1955*. Saigon, 1963. 71 pp., 73 plates.

Note also: John A. Novak: *A working aid for collectors of Annamese coins*. Longview, Washington: Ken Olmsted [1967]. 111 pp. Line drawings of coins, arranged by legend in character stroke order, to assist identification.

And: Désiré Lacroix: *Numismatique annamite*. Saigon: Ménard & Legros, 1900. 2 v. (231 + xxxiii pp., album of 40 plates). (Publications de l'Ecole Française d'Extrême-Orient [1].) Illustrates 510 specimens. For further details of the last three works see Cotter [30], pp. 73-4.

346

Quốc Sử Quán: *Việt sử thông giám cương muc*. Hanoi: Văn Sử Địa, 1957-60. 20 v. (2037 pp.).

Detailed year-by-year arrangement of Vietnamese history, from 2879 BC to AD 1789. A sequence of indexes (in vols 2, 4, 7, 8, 10, 12, 13, 15, 17, 20) covers personal and place names and lists major entries under subject categories. Quôc-ngu edition of a 19th century nôm publication.

Note also: Bùi Quang Tung: 'Tables synoptiques de chronologie vietnamienne' in *Bulletin de l'Ecole Française d'Extrême-Orient* no. 1 (1963). [Synoptic tables of Vietnamese chronology.]

L. Cadière, 'Tableau chronologique des dynasties annamites' in *Bulletin de l'Ecole Française d'Extrême-Orient* vol. 5 nos 1-2 (1905) pp. 77-145.

Georges Maspero: 'Tableau chronologique des souverains de l'Annam' in *T'oung pao* vol. 5 (March 1894) pp. 43-62.

347

Phan Huy Chú: *Lịch-triều hiến-chương loại-chí*. [1821?] 10 v. (49 parts).

[Study of dynastic institutions.] Encyclopaedia of the history of Vietnamese governments from 1010 to 1788. Entirely in Chinese characters. Contents: Vol. 1, Geography; vol. 2, biography; vol. 3, government; vol. 4, rites and ceremonies; vol. 5, examinations; vol. 6, finance; vol. 7, penal code; vol. 8, military affairs; vol. 9, publications; vol. 10, foreign relations.

Quôc-ngu edition: Hanoi: Viên Sủ Hoc, 1960-61. 4 v. For other, partial modern editions see the list in Cotter [30] pp. 23-4.

French translations: Vol. 6: R. Deloustal, translator: 'Les ressources économiques et financières de l'état dans l'ancien Annam' in *Revue indochinoise*, 1924-5. Vol. 7: R. Deloustal, translator: *Recueil des principales ordonnances royales éditées depuis la promulgation du code annamite et en vigueur au Tonkin*. Hanoi: Schneider, 1903. 221 pp., completed by: Raymond Deloustal: *La justice dans l'ancien Annam: traduction et commentaire du Code des Lê*. Hanoi: Imprimerie d'Extrême-Orient, 1911-12. 318 + 33 pp., reprinted from a series of articles in *Bulletin de l'Ecole Française d'Extrême-Orient*. Vol. 9 (rearranged): Emile Gaspardone: 'Bibliographie annamite' in *Bulletin de l'Ecole Française d'Extrême-Orient* vol. 34 (1934) pp. 1-174.

MALAYSIA, SINGAPORE, BRUNEI

348

K. Mulliner, Lian The-Mulliner: *Historical dictionary of Singapore*. Metuchen: Scarecrow, 1991. 251 pp. 0-8108-2504-X.
(Asian historical dictionaries, 7.)

Contents: Note on spelling and names, pp. xiii-xvi; Common abbreviations and acronyms; Chronology, pp. xxi-xxxii; Historical overview; The dictionary, pp. 23-164 (entries for people, places, events); List of heads of government and of cabinets 1959-91; General elections since 1955; Population by ethnicity; Percentage distribution of Chinese by dialect group; bibliography; index, pp. 241-251.

349

Steven Tan: *Standard catalogue of Malaysia-Singapore-Brunei coin and paper money*. Kuala Lumpur: International Stamp & Coin [1991]. 179 pp. 983-9650-02-5.

Eleventh edition of a well-illustrated valuation list. Banknotes, pp. 1-75 (illustrated in colour); coins and tokens, pp. 76-179.

Note also: Saran Singh: 'The coinage of the Sultanate of Brunei 1400-1980' in *Brunei Museum journal* vol. 4 no. 4 (1980) pp. 38-103. A brief historical discussion followed by genealogical table and the chronological illustrated catalogue (pp. 47-102), which allocates a standard reference number to each issue.

Another paper: J. A. Davidson: 'Brunei coinage' in *Brunei Museum journal* vol. 4 no. 1 (1977) pp. 43-81, is a useful companion, offering a historical study with information on banknotes and on foreign coins that circulated in Brunei.

350

C. S. Wong: *An illustrated cycle of Chinese festivities in Malaysia and Singapore*. Singapore: Malaysia Publishing House, 1987. 237 pp.

Part 1: the Chinese calendar as used in Malaysia and Singapore. Part 2: Chinese New Year: Part 3: other festivals.

Note also: S. Arasaratnam: *Indian festivals in Malaya*. Kuala Lumpur: University of Malaya, Department of Indian Studies, 1966. 51 pp. Details of all festivals celebrated by the Indian communities of Malaya, emphasising divergences with practice in India.

351
R. O. Daniel: *Cooperative societies in Singapore 1925-1985*. Singapore: Singapore National Co-operative Federation, 1987. 150 pp.

History accompanied by a list of societies arranged according to their aims.

352
Basant K. Kapur, editor: *Singapore studies: critical surveys of the humanities and social sciences*. Singapore: Singapore University Press, 1986.

By a group of academics from the National University of Singapore. Covers Historiography; Sociology and social work; Political science; Human and physical geography; Economic development; Demography; English, Chinese and Malay literature; English language in Singapore. Surveys of recent work (varying dates) with bibliographies.

353
John A. Lent, Kent Mulliner: *Malaysian studies: archaeology, historiography, geography and bibliography*. Detroit: Cellar Book Shop, 1985. 240 pp.
Northern Illinois University, Center for Southeast Asian Studies. (Monograph series on Southeast Asia. Occasional paper. 11.)

A survey of recent research in each field, keyed to a bibliography.

354
J. de V. Allen, A. J. Stockwell, I. R. Wright, editors: *A collection of treaties and other documents affecting the states of Malaysia, 1761-1963*. London: Oceana, 1981. 2 v.

Includes detailed introductions to each document.

Superseded: W. G. Maxwell, W. S. Gibbon: *Treaties and engagements affecting the Malay States and Borneo*. London: Truscott, 1924. 276 pp.

Earlier work: *Treaties and engagements entered into with or affecting the native states of the Malay Peninsula*. Singapore, 1889. 189 pp. Revised edition.

Arranged by state: 'Treaty of Holland, 1824'; Johor; Kedah; Perak; Selangor; Sungei Ujong; Rembau; Johol; Negri Sembilan; Jelebu; Pahang; Naning. Full texts of treaties dating between 1786 and 1889.

355

The Communist Party of Malaya: selected documents. N.p., 1979. 83 pp. South East Asia Documentation Group.

Twelve programmes and statements, and the new constitution of the Party (May 1972), recorded as transcripts from the Voice of the Malayan Revolution, a clandestine broadcasting service.

356

Colin Jack-Hinton: *A sketch map history of Malaya, Sarawak, Sabah and Singapore.* London: Hulton Educational, 1966. 96 pp.

A brief historical outline with numerous monochrome historical maps.

357

Leon Comber: *An introduction to Chinese secret societies in Malaya.* Singapore: Donald Moore, 1957. 77 pp.

Their history, activities and rituals. Included here for its appendix: List of societies active in Malaya and Singapore with details of their activities.

358

Gifford N. Symons: *The seventy-five years' Mohamedan-English calendar from the 1st Moharam, Anno Hijra 1266 to the 29th Zulhijjah, Anno Hijra 1340, being from the 17th November, Anno Domini 1849, to the 23rd August, Anno Domini 1922.* Singapore: Government Printing Office, 1897. 151 pp.

The author was Malay Interpreter to the Supreme Court, Singapore.

Note also: *Cheam cheow heng = The Anglo-Chinese and Mohamedan calendar for 60 years, 1855-1914.* Penang: Criterion Press, 1907. 60 ff. Both cited from Cordier [242].

INDONESIA

359

Chr. L. M. Penders, editor: *Indonesia: selected documents on colonialism and nationalism, 1830-1942.* St Lucia: University of Queensland Press, 1977. 367 pp. 0-7022-1324-1; 0-7022-1029-3.

72 documents of both official and unofficial origin.

'Part 1, Colonialism': the culture system 1830-70 (1-4); the impact of liberalism on Dutch colonial policy 1848-1900 (5-9); the ethical policy 1901-42 (economic policy 10-14, decentralization 15-23, education 24-35).

'Part 2, Nationalism': anticolonial movements in the 19th century (36-9); genesis of the modern nationalist movement (40-45); the Islamic movement (46-54); Communism (55-8); the Indonesia-centric nationalist movement 1922-42 (59-72).

Note also: *The Indonesian revolution: basic documents and the idea of guided democracy.* Jakarta: Department of Information, 1959. 122 pp. A compilation for propaganda purposes of 8 constitutional documents, 1945-59.

360

John G. Taylor: *The Indonesian occupation of East Timor 1974-1989: a chronology.* London: Catholic Institute for Internationmal Relations, 1990. 102 pp. 1-85287-051-6.

In association with University of Oxford, Refugee Studies Programme.

Ends with 22 June 1989. A series of 727 entries, briefly describing events, each with attribution to source (usually newspapers and news agency reports).

360a

L. De Jong: *Het Koninkrijk der Nederlanden in de Tweede Wereldoorlog. Deel 2: Nederlands-Indië.* The Hague: Staatsuitgeverij, 1984-6. 3 v. in 5.

[The Kingdom of the Netherlands in the Second World War. Part 2: Dutch East Indies.] A very extensive official historical narrative, rather sparing in references to sources.

Note also: S. H. Spoor, editor: *Nederlands-Indië contra Japan.* [The Hague: Staatsdrukkerij- en Uitgeverijbedrijf, 1949-61.] 7 v. (Ministerie van Oorlog. Generale Staf K. N. I. L., Hoofdkwartier, Kriegsgeschiedkundige Sectie.) [The Dutch East Indies versus Japan.] An official military history, planned on a grand scale (and in the event slightly reduced, from ten to seven volumes). Vol. 1-3: General and pre-war history. Vol. 4: Dutch Air Force. Vol. 5: Kalimantan and Sulawesi. Vol. 6: Ambon, Timor, Sumatra. Vol. 7: Java. Many folding maps in vols 4-7; statistics, documents.

PHILIPPINES

361

Philippine studies. DeKalb: Northern Illinois University, Center for

Southeast Asian Studies, 1974-81. 3 v.

A series of surveys of research trends, including the following volumes.

Frederick L. Wernstedt and others: *Geography, archaeology, psychology, and literature.* 1974. 104 pp. (Special report, 10.) Papers of a panel discussion under the auspices of the Association for Asian Studies.

Donn V. Hart, editor: *History, sociology, mass media, and bibliography.* 1978. (Occasional paper, 6.)

Kit G. Machado, Richard Hooley, Lawrence Reid: *Political science, economics, and linguistics.* 1981. (Occasional paper, 8.)

362

Ester G. Maring, Joel M. Maring: *Historical and cultural dictionary of the Philippines.* Metuchen: Scarecrow, 1973. 240 pp.
(Historical and cultural dictionaries of Asia, 3.)

Brief entries in simple English for places, people, historical events and cultural concepts.

363

Francisco R. Demetrio y Radaza: *Dictionary of Philippine folk beliefs and customs.* Cagayan de Oro City: Xavier University, 1970. 4 v.
Assisted by Teresita Veloso Pil, Corazon Avenir Manuel.

Arranged under 26 general subject headings, each subdivided. Headings and subheadings -- rather than individual entries -- are arranged alphabetically.

364

W. E. Retana, editor: *Archivo del bibliófilo filipino.* Madrid: Victoriano Suarez, 1895-1905. 5 v.

[The Philippine bibliophile's archive.] A collection of mainly unofficial documents and historical narratives, each with separate title page and pagination. Only selected contents are listed here.

Vol. 2 item 12: Fernando Blumentritt: *Diccionario mitológico de Filipinas.* 1895. 120 pp. [Mythological dictionary of the Philippines.] Definitions of religious terms and divine names in several Philippine languages.

Vol. 3 item 6: W. E. Retana, editor: *Documentos políticos de actualidad.* 1st ser. 1897. 361 pp. [Current political documents.] Selected political manifestos and documents, 1892-7.

Vol. 4 item 2: see **475**.

Vol. 4 item 7: W. E. Retana, editor: *Documentos políticos de actualidad*. 2nd ser. 1898. 185 pp. Selected political manifestos and documents, 1896-8.

Vol. 5 item 8: Felipe G. Calderón, editor: *Documentos para la historia de Filipinas*. 1st series [all publ.]. 1905. 93 pp. [Documents of Philippine history.] This consists of reprints of 12 decrees of the revolutionary leader Emilio Aguinaldo, two newly translated from Tagalog, all dated 1898, notably: *Instrucciones sobre el régimen de las provincias y pueblos*. Kabite, 1898. [Instructions on the administration of provinces and towns.]

Note also: E. H. Blair, J. A. Robertson, editors: *The Philippine islands 1493-1898*. Cleveland, 1903-9. 55 v. An almost unending compilation of reprinted texts and documents, arranged chronologically. Reprinted: Mandaluyong: Cachos Hermanos, 1973.

Topography

ATLASES

365

Richard Ulack, Gyula Pauer: *Atlas of Southeast Asia*. New York: Macmillan, 1989. 171 pp. 0-02-933200-1.

A geographical outline with small thematic maps (scales not stated). Contents: Regional overview, pp. 1-43, with maps of climate patterns, continental shelf with oil and gas resources, natural vegetation regions, political history (8th to 20th century: 5 maps), maritime claims, language families, religions, population (2 maps), refugees. After the overview come the national sections, usually including maps of major industries and trade, ethnolinguistic groups, major administrative divisions. There are additional maps of insurgent activities (Philippines, Burma) and of the post-1975 Vietnamization of Cambodia. Plans of capital cities.

Note also: Thomas F. Barton: *Southeast Asia in maps*. Chicago: Denoyer-Geppert, 1970. Not seen.

366

Atlas of physical, economic and social resources of the lower Mekong basin = Atlas des ressources physiques, économiques et sociales du bassin inférieur du Mékong. Washington: United States Government Printing Office, 1968.
Prepared under the direction of the United States Agency for International Development, Bureau for East Asia, by the Engineer Agency for Resources Inventories and the Tennessee Valley Authority for the Committee for Coordination of Investigations of the Lower Mekong Basin, United Nations Economic Committee for Asia and the Far East.

Maps at about 1:4,200,000, sometimes accompanied by detailed tabular data and statistics: data cover four countries, Cambodia, Laos, South Vietnam and Thailand (north-west and south Thailand excluded by the cut of the map). Very large page size.

Physical (2 maps), Climate (2 maps, 8 pages), Geology (4 maps, 6 pages), Soil mechanics (2 maps), Building materials, Mineral resources, Land use and agriculture (4 maps, 11 pages), Water resources (4 maps, 9 pages), Population, Ethnic and linguistic groups (2 maps, 10 pages), Education (13 pages), Health, Urban areas (28 pages: detailed tabulation of resources), Industries (19 pages), Fisheries, Tourism (15 pages: 190 places and 48 annual festivals described), Electric power (7 pages), Highways (5 pages), Railroads, Airfields (10 pages: list), Inland waterways and ports, Telecommunications,

Rural development, Mapping and aerial photography (4 maps: information from US Army Map Service and Cadastral Survey of Thailand). 15-page directory of institutions concerned with development.

367

Atlas of South-East Asia with an introduction by D. G. E. Hall. London: Macmillan; New York: St Martin's, 1964. 92 pp.

Arranged country-by-country, each on a slightly different scale. There are general hypsometric maps of each country, but at scales smaller than in *The Times atlas of the world* [11] and *The National Geographic atlas*; larger scale maps of large conurbations; thematic maps of climate, vegetation, land use, population, minerals, industries, communications. Ethnological/linguistic maps on very small scale. Three maps of 'Federation of Malaya' (Malay peninsula and Singapore) show density of population of Malay, Chinese, Indians separately, p. 36.

The coverage of Indochina is particularly weak: for general topography there are several better maps, e.g. *Cambodge-Laos-Viêt Nam 1/2 000 000*. Paris: Institut Géographique Nationale, 1966 (diacritical marks on major place-names only. First published 1945); *Viet Nam, Cambodia, Laos, and Thailand 1:1,900,800*. Washington: National Geographic Society, 1967 (no diacritical marks). For the latter an index is available: *Index to map of Viet Nam, Cambodia, Laos and Thailand with 9,669 place names*. 1967. 35 pp.

Thailand

368

Thailand: national resources atlas. 1972.
Prepared by the Royal Thai Survey Department, Supreme Command Headquarters.

Most maps at 1:2,500,000. Contents: Hypsometry, Climate (6 maps), Geology (with 8 pp. text), Soil (with 6 pp. text), Mineral resources (with 4 pp. text), Forests and national parks, Land registration, Land use (with 3 pp. statistics by province), Water resources (with 8 pp. list of rivers), Population, education, Industries, Fisheries (with 5 pp. statistics), Transport (2 maps, 6 pp. statistics), Administrative divisions.

First edition: 1969. 55 leaves.

Watts [29] cites a later publication on a smaller scale: *Natural resources atlas of Thailand*. Bangkok: Thailand Army Mapping Department, 1976- . A looseleaf publication intended to be updated from time to time.

369

Phaen thi tanon nai prathet Thai. [Bangkok:] Shell, 1961. 56 pp.
Prathet Thai Shell.

[Road atlas of Thailand.] 32 highly generalised maps at 1:1m; map of eastern
Asia; 13 town plans. Maps are in Thai and Roman scripts. Diagram of road
signs; 5-page list of major routes and inter-town distances (in Thai only).

Indochina

370

Guillaume Grandidier, editor: *Atlas des colonies françaises, protectorats
et territoires sous mandat de la France.* Paris: Société d'Editions
Géographiques, Maritimes et Coloniales [1934]. 39 plates and various
paginations.

[Atlas of the French colonies, protectorates and mandated territories.] A
total of over 150 maps and accompanying text, published in fascicles with
a loose-leaf binder. Large page size.

Indochina occupies plates 30-34 and a 20-page section of text. The whole
region is covered by good general hypsometric maps at 1:2,000,000,
Cochinchina and Tonkin at 1:500,000; large scale insets of Hanoi, Saigon,
Hue, Phnom Penh. Monochrome maps in the text of soil, climate,
ethnography, European plantations. The text forms a useful economic
survey with statistical tables.

Note also: P. Pollacchi: *Atlas colonial français: colonies, protectorats et pays sous
mandat.* Paris: L'Illustration, 1929. 319 pp. Smaller page size; maps of a more
old-fashioned style with relief hatching. Indochina: pages 205-216 with
numerous halftones in sepia; 8 map plates, with topographic coverage of the
region at 1:2,500,000, and an economic map (plate 29 ter).

371

Henri Russier, Henri Gourdon, Edouard Russier: *L'Indochine
Française: atlas indochinois.* Hanoi: Imprimerie d'Extrême-Orient, 1931.
131 pp.

[French Indochina: Indochinese atlas.] 29 plates; 100 photographs.

372

Atlas de l'Indochine. Hanoi, 1928.
Service Géographique de l'Indochine.

[Atlas of Indochina.] Not seen.

373

H. Brenier: *Essai d'atlas statistique de l'Indochine Française: Indochine physique, population, administration, finances, agriculture, commerce, industrie.* Hanoi: Imprimerie d'Extrême-Orient, 1914. 256 pp.
Gouvernement Général de l'Indochine.

[Attempt at a statistical atlas of French Indochina: physical geography, population, administration, finance, agriculture, trade, industry.] An early thematic atlas of the region; based on incomplete information, hence the 'attempt' of the title. 38 maps and 88 diagrams.

374

Atlas général de l'Indochine Française: atlas de Chabert--L. Gallois. Hanoi: Imprimerie d'Extrême-Orient, 1909. 63 pp.
'Contenant 169 cartes ou plans; documents puisés au Service Géographique, à la Direction Générale de l'Agriculture, des Forêts et du Commerce; renseignements de l'*Annuaire général de l'Indochine* [104].'

[General atlas of French Indochina.] Contains 169 maps and plans from official sources. Not seen.

375

P. Pelet: *Atlas des colonies françaises.* Paris: Armand Colin, [1900-]1902. 29 plates + 74 + 26 pp.

[Atlas of the French colonies.] Published in nine fascicles. Maps 20-22 cover Indochina (map 22: Tongking delta at 1:500,000), usefully showing explorers' routes and current French claims on Cambodia and Thailand.

Reissued as a bound volume, with some maps updated to about 1908, with undated title page.

376

Luc Mogenet: *Atlas de la ville de Louang-Phrabang.* Vientiane: Vithagna, 1973. 111 pp.
(Collection "Documents pour le Laos", 3.)

[Atlas of the city of Luang Phrabang.] The city is covered in a series of 10 very large scale plans (1:2500), not 'cadastral' but highly informative on land ownership and use, commerce etc.; 10 matching administrative plans. Smaller scale thematic plans: demography, population movement, types of housing, house ownership, vehicle ownership, water and electricity supply, location of administrative and religious buildings. Wider-ranging maps: education (Laos, Louang-Phrabang province, Louang-Phrabang city); migration (Laos, Louang-Phrabang province). Population statistics. Text on some plans is in French and Lao. A unique and fascinating depiction of a small royal city.

Malaysia

377

Atlas kebangsaan Malaysia. Kuala Lumpur: Dewan Bahasa dan Pustaka, 1977. 152 pp.

[National atlas of Malaysia.] In Bahasa Malaysia. Overwhelmingly concerned with Peninsular Malaysia. Large page size; well-printed colour maps. An impressive production.

Contents include: history, archaeology, ancient trade routes, administrative maps of each state, electoral maps including voting patterns by ethnic origin; physiography, geology, soil, climate, land use, population and ethnic origin (18 maps); agriculture, mining, communications and transport, education, health.

Then (pp. 84-109), notably, a pair of detail maps of each state at 1:500,000 (but Sabah and Sarawak much smaller) showing human topography, land use, infrastructure.

Accompanying notes and statistics: in Bahasa Malaysia, pp. 112-126; in English, pp. 127-139. Unfortunately these notes are not keyed to map numbers, which would have made the maps themselves much easier to use for English speakers.

Brunei

378

Ali Haji Hasan: *Ilmu alam ringkas Brunei.* Bandar Seri Begawan: Dewan Bahasa dan Pustaka, 1979. 51 pp.

[Geography of Brunei.] 23 maps: topography, climate, population, administrative divisions, natural resources, transport.

Indonesia

379

The land resources of Indonesia: a national overview atlas = Atlas tinjauan sumber daya lahan seluruh wilayah Indonesia. 1990. 28 sheets.
Land Resources Department NRI; United Kingdom Foreign and Commonwealth Office, Overseas Development Administration.

Vast page size, each pair of facing sheets opening out to display the whole of Indonesia at 1:2,500,000. Contents: Geology; Mineral and energy resources (including ofshore oil); Rainfall, with list of meteorological stations; climatic zones; groundwater potential; Land type, gradient, and development potential (2 maps); Soils; Forests, land use, zoning (2 maps); Volcanoes, seismology, landslides, flooding; Transmigrasi up to April 1989 (with list of settlements); Population distribution (very generalized); Regional infrastructure and development, an incomplete map dealing mostly with the western half of the country.

380

J. E. Romein and others: *Atlas nasional seluruh dunia untuk sekolah landjutan*. Jakarta: Ganaco, 1960. 72 pp.

[National and world atlas for high schools.] A small world atlas, but with a solid and useful central section of topographical and special maps of Indonesia.

Note also: *Atlas Indonesia. Vol. 1: Umum*. Jakarta: Bumirestu, 1977. [Atlas of Indonesia, vol. 1: general.] 'Third edition.' Poorly designed maps of each province, at varying scales, each with an index. I have not seen other volumes or editions.

381

Atlas van tropisch Nederland. [The Hague: Nijhoff] 1938. 31 plates. Koninklijk Nederlandsch Aardrijkskundig Genootschap. Topografische Dienst in Nederlandsch-Indië.

[Atlas of the tropical Netherlands.] Almost entirely devoted to the Dutch East Indies, modern Indonesia. The contents fall into two groups.

Topographical: Java, Bali and Lombok are mapped at 1:750,000, the remainder of the territory at about a third of that scale. There are many small detail maps of urban areas.

Special maps, of the whole territory and of various regions, include: Physiographical, volcanoes and earthquakes, landforms, plant and animal geography, climate, minerals, population, education, languages (an important step in the classification of the languages of eastern Indonesia), history, soils, agriculture, irrigation, forestry, roads and railways, administration.

See the review by E. Fischer in *Koloniale Rundschau*, 1939, pp. 138-142.

Philippines

382
The Philippine atlas. Manila: Fund for Assistance to Private Education, 1975. 2 v.

Vol. 1 contains the maps and forms an attractive pictorial atlas with useful accompanying text and statistics. Maps begin with a section on the geographical background: physiography; gradients; soil (2 maps); climate (6 maps). Then small, poorly designed road maps of each Philippine region (scales between 1:1,000,000 and 1:2,500,000); History. Then statistical maps, mainly not admitting detail below the province level, of majority ethnic groups, 'dialects', religion, population and migration (4 maps and statistics), literacy. Then economic maps, some in precise detail, of soil cover, land use, oil and gas, seismology, labour and local economy (7 maps), transport (6 maps), power, telecommunications, hospitals, mineral resources, fisheries, economic development, tourism (3 maps). Finally a long section of maps, charts and statistics of education (pp. 230-304).

Vol. 2: Index to vol. 1; register of public and private higher education institutions; list of sources of educational funds.

Note also: Robert S. Hendry, editor: *Atlas of the Philippines*. [Manila:] Phil-Asian Publishers [1959]. Maps of minerals, climate, population, industry and forestry, followed by very generalized maps of each province.

383
1972 national economic atlas. Manila: Department of National Defense, Philippine Coast and Geodetic Survey, 1973. 37 maps.

All maps are at 1:4,000,000. Administrative divisions (2 maps). Geography: relief, geology, mineralogy, soils, surface water resources (with list of 326 rivers), climate. Development: national parks, soil cover, irrigation, major agricultural produce, fisheries, mineral resources, population and labour, cultural-linguistic groups, literacy, domestic water supply, health (with statistics of hospitals), transport (with list of airports and seaports), telecommunications, power (with list of generators), industry, local trade patterns, banks, income. This is a more authoritative production than the *Philippine atlas* [382] but neither can be considered redundant.

Note also: *The Philippine economic atlas*. Manila: Presidential Economic Staff, 1966. Second edition. Not seen.

384
José Algué: *Atlas de Filipinas = Atlas of the Philippine Islands*.

Washington: United States Government Printing Office, 1900. 30 plates.
Treasury Department, United States Coast and Geodetic Survey. (Special publication, 3.)

Introduction with statistical tables and index of places. Special maps of ethnography, mountains, earthquakes; then topographical maps of provinces, plates 7-30. Exploration and survey of inland regions were far from complete, but the maps are highly informative on settlements and natural features then known and named. They are the work of Philippine draughtsmen.

INDEX-GAZETTEERS

385

Gazetteer of Vietnam. Names approved by the United States Board on Geographic Names. Washington: Defense Mapping Agency, 1986. 2 v. (1143 pp.).
One of a series Gazetteers, other members of which are listed below. Many, but not all, carry a number in the series: these numbers are given in brackets.

Published since 1973 by the Defense Mapping Agency. Editions of 1972, 1971 and 1970 were published by the United States Army Topographic Command. Earlier, some were published by the Department of the Interior, Office of the Geographer; others by the United States Government Printing Office. An even earlier series, published by the Hydrographic Office, is not listed here.

Tabulated names with coordinates, grid references, sheet number of Joint Operations Graphic map series. Many cross-references from alternative forms. The volume listed above replaced: *South Vietnam.* 1971. 337 pp. (58): *Southern Vietnam and the South China Sea.* 1961. 248 pp. (58): *Northern Vietnam.* 1971. 311 pp. (79): *Northern Vietnam.* 1964 (79).

In the same series: *Indonesia.* 1982. 2 v. (1529 pp.): *Indonesia and Portuguese Timor.* 1968. 901 pp. (13): *Indonesia, Netherlands New Guinea and Portuguese Timor.* 1955. 2 v. (1376 pp.) (13).

Laos. 1973. 348 pp. (69): *Laos.* 1962. 214 pp. (69).

Cambodia. 1971. 392 pp. (74): *Cambodia.* 1963. 199 pp. (74).

Malaysia, Singapore and Brunei. 1970. 1014 pp. (10): *British Borneo, Singapore and Malaya.* 1955. 463 pp. (10).

Thailand. 1966. 675 pp. (97).

Burma. 1966. 725 pp. (96): *Burma.* 1955. 175 pp. (9): *Burma: preliminary edition.* 1951.

Philippine Islands: preliminary edition. 1953. 2 v. (1303 pp.).

386

Gazetteer of Burma. [New Delhi] 1944. 575 pp.
'Published under the authority of the Director of Survey (India).' General Staff, Geographical Section.

Tabulated names 'from the largest scale standard topographical map available for each area,' giving coordinates and grid references. About 110,000 place names.

From the same source: *Gazetteer of Indo-China.* 1945. 498 pp. Nearly 100,000 names.

Gazetteer of Siam. 1946. 89 pp.

A gazetteer of Malaya. 1945. 122 pp.

Gazetteer of Sumatra and its outliers. 1945. 341 pp.

387

Index on AMS 1:50 000 maps of Thailand, series L 708. Washington: U. S. Army Map Service, 1968. 714 pp.

From the same source: *Index to names on 1:50 000 maps of Vietnam.* 1967. 2 v. (617 pp.) Volume 1 is South Vietnam, volume 2 North Vietnam.

Index to names on Topocom 1:50 000 maps of Laos, series L 7015. Washington: United States Army Topographic Command, 1970. 512 pp.

388

Lijst van de voornaamste aardrijkskundige namen in den Nederlandsch-Indischen Archipel. 1923.

[List of the main geographical names in the Dutch East Indian Archipelago.] Revised edition.

GUIDE BOOKS, DESCRIPTIVE GAZETTEERS

389

Joshua Eliot and others, editors: *Thailand, Indochina and Burma handbook* 1993. Bath: Trade & Travel Publications; New York: Prentice Hall, 1992. 816 pp. 0-900751-41-X.
(Travellers world guides.)

A guide book for serious travellers, objective, highly informative, well-written and closely printed. Contents: General practical and cultural information; Thailand, pp. 54-355; Burma, pp. 356-464; Vietnam, pp. 465-604; Laos, pp. 605-753; brief chapters on Singapore and Malaysia, see below. Index; list of maps and plans (of which there are about 100). Each country section includes a lengthy historical and cultural introduction, a descriptive section and concluding 'practical information for visitors'.

Accompanied by: Joshua Eliot and others, editors: *Indonesia, Malaysia and Singapore handbook 1993*. 1992. 0-900751-42-8. A work of similar size and usefulness.

Annual editions are promised.

390

Tony Wheeler: *South-East Asia on a shoestring*. Hawthorn: Lonely Planet, 1992. 912 pp. 0-86442-125-7.

Seventh edition. Excellent practical information on travel in the region.

Sixth edition: 1989. 684 pp. General section (pp. 7-28): practical advice, travel to and within south east Asia. Chapters for each country except Indochina (also includes Macau, Hong Kong, Papua New Guinea), arranged alphabetically: each chapter begins with practical information, followed by descriptions of places, emphasizing means of travel and the details and costs of tourist activities. E.g. Brunei, pp. 29-35; Malaysia, pp. 352-438. 'The other South-East Asia' (Laos, Cambodia, Vietnam): brief information on pp. 653-665. 'Stop press' (latest information, especially on Laos and Vietnam) after p. 678. Index. Over 100 maps, mostly of little general use.

More extensive information, with rather more interesting topographical description, is to be found in the series of 'travel survival kits' from the same publisher.

First edition: 1975.

391

Carl Parkes: *Southeast Asia handbook*. Chico: Moon, 1990. 873 pp.

A detailed, practical guide book to mainland south east Asia. 169 maps and 140 'charts'. For the accompanying volumes on Indonesia and the Philippines see **460, 470**.

More ephemeral: *Fodor's Southeast Asia*. New York: Fodor. An annual travel guide first published 1975. The 1975 edition (511 pp.) covered Thailand, Malaysia, Indonesia and the Philippines, each in about 40 pages; Burma, Brunei, Singapore, Cambodia, Laos and South Vietnam, very briefly.

392

Erhard Rathenberg, Tonny Rosiny, Christian Velder: *Kambodscha mit Angkor Wat, Birma, Laos*. Buchenhain vor München: Volk und Heimat, n.d. 164 pp. 3-87936-000-6.
(Mai's Auslandstaschenbücher, 30.)

[Cambodia including Angkor Wat, Burma, Laos.] Brief travel guide with solid preliminary factual information on each country. Last entry in bibliography 1967: covers some districts which were soon to become inaccessible to travellers. Separate contents pages for each country: separate indexes at end of volume.

393

Malaysia and Indo-China: information for visitors to British Malaya, Dutch-Indies (Java, Bali, Sumatra, etc.), Siam, French Indo-China. Singapore: Thomas Cook, 1929. 204 pp.

Previous edition: 1926. 164 pp. Both cited from the Library of Congress catalogue.

394

An official guide to eastern Asia. Tokyo.
Department of Railways, formerly Imperial Japanese Government Railways.

The official Japanese Railways guide book covered a much wider area than Japan, as indicated by the title. For south east Asia see the volume entitled: *East Indies including Philippine Islands, French Indo-China, Siam, Malay Peninsula and Dutch East Indies*. 1917. 519 pp.

There was a second edition published in 1920.

395

India, Ceylon, Burma, Malaya, Siam and Java. Leipzig: Baedeker, 1914. 358 pp.
'By Karl Baedeker.' Cover title: Baedeker's India.

Guide book with a 74-page introduction, 22 maps and 33 town plans. Chiefly devoted to India; but Java, for example, gets 36 pages of concise archaeological and topographical description.

Burma

396

Tony Wheeler: *Burma: a travel survival kit*. Hawthorn: Lonely Planet,

1989. [0-86442-134-6.]

Fourth edition. Emphasizes the practical aspects of travel but is also the most detailed topographical description of the country that is in print at present. Includes information and advice on areas not officially open to tourists.

First edition: 1979.

397

Paul Strachan: *Pagan: art and architecture of old Burma*. Whiting Bay: Kiscadale, 1989. 159 pp. 0-870838-25-4.

'A field-guide for the ever increasing number of visitors to Burma's foremost historical site' (blurb). Very full and useful architectural and artistic descriptions of 76 of the most important structures, preceded by a general historical introduction. Site names are given in Burmese script and romanization. Many plans and photographs. A beautiful book.

Note also: Than Tun: 'The preservation and study of Pagan' in Y. Ishizawa, Y. Kono, editors: *Study and preservation of historic cities of Southeast Asia*. Tokyo: Japan Times, 1986. 168 pp., pp. 67-84. A list of monuments requiring attention, with comments on previous restorations.

List of pagodas at Pagan under the custody of Government. Rangoon, 1901. (Archaeological Department.) Cited from Cordier [242].

398

Hans Johannes Hoefer, Wilhelm Klein and others: *Burma*. Hong Kong: Apa, 1988. 332 pp. [962-421-007-1.]
(Insight guides, 11.)

'Seventh edition.' Beautifully illustrated guide book beginning with a long general and historical survey. One or two plans of sites. A final section of practical information, on grey paper, is what is normally revised between editions.

First edition: 1981. 332 pp.

399

Ba Thann Win: *Highways and major bridges of Burma*. Rangoon, 1976. 179 pp.

Description of nine long distance roads and 21 new road bridges, with very poor photographs (one of which seems to be of a scale model, p. 108). May serve as a 'travel guide to tourists' according to a foreword: but actually of interest because nearly all the places described are closed to visitors.

400

The motor roads of Burma. Rangoon: Myanma Oil Corporation, 1974. 81 pp.

Brief practical description of motorable routes all over Burma, many of which have long been forbidden to visitors. Includes sketch maps. Business hours of filling stations, pp. i-v.

It is worth noting that detailed information on the road network at an earlier period is available in a series of district reports published under varying titles by the Government of Burma about 1903-7: see the list in Cordier [242] cols 506-8, reproduced from the *General catalogue of all publications of the Government of India and local Governments and Administrations.*

401

Aung Thaw: *Historical sites in Burma.* Rangoon: Ministry of Union Culture, 1972. 157 pp.

Readable illustrated survey of 14 major sites.

402

Pearl Aung, P. Aung Khin: *Pearl of the East: a guide to Burma and its people.* Rangoon: Pearl Publishers, 1961. 186 pp.

General information for travellers; Rangoon, pp. 63-122; other towns (very brief); contact and shopping directory.

Note also: Roy Hudson: *The magic guide to Burma.* Chiang Mai, 1977. 68 pp. Desultory but pithy information on travel problems in Burma.

403

Burma: information for travellers to Burma; specimen tours with notes on the climate, railway and steamer services, hotels and places of interest in Burma. Season 1926/1927. Rangoon: Thomas Cook, 1926.

Cited from the Library of Congress catalogue.

Two editions of an earlier publication (*Cook's guide to Burma.* London: Thomas Cook, 1896. 56 pp.; and 1903. 53 pp.) appear in the British Library catalogue.

Burma was covered in: *India, Burma and Ceylon: information for travellers and residents.* London: Thomas Cook. Published approximately annually from about 1895 to 1926. About 240 pp.

Note also the sections on Burma in the successive editions (under slightly

varying titles) of: *A handbook for travellers in India, Ceylon and Burma.*
London: John Murray, beginning with the second edition, 1891, and
continuing to the twenty-first, 1968.

404

Charles Duroiselle: *A guide to the Mandalay Palace.* Rangoon:
Superintendent, Government Printing, 1925.

405

J. H. G. Powell: *Mandalay to Bhamo.* Rangoon: American Baptist
Mission Press, 1922. 84 pp.

Discursive description of the steamer route for tourists. Includes practical
advice on group travel from Bhamo to Tengyüeh.

406

Amended list of ancient monuments in Burma. Rangoon [Superintendent,
Government Printing, about 1920?] Various paginations.

Detailed tabulation, arranged under administrative divisions, each list
divided ito 'Structural edifices' and 'Historical sites'. Notes on ownership
and preservation; some detailed information on boundaries.

Reprinted: 1960.

Superseded: *List of ancient monuments in Burma.* 1916. Various paginations.

List of objects of antiquarian and archaeological interest in British Burma.
Rangoon: Government Press, 1892. 45 pp. There had been an earlier edition:
1884. 39 pp. 'British Burma' is meant in its narrow sense of Lower Burma.
This list is thus paired with: *List of objects of antiquarian and archaeological
interest in Upper Burma.* Rangoon: Superintendent, Government Printing,
1901. 22 pp.

407

Burma. Calcutta: Superintendent of Government Printing, 1908. 2 v.
(Imperial gazetteer of India, Provincial series.)

Vol. 1 pp. 1-182: general survey. Statistical tables, pp. 145-157. Mountains,
Lake Indawgyi, Islands, Rivers, Canals, Tribes, pp. 158-182. Vol. 1 p. 183-vol.
2: Descriptions of districts arranged under divisions, with short entries for
subordinate townships. The hierarchical arrangement is difficult to follow
without use of the index.

Note also: *List of geographical names of which the Burmese orthography has been
authorized by the Text-Book Committee.* Rangoon: Superintendent, Government

Printing, 1903. 52 pp.; earlier edition: 1895. 50 pp. Both cited from Cordier [242].

408

Burma gazetteer. Rangoon: Superintendent, Government Printing.

These are the 'district gazetteers'. For each district of Lower and Upper Burma (but not the hill states) two volumes were issued.

Volume A described the district, its geography, its people, its economy and society; a final chapter, headed 'Minor articles', was a survey of the towns and villages. An appendix listed deputy commissioners who had held charge of the District since its inception. Volume A, a series published, most volumes in at least two editions, between 1910 and 1935, officially superseded the *British Burma gazetteer* [412] and the relevant entries in the *Gazetteer of Upper Burma* [409].

Volume B contained statistical tables, many of them reprinted from the most recent census, and appeared in three successive editions, in 1906-7 in foolscap format (in this edition the titles were *Akyab district gazetteer* etc.), in 1912-13, and in 1924-5. For the extension of the volume B series covering the hill states see **60**.

A detailed guide to these series is to be found in: Henry Scholberg: *The district gazetteers of British India: a bibliography*. Zug: IDC, 1970.

409

James George Scott: *Gazetteer of Upper Burma and the Shan States*. Rangoon: Superintendent, Government Printing, 1900. 5 v.
Assisted by J. P. Hardiman.

In two parts.

Part 1 (2 vols): Physical geography; 19th century history from Burmese sources; British 'pacification'; The Shan states and the Tai; The Kachin Hills and the Chingpaw; The Chin Hills and the Chin tribes; Ethnology; Alphabets; Vocabularies, vol. 1 pp. 626-727. Religion; Palace customs; extensive glossary of court language, vol. 2 pp. 105-133; honorific titles, pp. 134-152; plan of Mandalay Palace, p. 176; resources, revenue and trade; pre-British government and administration, with lists and statistics.

Part 2 (3 vols): gazetteer entries: some, for states and districts, very lengthy; also numerous brief entries for towns and villages. Those for some of the individual Shan States contain histories compiled from Shan and Burmese manuscripts collected by Scott. Entries for the districts of Upper Burma proper are superseded by the *Burma gazetteer* [408], but those for the Shan States remain indispensable. A vast quantity of statistical and ethnographical information gathered with tireless enthusiasm.

Reprint: New York: AMS Press, 1983.

Note also: *Tables for the transliteration of Shan names into English.* Rangoon: Superintendent, Government Printing, 1900. 13 pp. Classified list of place names in Shan script and romanization: States, circles, towns and villages; Rivers and streams; Mountains and hills.

410

Bertram S. Carey, H. N. Tuck: *The Chin Hills: a history of the people, our dealings with them, their customs and manners, and a gazetteer of their country.* Rangoon: Superintendent, Government Printing, 1896. 2 v.

Contents. Vol. 1: History of British involvement (pp. 12-117); History of the ethnic groups (pp. 118-164); Manners and customs; Law; Agriculture, manufactures and trade; Arms and warfare. Long genealogical tables of ruling families. Numerous fine photo-etchings. Vol. 2: Gazetteer of villages, arranged by ethnic group and indicating tribute-paying status; Very detailed 'road reports' (pp. 129-255) indicating stopping places and ease of march.

411

M. C. Nangle: *The Burma route book.* Calcutta: Superintendent of Government Printing, 1903-5. Vols 1-3.
Compiled for the Intelligence Branch, Quarter Master General's Department.

Highly detailed information including ease of route, fords, places to camp, supplies available. Compilers of original routes are named, with the date on which they travelled. Contents: Part 1: *Northern Burma.* 84 routes between the Irrawaddy and the Chindwin. Part 2: *North-eastern Burma.* 138 routes in the triangle Mandalay-Kunlong-Myitkyina. Part 3: *Western Burma.* 57 routes north of Thayetmyo and Akyab. There was to be a part 4: 'Southern Burma.' I do not know if it appeared. It would have been a big volume: much of the Shan States remained to be covered, as well as all of Burma proper south-east of Akyab.

Replacement of an earlier work which it described as the 'preliminary edition': A. B. Fenton: *Routes in Upper Burma including the Chin Hills and Shan States, to which are added a number of routes leading from Lower Burma and Siam into those districts.* 1894. 1195 pp. (Compiled for the Quartermaster-General of the Madras Army.) This older edition has been reprinted: Delhi: Cultural Publishing House, 1983. 2 v.

412

The British Burma gazetteer. Rangoon: Government Press, 1879-80. 2 v.

Preface signed by H. E. Spearman as compiler.

The official survey of what was soon to become 'Lower Burma'.

Vol. 1: general description. Script, pronunciation, transliteration; Physical geography; Geology and mineral resources; Forests and vegetation (survey by habitat); Ethnology; Religion; History; Manners and customs; Arts, agriculture, trade; Fauna (mammals, birds [by Eugene W. Oates, cf. 490], reptiles [by W. Theobald, cf. 483], fish [see 503], mollusca), detailed listings in systematic order with Burmese names; flora (see 566). Table of plants useful for oil, resin, gum, dye, fibre, pp. 131-140.

Vol. 2: Alphabetical gazetteer of places: very full entries for districts and major towns with much statistical information; many brief entries for villages. Vol. 2 was superseded by 408 (note also the briefer 407) but remains useful as a concise one-volume gazetteer.

Reprint: *Gazetteer of Burma*. Delhi: Cultural Publishing House, 1983. 2 v.

Note also: Malcolm B. S. Lloyd: *Gazetteer of the District of Rangoon, Pegu Province, British Burma, together with an historical account of that portion of the province which was formerly known as Han-tha-wa-dee*. Rangoon: Bartholomew, 1868. 123 pp. Cited from Cordier [242].

J. Butler: *Gazetteer of the Mergui District, Tenasserim Division, British Burma*. Rangoon: Government Press, 1884. 84 pp. An early general survey at the district level. 10-page statistical appendix; no descriptions of places.

Routes by land and water in British Burma. Rangoon: Rangoon Daily News Press, 1877. 20 pp. Cited from Cordier [242].

Thailand

413

Paul Gray, Lucy Ridout and others: *Thailand: the rough guide*. London: Rough Guides, 1992. 474 pp. 1-85828-016-8.

Contents: practical information for tourists, pp. 1-42. Then description of regions of interest to travellers: Bangkok, pp. 45-111; The central plains, pp. 112-174; The north, pp. 175-254; The east coast and northeast, pp. 255-328; The gulf coast, pp. 329-364; Andaman coast and deep south, pp. 365-429. Contexts (history, culture, glossary).

414

Joe Cummings: *Thailand: a travel survival kit*. Hawthorn: Lonely Planet, 1992. 0-86442-170-2.

Fifth edition of a similar work with a longer pedigree.

Fourth edition: 1990. 444 pp. Chapters of practical and background information, pp. 1-84; regional description, pp. 85-429 (Bangkok, 85-127).

First edition: 1982. 131 pp.

Note also: Joe Cummings: *Bangkok: a city guide*. Hawthorn: Lonely Planet, 1992. 0-86442-155-9.

Luca Invernizzi Tettoni: *A guide to Chiang Mai and northern Thailand*. Hong Kong: Guide Book Company, 1989. 254 pp. 0962-217-100-X. An illustrated guidebook with better than average maps.

Roy Hudson: *Hudson's guide to Chiang Mai and the North*. Chiang Mai, 1971. 170 pp. Fourth edition. Practical information as well as tourist guidance; gives place names in Thai script. Section on Laos, pp. 125-139. First edition: 1965.

415

Achille Clarac; Michael Smithies, editor and translator: *Guide to Thailand*. Kuala Lumpur: Oxford University Press, 1981. 219 + 35 pp. 0-19-580417-1.

Third edition of a landmark work, differing from those above in giving little space to the details and costs of travel: hence more permanently useful for its cultural and historical depth. 'For the serious tourist: we have made no attempt to cover restaurants and night life.' Bangkok, pp. 28-63; Around Bangkok, pp. 64-94; Regional survey. Some maps and plans. Index of places, which gives names in Thai script as well as in transliteration, 35 pp. at end. This, two generations late, is the Baedeker for Thailand that Karl Baedeker and his successors failed to provide.

Second edition: Achille Clarac, Michael Smithies: *Discovering Thailand: a guidebook*. Bangkok: Siam Communications, 1972. 458 pp.

First edition: 1971.

416

Thamniap thong thi = Directory of local administrative units. Bangkok: Ministry of the Interior, Department of Local Adminstration, 1975.

A list of tambons, the lowest administrative subdivision above the village, indicating the number of villages in each.

Note also: *The romanized spelling of provinces, districts and sub-districts*. Bangkok: Royal Institute, 1967. 90 pp.

417

Tri Amatayakul: *The official guide to Ayutthaya and Bang Pa-in*.

Bangkok: Fine Arts Department, 1972. 58 pp.

Brief survey of the ruined capital with a large scale plan.

Note also: Nidda Hongvivat, editor: *Ayutthaya: the former Thai capital.* Bangkok: Muang Boran, 1980. 63 pp. Cited from Watts [29].

418

Akkharanukrom phumisat Thai. Bangkok: Ratchabandit Sathan, 1963-6. 4 v.

[Dictionary of Thai geographical names. Royal Institute.] An encyclopaedic compilation, entirely in Thai.

Vol. 1: survey of the geography, flora and fauna (with scientific Latin names in the text), resources and ethnography of Thailand. There is an index at the end of the volume.

Vols 2-3 (1693 pp.): alphabetical, descriptive gazetteer of names of administrative districts, towns and natural features of Thailand. There are no separate entries at the village level.

Vol. 4 (213 pp.): small monochrome maps of each of the 71 changwats, each accompanied by an index of place names.

Note also: *Highways in Thailand.* Bangkok, 1971. (Department of Highways.)

419

Pierre Dupont: *L'archéologie mône de Dvaravati.* Paris: Ecole Française d'Extrême-Orient, 1959. 2 v. (329 pp., 152 plates).
(Publications de l'Ecole Française d'Extrême-Orient.)

[The Mon archaeology of Dvaravati.] Survey of architectural remains in Thailand from the first millennium.

Note also: E. Lunet de Lajonquière: 'Essai d'inventaire archéologique du Siam' in *Bulletin de la Commission Archéologique de l'Indochine* (1912 no. 1) pp. 19-181. [Preliminary archaeological inventory of Siam.] Cited from Cordier [242].

420

Erik Seidenfaden: *Guide to Bangkok with notes on Siam.* Bangkok: Royal State Railways, 1928. 324 pp. + advertisements.

Cultural and practical notes for travellers, pp. 1-132; description of Bangkok, pp. 133-284; general notes on Siam (but no description), pp. 285-318. Many halftone illustrations and some coloured plans.

Reprinted: Singapore: Oxford University Press, 1984. This omits the final section of advertisements.

Indochina

421

Daniel Robinson, Joe Cummings: *Vietnam, Laos and Cambodia: a travel survival kit*. Hawthorn: Lonely Planet, 1991. 561 pp. 0-86442-098-6.

A new guide book in a series well known for giving practical and cost-conscious advice to adventurous travellers. Divided into three sections. Vietnam: Facts about the country, pp. 14-61; Facts for the visitor, pp. 62-96; Travel, pp. 97-111; Saigon and Cholon, pp. 112-162; regional survey, pp. 163-359. Laos (pp. 363-458) and Cambodia (pp. 461-553) are dealt with similarly but on a smaller scale. Stop press section of latest news from travellers, pp. 557-561.

422

Michel Blanchard: *Cambodge, Laos, Vietnam*. Paris: Arthaud, 1989. 264 pp.
(Guide Arthaud.)

[Cambodia, Laos, Vietnam.] Under each country there is a general introduction and a practical section (with addresses; calendar of festivals) followed by descriptions of capital cities and other regions (including, briefly, districts not open to tourists).

Note also: Jacques Népote: *Indochine: Laos, Cambodge, Viet-Nam*. Geneva: Olizane, 1990. 396 pp. (Les guides Artou.)

423

Guide touristique générale de l'Indochine: guide alphabétique Taupin. Hanoi: Taupin, 1937. 450 pp. + portfolio of maps and plans.

[General tourist guide to Indochina: Taupin alphabetical guide.]

Note also: Georges Nores: *Itinéraires automobiles en Indochine: guide du touriste*. Hanoi: Imprimerie d'Extrême-Orient, 1930. 3 v. [Motor routes in Indochina: tourist's guide.] Vol. 1: Tongking, 110 pp.; Vol. 2: Cochinchina, Cambodia, 142 pp.; vol. 3: Annam, Laos, 146 pp. A series of descriptions of routes with detailed maps: also includes a large number of town plans.

Pierre-Edmond About: *Indochine. Cochinchine, Annam, Tonkin, Cambodge, Laos*. Paris: Société d'Editions Géographiques, Maritimes et Coloniales, 1931. 338 pp. (Guide des colonies françaises.) [Indochina: Cochinchina, Annam, Tongking, Cambodia, Laos.] A tourist guide in a series covering the French colonies. I have not seen these three competitors to the Madrolle guides.

424

Madrolle: *Indochina: Cochinchina, Annam, Yünnan, Cambodia, Tonkin, Laos, Siam.* Paris: Hachette, 1930. 280 pp.
(The Madrolle guides.) Half-title: *The traveller's handbook to French Indochina and Siam.*

An English abridgement based on the two French guide books of Claudius Madrolle, see below. Highly practical style: detailed route information as well as history and archaeology. Many maps and plans. Contents: General information on French Indochina and Siam, pp. i-xxxviii; Routes, Cochinchina and Cambodia, pp. 1-84 (also issued separately: *To Angkor.* 1930, 1939); Annam, pp. 86-132; Laos, pp. 133-157; Tonkin, pp. 158-216; Siam, pp. 217-260 (also issued separately). Index. List of hotels with advertisements, p. 263 ff. (also issued separately: *The hotels of French Indochina and Siam*).

Later issue: Paris: Société d'Editions Géographiques, Maritimes et Coloniales, 1939. 280 pp.

425

Madrolle: *Indochine du nord: Tonkin, Annam, Laos, Yunnan, Kouang-tcheou Wan.* Paris: Hachette, 1932. 74 + 384 pp.
(Guides Madrolle.) Half-title: *Manuel du voyageur en Indochine du Nord.*

[Northern Indochina: Tongking, Annam, Laos, Yunnan, Kwangchow.] 'Third edition.' Contents: General information, pp. i-xvi; outlines of Indochina, Annam and Tonkin, Laos, preliminary pages 1-74. Routes: Tonkin, pp. 1-207; northern and central Annam, pp. 208-285; northern and central Laos, pp. 286-350; Yunnan. Index. List of hotels with advertisements, p. 377 ff. Packed with maps and plans.

There was also an 'augmented 3rd ed.': ... *Hongkon, Kouang-tcheou Wan.* Paris: Société d'Editions Géographiques, Maritimes et Coloniales, 1939.

Previous editions or issues in 1923 and 1925.

426

Madrolle: *Indochine du sud: de Marseille à Saigon: Djibouti, Ethiopie, Ceylan, Malaisie; Cochinchine, Cambodge, Bas-Laos, Sud-Annam, Siam.* Paris: Hachette, 1928. lxxxiv + 80 + 344 pp.
(Guides Madrolle.) Half-title: *Manuel du voyageur en Indochine du Sud.*

[Southern Indochina. From Marseille to Saigon with Djibouti, Ethiopia, Ceylon, Malaysia; Cochinchina, Cambodia, southern Laos, southern Annam, Siam.] 'Second edition.' Contents: general information on Indochina, Cochinchina, Cambodia, Champa, Siam, pp. i-lxxxiv. Routes from France to

Indochina (Penang to Singapore, preliminary pages 66-80). Cochinchina, pp. 1-58; Cambodia, pp. 59-175; southern Laos, pp. 176-185; Annam, pp. 186-263; Siam, pp. 264-313 including the route Bangkok-Penang. Index. List of hotels with advertisements, p. 325 ff. Full of maps and plans, like its companion.

There was also an 'augmented 2nd edition:' Paris: Société d'Editions Géographiques, Maritimes et Coloniales, 1939. 344 pp.

Previous edition or issue: 1926.

427
Liste général de classement des monuments historiques de l'Indochine. Hanoi, 1930.
Ecole Française d'Extrême-Orient.

[General classification of the ancient monuments of Indochina.]

428
Claudius Madrolle: *De Marseille à Canton: guide du voyageur. Indochine, Canal de Suez, Djibouti et Harar, Indes, Ceylan, Siam, Chine méridionale.* Paris: Comité Asie Française, 1902. 133, 185 pp. etc.

[From Marseille to Canton: traveller's guide. Indochina, Suez Canal, Djibouti and Harar, East Indies, Ceylon, Siam, southern China.] The first pagination covers the sea-route to Indo-China, including 26 pp. on Siam. The second pagination deals with French Indochina in more detail (pp. 1-157), Yunnan, Guangdong and Macao. Plans of Saigon, Hanoi, and the ruins of Angkor. There is an unpaginated final section of shipping timetables and advertisements. No indexes.

This work was followed by a complicated series of more specialized guidebooks, including: Claudius Madrolle: *Guide du Tonkin du sud: Hanoi, Sontaison, Nam-thanh.* Paris: Challamel, n.d. [Guide to southern Tongking]; Claudius Madrolle: *Tonkin du Sud, Hanoï. Les Annamites, Hanoï, Pays de So'n-nam.* 1907. 96 pp. Madrolle: *La ligne du Yun-nan; Tonkin, Chine, excursions et itinéraires.* Paris: Hachette, 1913. 152 pp. [The Yunnan railway]; Madrolle: *De Saigon à Tourane: la Route Mandarine du Sud-Annam, les monuments Cham, le circuit des monts Pandarang, Dalat et le Lang-biang.* Paris: Hachette, 1936 [and earlier]. 78 pp.; Claudius Madrolle: *Annam central: Hué, tombes royales, Tourane, Mi-so'n.* Paris: Hachette, n.d. Various paginations.

For the latest versions see nos **425, 426, 424.**

429
E. Lunet de Lajonquière: *Atlas archéologique de l'Indochine: monuments du Champa et du Cambodge.* Paris: Imprimerie Nationale, 1901. 24 pp.,

5 maps.
(Publications de l'Ecole Française d'Extrême-Orient.)

[Archaeological atlas of Indochina: the monuments of Champa and Cambodia.] Maps of Annam and Cambodia at 1:500,000; remainder of Indo-China at 1:2,500,000; preceded by 14-page gazetteer of sites, which is arranged by province with an alphabetical index. See the review by: C. O. Blagden in *Journal of the Royal Asiatic Society* (July 1902) pp. 667-670.

Cambodia

430

Tony Wheeler: *Cambodia: a travel survival kit*. Hawthorn: Lonely Planet, 1992. 0-86442-174-5.

Rather more detailed than Robinson and Cummings [420].

431

Liste de khets (provinces), sroks (districts) et khums (villages) en caractères latins. Phnom Penh, 1967.
Forces Armées Royales Khmères, Service Géographique.

[List of names of provinces, districts and villages in roman script.]

432

J. Commaille: *Guide aux ruines d'Angkor*. Paris: Hachette, 1912. 241 pp.

[Guide to the ruins of Angkor.] With 154 figures and 3 plans. Cited from Cordier [242].

433

E. Lunet de Lajonquière: *Inventaire descriptif des monuments du Cambodge*. Paris: Imprimerie Nationale, 1902-1912. 3 v. and maps.
(Publications de l'Ecole Française d'Extrême-Orient, 4, 8, 9. Inventaire archéologique de l'Indochine, 1.)

[Descriptive inventory of the ancient monuments of Cambodia.] The maps are: Archaeological map of ancient Cambodia, 1:750,000; Map of the Angkor complex, 1:50,000.

See the review by: C. O. Blagden in *Journal of the Royal Asiatic Society* (April 1913) pp. 465-8. Cited from Cordier [242] col. 2693 refers to other reviews.

Additions were published by: Henri Parmentier: *Complément à l'Inventaire descriptif des monuments du Cambodge*. Hanoi: Imprimerie d'Extrême-Orient, 1913. 64 pp. (Bulletin de l'Ecole Française d'Extrême-Orient, vol. 13 no. 1.)

An interesting supplement on Angkor is provided by the finely-drawn architectural elevations, plans and details in: J. Dumarçay: *Documents graphiques de la conservation d'Angkor 1963-1973*. Paris: Ecole Française d'Extrême-Orient, 1988. 59 pp., 89 plates. 2-85539-545-3. (Collection de textes et documents sur l'Indochine, 17.)

Laos

434

Anna-Brita Rosell: *A guide to the wats of Vientiane*. Bangkok: Louis, 1989. 64 pp.

A description, illustrated with colour photographs, of a selection of the Buddhist temples of Vientiane, including the three which are now museums. Introduction: Buddhism in Laos; significance of Buddha images; how to visit a wat. Cited from Cordell [25].

435

Henri Parmentier: *L'art du Laos*. Paris: Ecole Française d'Extrême-Orient, 1988. 2 v. (404 pp., album of plates). 2-85539-542-9.
(Publications de l'Ecole Française d'Extrême-Orient, 35.)

[The art of Laos.] Revised edition by Madeleine Giteau. An inventory of the Buddhist religious architecture of Laos, originally compiled between 1911 and 1927 (and published posthumously) and thus listing many structures which have long since disappeared. Detailed inventory, pp. 13-158. Marginal numerals refer to the new notes by Giteau, pp. 333-359, commenting on the monuments and their current state.

The plates include 117 early photographs, plans of Vientiane and Luang Phrabang in 1912, location maps, architectural drawings and plans by Parmentier (plates v-li) and new detail sketches by Giteau (plates 1-17); there are also many plans in the text.

First edition: 1954. 2 v.

436

A. Baudenne: 'A travers le Laos: guide à l'usage des voyageurs' in *Bulletin économique de l'Indochine* (1911) pp. 285-330.

[Across Laos: travellers' guide.]

437

Annaliese Wulf: *Vietnam. Pagoden und Tempel im Reisfeld: im Fokus chinesischer und indischer Kultur*. Köln: DuMont, 1991. 548 pp. 3-7701-

2237-2.

[Vietnam: pagodas and temples in the ricefield: at the meeting point of Chinese and Indian culture.] A remarkably thorough cultural and architectural guide book. General, geographical, cultural and historical introduction, pp. 8-312; Detailed survey (Hanoi, pp. 313-342; Ho Chi Minh City, pp. 466-482); Glossary, pp. 494-502. Practical information for travellers on yellow pages 505-534. Index. Many maps and plans, including plans of historical monuments, of very high quality.

Note also: Hans Johannes Hoefer and others: *Vietnam*. Hong Kong: Apa, 1992. 962-421-126-4. An attractive picture guide book with a substantial descriptive section.

438
Guide touristique. Saigon, 1956. 206 pp.
Rotary Club, Saigon.

[Tourist guide.] Not seen.

439
Ph. Eberhardt: *Guide de l'Annam.* Paris: Challamel, 1914. 173 pp.

[Guide to Annam.]

440
Ant. Brébion: *Monographie des rues et monuments de Saigon.* Hanoi: Imprimerie d'Extrême-Orient, 1911. 40 pp.

[Survey of the streets and historical monuments of Saigon.] Includes a plan of Saigon at 1:20,000. The work was also serialized in the *Revue indochinoise*, October and November 1911. Cited from Cordier [242].

Note also: Delteil: *Guide du voyageur à Saigon: un an de séjour en Cochinchine.* Paris: Challamel, 1887. 213 pp. [Traveller's guide to Saigon: one year in Cochinchina.]

441
H. Parmentier: *Inventaire descriptif des monuments Cams de l'Annam.* Paris: Leroux, 1909-18. 2 v. in 4.
(Publications de l'Ecole Française d'Extrême-Orient, 11-12. Inventaire archéologique de l'Indochine, 2.)

[Descriptive inventory of the Cham monuments of Annam.] A volume of plates accompanies each volume of text.

In this same series the Ecole has much more recently published a survey of the archaeology of Lower Cochinchina, the Mekong Delta region, but in the form of a historical analysis rather than a geographical survey.

442

Géographie physique, économique et historique de la Cochinchine. Saigon: Ménard, Ardin, 1901- .
(Publications de la Société des Etudes Indo-Chinoises.)

[Physical, economic and historical geography of Cochinchina.] A series of provincial surveys of French Cochinchina, e.g. fasc. 1: *Monographie de la province de Biên-hoa.* 1901. 58 pp. This first fascicle includes a prospectus for the series and a map of Biên-hoa province at 1:250,000.

443

Ngô Vi Lien: *Nomenclature des communes du Tonkin, classés par cantons, phu, huyên ou châu et par provinces, suivies d'une table alphabétique détaillée contenant la transcription des noms en caractères chinois et divers renseignements gégraphiques.* Hanoi: Lê Van Tân, 1928. 426 pp.

[List of the communes of Tongking, arranged under cantons and provinces, with an alphabetical index giving Chinese transcriptions and various geographical information.]

Note also: 'Les provinces du Tonkin' in *Revue indo-chinoise*, 1904-8. [The provinces of Tongking.] A series of articles containing geographical and administrative information, published in successive issues of this periodical and forming a partial gazetteer.

Some slightly earlier surveys of this kind appeared as extra publications of the *Revue indo-chinoise*: *Notice sur la province de Ninh-binh.* Hanoi: Schneider, 1899. 75 pp.; *Notice sur la province de Hung-hoa.* 1899. 72 pp.; *Notice sur la province de Sontay.* 1900. 96 pp.; *Notice sur la province de Hung-yen.* [1900.] 71 pp.; *Notices sommaires sur les territoires militaires.* 1900. 122 pp. The last, with 11 maps, covers the territories of Cao-bang and Hà-giang.

444

Circonscriptions administratives. Hanoi: Schneider [1892-3].
Protectorat de l'Annam et du Tonkin.

[Administrative divisions.] A series of listings of administrative subdivisions for the French Protectorate of Annam and Tongking. Published for the Résidences of Hanoi (67 pp.), Son-tay (53 pp.), Haiphong (25 pp.), Bac-ninh (87 pp.), Hung-yên (33 pp.), Hung-hoa (25 pp.), Thai-nguyên (13 pp.), Thai-binh (49 pp.), Quang-yên (9 pp.), Ninh-binh (33 pp.), Hai-duong (79 pp.).

Note also: *Province de Nam-dinh: divisions administratives et renseignements statistiques.* Ke-So: Imprimerie de la Mission, n.d. 72 pp.

Province de Thanh-hoa: contrôle, divisions administratives et renseignements statistiques. Hanoi: Taupin, 1908. 93 pp. All cited from Cordier [242].

445

Đại-nam nhất-thống-chí. Saigon: Bộ Quốc-Gia Giáo-Dục, 1959-70. 29 v. (Văn hóa tùng thư, 2-42.)

Detailed gazetteer of Vietnam, arranged by nineteenth century provinces: includes districts already ceded to the French. Supplies nom forms of place names. Sections on geography, climate, customs, towns and villages, schools, fields, history, taxation, markets, temples and natural resources of each provinces and biographies of local figures. No index. Quôc-ngu edition of a nôm publication. Only the later volumes include reprint of original nôm text, but a reissue begun in 1973 (Văn hóa tùng thư, 52-) supplies the nôm text of the first three volumes. Original publication: 1865-82. For more bibliographical details see Cotter [30].

Note also: *Tên làng xã Việt Nam đần thế kỷ XIX, thuộc các tỉnh từ Nghệ Tĩnh trở ra, các tông trân xã danh bi lam.* Hanoi: Khoa Học Xã Hội, 1981. 654 pp. (Viện Nghiên Cứu Hán Nôm.) Edited by Dương Thị The, Phạm Thị Thoa. Quôc-ngu edition of a list of administrative divisions and their subdivisions, five levels in all, with statistics at each level; then, on pp. 25-121, an alphabetical list of places giving status, name in nôm, and administrative filiation. Relates to the pre-colonial period.

Malaysia

446

Tony Wheeler, Geoff Crowther and others: *Malaysia, Singapore and Brunei: a travel survival kit.* Hawthorn: Lonely Planet, 1991. 424 pp.

Fourth edition. In three sections: Singapore, pp. 12-106; Malaysia, pp. 108-399; Brunei Darussalam, pp. 402-415. The Malysia section, the largest, has about 60 pages of general and practical information followed by a detailed survey (Peninsular Malaysia, pp. 169-308; Sarawak, pp. 309-357; Sabah, pp. 358-399). Highly practical. Many small maps and plans.

First edition: 1982.

447

Hans Johannes Hoefer and others: *Malaysia.* Hong Kong: Apa, 1988. 348 pp.
(Insight guides.)

'Twelfth edition,' a reprint of the ninth. A guide book with a considerable general section, pp. 1-121, followed by descriptions of areas accessible to travellers. Includes Brunei, pp. 290-293. 'Guide in brief', pp. 297-337, is a section of practical information (festivals, pp. 308-315) followed by an appendix of addresses (hotels, restaurants, travel offices, diplomatic missions, etc.). Plans and maps; many beautiful photographs.

First edition: 1972.

448

Paul H. Kratoska: *The Penang guide*. Singapore: Graham Brash, 1986. 223 pp. 9971-947-99-4.

Practical information and local guide book. Glossary of food and drink, pp. 177-187.

449

S. Durai Raja Singam: *Port Weld to Kuantan: a study of Malay place names*. Kuantan, 1957. 282 pp.

Third edition of a roneoed compilation. Note on geographical terms, pp. 9-15; Introduction, pp. 16-40; Alphabetical dictionary of selected place names with etymology and historical references, pp. 78-266; supplement on Singapore.

Second edition: 1954; first edition: 1939.

Note also: Lo Man Yuk: 'Chinese names of streets in Penang' in *Journal of the Straits Branch of the Royal Asiatic Society* no. 33 (1900) pp. 197-246. Alphabetical list of official street names with Chinese equivalents (in characters and romanized) and historical notes; Similar list of major buildings; List of Chinese 'Kongsi-houses'; List of rural place names of Penang, in Malay with Chinese equivalents; Index of streets in romanized Chinese.

450

Colin McDougall: *Buddhism in Malaya*. Singapore: Donald Moore, 1956. 61 pp.

Included here for its lists of Buddhist associations, temples and relics.

451

Cuthbert Woodville Harrison: *An illustrated guide to the Federated Malay States*. London: Malay States Information Agency, 1923. 381 pp. Illustrations in colour by Mrs H. C. Barnard; photographs by Kleingrothe.

Revised edition. Contents: Through the Malay Peninsula from north to south, pp. 1-118 ('anyone travelling in the opposite direction must begin at the end and read backwards'); Notes for travellers and motorists, pp. 119-229 ('"Can we bring a lady?" There are 1,900 white women in the Federated Malay States: so no one need hesitate to bring his feminine belongings with him'); Game hunting; Museums, pp. 261-292; Mining. Appendices: glossary; statistics; route lists with distances. Folding map.

Reprinted: Singapore: Oxford University Press, 1985. 0-19-582625-6. This lacks the folding map.

First edition: [1910.] 358 pp.

Singapore

452

Norman Edwards, Peter Keys: *Singapore: a guide to buildings, streets, places.* Singapore: Times Books International, 1988. 599 pp.

A detailed description of the city, very fully illustrated with clear halftone photographs, concentrating on the history of buildings both public and private; names of architects; construction history. The location maps (general map, p. 10 and local maps at the beginning of each district section, A-S) are also a guide to postal codes. Solid glossary (cultural and architectural terms, flora) pp. 514-542. Index, pp. 548-579; additional indexes of places and of types of buildings; index of architects with lists of their works, pp. 586-598.

453

Singapore guide and street directory. Singapore: Ministry of Culture.

'First edition, new series': 1954. Regularly republished since. The 1972 edition contained: Directory of places of interest, businesses, schools; Index of streets, pp. 125-167; Atlas of street plans 1-137 [pp. 171-298]; List of bus services, pp. 299-330; post offices; police stations. 8 folding maps including postal districts and electoral divisions.

454

Jean-Pierre Mialaret: *Hinduism in Singapore: a guide to the Hindu temples of Singapore.* Singapore: Donald Moore, 1969. 72 pp.

An explanation of the Hinduism of Singapore and its festivals, followed by a guide to temples, many of which have since been demolished. Cited from Quah [28].

455

A. C. Willis: *Willis's Singapore guide*. Singapore, 1936. 166 pp.

Desultory but once useful guide and handbook without table of contents. Includes loose fold-out map of the island and street plan of the town, both produced by the Survey Department.

456

G. M. Reith: *Handbook to Singapore with map*. Singapore: Fraser and Neave, 1907. 133 pp.

Second edition, revised by Walter Makepeace. A travel guide.

Reprinted: G. M. Reith: *1907 handbook to Singapore*. Singapore: Oxford University Press, 1985.

First edition: Singapore: Singapore and Straits Printing Office, 1892. 135 pp. This included a plan of the Botanical Gardens: map and plan were optional extras.

Note also: B. E. d'Aranjo: *The stranger's guide*. Singapore: Singapore Free Press, 1890. 76 pp.; *MacJohn's guide book for Singapore and Johore*. Singapore: Kelly & Walsh, 1908. 66 pp.

457

H. T. Haughton: 'Notes on names of places in the island of Singapore and its vicinity' in *Journal of the Straits Branch of the Royal Asiatic Society* no. 20 (1889) pp. 75-82.

The first of a series of papers on Singapore place names by several authors. Note also: H. T. Haughton: 'Native names of streets in Singapore', ib. no. 23 (1891) pp. 49-65: H. W. Firmstone: 'Chinese names of streets and places in Singapore and the Malay Peninsula', ib. no. 42 (1905) pp. 53-208: Tan Kee Soon and others: 'An index in romanised Hokkien and Cantonese ... to the "Chinese names of streets and places in Singapore" ...', ib. no. 46 pp. 195-213: 'Chinese names of streets' by A. K., ib. no. 45 (1906) pp. 287-8.

Brunei

458

D. C. Mann, P. F. Lonergan: *Discover Brunei: things to do and see in Brunei*. Thornhill, Dumfriesshire: Tynron, 1990. 63 pp. 1-85646-015-0.

459

Abdul Latif Haji Ibrahim: 'Variations and changes in the names and locations of the wards of Brunei's Kampong Ayer over the last century' in *Brunei Museum journal* vol. 2 no. 3 (1971) pp. 56-73.

An attempt to pin down the historical topography and toponymy of the water-town of Brunei. Lists of names (tables 1-3), locations (maps 1-3), two historical views, analysis.

Indonesia

460

Bill Dalton: *Indonesia handbook.* Chico: Moon, 1991. 1073 pp.

Fifth edition. A truly encyclopaedic guide book. General, cultural and practical information, pp. 1-134; Java, pp. 135-376; Bali; Sumatra, notably well covered, pp. 457-632; Nusatenggara; Kalimantan; Sulawesi; Maluku; Irian Jaya, pp. 977-1018. Note on Bahasa Indonesia; glossary of useful phrases; bibliography; index. About 240 maps and plans. Much information on food and drink, and instructive use of Bahasa Indonesia words and phrases. Highly practical and impressively well-informed.

First edition: 1977.

461

Ginny Bruce and others: *Indonesia: a travel survival kit.* Hawthorn: Lonely Planet, 1992. 0-86442-163-X.

Third edition.

Second edition: 1990. 896 pp. Practical and general information, pp. 10-111; Java, pp. 112-316; Bali; Sumatra; Nusa Tenggara, in particular detail, pp. 536-678; Sulawesi; Maluku; Kalimantan; Irian Jaya. Many small maps and plans. For more detail on Bali and Lombok see Covernton and Wheeler [466] in the same series.

462

S. A. Reitsma: *Van Stockum's travellers' handbook for the Dutch East Indies.* The Hague: Van Stockum, 1930. 615 pp.

In almost perfect English. The author was 'chief editor of the periodical „Rail- and Tramways". Practical, pp. 3-32; General review of the Dutch East Indies, pp. 33-119. Then for each island or island group there is a lengthy 'general review' followed by 'local description': e.g. Sumatra, pp. 323-347, 348-426; Timor and dependencies, pp. 557-561, 561-570. Excludes Portuguese Timor and Dutch New Guinea. 35 good road maps and plans, mostly monochrome. Distance tables.

463

J. J. De Hollander: *Handleiding bij de beoefening der land- en volkenkunde van Nederlandsch Oost-Indie*. Breda: Broese, 1882. 2 v.
Koninklijke Militaire Academie.

[Guide to the geography and ethnography of the Dutch East Indies.] Contents: History, Population, Administration and finance, Military affairs. Then a highly detailed survey: Java and Madura, vol. 1 pp. 177-414; Bali and Lombok; Sumatra and neighbouring islands, pp. 496-834. Borneo, vol. 2 pp. 1-173 (including brief survey of British Borneo); Celebes, pp. 174-342; Moluccas, pp. 343-570 (including Dutch New Guinea, pp. 414-437); Timor and neighbouring islands, pp. 571-668. Addenda, pp. 669-684. A few statistical tables; no illustrations and very few local maps.

464

Aardrijkskundig en statistisch woordenboek van Nederlandsch Indie. Amsterdam: Van Kampen, 1869. 3 v.
Edited by H. van Alphen, P. J. Veth.

[Geographical and statistical dictionary of the Dutch East Indies.]

465

W. F. Stutterheim: *Gids voor de Boroboedoer*. Batavia: De Unie [1941]. 61 pp.

[Guide to Borobudur.] Replaces a similar work by N. J. Krom.

466

P. J. Veth: *Java, geographisch, ethnologisch, historisch*. Haarlem: Bohn, 1875-84. 4 v.

[Java: geographical, ethnographical, historical.] Contents: Vol. 1: Physical and human geography, with physical map showing river and mountain names; Arts; Economic life. Vol. 2: History, with historical map. Vol. 3: Topography: detailed survey, including Madura; 1098 pp., no illustrations. Vol. 4: Index and long list of amendments.

467

Mary Covernton, Tony Wheeler: *Bali & Lombok: a travel survival kit.* Hawthorn: Lonely Planet, 1992. 336 pp. 0-86442-133-8.

Fourth edition.

First edition: 1984. 208 pp. Contents: Facts about Bali; facts about Lombok; practical details; methods of travel. Topographical survey: Bali, Nusa

Penida, Lombok. Glossary, pp. 200-204; note on Indonesian language, pp. 41-3; food and drink with additional glossary, pp. 74-9. Discouraging note on Balinese language, p. 43.

Note also: A. Mason and others: *Bali*. London: Cadogan, 1988. 224 pp. 0-946313-86-5. (Cadogan guides.) There are many guide books to Bali, but none more detailed than these two.

468

Kal Muller: *Spice islands: the Moluccas*. Berkeley: Periplus Editions, 1990. 163 pp. 0-945971-07-9.

One of a series of beautiful picture guide books covering most of Indonesia, useful as fairly full introductions to some less-known regions. This volume is also cited as: Kal Muller: *Spice islands: exotic eastern Indonesia*. Chicago: Passport Books, 1990.

Note also: Kal Muller: *New Guinea: Irian Jaya*. Berkeley: Periplus Editions, 1990. 0-945971-07-9. Also cited as: Kal Muller: *New Guinea: journey into the stone age*. Chicago: Passport Books, 1990.

Helen Reid, Anthony Reid: *South Sulawesi*. Berkeley: Periplus Editions, 1988.

469

V. I. van de Wall: *De nederlandsche oudheden in de Molukken*. The Hague: Nijhoff, 1928. 314 pp.

[Dutch antiquities in the Moluccas.] A thorough survey of the region with detailed descriptions of houses and other architecture, inscriptions, etc., connected with Dutch trade and settlement. Large format: 93 halftone plates, 155 line drawings, 3 folding location maps at end. Divided into three regions: Banda, pp. 13-126; Ambon, pp. 129-224; Ternate, pp. 227-283. List of coats of arms, pp. 293-6; Superintendents of Banda, 1609-1796, pp. 297-8; Indexes of names and subjects.

Philippines

470

Jens Peters: *Philippines: a travel survival kit*. South Yarra: Lonely Planet, 1991. 456 pp. 0-86442-096-X.

Fourth edition. A handbook emphasizing the practicalities of independent and low-cost travel to all parts of the archipelago. Practical and general information, pp. 12-103; Manila and environs; Luzon and neighbouring islands, pp. 164-253; The Visayas, pp. 254-347; Mindanao and Palawan, pp. 348-425; Index; Addenda, pp. 432-4.

First edition: 1981.

Also published in German as *Philippinen: Reise-Handbuch.*

Note also: Peter Harper, Evelyn Peplow: *Philippines handbook.* Chico: Moon, 1991. 450 pp. 0-918373-62-X.

471

Jill Gale de Villa: *Philippine vacations and explorations.* Metro Manila: Devcon, 1988. 308 pp. 971-91082-3-1.

Attractively illustrated guide book, emphasizing accessibility. Metro Manila and environs, pp. 21-64; North Luzon; Bicol; Islands near Luzon; Palawan; central and Visayan islands, pp. 157-224; Mindanao. Transport guide, pp. 266-273; a good tabular list of 'lodging', pp. 274-297. Index; separate index to the many small clear maps and plans.

Note also: Lee Buenaventura: *The Philippines.* Hongkong: CFW; Ashbourne, Derbyshire: MPC, 1988. 144 pp. 0-86190-210-6. Copyright: South China Morning Post Ltd. (Postguide.) A handbook for visitors. General information, pp. 7-77, including a list of annual festivals on pp. 61-9. Metro Manila and environs, pp. 77-98: what to see, shopping, restaurants, etc.

Hans Johannes Hoefer and others: *Philippines.* Hong Kong: Apa, 1988. 335 pp. (The insight guides, 7.) 'Seventh edition' of a beautifully-illustrated guide book with a solid introductory section and detailed regional descriptions. First edition: 1980.

472

The ins and outs of Metro Manila. Manila: Philippine Guides, 1985. 104 pp.

A street atlas. Cited from Richardson [27].

Note also: *Metro Manila street directory.* Manila: Philippine Map Co. 60 pp. A similar work: maps at about 1:12,500 with detailed plans of shopping and business centres. Editions for 1983 and 1985 noted.

473

Luning B. Ira: *Streets of Manila.* Quezon City: GCF Books, 1977. 250 pp.
Historical research by Isagani R. Medina.

Origin of street names in the centre (Intramuros) and older suburbs. For other works on the history of Manila see Richardson [27] pp. 31-4.

474
Philippine geographical names. Manila, 1964-5. 2 v. in 4.
Bureau of the Census and Statistics.

Vol. 1, in 3 parts, lists political divisions and subdivisions. Vol. 2 (427 pp.) is a listing of natural features (rivers, mountains, coasts and marine and sea-bed details).

475
Information for travellers landing at Manila. Manila: Thomas Cook & Son.

Published regularly around 1913 to 1916: about 100 pp. Cited from the Library of Congress catalogue.

476
Relación de las encomiendas existentes en Filipinas el día 31 de mayo de 1591 años, ahora publicada por primera vez. Manila, 1898. 73 pp.
(W. E. Retana, editor: *Archivo del bibliófilo filipino* [see **364**] vol. 4 item 2.)

[Report of the areas of jurisdiction existing in the Philippines on the 31st May, 1591, now first published.]

NAVIGATION GUIDES

477
Bay of Bengal pilot: the east coast of India north of Point Calimere; the coast of Bangladesh; the coast of Burma; the west coast of Thailand from Pakchan River to Chong Pak Phra; Andaman Islands and Nicobar Islands. Taunton: Hydrographer of the Navy, 1978. 187 pp.
(N.P., 21.)

Tenth edition. First edition: 1887. A detailed description of coasts, harbours and navigation problems, one of a long series of pilots which form companions to the Admiralty charts. Other relevant volumes are described below.

China Sea pilot, vol. 1. The west side of the China Sea from Tanjong Lombat on the eastern side of Peninsular Malaysia to Zhalang Yan in China; Kepulauan Anambas, Hainan Dao and the islands and banks bordering the main route from Singapore Strait to Hong Kong. 1987. 305 pp. (NP, 30.) Revised printing of the fourth edition. First edition: 1937.

China Sea pilot, vol. 2. The western and north-western coasts of Borneo, the Philippine Islands from Balabac Island to Cape Bojeador in Luzon, and the outlying islands and dangers in the southern and eastern parts of the China Sea. 1982. 217 pp. (N.P., 31.) Revised printing of the fourth edition. First edition: 1936.

Malacca Strait and west coast of Sumatera pilot: Malacca Strait and its northern approaches, Singapore Strait, the west coast of Sumatera, and including Cocos Islands. 1987. (NP, 44.) Sixth edition. First edition: 1924.

Indonesia pilot, vol. 1. The western end of Java, the southern and eastern coasts of Sumatera, Sunda Strait, Selat Bangka, Selat Gelasa, Karimata Strait, the southern and western coasts of Borneo from Tanjung Puting to Pulau Pontijanak, Kepulauan Badas and Tambelan, Kepulauan Riau and Lingga, with the various routes leading to Singapore and the China Sea. 1975. 198 pp. (N.P., 36.) Spine title: Indonesian pilot.

Indonesia pilot, vol. 2. South coast of Java, north coast of Java east of Tanjung Awar Awar, east coast of Java, Nusa Tenggara, south coast of Kalimantan east of Tanjung Puting, east coast of Kalimantan south of the parallel of 4° 10' N, Sulawesi and the west part of Kepulauan Sula. 1983. 403 pp. (NP, 34.) Revised printing of the first edition (1976).

Indonesia pilot, vol.3. Islands between Mindanao and the north-east end of Sulawesi, Molucca Sea, Ceram Sea, Banda Sea, Arafura Sea, islands off the north-west end of Irian Jaya, north coast of Irian Jaya, north coast of Irian Jaya eastward to 141° 00' E and off-lying islands, south-west coast of Irian Jaya eastward to 104° 40' E and off-lying islands. 1980. 199 pp. (N.P., 35.)

Philippine Islands pilot: the northern and north-eastern coasts of Borneo to the Sabah/Indonesia border, the Philippine Islands (except for the western coasts of Palawan and Luzon between Cape Buliluyan and Cape Bojeador and the northern coast of Luzon between Cape Bojeador and Escarpada Point), Sulu Sea and Sulu Archipelago. 1978. 392 pp. (N.P., 33.)

Of historical interest are the following superseded titles in the series:

China Sea directory. 2 v. 1st edition, 1867-8; 5th edition, 1906, vol. 1 (734 pp.) 'containing directions for the approaches to the China Sea by Malacca, Singapore, Sunda, Banka, Gaspar, Carimata, Rhio, Berhala and Durian straits'; vol. 2 'containing directions for the China Sea between Singapore and Hongkong'. These volumes were replaced by:

China Sea pilot. 4 v. Of this set vol. 1 (1916) was replaced by the *Malacca Strait pilot.* Vol. 2 (1915) was replaced by vol. 4 of the *Eastern Archipelago pilot* (see below). Vols 3-4 (1st edition, 1912; 2nd edition, 1923) were replaced by the two-volume *China Sea pilot* of 1936-7 (see above).

Eastern Archipelago pilot. 4 v. Vol. 1 (1st edition, 1890: 7th edition, 1963) was replaced by the *Philippine Islands pilot.* Vol. 2 (1st edition, 1893; 7th edition, 1961) was replaced by *Indonesia pilot,* vols 1 and 2. Vol. 3 (published in 1890 as *Eastern Archipelago: eastern part, vol. 1:* 2nd edition, 1902; 1st edition as 'vol. 3', 1911; 6th edition, 1968) was replaced by *Indonesia pilot* vol. 3. Vol. 4 (1st edition, 1927; 4th edition, 1966) was replaced by *Indonesia pilot,* vol. 1.

An equally venerable and extensive French series (Instructions nautiques) published by the Service Hydrographique de la Marine has included the following titles: *Mer de Chine* [China Sea]; *Grand archipel d'Asie* [Great Asiatic Archipelago]; *Asie du Sud-Est* [south east Asia].

478

Gale Dixon: *Indonesian ports: an atlas-gazetteer.* Townsville: James Cook University of North Queensland, 1985. 159 pp.
(Centre of Southeast Asian Studies monograph, 16.)

Revised edition. An independent publication which, similarly, gives navigation details, summarizes harbour facilities, and indicates settlement type, referring to navigational charts.

Note also the Indonesian set *Kepanduan bahari Indonesia* (1980) and the older Dutch *Zeemansgids voor Indonesië* last published in 1957. [Mariner's guide to Indonesia.]

479

Philippine coast pilot. Manila, 1968. 2 v.

Fifth edition of an official Philippine publication.

Note the American guide to these waters: *Sailing directions for the Philippine Islands.* Washington: United States Government Printing Office, 1975-6. 3 v. (H.O., 90-92.)

The United States Hydrographic Office has also published: *Sailing directions for the western shores of the China Sea, from Singapore Strait to and including Hong Kong* (H.O., 125); *Sailing directions for Strait of Malacca and Sumatera* (H.O., 174); *Sailing directions for Soenda Strait and the western and northwest coasts of Borneo and off-lying islands* (H.O., 126); *Sailing directions for the north-east coast of Borneo* (H.O., 71); *Sailing directions for Celebes, south east Borneo, Java and islands* (H. O., 163); *Sailing directions for New Guinea* (H.O., 73).

480

Coasts of Siam, Indo-China and south China: atlas of tides, tidal streams and currents. Admiralty, Hydrographic Department, 1945. 12 pp.
(N.P., 215. H.D., 405.)

Monochrome chart followed by 4 pages of diagrams of tidal ranges at selected harbours, 6 pages of descriptions of harbours and landmarks with navigation problems.

Reprinted: 1972.

Companion work: *Coast of Burma and northern approaches to Malacca Strait.*
1945. 11 pp. (N.P., 213. H.D., 398.) Similar: detailed reprinted charts of the
Kaladan river estuary at Akyab.

Reprinted: 1974.

FRONTIERS

481

International boundary study. Washington: United States Government
Printing Office.
Department of State, Office of the Geographer.

A series of surveys of international boundaries, including: *Burma-Laos
boundary.* 1964. No. 33; *Cambodia-Laos boundary.* 1964. No. 32; *China-Laos
boundary.* 1964. No. 34; *Laos-Thailand boundary.* 1962. No. 20; *Laos-Viet-Nam
boundary.* 1966. No. 35. Revised edition; *Viet-Nam "demarcation line".* 1962.
No. 19.

Note also: J. R. V. Prescott, H. J. Collier, D. F. Prescott: *Frontiers of Asia and
Southeast Asia.* Melbourne: Melbourne University Press, 1977. A series of
one-page historical surveys of boundary problems and changes, each
accompanied by a map.

J. R. V. Prescott: *Map of mainland Asia by treaty.* 1975. 518 pp. A more
extensive work on similar lines.

482

Limits in the seas series. Washington: United States Government
Printing Office.
Department of State, Office of the Geographer.

A series of maritime boundary surveys. Includes: *Continental shelf boundaries:
Australia, Papua and Indonesia.* 1979. No. 87; *Continental shelf boundaries: India,
Indonesia, Thailand.* 1981. No. 93; *Indonesia-Malaysia boundary.* 1965. No.42.

Note also: J. R. Morgan, M. R. Valencia: *Atlas for marine policy in south east
Asian seas.* Berkeley: University of California Press, 1983. 144 pp. Not seen.

Fauna, flora, natural resources

483

Rev. F. Mason: *Burma: its people and productions; or, notes on fauna, flora and minerals of Tenasserim, Pegu and Burma.* Hertford: Stephen Austin, 1882. 2 v.
Rewritten and enlarged by W. Theobald. Published by order of the Chief Commissioner of British Burma.

On the complex history of Mason's work see Herbert [22] p. 37. This final edition is a survey (sometimes merely a list) in systematic order of Burmese fauna and (especially) flora of economic importance. Scientific names; appendix B in each volume is a Burmese-Latin glossary of popular names.

First edition: F. Mason: *The natural productions of Burmah.* Moulmein: American Mission Press, 1850-51. 2 v. (712 pp.), the second volume under the title *Tenasserim* and part of it also issued separately as *Flora Burmanica.*

The author's autobiography was published as: Francis Mason: *The story of a working man's life.* New York: Oakley, Mason, 1870. 462 pp.

484

Anat Arbhabhirama and others: *Thailand: natural resources profile.* Singapore: Oxford University Press, 1988.
Thailand Development Research Institute. (Natural resources of South-East Asia.)

Result of a major research project carried out in 1986-7. 'We are crossing the threshold beyond sustainable yields in the consumption of our natural resources.' Contents: Land, water, forest, mineral, mangrove, fishery resources; nature conservation; conclusions. Many tables, charts, maps. Lists of National Parks and wildlife sanctuaries; list of farmed/cultured aquatic species.

485

Charles Crévost, Ch. Lemarié: *Catalogue des produits de l'Indochine.* Hanoi: Imprimerie d'Extrême-Orient, 1917-35. 5 v.

[Catalogue of the natural products of Indochina.] Also published as a series of articles in *Bulletin économique de l'Indochine.*

486

I. H. Burkill and others: *A dictionary of the economic products of the Malay peninsula.* London: Crown Agents for the Colonies, 1935. 2 v. (2402 pp.).

Published on behalf of the Governments of the Straits Settlements and Federated Malay States.

Begun as a private guide to the collections of the botanic gardens of Singapore. 'Not a little information drawn from other parts of the Malay Archipelago has been interwoven.' Includes many recently introduced species.

Alphabetically arranged under entries for scientific Latin names of flora, fauna and minerals (thus, normally, under genera). No botanical/zoological description (the compiler refers to Ridley [528] for botanical descriptions). Alternative names; geographical range; economic, medicinal and food uses. Index (or rather, concise glossary) of Malay and English names, pp. 2309-2402.

Reprinted: Kuala Lumpur: Ministry of Agriculture and Cooperatives, 1966. I have not seen the reprint.

487

F. W. Roe: *The natural resources of Sarawak, comprising accounts prepared by members of the Natural Resources Board together with general information.* Kuching, 1952.

A second edition was published in 1962.

488

Datin Margaret Luping, Chin Wen, E. Richard Dingley, editors: *Kinabalu: summit of Borneo.* Kota Kinabalu: Sabah Society, 1978. 482 pp.
(Sabah Society monograph 1978.)

A reference volume on the natural history (not the human population) of the 301-square-mile national park in northern Borneo. Selected contents: D. V. Jenkins, 'The first hundred years: expeditions to Mt Kinabalu 1851-1950' (lists 53 in chronological order); G. Jacobson, 'Geology' with plates and maps; E. J. H. Corner and others, 'The flora' (pp. 113-252, coloured plates 1-32); 'The fauna' (pp. 254-457, coloured plates 33-49). Includes annotated lists of butterflies and moths, freshwater fishes, frogs and toads, birds, mammals.

489

Ricardo M. Umali and others: *Guide to Philippine flora and fauna.* Manila: Natural Resources Management Center, University of the Philippines, 1986. 13 v.

Covers about 3250 species: thus not comprehensive in any phylum, but highly useful as focusing on species of economic importance and on those that are endangered. Many line drawings and halftone plates.

Vol. 1: Zoosporic fungi, seaweeds, endemic mosses. Vol. 2: Economic ferns, endemic ferns, gymnosperms. Vol. 3: Trees (by Enriquito D. de Guzman and others. 414 pp.). Vol. 4: Bamboos, grasses, palms. Vol. 5: Corals. Vol. 6: Gastropods, pelecypods, annelids. Vol. 7: Zooplankton, barnacles, swimming crabs. Vol. 8: Water bugs, mites. Vol. 9: Fishes (by Prudencia V. Conlu. 495 pp.). Vol. 10: Amphibians, reptiles. Vol. 11: Birds, mammals. Vol. 12: Ectoparasites, poisonous animals. Vol. 13: general indexes to English and local names and to scientific names.

FAUNA

490

W. T. Blanford, editor: *The fauna of British India including Ceylon and Burma*. London: Taylor and Francis, 1888-1949.

A multi-volume work arranged systematically; 77 volumes in the set I examined. Concise descriptions of species in English: some fine illustrations, a few in colour. Vernacular names are given, but are not indexed.

The earlier volumes are described in detail by Cordier [242] cols 208-210. The last I have seen (Butterflies, vol. 2, by G. Talbot. 1947) was published with a slip giving a new series title: *Fauna of India including Pakistan, Ceylon and Burma*. The Library of Congress catalogue gives another late title, *The fauna of India including Pakistan, Ceylon, Burma and Malaya*.

The four volumes on birds were by W. T. Blanford and Eugene W. Oates. The two volumes on fish, by Francis Day, were an abridgement of a separate work by him [503]. The volume on reptiles and frogs (1890. 541 pp.) was by George A. Boulenger: see also **515**.

491

Chote Suvatti: *Fauna of Thailand*. Bangkok: Department of Fisheries, 1950. 1100 pp.

In English and Thai. Cited from Watts [29].

Mammals

492

G. B. Corbet: *Mammals of the Indomalayan region: a systematic review*. Oxford: Oxford University Press, 1992. 488 pp. 0-19-854693-9. (Natural History Museum publications.)

A descriptive listing of species with find-spots; some illustrations. Covers the Indian subcontinent, southern China, and mainland and insular south east Asia. Biographical notes on zoologists, pp. 424-9. Index of scientific Latin names. No vernacular names.

493

Earl of Cranbrook [Lord Medway]: *Mammals of South-East Asia.* Kuala Lumpur: Oxford University Press, 1991. 96 pp. 0-19-588568-6.
(Images of Asia series.)

'Second edition' of a readable overview incorporating a checklist (English and Latin) of over 650 known species.

First edition: Earl of Cranbrook [Lord Medway]: *Riches of the wild: land mammals of South-East Asia.* 1987. 95 pp. Not seen.

Note also: Boonsong Lekagul, Jeffrey A. McNeely and others: *Mammals of Thailand.* Bangkok: Saha Karn Bhaet, 1988. 758 pp. 974-86806-1-4. Second edition. First edition: Bangkok: Kuruspita, 1977. 691 pp.

Jean Deuve: *Les mammifères du Laos.* Vientiane: Ministère d'Education Nationale, 1972. 196 pp. [The mammals of Laos.]

Lord Medway: *The wild mammals of Malaya and offshore islands including Singapore.* Kuala Lumpur: Oxford University Press, 1968. 127 pp. Reprinted as: Lord Medway: *The wild mammals of Malaya (Peninsular Malaysia) and Singapore.* 1978.

494

Junaidi Payne, Charles M. Francis: *A field guide to the mammals of Borneo.* Kota Kinabalu: Sabah Society; Kuala Lumpur: World Wildlife Fund Malaysia, 1985. 332 pp.
Illustrated by Karen Phillipps.

About 220 land species (including 92 bats); also 27 marine mammals from Bornean or nearby waters; practically all are illustrated on 60 coloured plates accompanied by brief identification notes, keyed to main text which lists species in taxonomic order (English and Latin names, size, identification, ecology, distribution). Guide to footprints (pp. 302-311); Gazetteer and map of places referred to; Glossary of names 'in the major dialects of Sabah, Sarawak and Brunei including Malay' with English equivalents; Latin and English index. No names in Dutch or in the languages of Kalimantan.

Note also: Lord Medway: *Mammals of Borneo: field keys and an annotated checklist.* Kuala Lumpur: Malaysian Branch of the Royal Asiatic Society, 1977. 172 pp. (Monographs of the Malaysian Branch of the Royal Asiatic

Society, 7.) English and Latin names only. Many photographs, mostly supplied by the Sarawak Museum. Second, revised edition. First published as *Journal of the Malaysian Branch, Royal Asiatic Society* vol. 36 no. 3 (December 1963) and as a bound offprint.

495

Timothy Flannery: *The mammals of New Guinea*. Carina: Robert Brown, 1990. 439 pp. 1-86273-029-6.
The Australian Museum.

Introductory sections deal with geological history, vegetation, and introduced mammals. List of species, pp. 36-373 (readable descriptions, maps of findspots, coloured photographs, statistical information; scientific Latin, English, Indonesian and local names). Large format: about 1 species per page.

Birds

496

Ben F. King, Edward C. Dickinson: *A field guide to the birds of South-East Asia*. London: Collins, 1975. 480 pp., 64 plates.

Arranged systematically. 1192 species are concisely described with excellent colour illustrations. 'English' names (some invented by the authors, see pp. 11-14) and scientific Latin names, with index to both. No vernacular names.

Recent reprints under new title: Ben F. King, Edward C. Dickinson: *The Collins field guide to the birds of south-east Asia*. 0-00-219207-1.

Note also: Eugene W. Oates: *Handbook to the birds of British Burmah, including those of Karennee*. 1883. 2 v. Cited from Cordier [242] col. 2841.

Boonsong Lekagul, E. W. Cronin: *Bird guide of Thailand*. Bangkok, 1972. 374 pp. Second edition of a field guide describing 829 species.

497

H. C. Robinson, F. N. Chasen: *The birds of the Malay peninsula. A general account of the birds inhabiting the region from the Isthmus of Kra to Singapore with the adjacent islands*. London: Witherby, 1927-76. 5 v.

Of particular reference use is vol. 5, by Lord Medway and David R. Wells: *Conclusion and survey of every species*. Co-published: Kuala Lumpur: Penerbit Universiti Malaya. 1976. 448 pp. 0-85493-104-X. The main feature of this volume is the systematic survey; but few colour illustrations and no Malay names. History of the work, pp. v-vii.

Note also: A. G. Glenister: *The birds of the Malay peninsula, Singapore and Penang: an account of all the Malayan species, with a note of their occurrence in Sumatra, Borneo and Java and a list of the birds of those islands.* London: Oxford University Press, 1951. 291 pp. Introduction followed by systematic survey. Appendices: Glossary (i.e. index) of Malay bird names; List of birds of western Indonesia. Many colour illustrations. Reprinted: Kuala Lumpur: Oxford University Press, 1971.

Sir J. A. S. Bucknill, F. N. Chasen: *The birds of Singapore Island.* Singapore, 1927.

498

John MacKinnon and others: *Field guide to the birds of Borneo, Sumatra, Java and Bali.* Kuala Lumpur: Oxford University Press, forthcoming. 0-19-854035-3.

Announced for Summer 1993. This will no doubt supersede:

John MacKinnon: *Field guide to the birds of Java and Bali.* Yogyakarta: Gadjah Mada University Press, 1988. 390 pp. 979-420-092-1. (In collaboration with Yayasan Indonesia Hijau.) Introduction; Guide to families; Coloured plates with captions, between pp. 45-6; systematic list of 488 species with English and Indonesian names; separate English, scientific Latin and Indonesian indexes. 'The species order and English names follow those used in King [496].'

499

Bertram E. Smythies: *The birds of Borneo.* Kota Kinabalu: Sabah Society; Kuala Lumpur: Malayan Nature Society, 1981. 473 pp. Revised by the Earl of Cranbrook [Lord Medway].

Third edition. A systematic catalogue with detailed, discursive descriptions keyed to 45 colour plates. English and Latin names. The catalogue is in essence reprinted from the second edition, but the arrangement and nomenclature have been revised to match those of King [496], and notes on recent work have been added. Guide to place names; short glossary of Malay and Iban names (the two are not distinguished); index of English and Latin names.

Second edition: Edinburgh: Oliver & Boyd, 1968. 593 pp.

First edition: 1960. 562 pp. The two earlier editions included chapters on ethnoornithology, by Tom Harrisson ('Birds and men in Borneo', pp. 20-61), J. D. Freeman ('Iban augury', pp. 73-98), and by Smythies and Medway, that were excluded from the third: 'there is probably no other part of the world where birds and men are more intimately intermixed than in Borneo'

(Smythies).

500

Bruce M. Beehler, Thane K. Pratt, Dale Zimmermann: *Birds of New Guinea*. Princeton: Princeton University Press, 1986. 293 pp., 55 plates. Wau Ecology Institute handbook, 9.

A field guide, listing about 700 species (600 illustrated) in systematic order under 'common' [invented English] names with scientific Latin names also. Cited from McConnell [24].

Note also: Austin L. Rand, E. Thomas Gilliard: *A handbook of New Guinea birds*. London: Weidenfeld & Nicolson, 1967. 612 pp. + index. A readable, systematic survey, keyed to 76 monochrome and 5 colour plates. The final editing appears to have been done somewhat hastily. The tipped-in index of scientific and 'popular' [invented English] names is not paginated.

501

John Eleuthere duPont: *Philippine birds*. Greenville, Delaware: Delaware Museum of Natural History, 1971. 480 pp.
Colour illustrations by George Sandstrom, John R. Pierce.

Latin and 'popular' [English] names, description: many species illustrated in colour.

Note also: Jean Delacour, Ernst Mayr: *Birds of the Philippines*. Nw York: Macmillan, 1946. 309 pp. A systematic list with informal descriptions. Many invented English names: 'native names have been avoided as too often they vary from one locality to another.'

Fish; fisheries

502

Alan Davidson: *Seafood of south-east Asia*. Singapore: Federal Publications, 1976. 366 pp.

Part 1: illustrated catalogue of edible fish and other seafood, pp. 13-198. Part 2: recipes. Index of names, English, Latin and vernacular.

Reprinted: London: Macmillan, 1978.

503

U Khin: *Fisheries in Burma*. Rangoon: Superintendent, Government Printing, 1948. 180 pp.

Note appendix A (pp. 111-7): Provisional list of food fishes of Burma, in systematic order, giving scientific name; English name if any; Burmese name. Notes on selected species, pp. 9-27; 40 monochrome plates.

Note also: Francis Day: *The fishes of India, being a natural history of the fishes known to inhabit the seas and fresh waters of India, Burma and Ceylon.* London: Bernard Quaritch, 1875-8. 2 v. (778 pp.) + Atlas (145 plates). This work formed the basis of the section on ichthyology in the *British Burma gazetteer* [411].

504

J. Thiemmedh: *Fishes of Thailand: their English, scientific and Thai names.* Bangkok, 1966. 112 pp.
Kasatsart University. (Fisheries research bulletin, 4.)

Cited from Watts [29].

Note also: Chote Suvatti: *Checklist of the acquatic fauna of Siam (excluding fishes).* Bangkok: Bureau of Fisheries, 1937. 116 pp.

505

Loys Pétillot: *Une richesse du Cambodge: la pêche et les poissons.* Paris: Challamel, 1911. 167 pp.

[One of Cambodia's riches: fish and fisheries.] 14 plates; map. Cited from Cordier [242].

506

Alan Davidson: *Fish and fish dishes of Laos.* Vientiane, 1975.

First section: catalogue of fish species, giving Lao, English and Latin names with excellent line drawings and notes on the species and its use in cooking. Second section: recipes.

Also published: Rutland: Tuttle, 1975.

Note also: *Traditional recipes of Laos, being the manuscript recipe books of the late Phia Sing from the Royal Palace at Luang Prabang, reproduced in facsimile and furnished with an English translation.* London: Prospect Books, 1981. 318 pp.

507

Viện Nghiên Cứu Biển: *Cá kinh tế vịnh bắc bộ.* Hanoi: Khoa Học và Kỹ Thuật, 1971. 159 pp.

Illustrated catalogue of 40 Vietnamese marine fish, arranged by taxonomic families, with scientific names.

508

Istilah perikanan bahasa inggeris-bahasa Malaysia bahasa Malaysia-bahasa inggeris. Kuala Lumpur: Dewan Bahasa dan Pustaka, 1988. 270 pp. 983-62-0569-1.

[English and Bahasa Malaysia glossary of fisheries.] Tabular format. Includes a four-column glossary of fish names, Bahasa Malaysia-scientific Latin-standard English-local English.

509

Donald L. Lovett: *A guide to shrimps, prawns, lobsters and crabs of Malaysia and Singapore.* Selangor: Faculty of Fisheries and Marine Science, 1981. 156 pp.
(Occasional publication, 2.)

Descriptions with anatomical diagrams.

510

Theodore Cantor: *Catalogue of Malayan fishes.* Calcutta, 1849. Pp. 983-1443.
(Journal of the Asiatic Society of Bengal, vol. 18 part 2 [1849].)

Note also: Albert W. C. T. Herre, G. S. Myers: 'A contribution to the ichthyology of the Malay Peninsula' in *Bulletin of the Raffles Museum, Singapore, Straits Settlements* no. 13 (August 1937) pp. 5-74.

511

M. Weber, L. F. de Beaufort and others: *The fishes of the Indo-Australian archipelago.* Leiden: Brill.

512

Thomas Gloerfelt-Tarp, Patricia J. Kailola: *Trawled fishes of southern Indonesia and northwestern Australia.* [Canberra? 1982?] 0-642-70001-X. Published by the Australian Development Assistance Bureau; the Directorate General of Fisheries, Indonesia; the German Agency for Technical Cooperation.

A fish identification guide for use by fishery workers in the field: the result of a survey during 1979-81. Covers Indian Ocean coasts from north west Sumatra to north west Australia and Timor. Survey in taxonomic order with English, scientific Latin and Indonesian names, descriptions and illustrations, usually from coloured photographs, pp. 1-299; species list, pp. 300-364; English, Latin, and Indonesian indexes.

513

I. S. R. Munro: *The fishes of New Guinea*. Port Moresby: Department of Agriculture, Stock and Fisheries, 1967. 650 pp.

Covers both marine and freshwater species. Illustrations (photographs and line-drawings). Not seen.

514

Norbert Rau, Anke Rau: *Commercial marine fishes of the central Philippines*. Eschborn: German Agency for Technical Co-operation, 1980. 623 pp.
Cover title: *Commercial fishes of the Philippines*.

Alphabetical by family: emphasizes external, easily recognizable features to aid rapid identification. Questionnaire format. Latin, 'common' [English] and local names (but local languages not identified): many line drawings. No notes on uses. Indexes of scientific and common but not of local names.

Other animals

515

George A. Boulenger: *A vertebrate fauna of the Malay Peninsula from the Isthmus of Kra to Singapore, including the adjacent islands: Reptilia and batrachia*. London: Taylor and Francis, 1912. 294 pp.
Edited by H. C. Robinson.

Much of this work duplicates the author's volume on reptilia and batrachia in the *Fauna of British India* [490]: '80% of the species in Malaya are also found in Tenasserim.' The planned series, paralleling the *Fauna of British India*, of which this was to be the first volume, was not continued.

516

Frank F. Reitinger: *Common snakes of south east Asia and Hong Kong*. Hong Kong: Heinemann, 1978. 114 pp., 31 plates.

The listing is on pp. 45-95, 'intended to serve as a guide to some of the more common species and a few rare ones'. English and Latin names, half-page descriptions: good colour photographs.

Note also: René Bourret: *Les serpents de l'Indochine*. Toulouse, 1936- . 2 v. [The snakes of Indochina.]

Jean Deuve: *Serpents du Laos*. Paris, 1970. 251 pp. (Mémoires de l'ORSTOM, 39.) [Snakes of Laos.] Description of about 100 species, preceded by an introduction which discusses Lao names.

M. W. F. Tweedie: *The snakes of Malaya*. Singapore: Government Printing Office, 1957. 143 pp. Second edition. Brief descriptions of 129 species of land and sea snakes, with line drawings. There are notes on distribution of these species outside Malaya.

517

Edward H. Taylor: 'The amphibian fauna of Thailand,' 'The lizards of Thailand,' 'Serpents of Thailand and adjacent waters,' articles in *University of Kansas science bulletin* vols 43-5 (1962-5).

For full references see Watts [29].

518

Theodore Cantor: 'Catalogue of reptiles inhabiting the Malayan Peninsula and Islands' in *Journal of the Asiatic Society of Bengal* vol. 16 (1847) pp. 607-656, 897-952, 1026-1078.

Note also: R. Shelford: 'A list of the reptiles of Borneo' in *Journal of the Straits Branch of the Royal Asiatic Society* no. 35 (1902) pp. 43-68. In taxonomic order. Latin names only: no index.

519

P. Y. Berry: *The amphibian fauna of Peninsular Malaysia*. Kuala Lumpur: Tropical Press, 1975. 130 pp.

Notes on each of about 80 species; some photographs.

Note also: René Bourret: *Les batraciens de l'Indochine*. Hanoi: Gouvernement Général de l'Indochine, 1942. 547 pp. (Mémoires de l'Institut Océanographique de l'Indochine, 6.) [Frogs of Indochina.]

520

G. F. L. Marshall, Lionel de Nicéville: *The butterflies of India, Burmah and Ceylon*. Calcutta: Calcutta Central Press, 1882-90. 3 v.

Cited from Cordier [242].

521

Boonsong Lekagul and others: *Field guide to the butterflies of Thailand*. Bangkok: Association for the Conservation of Wildlife, 1977. 260 pp.

Names and descriptions in English and Thai: colour photographs. Over 800 species.

Note also: Brother Amnuai Pinratana, F. A. Degeorges: *Butterflies in Thailand*.

Bangkok: Viratham, 1975-81. 4 v. Cited from Watts [29] who gives the complex details of this publication.

522

A. Steven Corbet, H. M. Pendlebury: *The butterflies of the Malay peninsula*. Kuala Lumpur: Malayan Nature Society, 1978. 649 pp.

Third edition, revised by J. N. Eliot. Systematic survey; 35 plates, mostly in colour; checklist of species and distribuion, pp. 420-468; general index; index of scientific Latin names.

Second edition: 1956; first edition: 1934.

Note also: W. A. Fleming: *Butterflies of West Malaysia and Singapore*. Faringdon: E. W. Classey; Singapore, Kuala Lumpur: Longman, 1975. 2 v. 0-900848-71-5, 0-900848-72-3. Very brief systematic listing with colour illustrations of all species (90 plates). Includes information on distribution outside Malaysia, and on the butterflies' food plants.

523

Bernard D'Abrera: *Butterflies of the Australian region*. Melbourne: Lansdowne, 1977. 415 pp.

Second edition. A systematic catalogue with some information on ecology and behaviour. The region includes eastern Indonesia. Most species illustrated in colour.

FLORA

Major floras

524

J. D. Hooker: *The flora of British India*. London: Reeve, 1872-97. 7 v. (23 fascicles).

'Concise, briefly descriptive flora of seed plants with keys: includes synonymy, range, notes on habitat, etc.' (Frodin). In English with many technical abbreviations: on botanical terminology see the useful 'Outlines of elementary botany', vol. 1 pp. i-xl [*bis*]. No vernacular names; no illustrations. There is a cumulative index to botanical names in vol. 7 pp. 425-842, superseding the separate volume indexes in vols 1-6. Besides the Indian subcontinent the work covers Burma, southwestern Thailand and Malaya, but less comprehensively. Malaya was meanwhile more completely covered in the work of King, Gamble and Ridley [528]. Ferns were originally to be included but were in the end omitted: for these see van Rosenburgh

[531] and Holttum [527].

Volumes have been variously reprinted, more recently under the title *Flora of India*.

Supplemented by: C. C. Calder and others: *List of species and genera of Indian phanerogams not included in Sir J. D. Hooker's 'Flora of British India'.* 1926. 157 pp. (Records of the Botanical Survey of India, 11 i.) Subsequent supplementary publications (for references see Frodin [1]) did not extend to south east Asia.

Superseded: J. D. Hooker, Thomas Thomson: *Flora Indica; being a systematic account of the plants of British India, together with observations on the structure and affinities of their natural orders and genera.* London: W. Pamplin, 1855. Vol. 1 [no more published]. This work, in botanical Latin with English notes, covered the families Ranunculaceae to Fumariaceae, with a long introductory essay. Here too India was taken in the broad sense 'from Persia to the Chinese dominions'.

525

T. Smitinand, K. Larsen, editors: *Flora of Thailand.* Bangkok: Applied Scientific Research Corporation of Thailand, 1970- .

'Briefly descriptive flora of vascular plants, with keys, synonymy, references, vernacular names, detailed range, notes on habitat, ecology, uses, etc.' (Frodin [1]). Names in several vernacular languages. Some species are illustrated: fine colour photographs. Each fascicle contains one or more families, in a random sequence. Last seen: vol. 5 part 3, 1991.

Smitinand and Larsen will supersede: W. G. Craib; A. F. G. Kerr, editor: *Florae Siamensis enumeratio: a list of the plants known from Siam with records of their occurrence.* Bangkok: Bangkok Times Press; London: Luzac, 1925-62. Vols 1-3. (Under the auspices of the Siam Society.) [An enumeration of the flora of Thailand.] In English. No descriptions of species. Often gives vernacular names in several languages, including Shan and Lao. Published in fascicles; errata and index of botanical names at head of each volume: a discussion of vernacular names, by Kerr, in the introduction. This work remained incomplete, having covered families (in taxonomic order) from Ranunculaceae to Gesneriaceae.

526

A. Aubréville and others, editors: *Flore du Cambodge, du Laos et du Viêt-nam.* Paris: Musée Nationale d'Histoire Naturelle, 1960- .

[Flora of Cambodia, Laos and Vietnam.] 'Large-scale descriptive research flora of vascular plants: keys, synonymy, references, localities and range, notes on habitat, uses, etc.' (Frodin [1]). Dealing with families, or groups of families, in a random order (see list of published fascicles, inside back cover of each) and as yet far from complete. 26 fascicles published up to 1992, each containing two indexes, to scientific Latin and to vernacular names: no cumulative indexing. Vernacular includes Vietnamese, Khmer, Lao, 'Proto-Indochinois' (the Montagnard languages of Vietnam) and occasionally others.

The first fascicle was intended to begin a second supplementary volume of the *Flore générale de l'Indochine*. With the second fascicle the plan was changed: the *Flore générale* is to be replaced.

The predecessor: H. Lecomte, H. Humbert, editors: *Flore générale de l'Indochine*. Paris: Masson; Musée Nationale d'Histoire Naturelle, 1907-52. 7 v. + Preliminary volume + Supplementary vol. 1. [General flora of Indochina.] Botanical descriptions, with ranges and findspots, entirely in French: a few line drawings. Includes eastern Thailand and the island of Hainan as well as French Indochina. The preliminary volume contains a biographical dictionary of collectors and contributors, as well as indices to families and to vernacular names. The latter are given without diacritics. The supplement, published in 10 parts 1938-51, is a series of additions and corrections.

527

R. E. Holttum and others: *A revised flora of Malaya*. Singapore: Government Printer, 1953-71. Vols 1-3.

'A large number of our species were first found by Mr. H. N. Ridley, but unfortunately his descriptions of them [528] are often unsatisfactory.' Intended to replace Ridley, this work remained incomplete. The task is subsumed in that of the *Flora Malesiana* [529], to which Holttum has contributed.

Vol. 1: Orchids (3rd edition, 1968), including cultivated species, the non-Asian ones more briefly; a few coloured plates. Vol. 2: Ferns (2nd edition, 1968): some line drawings only; cf. van Rosenburgh [531]. Vol. 3: Grasses, by H. B. Gilliland and others. 1971. 321 pp. Line drawings and some coloured illustrations; index includes vernacular names.

528

Henry N. Ridley: *Flora of the Malay Peninsula*. London, Ashford: Reeve, 1922-5. 5 v.

Brief botanical descriptions with notes on range: some line drawings. Includes vernacular names. This work has been criticised for its inaccurate descriptions. The introduction in volume 1 includes a list of botanists, pp. xiv-xix. Vol. 5 pp. 286-344 is a supplement to the preceding volumes; this is followed by an index of Malay names (pp. 346-371), a list of illustrations, and an index of Latin names (pp. 377-470).

Reprinted: Amsterdam: Asher, 1968.

The set was intended to cumulate and supersede:

G. King, J. S. Gamble: *Materials for a flora of the Malay Peninsula*. Calcutta, 1889-1936. 26 parts, reprints of a series of papers in the *Journal of the Asiatic Society of Bengal*: Cordier [242] cols 1299, 2905 gives references to most of them. The work was largely completed by 1914 except for A T. Gage's paper on 'Euphorbiaceae', 1936. As observed by Craib [525], references made by others to this work sometimes give the journal's pagination or and sometimes that of the reprints.

Accompanied by: H. N. Ridley: *Materials for a flora of the Malay Peninsula: Monocotyledons*. Singapore: Government Printer, 1907-8. 3 v. Supported by several of the governments of the peninsula, these two series aimed to extend the coverage of Hooker [524].

An index to the two series, up to 1908, was provided by: H. N. Ridley: *Index to 'Materials for a flora of the Malay Peninsula'*. Singapore: Methodist Publishing House, 1908. 75 pp.

529

C. G. G. J. van Steenis, R. E. Holttum, editors: *Flora Malesiana, being an illustrated systematic account of the Malaysian flora*. Jakarta, etc.: Noordhoff, 1948- .
Republic of Indonesia, Ministry of Agriculture.

Covers Malaysia (Malesia) in the biogeographical sense: of current political units this includes Malaysia, Singapore, Brunei, Indonesia, the Philippines and Papua New Guinea.

Series 1: General introductory sections and Spermatophyta [seed plants], vol. 1- . Series 2: Pteridophyta [ferns], vol. 1- . 'Comprehensive descriptive floras with keys, synonymy, vernacular names (with their provenance), range (with some maps), notes on habitat, ecology' (Frodin's annotation [1], adapted). Series 1 volume 1 consists largely of a biographical dictionary of collectors by M. J. van Steenis-Kruseman (pp. 1-639, with many photographs. Index of proper names, pp. 607-639). There is also introductory material in series 1 vols 4 and 5. The volumes appear in fascicles, each dealing with one or more families in no systematic order. Frodin estimated in 1980 that the *Flora* at its current rate of progress would reach completion in 120 years.

There is an annual bulletin attached to the project: *Flora Malesiana bulletin*. Leiden: Flora Malesiana Foundation, 1948- .

Series 2 will supersede van Rosenburgh [531]; series 1 will supersede Miquel [530].

530

F. A. W. Miquel: *Flora van Nederlandsch Indië* = *Flora Indiae Bataviae*. Amsterdam: van der Post, 1855-9. 3 v. in 4.

[Flora of the Dutch East Indies.] 'Descriptive flora with keys, synonymy, references, vernacular names, range, notes on habitat and uses'. There is an index to species in each volume. The botanical descriptions are in Latin, the remaining text in Dutch. Cited from Frodin [1], where fuller details will be found.

For a supplement see 553.

531

C. R. W. K. van Alderwerelt van Rosenburgh: *Malayan ferns: handbook to the determination of the ferns of the Malayan Islands (incl. those of the Malay Peninsula, the Philippines and New Guinea)*. Batavia: Department of Agriculture, 1908. 899 pp.

'Briefly descriptive comprehensive treatment, with keys; synonymy, distribution, and other notes' (Frodin [1]).

Accompanied by: C. R. W. K. van Alderwerelt van Rosenburgh: *Malayan fern allies: handbook to the determination of the fern allies of the Malayan Islands*. 1915. 261 pp.

The two works were supplemented in: C. R. W. K. van Alderwerelt van Rosenburgh: *Malayan ferns and fern allies: supplement 1*. 1917. 577 + 73 pp. There is a Latin index in each of the three works.

Of historical interest: R. H. Beddome: *Handbook to the ferns of British India, Ceylon and the Malay Peninsula*. Calcutta: Thacker, Spink, 1892. 500 + 110 pp. 'Second edition': a reprinted text with a 110-page supplement. 'Briefly descriptive fern flora with keys, citations, range; index to botanical names' (Frodin [1]). 300 line drawings in the text. List of illustrations, pp. 477-481; Latin index pp. 482-500. This edition was reprinted: Delhi: Today's and Tomorrow's Printers and Publishers, 1969.

First edition: 1883. 500 pp.

Local and specialized lists of plants

532

D. M. Nath Nair: *The families of Burmese flowering plants*. Rangoon: Rangoon University Press, 1963. 2 v.

Not seen: cited from Frodin [1].

533

S. Kurz: 'Contributions towards a knowledge of the Burmese flora' in *Journal of the Asiatic Society of Bengal*, 1874-7. 4 parts.

Eight parts were planned: Kurz's work was broken off by his early death in 1877.

534

Dewan Mohinder Nath: 'Botanical survey of the Southern Shan States, with a note on the vegetation of the Inle Lake' in *Burma Research Society fiftieth anniversary publication* (Rangoon, 1961) vol. 1 pp. 157-418.

Gives Shan names of species.

535

H. G. Hundley, U Chit Ko Ko: *List of trees, shrubs, herbs and principal climbers, etc., recorded from Burma, with vernacular names*. Rangoon: Superintendent, Government Printing and Stationery, 1961. 532 pp.

Third edition. Systematic order; tabular format. Gramineae (see also Rhind [536]) are covered selectively. About 6000 entries. Against each scientific name are given synonyms, transliterated Burmese name if any, English name if any, locality. Part 2: pp. 325-456, Burmese-Latin glossary and index; pp. 457-508, briefer Chin, Kachin, Karen, Mon, Shan and English indexes. Pp. 509-532, Latin index.

Second edition: J. H. Lace, Alex. Rodger: *List of trees, shrubs and principal climbers, etc., recorded from Burma, with vernacular names*. 1922. 366 pp.

First edition, by Lace alone, 1912. 291 pp.

536

D. Rhind: The *grasses of Burma*. Simla: Director of Agriculture, Burma, 1945. 99 pp.

'An attempt to gather the scattered information about the Burmese grass flora and to place it on record. The list of species is undoubtedly incomplete because it lacks all but a few collections from the high hills ... Some of the important herbaria have not been available for consultation.' Systematic arrangement, giving scientific name, brief scientific description, habitat, uses, local name; about 500 entries. List of fungi recorded on grasses in Burma, pp. 80-81; glossary of Burmese and other local names, pp. 83-91; Latin index.

537

Bartle Grant: *The orchids of Burma (including the Andaman Islands) described*. Rangoon: Hanthawaddy Press, 1895. 424 pp.

Intended as a more accessible reference work than parts 5-6 of Hooker [524]. Brief description in English; notes on findspots and on cultivation.

Reprinted about 1980: Dehra Dun: Bishen Singh, n.d.

538

Tem Smitinand: *Thai plant names: botanical name, vernacular name*. Bangkok: Royal Forest Department, 1980. 379 pp.

Not seen. There was also an earlier version: *Siamese plant names*. 1948. 504 pp. In Thai and English. Includes alternative names and names in minority languages, an index to which was published later.

539

Chote Suvatti: *Flora of Thailand*. Bangkok: Royal Institute of Thailand, 1978. 2 v. (1503 pp.).

A useful simple list, with notes on each species in Thai and English, but no descriptions and no illustrations.

540

S. Lewitz, B. Rollet: 'Lexique des noms d'arbres et d'arbustes au Cambodge' in *Bulletin de l'Ecole Française d'Extrême-Orient* vol. 60 (Paris, 1973) pp. 117-162.

[Dictionary of names of trees and shrubs of Cambodia.]

541

J. E. Vidal: 'Noms vernaculaires de plantes (lao, mèo, kha) en usage au Laos' in *Bulletin de l'Ecole Française d'Extrême-Orient* vol. 49 no. 2 (1959) pp. 435-608.

[Vernacular plant names (Lao, Mieo, Kha) in use in Laos.] Second edition.

A two-way vernacular/Latin glossary, the Lao names both in Lao script and romanized: a few illustrations.

A revised edition, which I have not seen, appeared in 1962.

Note also: Jules Vidal, Jacques Lemoine: 'Contribution à l'ethnobotanique des Hmong du Laos' in *Journal d'agriculture tropicale et de botanique appliquée* vol. 17 (1970) pp. 1-59. [On the ethnobotany of the Hmong (Mieo) of Laos.] Principally a list of Mieo names with taxonomic, Latin, French and pharmacological indexes. Two articles by Vidal in vols 6-7 of the same journal (1959-60) are also relevant.

542

Nguyễn Nhu Hiền, Phạm Bình Quyển, S. V. Smirnova [X. V. Xmirnop]: *Từ điển tên sinh vật Nga-Việt = Russko-v'etnamskii slovar' biologicheskikh nazvanii*. Hanoi: Khoa Học và Kỹ Thuật; Moscow: Russkii Yazyk, 1985. 334 pp.

[Russian-Vietnamese-Latin dictionary of zoological and botanical names.] About 15000 entries. No Vietnamese or Latin index.

543

Phạm-Hoàng Hộ: *Cây-cỏ miền nam Việt-Nam = An illustrated flora of South Vietnam*. Saigon: Bộ Van-Hoa Giáo-Dục, 1970-72. 2 v.

Second edition. Omits medicinal plants and marine algae (for the latter see **544**) but includes mushrooms (vol. 1 pp. 24-42), lichen and mosses. Arranged systematically: each species entry gives Latin and Vietnamese name. About 5300 plants described (3 per page) and illustrated with line drawings. Index of Vietnamese names in each volume.

First edition: Phạm-Hoàng Hộ, Nguyễn Văn Dương: *Cây-cỏ miền nam Việt-Nam*. Saigon: Bộ Quốc-Gia Giáo-Dục, 1960. 803 pp. About 1600 plants described, most illustrated. This first edition included medicinal plants and algae. For a full analysis see Cotter [30].

544

Phạm-Hoàng Hộ: *Rong biển Việtnam = Marine algae of South Vietnam*. Saigon: Bộ Giáo-Dục, 1969. 558 pp.

Exhaustive catalogue arranged by scientific family. Each entry gives Latin name, Vietnames name if any, detailed description, line drawing. Supersedes entries for marine algae in the first edition of **543**.

545

Võ Văn Chi and others: *Cây cỏ thường thấy ở Việt Nam*. Hanoi: Nhà

Xuất Bản Khoa Học, 1969-1975. 5 v.

[Common plants of Vietnam.] Vols 1-4 cover dicotyledons in alphabetical order of botanical families; vol. 5, monocotyledons. Sub-arrangement is by botanical name of species, with synonyms and Vietnamese names. About 2000 entries of roughly 1 page in length, most of them illustrated with line drawings. I have not seen vols 4-5, and have drawn some details from Cotter [30].

546

Lê-Văn-Thới and others: *Danh-từ thực-vật-học Pháp-Việt, có phần đối-chiếu Việt-Pháp.* [Saigon:] Bộ Quốc-Gia Giáo-Dục, 1963. 279 pp.

[French-Vietnamese glossary of botany, with Vietnamese index.] Tabular format.

547

Joannes de Loureiro: *Flora Cochinchinensis, sistens plantas in Regno Cochinchina nascentes, quibus accedunt aliae observatae in Sinensi Imperio, Africa orientali, Indiaeque locis variis; omnes dispositae secundum systema sexuale Linnaeanum.* Lisbon: expensis Academicis, 1790. 2 v. (744 pp.).

[Flora of Cochinchina, being plants native to the Kingdom of Cochinchina, with others observed in the Chinese Empire, eastern Africa and various parts of the Indies, arranged according to Linnaean taxonomy.] In botanical Latin: also gives vernacular names in Vietnamese (marked *alpha*), Chinese (marked *beta*), both with indications of tone, and occasionally in other languages. Includes a Latin index, pp. 699-722, and a Vietnamese index, pp. 723-744. Erratum sheet. No illustrations.

Later edition: Berlin: Haude & Spener, 1793. 2 v. (882 pp.). With notes by Carolus Ludovicus Willdenow. I have not seen this.

On Loureiro's work see: Elmer D. Merrill: *Commentary on Loureiro's Flora Cochinchinensis.* Philadelphia, 1935. 445 pp. (Transactions of the American Philosophical Society, N. S. 24 i.) This gives details of the fate of Loureiro's botanical specimens, which illustrate his work and some of which survive in the British Museum (see pp. 12-23) and discusses the identification and synonymy of each species listed. Index to all vernacular names in the original work (without corrections), pp. 405-412; to Latin names and synonyms, pp. 413-445.

548

H. Keng: *Orders and families of Malayan seed plants.* Singapore: Singapore University Press, 1983. 500 pp.

Third edition. 'Synopsis of orders and families of Malayan gymnosperms, dicotyledons and monocotyledons.' Includes naturalized and some cultivated plants. Numerous illustrations.

Second edition: 1978. 437 pp.

First edition: 1969.

549

M. R. Henderson: *Malayan wild flowers*. Kuala Lumpur: Malayan Nature Society, 1949-54. 2 v.

Intended to assist identification of 'a majority of the smaller plants' of the peninsula. Vol. 1: Dicotyledons (472 pp.) was published as the December 1949, September 1950 and June 1951 issues of the *Malayan nature journal*. There is no volume index, but a scientific Latin index in each fascicle. English and Malay names appear in the text but are not indexed. Vol. 2: Monocotyledons, appeared in 1954 (not seen).

Note also: E. J. H. Corner: *Wayside trees of Malaya*. Singapore: Government Printing Office, 1940. 2 v. (Vol. 1, 772 pp.; vol. 2, 228 monochrome photographs). A systematic list in alphabetical order of families, with line drawings and Malay and English names, with notes on occurrence and uses. English index, pp. 729-745; Malay index, pp. 746-766; Latin index.

'Second edition' (only slightly revised): 1952.

550

Anne Johnson: *Mosses of Singapore and Malaysia*. Singapore: Singapore University Press, 1980. 126 pp.

Illustrated with line drawings.

551

H. Keng: 'Annotated list of seed plants of Singapore' in *Gardens bulletin Singapore*.

A series of articles beginning in vol. 26 (1973) with gymnosperms.

An earlier work: H. N. Ridley: 'The flora of Singapore' in *Journal of the Straits Branch of the Royal Asiatic Society* no. 33 (1900) pp. 27-196. A List of Latin names in taxonomic order with brief descriptions: Malay and English names where available. No index.

552

F. S. A. de Clercq: *Nieuw plantkundig woordenboek voor Nederlandsch Indië, met korte aanwijsingen van het nuttig gebruik der planten en hare beteekenis in het volksleven, en met registers der inlandsche en wetenschappelijke benamingen.* Amsterdam: De Bussy, 1927. 443 pp.

[New botanical dictionary of the Dutch East Indies, with concise notes on the uses of the plants and their popular significance, and indexes of native and scientific nomenclature.] Second edition, revised by A. Pulle with linguistic revision by A. H. J. G. Walbeehm. The 'native' names are Malay.

First edition: 1909. 395 pp. Edited by M. Greshoff.

553

F. A. W. Miquel: *Prodromus florae Sumatranae = Sumatra: zijne plantenwereld en hare voortbrengselen.* Amsterdam: van der Post, 1860-61. 656 pp.
(Florae Indiae Batavae supplementum 1.) For the parent work see 529.

[Sumatra: its plants and their products.] An enumeration of the known seed plants of the island (pp. 104-276); longer notes on genera etc.

There was also a German edition: F. A. W. Miquel: *Sumatra: seine Pflanzenwelt und deren Erzeugnisse.* 1862. 656 pp.

554

E. D. Merrill: *A bibliographic enumeration of Bornean plants.* Singapore, 1921. 637 pp.
(Journal of the Straits Branch of the Royal Asiatic Society, special number.)

In systematic order: useful not only as a bibliography but also as a flora, since it indicates range and findspots and includes some descriptive and taxonomic information.

On this were based two later works which I have not seen: G. Masamune: *Enumeratio phanerogamarum bornearum.* Taihoku: Taiwan Sotukufu Gaijabu, 1942. 739 pp. [Enumeration of Bornean seed plants.] G. Masamune: *Enumeratio pteridophytarum bornearum.* 1945. 124 pp. [Enumeration of Bornean ferns.] Cited from Frodin [1].

555

C. A. Backer, R. C. Bakhuizen van den Brink: *Flora of Java (spermatophytes only).* Groningen: Noordhoff, 1963-8. 3 v.

Highly technical description of over 6000 species of seed plants (well over 1000 of which are non-native) in 238 families. General chapter on the vegetation of Java in vol. 2; scientific Latin index, vol. 3 pp. 661-761. No illustrations. No vernacular names.

Earlier version: C. A. Backer: *Beknopte flora van Java.* Leiden: Rijksherbarium,

1942-61. 22 parts. [Concise flora of Java.] Roneoed.

Accompanied by: C. A. Backer, O. Posthumus: *Varenflora voor Java*. Buitenzorg: s'Lands Plantentuin, 1939. 370 pp. [Fern flora of Java.] Nearly 100 illustrations.

For illustrations of many species, and for vernacular names, see the older work: S. H. Koorders: *Exkursionsflora von Java, umfassend die Blütenpflanzen*. Jena: Fischer, 1911-37. 3 v. + Atlas. Over 1100 plates were issued for the atlas before publication ceased. For full discussion of this work see Frodin [1].

556

S. H. Koorders: *Verslag eener botanische dienstreis door de Minahasa, tevens eerste overzicht der flora van N. O. Celebes*. Batavia, 1898. 716 pp.

[Report on a botanical mission in Minahasa, forming a preliminary survey of the flora of north east Sulawesi.] Contents include: Geography; History of botanical studies; Author's itinerary; Useful plants, pp. 111-252; Enumeration of species of seed plants, pp. 253-645; index to vernacular names. For references to supplementary publications, and to works by H. Christ on ferns, see Frodin [1] pp. 491-2.

557

Georgius Everhardus Rumphius: *Herbarium amboinense = Het Amboinsch kruid-boek, dat is, beschryving van de meest bekende boomen, heesters, kruiden, land- en water-planten, die men in Amboina en de omleggende eylanden vind, na haare gedaante, verscheide benamingen, aanqueking en gebruik*. Amsterdam: Uytwerf, 1741-50. 6 v.

[The Ambon herbal.] Parallel Latin and Dutch texts. A pre-Linnaean, generously illustrated survey of the plants of Ambon, with much ethnobotanical information. Includes vernacular names. Never superseded. Rumphius had died in 1693: the work was edited by Joannes Burmannus.

Accompanied by: *Georgii Everhardi Rumphii herbarii amboinensis auctuarium = Het auctuarium ofte vermeedering op het Amboinsch kruyd-boek*. 1755. 74 pp., 30 plates. [Supplement to G. E. Rumphius's Ambon herbal.] This ends with a cumulated index to the whole set, marking Linnaean equivalents against some names.

For more Linnaean 'translations' and a thorough commentary on these works see: Elmer D. Merrill: *An interpretation of Rumphius's Herbarium amboinense*. Manila, 1917. 595 pp.

Merrill's work had been prefigured on a smaller scale, and with attention to medical uses of plants, by: Aug. Guil. Ed. Th. Henschel: *Clavis Rumphiana botanica et zoologica: accedunt vita G. E. Rumphii, Plinii Indici, specimenque materiae medicae amboinensis*. Bratislava: Schulz, 1833. 215 pp. [Botanical and zoological key to Rumphius, with a life of G. E. Rumphius, "Pliny of the Indies," and some pages of a materia medica of Ambon.] 'Zoology' is in the title because this work also provides an index to the spectacular illustrated catalogue of Rumphius's shells, crustacea and other marine jetsam, *D'Amboinsche Rariteitkamer* (Amsterdam: Halma, 1705. 340 pp., 60 plates).

Note also: H. C. De Wit, editor: *Rumphius memorial volume*. Baarn: Hollandia, 1959. This includes: H. C. De Wit: 'A checklist to Rumphius's Herbarium amboinense,' pp. 339-460.

558

E. E. Henty: *A manual of the grasses of New Guinea*. Lae: Department of Forests, Division of Botany, 1969. 214 pp.
(Botany bulletin, 1.)

Arranged systematically; descriptions and line drawings.

559

P. van Royen: *Keys to the families and genera of higher plants in New Guinea*. Leiden [1959]. 3 v.

Roneoed. For guidance beyond this basic listing through the complex bibliography of New Guinea botany see the relevant sections (from 903 to 931) of Frodin [1], whose special field this is.

560

Elmer D. Merrill: *An enumeration of Philippine flowering plants*. Manila: Department of Agriculture, 1922-6. 4 v. (15 fascicles).
Bureau of Science. (Publication, 18.)

No illustrations and little description; bibliographical guidance, information on range, and a useful listing of vernacular names. Vol. 4 consists of addenda and general introductory chapters (geography, climate, history of botanical work), a bibliography and separate cumulated indexes to scientific Latin and vernacular names.

Reprinted: Amsterdam: Asher, 1968.

Note also: Manuel Blanco: *Flora de Filipinas*. Manila: Provincia de Agustinos Calzados de Filipinas, 1877-83. 4 v. + 2 portfolios of plates. [Third edition.] With additions based on work of Ignacio Mercado and Antonio Llanos, edited by Andrés Naves and Celestino Fernández-Villar. 'For a detailed description see W. E. Retana, *Aparato bibliográfico*, Madrid, 1906, vol. 2 pp. 849-50' (Library of Congress catalogue).

Second edition: 1845. 619 pp.; first edition: 1837. 877 pp. A pioneering flora, but not linked to any preserved collection of botanical specimens.

561

Elmer D. Merrill: *A dictionary of the plant names of the Philippine Islands*. Manila: Department of the Interior, 1903. 192 pp.
Bureau of Government Laboratories. (1903 no. 8.)

Covers ten Philippine languages, in addition to Spanish and 'Spanish-Filipino', in a single vernacular-Latin alphabetical dictionary, pp. 11-117. Latin-vernacular dictionary pp. 119-192. Abbreviations of language names, p. 9.

562

Edwin B. Bartram: *Mosses of the Philippines*. Koenigstein-Taunus: Otto Koeltz, 1972. 437 pp.

Illustrated with line drawings.

Previously published as *Philippine journal of science*, vol. 68 nos 1-4 (1939).

563

Edwin B. Copeland: *Fern flora of the Philippines*. Manila: National Institute of Science and Technology, 1958-61. 3 v. (557 pp.)
(Monographs of the Institute of Science and Technology, 6.)

Covers 943 species of true ferns, arranged taxonomically, with notes on distribution. No index.

Trees; forestry

564

Native woods for construction purposes in the South China Sea region: Burma, Malay Peninsula, Thailand, Sumatra, Java, Borneo, French Indo-China and southeast China including Hainan and Formosa. Washington: Navy Department, Bureau of Yards and Docks, 1945. 277 pp.
'Prepared by Dr J. H. Kraemer.' (Navdocks, P-163.)

Descriptions of the trees and their woods, pp. 33-260: about a page of description and a line-drawing of leaves and flower. Includes 'local names', which are drawn exclusively from Java and other Indonesian islands. Index to botanical and local names of trees, pp. 266-277.

565

Alex. Rodger: *A handbook of the forest products of Burma*. 1935. 162 pp.

Revised edition. Arranged according to use: Timbers, fuel, charcoal, bamboos, canes, tanning and dyeing materials, paper-making, resins and gums, oils, rubber, fibres, animal products, miscellaneous products. Under each, useful trees are listed with brief descriptions, giving Burmese and scientific name (and English if any). Medicinal plants (pp. 96-105): list in systematic order of about 175 species. Appendices: strengths of timbers; list of reserved trees; estimated supplies of chief timbers. English, Burmese and Latin indexes. Reprints: Bombay, 1943 (with additions); Rangoon, 1951. First edition: 1921. 128 pp. This contained a survey in systematic order (pp. 2-54).

Note also: V. Desraj: *Some common Burmese timbers: and other relevant information*. Rangoon: Student Press, 1961. 170 pp.

Earlier work: C. B. Smales: *A simple key to one hundred common trees of Burma*. Rangoon: Superintendent, Government Printing, 1922. 40 pp. A laconic identification guide keyed to descriptions on pp. 17-35, which are headed by Latin and Burmese names. Latin and Burmese indexes.

Reprinted with additional prefatory matter, Simla: Director of Public Relations, Burma, 1945.

566

S. Kurz: *Forest flora of British Burma*. Calcutta: Superintendent of Government Printing, 1877. 2 v.

Descriptions in English of about 2000 species of 'woody plants'. The information was incorporated in the *British Burma gazetteer* [411] and in Hooker [524]. There are indexes to English, Burmese and scientific Latin names in vol. 2.

Partly superseded: Sulpice Kurz: *Preliminary report on the forest and other vegetation of Pegu*. Calcutta: Baptist Mission Press, 1875. Various paginations. Note especially the appendices: Burmese forest trees (tabular format: Latin, Burmese script, transcription: 138 pp.); Key to families and genera, 93 pp.; List of non-arboreous plants for which Burmese names have been obtained, 24 pp.; Extracts from Kurz's journal of his tours in Burma, 34 pp.

Some references to the *Preliminary report* give the imprint: Calcutta: Superintendent of Government Printing, 1876.

There is a cumulative index: *List of the Burmese names of trees and plants given in Kurz's Forest flora of British Burma and in appendices A to C to Kurz's Preliminary report on the forest and other vegetation of Pegu*. Rangoon: Superintendent, Government Printing, 1895.

567

K. Suvarnasuddhi: *Some commercial timbers of Thailand: their properties and uses.* Bangkok: Royal Forest Department, 1950.

Note also: D. G. Neal: *Statistical description of the forests of Thailand*. Bangkok: Joint Thai-U.S. Military Research and Development Center, 1967.

568

Henri Lecomte: *Les bois de l'Indochine: avec un appendice sur les caractères généraux de la forêt indochinoise*. Paris: Agence Economique de l'Indochine, 1925-6. 310 pp. and atlas.
(Publications, 13.)

[Timbers of Indochina, with an appendix on the general characteristics of the Indochinese forest.] The appendix is by H. Guibier.

569

M. Béjaud, M. L. Conrard: *Essences forestières du Cambodge*. Phnom Penh: Service Forestière, 1932. 4 v.

[Forest species of Cambodia.] Vol. 1 is the text (484 pp.); vols 2-4 a series of 830 plates. Cited from Frodin [1].

570

L. Pierre: *Flore forestière de la Cochinchine*. Paris: Octave Doin, 1881-1907. 5 v. (800 pp., 400 plates).

[Forest flora of Cochinchina.] Published as a series of 25 fascicles, 1881-99, followed after the author's death by a 26th containing a preface and an index of botanical names. Monochrome lithographic plates by E. Delpy.

Reprinted: Lehre: Cramer, n.d.

Note also: Emilien Richard: *Nomenclature des principales essences forestières de Cochinchine, avec leurs familles, caractéristiques, usages, noms annamites, cambodgiens, français, scientifiques, classement par catégories et dimensions minima d'abatage fixées par l'arrêté du 5 janvier 1895*. Saigon: Imprimerie Coloniale, 1898. 179 pp. [List of the major forest species of Cochinchina, their families and characteristics, uses, Vietnamese, Khmer, French and scientific names, categorization and minimum felling dimensions as prescribed by the regulation of 5 January 1895.]

571

T. C. Whitmore, F. S. P. Ng, editors: *Tree flora of Malaya: a manual for foresters*. London, Kuala Lumpur: Longman, 1972-89. 4 v. 0-582-72412-0, 0-582-72413-9, 0-582-72425-2, 967-976-202-5.
(Malayan forest records, 22.)

A flora, illustrated with a few line drawings, and at each entry a section on uses. In each volume families are dealt with in alphabetical order. Separate indexes, in each volume, of scientific Latin and Malay names. Cumulated indexes of scientific Latin names, vol. 4 pp. 484-544; of Malay names, pp. 545-9.

Omits Dipterocarpaceae: for these see: C. F. Symington: *Foresters' manual of dipterocarps*. Kuala Lumpur, 1943. 244 pp. (Malayan forest records, 16.) Reprinted with halftone illustrations (omitted from the first edition): Kuala Lumpur: University of Malaya Press, 1976.

572

Istilah perhutanan bahasa inggeris-bahasa Malaysia bahasa Malaysia-bahasa inggeris. Kuala Lumpur: Dewan Bahasa dan Pustaka, 1987. 317 pp.

[English and Bahasa Malaysia glossary of forestry.] Tabular format.

573

F. G. Browne: *Forest trees of Sarawak and Brunei and their products*. Kuching: Government Printing Office, 1955. 369 pp.

Deals with trees of economic importance: 'a preliminary survey of the forest wealth of Sarawak and Brunei for foresters and timbermen.' Key to trees and woods; survey of 47 families in alphabetical order. 'I am not a botanist nor a wood technologist but only a plain forester.' Index including vernacular names.

P. S. Ashton and Paul P. K. Chai are developing a multi-volume manual of forest trees of northern Borneo, with full illustrations and information on vernacular names, beginning from his *Manual of the dipterocarp trees of Brunei State* (Oxford: Oxford University Press, 1964. 242 pp.). The two continuations I have noted are: *A manual of the dipterocarp trees of Brunei State and of Sarawak. Supplement* (Kuching: Borneo Literature Bureau, 1968. 129 pp.) and *Manual of the non-dipterocarp trees of Sarawak. Vol. 2* (Dewan Bahasa dan Pustaka, Sarawak Branch, 1988. 983-62-0155-6). Vol. 1 of the non-dipterocarps had not yet appeared.

Note also: *Potential tree species for Negara Brunei Darussalam*. Bandar Seri Begawan: Ministry of Development, 1985. 65 pp. (Town and Country Planning Department.) Deals with 40 species: botany, habit, economic potential. Colour illustrations.

574

Tree flora of Indonesia. Bogor: Forestry Research and Development Centre.

Planned as a series of six volumes for the regions of Indonesia, each volume to be arranged alphabetically by family. Covers only genera which are represented by at least one big tree species: but for these genera all species known in the region are listed. Brief notes on form, habitat, range, uses. Index of vernacular names.

Includes: T. C. Whitmore, I. G. M. Tantra, U. Sutisna, editors: *Check list for Bali, Nusa Tenggara and Timor*. 1989. 119 pp.

This series is the successor to one begun at Bogor in 1940, each part covering a residence/province of Indonesia. The first editions were by F. H. Hildebrand and most of them carried titles beginning *Lijst van boomsoorten* ...; they were succeeded by slightly revised versions entitled *Daftar nama pohon-pohonan* ... [List of tree species]. For bibliographical details see Frodin [1] pp. 483-500 passim.

575

H. N. Whitford: *The forests of the Philippines*. Manila, 1911. 2 v. Department of the Interior, Bureau of Forestry. (Bulletin, 10.)

Part 1: *Forest types and products*. Illustrations, tables, many photographs; large folding map. Part 2: *The principal forest trees*. Arranged under families, with informal notes on each species and many photographs and line drawings.

Useful plants; food plants

576

Christiane Jacquat: *Plants from the markets of Thailand: descriptions and uses of 241 wild and cultivated plants, with 341 colour photographs*. Bangkok: Duang Kamol, 1990. 251 pp. 947-210-103-3.

Arranged by species: Latin and Thai names (in Thai script and romanization), description of the plant, notes on culinary use. Indexes of Latin and romanized Thai names. Fine illustrations: a most attractive book.

577

Tem Smitinand, T. Santiruk: 'The spices and essential oil crops of Thailand' in *Natural history bulletin of the Siam Society* vol. 29 (September 1981) pp. 85-128.

Deals with cultivation, management, marketing and export.

578

L. Houel: *Plantes et fleurs comestibles de l'Indochine*. Haiphong:

Imprimerie Van-minh, 1911. 54 pp.

[Edible plants and flowers of Indochina.]

Note also: J. Pouchat: *Légumes indigènes susceptibles d'être consommés par les Européens.* Hanoi: Schneider, 1905. 55 pp. (Gouvernement Général de l'Indo-Chine. Notices publiées par la Direction des Forêts et du Commerce de l'Indo-Chine en vue de l'Exposition de Marseille.) [Native vegetables which can be eaten by Europeans.] Also published in *Bulletin économique de l'Indo-Chine* no. 48 (December 1905) pp. 1097-1151.

579

M. A. Martin: *Introduction à l'ethnobotanique du Cambodge.* Paris: Centre National de la Recherche Scientifique, 1971. 257 pp.

[Introduction to Cambodian ethnobotany.]

580

Nguyễn Năng Vinh, Nguyễn Trọng Biểu, A. I. Sorokina [A. I. Xôrôkin]: *Từ điển công nghiệp thực phẩm Nga-Việt = Russko-v'etnamskii slovar' po pishchevoi promyshlennosti.* Hanoi: Nhà Xuất Bản Khoa Học và Kỹ Thuật; Moscow: Russkii Yazyk, 1984. 255 pp.

[Russian-Vietnamese dictionary of food and nutrition.] About 15000 entries. Includes scientific Latin names of food animals and plants. No Vietnamese or Latin index. Glossary of Russian abbreviations, pp. 251-3.

581

Phan-Văn-Tây: *Trồng cây ăn trái.* Saigon, 1974. 308 pp.

[Important fruit trees.] Illustrated manual of 35 Vietnamese edible fruits of commercial importance, with scientific names.

582

Karl Schroeder, Albert Schroeder: 'Enumération des végétaux cultivés en Cochinchine avec leurs dénominations française, latine, annamite, mandarine et cambodgienne (Prodromus)' in *Bulletin du Comité Agricole et Industriel de la Cochinchine* n. s. vol. 1 no. 5 (1876) pp. 287-375.

[Enumeration of vegetables grown in Cochinchina with French, Latin, Vietnamese, Chinese and Khmer names.]

Note also: Charles Crévost: *Matières alimentaires du Tonkin.* Hanoi: Imprimerie d'Extrême-Orient, 1918. 17 pp. (Congrès d'Agriculture Coloniale,

Paris, 1918. Série Hanoi, 2.) [Food substances of Tongking.]

583
G. A. C. Herklots: *Vegetables in south-east Asia.* London: Allen & Unwin, 1972. 0-04-635008-X.

Centres on Singapore, Malaya and Hong Kong. The main survey, pp. 127-507, is subdivided thus: Salads, spinaches and other greens; Cabbages; Beans and peas; Cucurbits; Fruits other than cucurbits; Bulbs, roots and turbers; 'Market vegetables'. The latter includes Herbs and spices, Water plants and a miscellaneous group. Introduction, including information on nutritional values. Brief index.

Note also: Betty Molesworth Allen: *Malayan fruits: an introduction to the cultivated species (with Thai and Tamil names).* Singapore: Donald Moore, 1967. 245 pp. Cited from Watts [29].

584
Istilah sains dan teknologi makanan bahasa inggeris-bahasa Malaysia bahasa Malaysia-bahasa inggeris. Kuala Lumpur: Dewan Bahasa dan Pustaka, 1988. 223 pp. 983-62-0584-5.

[English and Bahasa Malaysia glossary of food science and technology.] Tabular format.

Note also: *Istilah tadbir rumahtangga inggeris-Malaysia-inggeris.* 1973. 376 pp. [English and Bahasa Malaysia glossary of home economics.] Includes cookery.

Daftar istilah pertanian Indonesia-asing. Jakarta: Departemen Pendidikan dan Kebudayaan, 1979. 85 pp. (Seri Cd, 14.) [Bahasa Indonesia-English glossary of farming.] Tabular format.

585
Jacob Jonas Ochse, R. C. Bakhuizen van den Brink: *Vegetables of the Dutch East Indies: edible tubers, bulbs, rhizomes and spices included. Survey of the indigenous and foreign plants serving as pot-herbs and side-dishes.* Amsterdam: Ascher, 1931. 1006 pp.

An exhaustive work, illustrated with line drawings. Systematic list in alphabetical order of botanical families, pp. 1-770; Index of vernacular names 'used in the Dutch provinces *outside* Java and Madoera', pp. 771-927; Glossary of vernacular words [excluding names of plant species] used in the text, pp. 943-970; General index including scientific Latin names.

Reprint with new preface and addenda: 1975. The addenda, a 10-page list after p. 1006, consist of revisions to scientific names and identifications.

Based on a preceding Dutch work which the author modestly describes as a 'booklet': Jacob Jonas Ochse: *Tropische groenten*. Volkslectuur, 1925. [Tropical vegetables.]

586

K. Heyne: *De nuttige planten van Nederlandsch-Indië, tevens synthetische catalogus der verzamelingen van het Museum voor Economische Botanie te Buitenzorg*. Buitenzorg, 1927. 3 v.

[The useful plants of the Dutch East Indies; a catalogue of the collections of the Museum of Economic Botany at Buitenzorg.] Second edition. A systematic listing with many vernacular names and much detail of uses: some statistics of products of economic importance. A true encyclopaedia. The 'third edition' (Wageningen, 1950. 2 v. [1660 + ccxli pp.]) is said to be a reprint of the second.

First edition: 1913-17. 3 v. Indexes of Latin and vernacular names in each volume: no cumulative index.

587

Claudine Friedberg: *Le savoir botanique des Bunaq: percevoir et classer dans le Haut Lamaknen (Timor, Indonésie)*. Paris: Muséum National d'Histoire Naturelle, 1990. 155 pp.

[The botanical knowledge of the Bunak: observing and classifying in Upper Lamaknen.] Research into folk taxonomy and ethnobotany of a people of Timor. Included here because of its inventory of plants known to the Bunak, with an index of Bunak names. Cited from Rowland [209], who refers to further relevant works by Friedberg.

588

Nicole Revel: *Fleurs de paroles: histoire naturelle palawan. Vol. 1: Les dons de Nägsalad*. Paris: Peeters, 1990. 374 pp. 2-87723-022-8.

[Word flowers: Palawan natural history. The gifts of Nägsalad.] A survey of Palawan ethnobotany and ethnozoology, sufficiently comprehensive to be of reference value. Botanical classification based on food plants, pp. 129-214; Classification of animals, pp. 241-330; Palawan-scientific Latin glossaries of plant and animal names, pp. 335-368.

589

Bernard Vercourt: *A manual of New Guinea legumes*. Lae: Office of Forests, Division of Botany, 1979. 645 pp.

(Botany bulletin, 11.)

Includes geographical distribution. Index of scientific Latin names.

Materia medica

590

Lily M. Perry, Judith Metzger: *Medicinal plants of East and Southeast Asia: attributed properties and uses.* Cambridge, Mass.: MIT Press, 1980. 620 pp. 0-262-16076-5.

'A compilation of the published medicinal and chemical studies of the plants of the area.' Research completed in 1961. A very useful systematic survey, arranged alphabetically by family. Vernacular and English names seldom mentioned. Indexes: therapeutic properties, pp. 495-542; disorders and remedies, pp. 543-586; scientific Latin names, pp. 587-620.

591

San Khin: *Some medicinal and useful plants, both indigenous and exotic, of Burma.* Rangoon: Student Press, 1970. 147 pp.
Edited by Tha Myat.

In English and Burmese.

592

Dhavadee Ponglux and others: *Medicinal plants.* Bangkok, 1987. 279 pp. 974-7317-03-6.
International Congress on Natural Products, First Princess Chulabhorn Science Congress 1987, Medicinal Plants Exhibition Committee.

An exhibition catalogue of 137 species, listed alphabetically under scientific Latin names. Includes Thai names, chemical constituents, uses and a full page line drawing, with references to medical and pharmaceutical literature.

593

Alfred Pételot: *Les plantes médicinales du Cambodge, du Laos et du Viêtnam.* Saigon: Centre de Recherches Scientifiques et Techniques, 1952-4. 4 v.
(Archives des recherches agronomiques au Cambodge, au Laos, et au Viêtnam, 14. Archives des recherches agronomiques et pastorales au Viêt-Nam, 18, 22, 23.)

[Medicinal plants of Cambodia, Laos and Vietnam.] Vols 1-3: encyclopaedic catalogue, arranged taxonomically, giving Latin, Chinese, 'vulgaire' (English,

French etc.) and 'vernaculaire' (Vietnamese and occasionally Lao, Khmer, Srê etc.) names, botanical description, properties and use. Vol. 4: Index of therapeutic properties, pp. 9-72; Latin index, pp. 75-174; 'vulgaire' index, pp. 177-194; Vietnamese index, pp. 197-244; separate Khmer, Lao, Montagnard, Chinese and Sino-Vietnamese indexes.

594

M. Menault: *La matière médicale cambodgienne.* Hanoi, 1929. 197 pp. (Bulletin économique de l'Indochine, 200-201.)

[Cambodian materia medica.]

Note also: Douk Phana: *Contribution à l'étude des plantes médicinales du Cambodge.* Quimper, 1966. 246 pp. [Contribution to the study of Cambodian medicinal plants.]

595

Nguyễn Văn Dương and others: *Danh-từ dược-học Pháp-Việt có phần đối chiếu Việt-Pháp.* Saigon: Bộ Giáo-Dục, 1970. (Tủ sách khoa học.)

[French-Vietnamese dictionary of pharmacy, with Vietnamese index.] In tabular format, with few phrases and no examples of usage. Includes many Latin botanical names for which no precise equivalents could be given in either French or Vietnamese.

596

D. S. Vũ Văn Chuyên: *Tóm tắt đặc điểm các họ cây thuốc.* [Hanoi:] Y Học và Thể Dục Thể Thao [1966]. 120 pp. Tủ Sách Hội Dược Học Việt-Nam.

[Outline of the characteristics of medicinal plants by family.] Arranged under botanical families: brief general observations followed by an unannotated list of useful species, giving Latin and Vietnamese names. Vietnamese-Latin glossary (about 1800 entries), pp. 83-116.

597

Paul Hurrier: *Matière médicale et pharmacopée sino-annamites.* Paris: Vigot Frères, 1907. 292 pp. Université de Paris, Ecole Supérieure de Pharmacie. (1906-1907 no. 7.)

[Sino-Vietnamese materia medica and pharmacopoeia.] Based on specimens at the Ecole. Contents: History, including influence of American, Indian and Japanese medicine on the current Sino-Vietnamese materia medica; Principles; Relation of pharmacy to medicine; Drugs also used in European medicine, pp. 51-56; Systematic list of botanical sources of drugs specific to Vietnamese medicine, pp. 57-198 (concise list of uses; no botanical descriptions). A few illustrations of plants and products. Separate indexes in Latin, Chinese (in transcription), Vietnamese (quoc-ngu), Japanese (in transcription), Khmer. Chinese characters are given in the text.

Note also: G. Dumoutier: *Essai sur la pharmacie annamite: détermination de 300 plantes et produits indigènes avec leur nom en annamite, en français, en latin et en chinois et l'indication de leurs qualités thérapeutiques d'après les pharmacopées annamites et chinoises.* Hanoi: Schneider, 1887. 54 pp. [Study of Annamite pharmacy: identification of 300 indigenous plants and products with their names in Vietnamese, French, Latin and Chinese and a guide to their therapeutic properties according to Vietnamese and Chinese pharmacopoeias.]

598

John D. Gimlette: *A dictionary of Malayan medicine.* Oxford: Oxford University Press, 1939. 259 pp.

A concise encyclopaedia of indigenous medicine, including many botanical terms for plants of use in the materia medica. A mixture of short, glossary entries and long descriptive ones. Partial classified English-Malay index, pp. 251-9 (no index of plants or drugs).

Note also: John D. Gimlette: *Malay poisons and charm cures.* London: Churchill, 1929. 301 pp. Third edition ('preface to first edition' dated 1915). Part 2 (pp. 118-269) is a systematic list of animal, vegetable and inorganic poisons. Appendix 2 is a classification by natural orders. The index includes scientific Latin and Malay names.

599

Eduardo Quisumbing: *Medicinal plants of the Philippines.* Quezon City: Katha, 1978. 1262 pp.

'Revised edition.' Covers about 850 species known or supposed to have medicinal properties. Taxonomic arrangement. Names (with botanical synonymy and many local names), description, range, active constituent, uses of derivatives. Indexes of uses and of scientific and local names.

First published: Manila, 1951. 1234 pp. (Department of Agriculture and Natural Resources. Technical bulletin, 16.) The 1978 edition is a reprint of the first with substantial addenda (pp. 1235-1262).

Note also: T. H. Pardo de Tavera: *The medicinal plants of the Philippines.* Philadelphia: Blakiston, 1901. 269 pp. Translated by Jerome B. Thomas, who supplied or revised the botanical descriptions. Systematic order: discursive notes on range and usage, with usual doses, and lists of vernacular names, Spanish, Spanish-Filipino, Tagalog, Ilocano, Visayan, Bicol, Pampangan, Pangasinan. Index of all names, pp. 257-269.

First published in Spanish: T. H. Pardo de Tavera: *Plantas medicinales de Filipinas*. Madrid: Bernardo Rico, 1892. 341 pp.

MINERAL RESOURCES

600

H. L. Chhibber: *The mineral resources of Burma*. London: Macmillan, 1934. 320 pp.

Main contents: Gemstones; Jadeite; Amber; Iron ore; Coal and lignite; Gold; Lead, silver and zinc; Petroleum; Tin; Tungsten; Salt; Other minerals. Under each is a survey of known sites, with a history of their exploitation if any. Sketch maps; index of places.

Some additional material in a similar work: N. M. Penzer: *The mineral resources of Burma*. London: Routledge, 1922. 176 pp. (Federation of British Industries, Intelligence Department.) This includes a brief English-Burmese glossary of mineralogical terms and an etymological guide to some Burmese place-names.

Note also: Edwin Hall Pascoe: *The oil fields of Burma*. Calcutta: Geological Survey of India; London: Kegan Paul, 1912. 269 pp. Surveys each district in turn.

601

Gaston Dupouy: *Etudes minéralogiques sur l'Indochine Française: minéraux, minerais, gisements, eaux et limons, industrie minérale indigène, statistique*. Paris: Larose, 1913. 438 pp.

[Mineralogical researches in French Indochina: minerals, ores, deposits, rivers and alluvia, indigenous mineral industries, statistics.] The author was a scientist with the Service des Mines de l'Indochine. Cited from Cordier [242].

Note also: F. Blondel: 'La géologie et les mines de l'Indochine Français' in *Annales de l'Académie des Sciences Coloniales* vol. 6 (1933) pp. 167-322. Includes a geological map of Indochina at 1:4,000,000.

602

D. M. D. James, editor: *The geology and hydrocarbon resources of Negara Brunei Darussalam*. Bandar Seri Begawan: Muzium Brunei, 1984. 169 pp.

Based on explorations by Brunei Shell and the Geologic Survey Department.

Contents: Geographical overview; Regional geological setting; Lithostratigraphy, pp. 43-75; Palaeontology, pp. 76-92; Structure; Oil and gas resources of Brunei, pp. 103-139; Coal resources of Brunei; Other mineral resources. Generously illustrated with maps, charts and tables. Includes results of intensive offshore exploration.

For other works on the geology of Brunei and neighbouring districts see Krausse [21] p. 21.

603

Reinout Willem van Bemmelen: *The geology of Indonesia*. The Hague: Government Printing Office, 1949. 2 v.

Volume 1a: general geology. Vol. 1b: portfolio of maps. Vol. 2: economic geology.

604

W[arren] D[u Pré] Smith: *Geology and mineral resources of the Philippine Islands*. Manila, 1924. 539 pp.

With 6 folding maps, many other maps and figures. Appendices: Outline of Philippine government; Abstract of Philippine mining laws; Philippine forests and timbers; Mining lands and mine operators; Glossary of Philippine mining terms.

Languages and peoples

605

Stephen A. Wurm, Shirô Hattori, editors: *Language atlas of the Pacific area*. Canberra: Australian Academy of the Humanities, 1981-3. Portfolio of 47 plates and accompanying pages. 0-85883-239-9.
Australian National University, Research School of Pacific Studies. 'In collaboration with the Japan Academy.' Cartography by Theo Baumann. (Pacific linguistics, series C, 66-7.)

Issued in two parts: part 1: New Guinea area, Oceania, Australia (24 plates); part 2: Japan area, Philippines and Formosa (corrected to 'Taiwan' in addenda), mainland and insular south east Asia (23 plates). Excludes Burma, except Tenasserim, Kayah and southern Shan State. Beautifully printed in colour (by Kummerly & Frey). Each map is accompanied by blue text/index pages, including bibliography and detailed evaluation of sources. There is a preliminary key map; note also map 25, Language groups included in the Atlas. Five sheets of errata.

Maps 1-14: New Guinea mainland and adjacent islands: note especially 1, general map of Irian Jaya; 2-4, larger scales. Map 24, Pidgin languages, trade languages and lingue franche in New Guinea, Oceania and Australia. Maps 31-4, Philippines. Maps 35-6, Mainland south east Asia. Map 37, Peninsular Malaysia with Andaman and Nicobar Islands. Maps 38-45, Insular south east Asia: note map of Jakarta, 39 verso. No attempt is made to show results of recent population mobility and transmigrasi in Indonesia, for mapping of which see *Land resources of Indonesia* [379]. Map 46, Pidgin languages, trade languages and lingue franche in the Philippines and mainland and insular south east Asia. Map 47, Distribution of varieties of Chinese in the greater Pacific area.

606

Richard Salzner: *Sprachenatlas des indopazifischen Raums*. Wiesbaden, 1960. 2 v.

[Language atlas of the Indo-Pacific region.] Excludes Sino-Tibetan and Tai languages and those only recently introduced to the region. Includes Madagascar, Australasia and the south Pacific.

Vol. 1 sets out a classification: the Austroasiatic [Mon-Khmer], Austronesian, North Halmaheran, Papuan, Australian, Andaman, Malaccan and Kadai families are carefully subdivided and individual languages listed, pp. 1-54. Index of language names, pp. 55-107. Bibliography of sources, pp. 108-117. General legend to the maps, pp. 135-7.

Vol. 2 contains the maps (64 plates). These are neatly hand-drawn in 2 or

3 colours: languages are indicated by their classification numbers, referring to the scheme set out in vol. 1. Many place-names are also replaced by numbers, to which there is a key in vol. 1, pp. 118-134. Note general map of linguistic families, plate 1; key maps, plates 2, 19, 31, 32.

The maps are arranged in a roughly systematic sequence matching the classification, including: Mon-Khmer, plates 3-7; Austronesian languages of Malaysia, Indonesia and the Philippines, plates 10, 12-18, 20-28 (but plate 25 includes the Papuan languages of Timor); Malaccan languages, plate 11; North Halmahera, plate 29; Austronesian and Papuan languages of New Guinea, plates 46-54; Kadai, plate 64.

Very complicated to use owing to the attempt to map the finest shades of linguistic kinship, which, after all, do not always bear much relation to geography. The maps of mainland south east Asia are the least helpful, omitting two major language families and being at much too small a scale considering the great complexity of the data.

Now for most purposes superseded by Wurm [605].

607

Thomas A. Sebeok, editor: *Linguistics in east Asia and south east Asia.* The Hague: Mouton, 1967. 979 pp.
(Current trends in linguistics, 2.)

The series was planned as a survey of linguistic research on a country-by-country basis from about 1945: by the time vol. 2 appeared, fortunately, the aim had begun to change, and the five papers on south east Asia in this volume deal with research relevant to south east Asian languages carried out all over the world.

Selected contents: William S. Cornyn, 'Burma' (only 5 pp.); William J. Gedney, 'Thailand and Laos'; Laurence C. Thompson and David D. Thomas, 'Vietnam'; E. M. Uhlenbeck, 'Indonesia and Malaysia' (the longest, 52 pp., in part a condensation of and supplement to works described at 631 and 712); Judith M. Jacob, 'Linguistics in Cambodia and on Cambodian'. Note also, in the same volume, Mineya Tôru, 'Languages of south east Asia' [survey of Japanese research].

Mainland south east Asia

608

Robert Parkin: *A guide to Austroasiatic speakers and their languages.* Honolulu: University of Hawaii Press, 1991. 213 pp. 0-8248-1377-4.
(Oceanic linguistics special publications, 23.)

Arranged by linguistic subgrouping: Mon-Khmer sub-family, pp. 57-115. A dispassionate survey of the literature on this one language family, clarifying alternative namings and classifications. Index to names of ethnic groups, languages and language families, pp. 185-198. 13 location maps.

609

Introduction à la connaissance de la péninsule indochinoise. Paris, 1983. 145 pp. 2-904955-00-3.

[Introduction to the study of mainland south east Asia.] A handbook of the written languages and literatures of Burma, Cambodia, Laos, Thailand and Vietnam. Each country has a chapter: additional chapters on the Cham, the Hmong and 'the proto-Indochinese' (e.g. Bahnar, Rhadé). Each chapter covers chronology and dating (lists of month names, year names etc.), religion, language, script, printing and the press, literature, minority languages and literatures. 15 tables of scripts including Shan, Khün, Lü, Tai Neua, Red Tai, Black Tai, Yüan, Cham, Roman for Vietnamese, Roman for Montagnard languages.

610

András Höfer and others: *Die Religionen Südostasiens.* Stuttgart: Kohlhammer, 1975. 578 pp. 3-17-001158-8.
(Die Religionen der Menschheit, 23.)

[Religions of south east Asia.] A volume in an encyclopaedic series on the religions of mankind. Largely organised on an ethnological principle. Contents: Religions of the Asian negritos; Religions of the ethnic groups of further India; Religions of the minorities of Southern China; Religions of the aboriginals of Taiwan; Religions of Vietnam (pp. 293-382); Religions of Cambodia, Burma, Laos, Thailand and Malaya (pp. 384-560). Does not cover Indonesia, nor the Muslims and Christians of south east Asia.

611

Frank M. LeBar, Gerald C. Hickey, John K. Musgrave and others: *Ethnic groups of mainland Southeast Asia.* New Haven: HRAF Press, 1964. 288 pp.

A pioneer work, arranged by linguistic family. Under each language name: Orientation (i.e. identification, nomenclature, location), Settlement pattern and housing, Economy, Kin groups, Marriage and family, Sociopolitical organization, Religion. There is an index of alternative language names and a 2-sheet coloured map. On the sources of the map, which is still about the best available, see pp. ix-x.

Superseded: J. Embree, W. L. Thomas jr.: *Ethnic groups of northern Southeast Asia*. New Haven: Yale University Press, 1950; J. Embree, W. L. Thomas jr: *Ethnic map and gazetteer of northern Southeast Asia*. 1950.

There is much useful information in a collection of papers, Peter Kunstadter, editor: *Southeast Asian tribes, minorities and nations*. Princeton: Princeton University Press, 1967. 2 v. (902 pp., 15 maps).

612

L. Finot: 'Les écritures lao' in *France-Asie* nos 118-119 (March-April 1956) pp. 981-998.

[Lao scripts.] Traces the general history of the Indian-type scripts as applied to Tai languages, then describes the Lao script in detail.

Note also: Pierre-Bernard Lafont: 'Les écritures tay du Laos' and 'Les écritures du pali au Laos' in *Bulletin de l'Ecole Française d'Extrême-Orient* vol. 50 (1962) pp. 367-405 [Tai scripts of Laos; scripts used for Pali in Laos], including locations, and population estimates, for minority Tai language speakers in Laos.

Sixteen tables of Thai alphabets current in Siam. Bangkok: Vajiranana National Library, 1914. Cited from Cordier [242].

Burma

613

Makatuku Pemeke (na Nohi Pibni), C. Un Gang: *Draft of a short list of names attributed in the past and present times to one or other of the Karen tribes ... along with a temptative listing of the Karenni linked ethnological photographies*. Chiang Mai: Teroppin Hail, 1983. 44 pp.

A list of tribal names used in European publications, with many alternative spellings and etymological notes; followed by a guide to published photographs of Karenni subjects.

614

C. M. Enriquez: *Races of Burma*. Calcutta: Government of India, Central Publication Branch, 1924. 79 pp.

Compiled under the orders of the Government of India. (Handbooks for the Indian Army.)

Contents: Recruiting: seasons, methods and policy; Physique; Recruiting areas: an ethnological survey; Migrations and history. Then a more detailed ethnic survey: Mon-Khmer, pp. 29-32; Tibeto-Burmans, pp. 33-60; Tai-Chinese, pp. 61-68. Index, pp. 75-80.

615

Ethnographical survey of India: Burma. Rangoon: Office of the Superintendent, Government Printing.

A series which never attained the comprehensiveness implied by its title. No. 1: C. C. Lowis: *A note on the Palaungs of Hsipaw and Tawngpeng.* 1906. 43 pp.

No. 2: W. J. S. Carrapiett: *The Salons.* 1909. 27 pp.

No. 3: E. Jamieson: *Description of habits and customs of the Muhsös (Black and Red) also known as Lahus.* 1909. 6 pp. in questionnaire format ('**Morals.**--I cannot give an opinion').

No. 4: C. C. Lowis: *The tribes of Burma.* 1910. 111 pp. This last consists of a general survey followed by a list of authorities in tabular form. '"Tribe" means the collections of indigenous folk [that] have not attained to political cohesion; it excludes the Burmans, the Arakanese, the Talaings and the Shans.'

The *Linguistic survey of India* excludes Burma, though its surveys of linguistic groups represented in south east Asia have been useful to linguists specializing in the region. As a scion of this survey an *Ethnographical and linguistic survey of Burma* was planned, but the materials that were collected for it by Leslie Taylor were not published. See: *Ethnographical survey of Burma: questions on the social structure, beliefs, customs and economic life of the indigenous races of Burma.* 1927. 39 pp. A list of 402 questions for field work on the survey. See also: L. F. Taylor: *History of the "Ethnographical and linguistic survey of Burma" and of attempts made to save it.* London, 1933. 111 pp., a sad, if evidently one-sided, story.

Thailand

616

Jerry W. Gainey, Theraphan L. Thongkum: *Language map of Thailand handbook.* [Bangkok,] 1977. 24 pp. with folding map.
Office of State Universities, Central Institute of English Language, Indigenous Languages of Thailand Research Project.

Contents: Stages in the collection of data and preparation of map (Thai and English); List of secondary sources used to fill in incomplete data; List of provinces and districts (Thai and Roman scripts parallel). The map gives a background of administrative divisions on which coloured numerals identify locations where 39 minority languages are spoken: key to languages in Thai and English.

617

Joann L. Schrock and others: *Minority groups in Thailand*. Washington: United States Government Printing Office, 1970. 1135 pp.

American University, Cultural Information Analysis Center, Center for Research in Social Systems. (Ethnographic study series [2]. DA pam, 550-107.)

Indochina

618

S. I. Bruk: *Karta narodov Indokitaya*. Moscow, 1959. 23 pp., map.

[Map of the peoples of Indochina.] Ethnographical map and accompanying booklet.

Note also: *Carte ethnolinguistique de l'Indochine*. Hanoi: Ecole Française d'Extrême-Orient, 1949. [Ethnolinguistic map of Indochina.] One of a series of special maps based on the *Carte de l'Indochine au 2.000.000e*.

619

Louis Malleret: *Groupes ethniques de l'Indochine Française*. Saigon: Société d'Etudes Indochinoises, 1937. 62 pp., 100 plates.

[Ethnic groups of French Indochina.] Arranged according to ethnic group: each entry gives geographical location and details of customs, with an emphasis on costume both in text and illustrations. Includes ethnographical map.

The text (without map and plates) is available in English: Louis Malleret: *Ethnic groups of French Indochina*. Washington: US Joint Publications Research Service, 1962. 110 pp. (JPRS, 12359.)

620

F. M. Savina: *Guide linguistique de l'Indochine Française*. Hong Kong: Société des Missions-Etrangères, 1939. 2 v. (1198 pp.)

[Linguistic guide to French Indochina.] An eight-language glossary in tabular format: French-Vietnamese-Tho (Tai)-Man (Yao)-Miao-Cantonese-Hoclo (Hainan)-Mandarin, in alphabetical order of the French entries. Includes Sino-Vietnamese forms and corresponding Chinese characters: note the 107-page supplement at the end of vol. 1, which completes these. Appendix to vol. 2: Chinese characters for foreign and Chinese place names, for French Christian names, and for the 60-year cycle and year divisions. As regards the minority languages the work is based on bilingual dictionaries which Savina had published earlier.

Vietnam

621

Ethnographical data. Hanoi: Xunhasaba, 1972-5. 3 parts.
(Vietnamese studies, 32, 36, 41.)

Includes Lê Văn Hảo: 'Ethnological studies and research in North Vietnam',
a survey article previously published in Vietnamese in *Nghiên-cứu lịch-sử* no.
133 (July-August 1970). French edition: *Données ethnographiques.* 1972-5. 3
parts. (Etudes vietnamiennes, 32, 36, 41.)

Note also: *Mountain regions and national minorities in the Democratic Republic
of Viet Nam.* Hanoi: Xunhasaba, 1968. 225 pp. (Vietnamese studies, 15.)
French edition: *Régions montagneuses et minorités nationales en RDV.* 1967. 246
pp. (Etudes vietnamiennes, 15.)

622

Joan L. Schrock and others: *Minority groups in North Vietnam.*
Washington: United States Government Printing Office, 1972. 653 pp.
Department of the Army, Ethnographical Studies Service. (DA pam 550-110.)
Prepared by the American Institutes for Research, Kensington Office.

Part 1: *tribal* groups, with introductory section on government policy: Black
Tai; Laqua; Lati; Lolo; Man; Meo; Muong; Nhang; Nung; Puok; Red Tai;
Tho; White Tai. Part 2: *other* minorities (Catholics, pp. 535-556; Chinese, pp.
557-626). Index of variant names, followed by 16 separate indexes to the
above sections. A few illustrations and maps.

Note also: *Les minorités ethniques du Vietnam (provinces du nord).* Hanoi, 1978.
454 pp. (Institut d'Ethnologie.)

E. Diguet: *Les montagnards du Tonkin.* Paris: Challamel, 1908. 159 pp. An
early survey with some good photographs.

623

Joann L. Schrock and others: *Minority groups in the Republic of
Vietnam.* Washington: United States Government Printing Office,
1967. 1163 pp.
Department of the Army, Headquarters. Prepared by American University,
Cultural Information Analysis Center. (Ethnographic study series. DA pam
550-105.)

Insular south east Asia

624

Frank M. LeBar: *Ethnic groups of insular Southeast Asia*. New Haven: Human Relations Area Files Press, 1972-5. 2 v.

Vol. 1: *Indonesia, Andaman Islands* (pp. 4-11) *and Madagascar* (pp. 1-3). Borneo, pp. 147-197, is the longest section of this volume. Vol. 2: *Philippines and Formosa* (pp. 1-14). Under each language name, in a brief monograph (usually less than a page), information is given on nomenclature, identification, location, linguistic affiliation, demography, settlement pattern and housing, economy, kinship, marriage and family, sociopolitical organization, religion.

Malaysia

625

Asmah Haji Omar: *The Malay peoples of Malaysia and their languages*. Kuala Lumpur: Dewan Bahasa dan Pustaka, Kementerian Pelajaran Malaysia, 1983. 682 pp.

Descriptive analysis of twenty-three languages of the Austronesian family spoken in Malaysia: Malay, twelve languages of Sabah, ten of Sarawak. The language data are accompanied by an ethnographical description of each language community: settlement history, economy, religion, art and craft, social organization. Excludes related languages of Indonesia.

626

Walter William Skeat, Charles Otto Blagden: *Pagan races of the Malay peninsula*. London: Macmillan, 1906. 2 v.

Detailed ethnographic description of the aboriginal peoples (excluding Malay, Indian, Chinese and European) of West Malaysia. Contents: Vol. 1: Race (including a note on *Fasciculi Malayenses* [18] by W. L. Duckworth); Way of life. Vol. 2: Religion and folklore; Language, with comparative vocabulary.

Among many reviews (see the list in Cordier [242] col. 1259) note: R. C. Temple in *Journal of the Royal Asiatic Society* (October 1907) pp. 1099-1103.

627

Henry Ling Roth: *The natives of Sarawak and British North Borneo*. Kuala Lumpur: University of Malaya Press, 1968. 2 v.

Extensive collectanea of extracts from earlier publications and reports, based on a manuscript compilation by Hugh Brooke Low. Arranged thematically after a very thin first chapter on 'Geographical distribution', with 1 map. Many illustrations. Appendices: unpublished vocabularies of about 30 languages of Borneo, some very sketchy, of various origins and dates.

Indonesia

628
W. A. L. Stokhof, editor: *Holle lists: vocabularies in languages of Indonesia*. Canberra: Australian National University, Research School of Pacific Studies, 1980-87. 11 v. in 20.
(Pacific linguistics, series D, 17, 28, 35, 44, 49-53, 59-62, 66, 69, 71, 74-6. Materials in languages of Indonesia.)

Publication from manuscripts in the Museum Nasional, Jakarta, of 234 surviving wordlists from those collected for K. F. Holle in the late nineteenth century, translating a standard set of up to 1546 words into about 250 languages of Indonesia. Vol. 1 includes the master list with Bahasa Indonesia, Dutch and English indexes: the remaining volumes are arranged regionally. Vol. 11 ends with an index to language and dialect names for the set, and an index to maps. Contents of set, vol. 11 p. 349.

629
Koentjaraningrat: *Anthropology in Indonesia: a bibliographical review*. 343 pp. 90-247-1827-9.
Koninklijk Instituut voor Taal-, Land- en Volkenkunde. (Bibliographical series, 8.)

Listed here as a dispassionate survey of anthropological work in the Dutch East Indies and Indonesia, keyed to a bibliography, pp. 254-329.

630
B. Alkema, T. J. Bezemer: *Beknopt handboek der volkenkunde van Nederlandsch Indie*. Haarlem, 1937.

[Concise handbook of the ethnology of the Dutch East Indies.]

631
A. A. Cense, E. M. Uhlenbeck: *Critical survey of studies on the languages of Borneo*. The Hague: Nijhoff, 1958. 82 pp.
Koninklijk Instituut voor Taal-, Land- en Volkenkunde. (Bibliographical series, 2.)

The introduction surveys the language situation of Borneo. For some more recent information see Uhlenbeck's article in Sebeok [607]. Note an earlier work: Sidney H. Ray: 'The languages of Borneo' in *Sarawak Museum journal* vol. 1 no. 4 (1913) pp. 1-196.

Cense and Uhlenbeck's survey is one of a series. Note also: J. Noorduyn: *A critical survey of studies on the languages of Sulawesi*. Leiden: KITLV Press, 1991. 245 pp. 90-6718-028-9. (Bibliographical series, 18); E. M. Uhlenbeck: *A critical survey of studies on the languages of Java and Madura*. The Hague: Nijhoff, 1964. 207 pp. (Bibliographical series, 7); P. Voorhoeve: *Critical survey of studies on the languages of Sumatra*. The Hague: Nijhoff, 1955. (Bibliographical series, 1.)

632

A. Teeuw: *Dialect-atlas van/of Lombok (Indonesia)*. Djakarta, 1951. 78 sheets in portfolio.

A series of word maps based on survey in 1949-50.

This is to be consulted with: A. Teeuw: *Lombok. Een dialectgeografische studie*. 1958. 247 pp. (Verhandelingen van het Koninklijk Instituut voor Taal-, Land- en Volkenkunde, 25.) [Lombok: a study in dialect geography.]

633

C. L. Voorhoeve: *Languages of Irian Jaya: checklist, preliminary classification, language maps, wordlists*. Canberra: Australian National University, Research School of Pacific Studies, 1975.
(Pacific linguistics, series B, 31.)

Contents: Index of language names; Classification; Main list of languages (199 entries) with bibliographical references, pp. 21-60; Maps, pp. 62-79, now superseded by Wurm [605] sheets 1-4; glossary of forty words in 191 languages.

Philippines

634

Harold C. Conklin: *Ethnographic atlas of Ifugao: a study of environment, culture and society in northern Luzon*. New Haven: Yale University Press, 1980. 116 pp. 0-300-02529-7.
With the special assistance of Pugguwon Lupaih and Miklos Pinther; with the co-operation of the American Geographical Society of New York.

Introduction, with many photographs, on the local culture of Ifugao and its relation to the environment. About 120 maps in fine colour, 184 figures, 9 tables: a remarkably successful demonstration of the power of cartography, in conjunction with text and illustration, in explaining human culture.

Note also: Curtis D. McFarland: *A linguistic atlas of the Philippines*. Tokyo, 1980; Manila: Linguistic Society of the Philippines, 1981. 131 pp.

635
Teodoro A. Llamzon: *Handbook of Philippine language groups*. Quezon City: Ateneo de Manila University Press, 1978. 152 pp.
For UNESCO.

25 chapters each devoted to an ethnolinguistic group, surveying customs, beliefs, institutions and language. Location maps. Introductory chapter discusses classification.

Note also: Lawrence A. Reid, editor: *Philippine minor languages: word lists and phonologies*. Honolulu: University of Hawaii Press, 1971. (Oceanic linguistics special publications, 8.)

Juan R. Francisco: *Philippine palaeography*. Quezon City: Linguistic Society of the Philippines, 1973. 135 pp. (Philippine journal of linguistics. Special monograph issue, 3.)

636
Frederic H. Sawyer: *The inhabitants of the Philippines*. London: Sampson Low, 1900. 422 pp.

A series of chapters, one on each ethnic group, giving their locations, way of life, economy, etc., with photographs. Preceded by a discusrive introductory section (pp. 1-200) on history and general culture.

NATIONAL LANGUAGES

637
Bernard Comrie, editor: *The major languages of east and south-east Asia*. London: Routledge, 1990. 234 pp. 0-415-04739-0.

Chapters by academic linguists on: Tai languages; Thai; Vietnamese; Sino-Tibetan languages; Chinese; Burmese; Japanese; Korean; Austronesian languages; Malay; Tagalog. Brief surveys of linguistic history, writing systems, phonology and grammar.

Extracted from: Bernard Comrie, editor: *The world's major languages*. London: Croom Helm, 1987. Note the 'new edition' of this: London: Routledge, 1991. 1040 pp. 0-415-04516-9.

638

Patricia Herbert and Anthony Milner, editors: *South-East Asia languages and literatures: a select guide*. Whiting Bay, Arran: Kiscadale [1988]. 182 pp. 1-870838-10-6.

A collective work instigated by the South East Asia Library Group. Deals with the ruling languages of Burma, Cambodia, Indonesia, Laos, Malaysia, the Philippines, Thailand, Vietnam; some information on minority languages and literatures of Indonesia; also chapter on 'Overseas Chinese', pp. 171-182. Each chapter covers dating system, language, script (no tables), manuscripts, printing and the press, literature.

639

Alessandro Bausani: *Le letterature del sud-est asiatico: birmana, siamese, laotiana, cambogiana, viêtnamita, giavanese, malese-indonesiana, filippina*. Firenze: Sansoni; Milano: Accademia, 1970. 442 pp.
(Le letterature del mondo, 37.)

[The literatures of south east Asia: Burmese, Thai, Laotian, Cambodian, Vietnamese, Javanese, Malay/Indonesian, Philippine.] Historical surveys of the national language literatures plus Javanese. Laotian is included as an appendix to Thai; Philippine literature gets in only as a brief section (pp. 71-4) in the introduction. Separate indexes for each chapter, six in all.

Note also: P.-B. Lafont, D. Lombard, editors: *Littératures contemporaines de l'Asie du Sud-Est*. Paris: L'Asiathèque, 1974. 327 pp. (Colloque du XXIXe Congrès des Orientalistes.) [Contemporary literatures of south east Asia: a workshop of the 29th Congress of Orientalists.] Contains useful surveys of contemporary national literatures, especially popular publishing, in most countries of the region (no papers on Singapore or Brunei). No index.

BURMESE

Burmese dictionaries and encyclopaedias

640

Myanma abidan akyin-gyok. Rangoon, 1982-[1985?]. 5 v.

[Big Burmese dictionary.] Modern encyclopaedic dictionary of the Webster kind, entirely in Burmese, illustrated with line drawings. About 37,000 entries.

641

Myanma swèzon kyan. Rangoon, 1954-?. 15 v.

[Burmese encyclopaedia.] Large scale alphabetical encyclopaedia, entirely in Burmese, fully illustrated in monochrome. Each volume contains a list of foreign names occurring in the text with roman (English) equivalents, but no index. Complete table of contents at end of vol. 15.

Accompanied by an annual supplement, 1978- . This contains a chronology of the year and an alphabetical section with articles on significant personalities and events. Last edition seen: 1986.

642

Maung Kyaw Htun: *Pakinnaka-dipani kyan*. Rangoon, 1873. 467 pp.

An old-fashioned encyclopedic miscellany, entirely in Burmese.

Burmese bilingual dictionaries

643

U Hoke Sein: *The universal Burmese-English-Pali dictionary*. Rangoon, 1981. 1066 pp.

A remarkable, perhaps unique, work offering Pali translations for many modern and scientific terms. Large enough (about 60,000 entries) to be of considerable use as a Burmese-English dictionary in spite of the brevity of individual entries. Includes scientific Latin names for flora and fauna. The Pali is naturally in Burmese script.

644

J. A. Stewart, C. W. Dunn and others: *A Burmese-English dictionary*. Parts 1-6 [no more published]. [London: School of Oriental and African Studies] 1940-81. 0-7286-0092-7.
Parts 1-2 'under the auspices of the University of Rangoon'; parts 3-6 published by the School of Oriental and African Studies.

Compilation was begun by the Burma Research Society in 1925. A large scale work modelled on the *Oxford English Dictionary*, with many examples of usage, covering written Burmese from the fifteenth century. Abandoned before reaching the end of the first letter of the alphabet (which, in the sequence adopted here, is A). Continuation of the work at the same speed, incidentally, would have produced a complete dictionary in 320 years.

For the history of the project see: Hla Pe: 'A short history of *A Burmese-English dictionary*, 1913-1963' in C. D. Cowan, O. W. Wolters, editors: *Southeast Asian history and historiography: essays presented to D. G. E. Hall*. Ithaca: Cornell University Press, 1976, pp. 86-99.

645

The Judson Burmese-English dictionary. Rangoon: American Baptist Mission Press, 1921. 1123 pp.

Revised and enlarged by Robert C. Stevenson; revised and edited by Rev. F. H. Eveleth.

This may be regarded as the fourth edition. With about 27,500 entries it is still in many ways the best complete Burmese-English dictionary (but note also U Hoke Sein [643]). Appendices: Notes (brief encyclopedic entries for Buddhist concepts) pp. 1062-1099; Buddhist proverbs and quaint sayings, pp. 1100-04; Formal and colloquial phraseology contrasted, pp. 1105-11; Antonyms, pp. 1112-23.

Reprinted: *Judson's Burmese-English dictionary.* Rangoon: Baptist Board of Publications, 1953, with a 'Preface to the Centenary edition' by F. G. Dickason; and several other reprints.

[Third edition:] *Judson's Burmese-English dictionary.* Rangoon, 1893. Revised and enlarged by Robert C. Stevenson, Burma Commission. 1194 pp. Burmese proverbs, aphorisms and quaint sayings, pp. 1189-94. See the review of this 1893 edition: R. F. St. Andrew St. John: 'The new Burmese dictionary' in *Journal of the Royal Asiatic Society* (July 1894) pp. 556-8.

Second edition: A. Judson: *A dictionary, Burmese and English.* Rangoon: American Baptist Mission Press, 1883. 783 pp. 'Preface to the second edition' by Edward O. Stevens. Appendices: 'A grammar of the Burmese language' by A. Judson, pp. 657-704 [this was also issued separately: 1883. 52 pp.]; Geographical names, Burmese and foreign, pp. 707-737; Scripture proper names (from a manuscript by Judson), pp. 740-780; Hebrew and Greek loanwords used in the Burmese Bible, pp. 781-2.

First edition: Moulmein: American Mission Press, 1852. This was prepared for the press by E. A. Stevens, father of the foregoing, who added some terms (particularly for flora and fauna) in square brackets.

An earlier version of Judson's material had been published as: *A dictionary of the Burman language with explanations in English: compiled from the manuscripts of A. Judson, D. D. and of other missionaries in Burmah.* Calcutta: Thacker, 1826. 411 pp.

These Burmese-English dictionaries are paired with: *Judson's English and Burmese dictionary.* Rangoon: American Baptist Mission Press, 1901. 928 pp. Fifth edition. This is the latest version, having been revised and enlarged successively by Rev. E. O. Stevens, Dr Francis Mason, Rev. F. H. Eveleth and Miss Phinney. Judson's English-Burmese dictionary, with about 20,000 concise entries, is a smaller work than its companion, and is now for most practical purposes superseded.

Subsequent editions of it are reprints of the fifth, e.g. the 'unabridged tenth edition': Rangoon: Baptist Board of Publications, 1966. 928 pp.

First edition: A. Judson: *A dictionary, English and Burmese.* Moulmein, 1849. 589 pp.

On the author of these dictionaries see (among many other sources): Francis Wayland: *A memoir of the life and labours of the Rev. Adoniram Judson, D. D.* Boston: Phillips, Sampson, 1853. 2 v. Also published: London: Nisbet, 1853. 2 v.

646

Maung Ba Han: *The University English-Burmese dictionary.* Rangoon: Hanthawaddy Press, 1951-66. 2292 pp.

A vast work by a scholar well versed in both languages (Barrister of Lincoln's Inn; Professor Emeritus of Law, Rangoon): about 80,000 entries, many of some length and complexity, with lively examples. The best available.

Note also: *The Khit Pyin English English Burmese dictionary.* Rangoon: Moe Wai, 1960. Various paginations. Compiled by Sun Htoo editorial staff. This does not match its competitor in size, but is still a massive work. Some of the space is taken up (as indicated by the title) in the provision of English as well as Burmese definitions of headwords. The English is far from infallible (e.g. 'auxilliary') and many headwords are of doubtful value (e.g. 'availably').

647

Denise Bernot: *Dictionnaire birman-français.* Paris: SELAF, Peeters, 1978- .

[Burmese-French dictionary.] A large scale dictionary, reproduced from typescript of unfortunately poor legibility, with numerous illustrations. Almost complete in 14 volumes of about 250 pp. each. Will end with the vowel characters, and thus has not yet duplicated the *Burmese-English dictionary* [644]. The total number of entries will be around 35,000, many quite lengthy.

648

Annemarie Esche: *Wörterbuch Burmesisch-Deutsch.* Leipzig: Verlag Enzyklopädie, 1976. 546 pp.

[Burmese-German dictionary.] Only about 15,000 entries: worth noting, however, because of the shortage of modern bilingual Burmese dictionaries.

649

N. N. Novikov, V. P. Kolobkov, U Ei Shwe: *Russko-birmanskii slovar'*.
Moscow: Sovetskaya Entsiklopediya, 1966. 880 pp.

[Russian-Burmese dictionary.] About 27,000 entries. Appendix of
geographical names, pp. 872-880.

Burmese specialized dictionaries

650

The political, social and economic terminology, English-Burmese. Rangoon:
Myo Myint Aye, 1970. 524 pp.
'All rights reserved by Daw Myo Myint Aye, Daw Oo Khin.'

A fairly wide-ranging supplement to English-Burmese dictionaries; includes
entries for proper names ('Zeno of Elea'; 'Zinoviev, G. E.' On pp. 503-524 are
English-Burmese glossaries of Burmese and international associations.

Note also: Ngwe Daung Byu: *The dictionary of current Burmese words*.
Rangoon, 1969. 480 pp. Intended as an appendix to Burmese dictionaries,
this gives explanations for neologisms relevant to current affairs. Entirely
in Burmese, except that English forms are appended to entries for English
loanwords.

651

Daw Yi Yi: *Thu-tei-thana abidan-mya hmat-su*. Rangoon, 1974. 512 pp.

[Dictionary of historical terminology.] An explanatory dictionary, entirely
in Burmese.

652

Scientific and technical terms, A-Z. Rangoon: Ministry of Education,
1980. 1202 pp.

An English-Burmese dictionary of technical terms in compact tabular
format. About 80,000 entries. Previously issued in 8 parts, 1971-4.

Burmese idioms and phrases

653

Hla Pe: *Burmese proverbs*. London: Murray, 1962. 114 pp.

Almost 500 proverbs, arranged thematically, with English translations.

Burmese language and script

654

John Okell: *A reference grammar of colloquial Burmese*. London: Oxford University Press, 1969. 2 v. 0-19-713558-7.

A modern scientific analysis of the language. Vol. 1: Sounds; Verbs; Nouns and noun phrases; Interjections; Particles; Complements in verb phrases; Clauses and sentences; Co-ordination; Postpositions; Counting and measuring. Part 2: Alphabetical list of particles and common words with grammatical notes and examples, forming an important supplement to existing Burmese dictionaries.

Note also: Maun Maun Nyun [Maung Maung Nyunt] and others: *Birmanskii yazyk*. Moscow: Nauka, 1963. [The Burmese language.] Brief grammar in Russian in a standard format.

And: U Pe Maung Tin: *Myanma thada*. Rangoon: Burma Translation Society, 1954. [Burmese grammar.] A traditional grammar, entirely in Burmese.

655

John Okell: *A guide to the romanization of Burmese*. London: Royal Asiatic Society, 1971. 69 pp.
(James G. Furlong fund, 27.)

A survey of available systems, with a recommended standard.

Among earlier works on the subject note: Ch. Duroiselle: 'The literal transliteration of the Burmese alphabet' in *Journal of the Burma Research Society* vol. 6 (1916). This kind of transliteration is normally adopted for early inscriptions.

I have not seen: R. B. Hancock: *Phonetic transliteration for the writing of English names in Burman signs and Burman names in English signs*. Rangoon: American Baptist Mission Press [1883]. 44 pp. Cited from Cordier [242].

KHMER

Khmer dictionaries

656

Vacananukrama Khmera = Dictionnaire cambodgien. Phnom-Penh, 1967-8. 2 v. (1858 pp.).
Institut Bouddhique.

[Khmer dictionary.] Fifth edition of a medium-scale work (about 25,000 entries, many of some length), the only seriously useful dictionary that is entirely in Khmer.

Reprinted: n.p. [1981]. 1888 pp. 'Under the auspices of the Japan Committee for the Republication and Relief of Cambodian Buddhist Books.'

Fourth edition: 1962; second edition: 1951.

First edition: Phnom Penh: Editions de la Bibliothèque Royale du Cambodge, 1938-43.

Khmer bilingual dictionaries

657

Robert K. Headley and others: *Cambodian-English dictionary*. Washington: Catholic University of America Press, 1977. 2 v. (1495 pp.)
Bureau of Special Research in Modern Languages. (Publications in the languages of Asia, 3.)

A very comprehensive work; about 30,000 entries with many sub-entries. Khmer script, phonetic transcription, gloss; includes indication of origin of loanwords. 'The text was prepared on a Varityper machine with a Khmer font which inexplicably lacked certain letters:' nonetheless clear printing. 13 plates (at end of vol. 2) giving terminology for agricultural implements, musical instruments, etc. Brief introduction includes notes on script and alphabetical order.

Note also: Judith M. Jacob: *A concise Cambodian-English dictionary*. London: Oxford University Press, 1974. 242 pp. 0-19-713574-9. (School of Oriental and African Studies.) About 8000 entries: spacious layout makes the work easy to read. Khmer script followed by phonetic transcription and English glosses. Extensive notes on orthography, transcription, alphabetical order etc., pp. xi-xxxii.

658

Franklin E. Huffman, Im Proum: *English-Khmer dictionary*. New Haven: Yale University Press, 1978. 690 pp. 0-300-02261-1.
(Yale linguistic series.)

About 28,000 brief entries, very clearly printed in a letter-quality typewriter face. Short introduction.

Note also: Preap-Sokh: *Dictionary, English-Cambodian*. Phnom Penh, 1957. 992 pp. In tabular form: English, English pronunciation in Khmer script, Khmer gloss.

659

J. Guesdon: *Dictionnaire cambodgien-français.* Paris: Plon, 1930. 2 v. (1982 pp.).

[Khmer-French dictionary.] The work was compiled in the late 19th century and long remained in manuscript. About 20,000 entries, many of considerable length, with cross-references and notes to explain etymology. Outdated but still useful. Tables of alphabet and numerals, pp. 7*-12*.

660

Tep Yok, Thao Kun: *Dictionnaire français-khmer.* Phnom-Penh: Librairie Bouth-Neang, 1962-4. 2 v.

[French-Khmer dictionary.] The largest bilingual dictionary of Khmer: about 50,000 entries with many phrases and specimen sentences. Some addenda in preliminary pages. Intended for Cambodian users.

Since this is not widely available it may be worth noting some briefer alternatives: Sam-Thang: *Lexique franco-khmère.* Phnom Penh, 1961. 891 pp. [French-Khmer dictionary.] About 32,000 brief entries. Aimed at Cambodian users. Very poor printing. Paired with: Sam-Thang: *Lexique khmère-français.* Phnom Penh, 1962. [Khmer-French dictionary.]

A similar work: Tep Yok, Ly Vouong, Thao Kun: *Petit dictionnaire français-cambodgien.* Phnom-Penh: Librairie Phnom-Penh, 1969. 1003 pp. [Little French-Cambodian dictionary.]

Somewhat larger than these: Tep Yok, Thao Kun: *Petit dictionnaire français-khmer.* Phnom-Penh: Librairie Phnom-Penh, 1967. 1377 pp. [Little French-Khmer dictionary.] About 35,000 entries with some exemplification.

A work of similar parentage to the last two was reprinted about 1977 without authors' names as: *Petit dictionnaire français khmer.* Boulogne Billancourt: Alliance Christian et Missionaire [*sic*]; Groningen: Comite Hulpverlenning Z. O. Asie, n.d. 808 pp.

661

S. Tandart: *Dictionnaire français-cambodgien.* Hong Kong: Société des Missions-Etrangères, 1910-11. 2 v.

[French-Khmer dictionary.] In tabular format: gives Khmer terms in script and transliteration. Very outdated, but not entirely superseded. See the review by: E. Huber in *Bulletin de l'Ecole Française d' Extrême-Orient* vol. 10 (July-September 1910) pp. 623-5.

Paired with: S. Tandart: *Dictionnaire cambodgien-français.* Phnom-Penh: Imprimerie Albert Portail, 1935. 2 v. (1272 pp.) [Khmer-French dictionary.]

About 24,000 brief entries in tabular format. Now seldom used.

662

Yu. A. Gorgoniyev; Long Seama, editor: *Kkhmersko-russkii slovar'*. Moscow: Russkii Yazyk, 1984. 983 pp.

[Khmer-Russian dictionary.] 'Second edition.' About 20,000 entries in a very large typeface. Russian index, compiled by V. I. Tomilov, pp. 953-983.

First edition: Y. A. Gorgoniev: *Dictionnaire khmer-russe*. 1975. 952 pp. [Khmer-Russian dictionary.] Not seen: I wonder if this differs only in having no Russian index?

Khmer idioms and phrases

663

R. Kovin: *Mots culturels khméro-français expliqués*. Phnom Penh, 1964.

[Cambodian-French glossary of cultural terms.] Cited from Aschmoneit [23].

664

P. S. Dhammarama, Ly Vou-Ong: *Lexique français-cambodgien expliqué*. Phnom-Penh: Librairie Phnom-Penh, 1963. 1016 pp.

[French-Khmer explanatory dictionary.] An alphabetically arranged phrasebook giving sample sentences in French and Khmer arranged under French keywords. Appendix of country and nationality names, pp. 1005-1016.

665

Hoàng-Hoc: *Tù diên Viêt-Khome*. Hanoi: Nhà Xuât Ban Khoa Hoc Xa Hôi, 1978. 2 v. (1803 pp.)

[Vietnamese-Khmer dictionary.] Very poor paper and printing, though the Khmer text is typeset.

Khmer language and script

666

Judith M. Jacob: *Introduction to Cambodian*. London: Oxford University Press, 1968. 341 pp. 0-19-713556-0.

A textbook for learning the language and script, but sufficiently systematic to be useful as a reference grammar. In section 1 'Pronunciation and orthography' (pp. 3-53) Khmer script and IPA are used in parallel; in the 'Grammar' and 'Vocabulary', unfortunately, only IPA is given.

Note also: Y. A. Gorgoniyev: *The Khmer language*. Moscow: Nauka, 1966. (Languages of Asia and Africa.) A brief scientific description of the language, using phonetic transcription only.

Previously published in Russian: Yu. A. Gorgoniyev: *Kkhmerskii yazyk*. 1961.

667
Georges Maspero: *Grammaire de la langue khmère (cambodgien)*. Paris, 1915.
Ecole Française d'Extrême-Orient.

[Grammar of the Khmer (Cambodian) language.]

LAO

Lao dictionaries

668
Vacananukom phasa law. Vientiane, 1962. 1145 pp.
Comité Littéraire. Edited by Maha Sila Viravong.

[Dictionary of the Lao language.] Small page size. A modest, 10,000-entry dictionary, but the only one entirely in Lao. No guidance on pronunciation. Innovative filing order based on initial and final consonants.

Lao bilingual dictionaries

669
Allen D. Kerr: *Lao-English dictionary*. Washington: Consortium Press, Catholic University of America Press, 1972. 2 v. (1223 pp.).
(Publications in the languages of Asia, 2.)

Lao in both script and phonetic transcription: about 24,000 entries. 'The first reasonably comprehensive dictionary of the Lao language' (forgetting Reinhorn [670] and Guignard [671]!). 'Every [entry] has been discussed with at least three different [Lao] speakers.' Sources for botanical and zoological terms, carefully acknowledged, include Vidal [541] and Deuve [516]. Includes indication of Pali and Sanksrit origin of loanwords. Tables of alphabetical order, pp. xii-xvii. List of classifiers, pp. xxi-xxiii.

Note also: Russell Marcus: *English-Lao Lao-English dictionary*. Rutland: Tuttle, 1970. 416 pp. 0-8048-0909-7. A pocket dictionary. The English-Lao part includes both phonetic and Lao scripts. Brief guidance on pronunciation and filing order. Partly based on the larger dictionary by Kerr, which already existed in manuscript.

I have seen a reference to a 'revised edition' (1983. 416 pp.) of Marcus, but I believe it is a ghost.

670

Marc Reinhorn: *Dictionnaire laotien-français*. Paris: Centre National de la Recherche Scientifique, 1970. 2 v. (2151 pp.).
Centre de Documentation sur l'Asie du Sud-Est. (Atlas ethno-linguistique, 4e série: Dictionnaires.)

[Lao-French dictionary.] A fourth edition, much larger than its predecessors: about 40,000 entries. Entries give both Lao script and phonetic transcription. Annotations include etymology of loanwords and references to sources, e.g. Vidal [541]. Introductory matter: Language and script; Alphabetical order, pp. xvii-xviii; Weights and measures, pp. xxix-xxx; Money; Chronology, pp. xxxii-vi (with Lao calendar reproduced on xliii-xlviii); List of classifiers; Administrative map; Compass points, p. xlix. Note long list of corrigenda, pp. 2143-50.

The bibliography (pp. xxv-xxviii) includes several specialized Lao-French glossaries on military and administrative subjects.

See the review by: J. Filliozat in *Revue asiatique* vol. 259 pp. 387-390.

Earlier edition: Vientiane: Mission Militaire Française d'Instruction, 1968. 676 pp. Roneoed. Claims to represent only a slight revision of its predecessor. General guidance on pronunciation: headwords are in Lao script without romanization.

Earlier edition(s): Paris: CMISOM. 5 v. (634 pp.) Roneoed. Not seen, and variously dated 1954, 1955, 1956 in references.

671

Théodore Guignard: *Dictionnaire laotien-français*. Hong Kong: Imprimerie de Nazareth, 1912. 959 pp.

[Lao-French dictionary.] Tabular format in three columns: script, romanization, gloss. Prefatory matter includes: Note on geography, history and ethnography, pp. iv-xvi; Grammar, pp. xvii-xlviii; Chronology; Weights, measures and money; Kinship terms; Script, pp. lvii-lxx. Folding comparative chart of Tai alphabets.

See the review by: [Henri Cordier] in *T'oung pao* (May 1913) pp. 299-302.

672

M.-J. Cuaz: *Lexique français-laotien*. Hong Kong: Société des Missions-Etrangères, 1904. 490 pp.

[French-Lao dictionary.] With an introductory ethnolinguistic survey of Laos and a brief grammatical outline of Lao. Not seen.

673

L. N. Morev: *Russko-laosskii uchebnyi slovar' dlya prodvinutogo etapa.* Moscow: Russkii Yazyk, 1985. 560 pp.

[Concise Russian-Lao dictionary for advanced students.] About 5000 entries: beautifully printed Lao script. Appendices: Names of republics of the USSR, pp. 556-7; Names of socialist countries and international organizations; Numerals.

Lao idioms and phrases

674

T. Hishino: *Lao phrase book.* Vientiane: Kats Books, 1969. 169 pp.

Lao script, phonetic rendering, English translation. From typescript. Intended for toursits: worth noting in view of the shortage of Lao dictionaries.

675

Russell Marcus: *Lao proverbs.* Bangkok: Craftsman Press, 1969. 56 pp.

Arranged under theme. For each proverb is given Lao text, transcription, literal translation, attempted equivalent. An illustrated, popular work.

Based on a selection from: *Supasit buran.* Vientiane: Comité Littéraire, 1961. [Traditional proverbs.]

Lao language and script

676

L. N. Morev, A. A. Moskalev, Y. Y. Plam: *The Lao language.* Moscow: Nauka, 1979. 129 pp.
(Languages of Asia and Africa.)

A grammar intended for comparative linguists. Contents: Phonology; Script, pp. 24-30; Lexicon and word formation; Parts of speech; Syntax. Both Lao script (mostly handwritten) and a semi-phonological transcription are given throughout. One of a very extensive and important series of brief descriptive grammars.

First published in Russian: L. N. Morev, A. A. Moskalyov, Yu. Ya. Plam: *Laoskii yazyk.* 1972.

Note also: Marc Reinhorn: *Grammaire de la langue lao*. Paris: Samuelian, 1980. 204 pp. [Grammar of the Lao language.] Lao script and a literal transliteration throughout. Includes a chapter on verse prosody.

677

Maha Sila Viravong: *Lak phasa lao*. Bangkok, 1962.

[Principles of the Lao language.] A grammar on traditional Pali principles, adapted from the Thai grammar of Upakit Silpasarn [**729**]. Cited from Gedney's paper in Sebeok [**607**]. The same author published a Pali grammar in Lao: Vientiane, 1960. 3 v.

MALAY

Malay dictionaries and encyclopaedias

678

Kamus Dewan. Kuala Lumpur: Dewan Bahasa dan Pustaka, 1989. 1480 pp. 983-62-0979-4.

[Bureau dictionary.] Second edition. A big monolingual Bahasa Malaysia dictionary, beautifully printed. About 45,000 entries, with many subheadings and examples.

First edition: 1970. 1352 pp. Edited by Teuku Iskandar.

679

Kamus besar bahasa Indonesia. Jakarta: Balai Pustaka, 1988. 1090 pp. 979-407-182-X.
Pusat Pembinaan dan Pengembangan Bahasa, Tim Penyusun Kamus. (BP, 3658.)

[Big Bahasa Indonesia dictionary.] A large scale monolingual dictionary: about 50,000 entries. Appendices: Grammar and stylistics, pp. 1024-55; Scripts used in Indonesia; Abbreviations, pp. 1058-68; Gazetteer of administrative subdivisions of Indonesia, pp. 1069-82; Currencies (and, incidentally, names of countries), pp. 1083-5.

On a smaller scale: W. J. S. Poerwadarminta: *Kamus umum bahasa Indonesia*. 1976. 1156 pp. (BP, 1866.) [Popular Bahasa Indonesia dictionary.] Fifth edition: about 30,000 entries.

Fourth edition: 1966. 632 pp. Third edition: 1960. 903 pp. Second edition: 1954. 903 pp. First edition: 1952.

680

Ensiklopedi nasional Indonesia. Jakarta: Cipta Adi Pustaka, 1988-91. 18 v.

[Indonesian national encyclopaedia.] A long-entry comprehensive illustrated alphabetical encyclopaedia in Bahasa Indonesia, with signed articles. Vol. 18 is the index for the set.

681

Hassan Shadily, editor: *Ensiklopedi Indonesia.* Jakarta: Ichtiar Baru-van Hoeve, 1980. 7 v. (4389 pp.).

[Indonesian encyclopaedia.] A short-entry illustrated encyclopaedia lacking a full index, though there is a long list of cross-references in vol. 7 (pp. 4081-4296). This is followed by a section of national information. Thematic sections in preliminaries of each volume: vol. 1: Indonesian constitution; vol. 2: Astronomy and geology; vol. 3: languages; vol. 4: botany; vol. 5: world geography; vol. 6: mathematical and chemical data; vol. 7: historical chart (reprinted from first edition).

First edition: *Ensiklopedia Indonesia.* Bandung: van Hoeve, n.d. [c. 1954]. 3 v. (1446 pp.). Already illustrated, and with similar thematic information in preliminaries: note list of Indonesian cabinets, 1945-53, in vol. 1.

682

R. O. Winstedt: *Kamus bahasa Melayu.* Singapore, 1960. 338 pp.

[Dictionary of Malay.] A concise monolingual dictionary recording an earlier stage of the fast-developing language.

Malay bilingual dictionaries

683

A. Teeuw: *Indonesisch-Nederlands woordenboek.* Leiden: KITLV, 1990. 764 pp. 90-6718-021-1.
Koninklijk Instituut voor Taal-, Land- en Volkenkunde.

[Bahasa Indonesia-Dutch dictionary.] The current representative of a long tradition of Malay-Dutch lexicography. About 28,000 entries.

Earlier version: W. J. S. Poerwadarminta and A. Teeuw: *Indonesisch-Nederlands woordenboek.* Groningen: Wolters, 1952. 383 pp. Second edition of a work strong in the traditional literary vocabulary of Malay.

First edition: 1950. 369 pp.

684

H. C. Klinkert: *Nieuw maleisch-nederlandsch woordenboek met arabisch karakter*. Leiden: Brill. 1047 pp.

[New Malay-Dutch dictionary in Arabic script.] About 20,000 entries: headwords in Jawi followed by romanization.

Fourth printing: 1930.

685

John M. Echols and Hassan Shadily: *An Indonesian-English dictionary*. Ithaca: Cornell University Press, 1989. 618 pp.
Revised by John U. Wolff, James T. Collins.

The standard Bahasa Indonesia-English dictionary, an important feature of which is that it resolves a defect of the romanization of Malay by distinguishing the open 'e' vowel as *é*.

Second edition: 1963. 431 pp. 0-8014-0112-7. About 16,000 entries: expanded by including many loanwords omitted from its predecessor.

First edition: 1961. 384 pp.

Note also: A. E. Schmidgall-Tellings, Alan M. Stevens: *A contemporary Indonesian-English dictionary*. Athens, Ohio: Ohio University Press, 1981. 388 pp. This was useful as a supplement to the standard dictionaries owing to its concentration on neologisms and new meanings.

686

R. O. Winstedt: *An unabridged Malay-English dictionary*. Kuala Lumpur, Singapore: Marican & Sons, 1965. 390 pp.

Sixth edition. By no means as comprehensive as its title would suggest. I have noted no more recent Bahasa Malaysia-English dictionary.

The author's first Malay-English dictionary was: R. Winstedt: *Dictionary of colloquial Malay*. Singapore, 1920. 175 pp. On his contribution to Malay studies see: *Malayan and Indonesian studies: essays presented to Sir Richard Winstedt*. 1964.

687

R. J. Wilkinson: *A Malay-English dictionary (romanised)*. Mytilene, 1932. 2 v.

About 26,000 entries: never superseded as a large scale dictionary of older literary Malay. The eventful history of the work, its loss in the sack of Smyrna in 1922 and obstinate recompilation, can be read in the preface (pp.

i-iv). 'Mytilene [on the Greek island of Lesbos] is a poor centre for Malay studies. My only local helper has been my wife. Printing also was hard in a place where no compositor knows English, much less Malay,' but the printers, Salavopoulos & Kinderlis, did well. Malay manuscripts had provided the initial vocabulary (precise references to sources are given) but 'many Malay terms lie quite outside literature'. Indicates origin of loanwords. Scientific Latin names are given for plants and animals: 'in most cases that meant catching the fish and having it identified by a zoologist.'

688

R. J. Wilkinson: *A Malay-English dictionary*. Singapore: Kelly & Walsh, 1901-3. 776 pp.

A lavishly printed dictionary of Malay in jawi (romanization is also given). In Arabic alphabetical order: index in roman script, 54 pp. at end, followed by 'Malay names of snakes', 1 page.

689

Kamus inggeris-melayu Dewan = An English-Malay dictionary. Kuala Lumpur: Dewan Bahasa dan Pustaka, 1992. 1945 pp.

Begun by the Australian National University and taken over by the Malaysian Language and Literature Bureau in 1977. A large scale work with over 40,000 entries. 'What distinguishes it from other English-Malay dictionaries published to date is that it does not give definitions, but instead provides Malay equivalents based on context and usage.' Intended for people who speak English as their first or second language. A highly professional, well-planned and well-produced dictionary.

Contrasted with: *Kamus dwibahasa: bahasa inggeris-bahasa Malaysia*. Kuala Lumpur: Dewan Bahasa dan Pustaka, Kementerian Pelajaran Malaysia, 1981. 1457 pp. [Bilingual dictionary, English-Bahasa Malaysia.] Intended for Malay speakers: about 28,000 entries, often with explanation rather than translation in Malay.

690

Peter Salim: *The contemporary English-Indonesian dictionary*. Jakarta: Modern English Press, 1989. 2358 pp.

Fourth edition. 'A colossal work of art' (Salim). Over 60,000 entries, some very lengthy with useful phrases and sentences, but also some rather odd English. Reproduced from neat typescript: some line drawings.

First edition: 1985.

Note also: John M. Echols, Hassan Shadily: *Kamus Inggris-Indonesia*. Jakarta:

Gramedia, 1975. 660 pp. About 33,000 concise entries: a very practical work, well printed and compact, 'primarily for the use of Indonesians.' Also published as: John M. Echols, Hassan Shadily: *An English-Indonesian dictionary.* Ithaca: Cornell University Press, 1975. 0-8014-0728-1.

691

William Marsden: *A dictionary and grammar of the Malayan language.* 1812. 2 v.

Vol. 1 (589 pp.) is the dictionary, Malay-English and English-Malay. Malay headwords and glosses are given in jawi and roman; examples and sub-headings in roman only. Vol. 2: Grammar (225 pp.). Both dictionary and grammar may still be useful as forming a substantial description of the language before significant English and Dutch influences and before the division between Malaysian and Indonesian usage.

Reprinted: Singapore: Oxford University Press, 1984. (Oxford in Asia historical reprints.) With an introduction by Russell Jones.

692

Pierre Labrousse: *Dictionnaire général indonésien-français.* Paris: Association Archipel, 1984. 934 pp.
(Cahier d'Archipel, 14.)

[General Bahasa Indonesia-French dictionary.] About 27,000 entries, with generous exemplification; many sub-entries. Very well laid out.

693

Farida Soemargono, Winarsih Arifin: *Dictionnaire français-indonésien.* Paris: Association Archipel, 1991. 1115 pp. 979-511-388-7.
(Cahier d'Archipel, 18.)

[French-Bahasa Indonesia dictionary.] About 25,000 detailed entries: an impressive work, with generous exemplification, on the basis of the French *Micro Robert.*

694

P. Favre: *Dictionnaire malais-français.* Vienna: Imprimerie Impériale et Royale; Paris: Maisonneuve, 1875. 2 v.

[Malay-French dictionary.] A large scale work in jawi with romanization; includes etymological notes.

Paired with: P. Favre: *Dictionnaire français-malais.* Vienna: Imprimerie Impériale et Royale; Paris: Maisonneuve, 1880. 2 v.

695

Taketomi Masakazu: *Marai-go daijiten.* 1942. 1075 pp.

[Malay-Japanese dictionary.]

More concise: Seidô Miyatake: *Hyôjun marai-go daijiten = Kamoes bahasa melajoe (Indonesia)-nippon jang lengkap.* Tokyo, 1943. 1774 pp. [The complete Malay (Bahasa Indonesia)-Japanese dictionary.] Both works extend to about 30,000 entries and indicate origin of loanwords.

Malay specialized dictionaries

696

Safian Husain and others: *Glosari istilah kesusasteran.* Kuala Lumpur: Dewan Bahasa dan Pustaka, 1988. 395 pp. 983-62-0385-0.

[Glossary of literary terms.] An explanatory dictionary in Bahasa Malaysia, with one-word English glosses. English index, pp. 365-387.

Note also: Mansor Puteh: *Glosari perfileman.* 1989. 144 pp. 983-62-0861-5. [Glossary of film.] A similar work, also with one-word English glosses, but without an English index.

Glossaries in tabular format: *Istilah drama dan teater bahasa inggeris-bahasa Malaysia bahasa Malaysia-bahasa inggeris.* 1987. 81 pp. [English and Bahasa Malaysia glossary of theatre and drama]; *Istilah seni lukis inggeris-Malaysia-inggeris.* 1974. 255 pp. [English and Bahasa Malaysia glossary of art]; *Istilah percetakan, penerbitan dan komunikasi massa inggeris-Malaysia-inggeris.* 1978. 594 pp. [English and Bahasa Malaysia glossary of printing, publishing and mass communication.] Guide to proof-reading marks, pp. 591-4.

697

Simon Barraclough: *A dictionary of Malaysian politics.* Singapore: Heinemann Asia, 1988. 99 pp. 9971-64-115-1.

Dictionary of terms of both English and Malay origin which have special significance in English-language writing on Malaysian affairs. Guide to abbreviations and acronyms, pp. xiii-xiv.

698

Istilah perdagungan, perusahaan dan ilmu akaun inggeris-Malaysia-inggeris. Kuala Lumpur: Dewan Bahasa dan Pustaka, 1973. 489 pp.

[English and Bahasa Malaysia glossary of business and management.] In tabular format.

699

Istilah pendidekan melayu-inggeris-melayu. Kuala Lumpur: Dewan Bahasa dan Pustaka, 1966. 234 pp.
(Siri istilah DBP, 6.)

[Malay and English glossary of education.] In tabular format, with separate sections dealing with physical education (pp. 91-124, 205-234).

700

Daftar istilah geografi asing-Indonesia Indonesia-asing. Jakarta: Departemen Pendidikan dan Kebudayaan, 1979. 85 pp.
(Seri Cd.)

[English and Bahasa Indonesia glossary of geography.] In tabular format.

Note also: *Istilah geologi bahasa inggeris-bahasa Malaysia bahasa Malaysia-bahasa inggeris.* Kuala Lumpur: Dewan Bahasa dan Pustaka, 1988. 573 pp. 983-62-0529-2. [English and Bahasa Malaysia glossary of geology.]

701

John D. Gimlette: *A dictionary of Malayan medicine.* Oxford: Oxford University Press, 1939. 259 pp.

A concise encyclopaedia of indigenous medicine, including many botanical terms for plants of use in the materia medica. A mixture of short, glossary entries and long descriptive ones. Partial classified English-Malay index, pp. 251-9 (no index of plants or drugs).

702

Istilah perubatan bahasa inggeris-bahasa Malaysia bahasa Malaysia-bahasa inggeris. Kuala Lumpur: Dewan Bahasa dan Pustaka, 1987. 444 pp. 983-62-0441-5.

[English and Bahasa Malaysia glossary of medicine.] Tabular format: a dictionary of modern terminology.

In the same series: *Istilah biologi bahasa inggeris-bahasa Malaysia.* 1988. 414 pp. 983-62-0397-4 [English-Bahasa Malaysia glossary of biology]; *Istilah pergigian inggeris-bahasa Malaysia bahasa Malaysia-bahasa inggeris.* 1988. 303 pp. 983-62-0353-2 [English and Bahasa Malaysia glossary of dentistry].

Note also: *Daftar istilah biologi asing-Indonesia Indonesia-asing.* Jakarta: Departemen Pendidikan dan Kebudayaan, 1979. 174 pp. [English and Bahasa Indonesia glossary of biology]; *Daftar istilah anatomi asing-Indonesia Indonesia-asing.* 1979. 87 pp. [English and Bahasa Indonesia glossary of anatomy.]

From an older period: P. N. Gerard: *A vocabulary of Malay medical terms.*

Singapore: Kelly & Walsh, 1905. 107 pp. English and romanized Malay. Cited from Cordier [242].

Malay idioms and phrases

703

Tesaurus umum bahasa Melayu. Kuala Lumpur: Dewan Bahasa dan Pustaka, 1990. 790 pp. 983-62-1602-2.

[Popular thesaurus of Malay.] A monolingual thesaurus: a sequence of main articles, arranged alphabetically, pp. 1-263, followed by an index, pp. 265-787.

704

Hadi Podo, Joseph J. Sullivan: *Kamus ungkapan Indonesia-inggris.* Jakarta: Gramedia, 1986. 1243 pp.
Pandai Berbahasa Inggris.

A remarkably comprehensive dictionary of English phrases with Bahasa Indonesia translations, arranged alphabetically under Indonesian keywords: about 12,000 headings.

705

Sir Richard Winstedt: *Malay proverbs = Bidalan Melayu.* Singapore: Graham Brash, 1981. 112 pp. 9971-947-15-3.
Revised by T. C. Kwang.

Arranged by subject. Appendix B: Minangkabau proberbs of Negeri Sembilan. Index of Malay proverbs, pp. 103-112.
Reprinted 1986.

706

Jeffery R. Crockett: *Indonesia: dictionary of abbreviations and acronyms used in Indonesian publications = Kamus singkatan2 dan akronama2 jang dipergunakan di penerbitan2 Indonesia.* Washington, 1971. 174 pp.

Photocopied from typescript. A useful, expalnatory list: about 4500 entries. For institutions, full names in Indonesian are followed by English translations. Includes much information from Dutch and Japanese periods.

Malay standards and dialects

707

Leo Suryadinata: *Times comparative dictionary of Malay-Indonesian synonyms.* Singapore: Times Books International, 1991. 486 pp. 981-204-215-6.

About 6000 entries with full, readable explanations in English. Headwords are normally Bahasa Malaysia terms, but there are full cross-references from Bahasa Indonesia.

Note also: Harimurti Kridalaksana: *Leksikon Malaysia.* Jakarta: Lembaga Riset Kebudayaan Nasional, 1974. 45 pp. (Seri pata dasar, 6.) A brief alphabetical Bahasa Malaysia-Bahasa Indonesia glossary, to be used with care: e.g., 'Jawi = Melayu' is not a helpful gloss on all or even most occurrences of these words.

708

H. B. Marshall: 'A vocabulary of Brunei Malay' in *Journal of the Straits Branch of the Royal Asiatic Society* no. 83 (1921) pp. 45-74.

Lists about 500 words.

Superseded: H. S. Haynes: 'A list of Brunie-Malay words' in *Journal of the Straits Branch of the Royal Asiatic Society* no. 34 (July 1900) pp. 39-48. A first alphabetical list of 295 local words: transcription unreliable.

709

F. S. A. de Clercq: *Petit dictionnaire des principaux mots étrangers différant du malais ordinaire et employés dans les Résidences de Manado, Ternate, Amboine, Banda et Timor-Coupang.* Batavia: W. Bruining, 1876. Publié par la Société des Arts et des Sciences de Batavia.

[Little dictionary of the principal foreign words used in (the Malay of) the residences of Manado, Ternate, Banda and Timor-Coupang and not used in Common Malay.] Cited from Cordier [242].

Malay language and script

710

Tata bahasa baku bahasa Indonesia. Jakarta: Balai Pustaka, 1988. 475 pp. (BP, 3657.)

[Modern grammar of Bahasa Indonesia.] A clear, well-laid-out reference grammar, strong on word formation and the adaptation of loanwords.

711

A. A. Fokker: *Beknopte grammatica van de Bahasa Indonesia*. Groningen, 1950. 160 pp.

[Concise grammar of Bahasa Indonesia.] Fourth edition.

First published as: A. A. Fokker: *Beknopte Maleise grammatica*. Groningen, 1941. [Concise Malay grammar.]

Note also: A. S. Tesyolkin, N. F. Aliyeva: *Indoneziiskii yazyk*. Moscow: Nauka, 1960. [The Indonesian language.] A brief grammatical description in Russian.

For a survey of grammars of Malay in its several standards see Uhlenbeck's article in Sebeok [607].

712

A. Teeuw, H. W. Emanuels: *A critical survey of studies on Malay and Bahasa Indonesia*. The Hague: Nijhoff, 1961. 176 pp.
Koninklijk Instituut voor Taal-, Land- en Volkenkunde. (Bibliographical series, 5.)

The second half of this work is an alphabetical bibliography, pp. 91-157. For some more recent information see Uhlenbeck's article in Sebeok [607].

713

Yunus Maris: *Kamus fajar rumi-jawi*. Petaling Jaya: Penerbit Fajar Bakti, 1984. 585 pp.

[Fajar roman-jawi dictionary.] A monolingual dictionary of the basic, older vocabulary of Malay, with the added feature of jawi (Arabic script) forms following the rumi (roman) headwords. Strong coverage of the Arabic-based vocabulary of Islam.

PILIPINO

Pilipino bilingual dictionaries

714

Leo James English: *Tagalog-English dictionary*. Manila: Congregation of the Most Holy Redeemer, 1986. 1583 pp. 971-91055-0-X.

A comprehensive modern dictionary wth over 15000 entries and many sub-entries. Numerous phrases and example sentences. Origin of loanwords indicated. English loanwords are given in Tagalog spellings, a feature which the author came to regret (see preface) but which is evidently more useful to non-Philippine readers in a reference book of this kind than the alternative English spellings would have been. These are in any case listed in an initial appendix.

Paired with: Leo James English: *English-Tagalog dictionary*. Manila: Department of Education, 1965. 1211 pp. About 13000 entries of some length, with many examples.

715

José Villa Panganiban: *Diksyunaryo-tesauro Pilipino-Ingles*. Quezon City: Manlapaz, 1973. 1027 pp.

[Pilipino-English dictionary-thesaurus.] A remarkably hospitable and endlessly enjoyable work offering not only English glosses but also synonyms in other Philippine languages; sub-entries for phrases and compound words. Notes on origin of loanwords. 'Begun as a curiosity venture in 1935 by studying the *Artes y reglas* and *Vocabularios* on different Philippine ethnic groups written by Spanish missionaries.'

Paired with: Jose Villa Panganiban: *Tesauro diksiyunaryo ingles-pilipino*. San Juan Rizal, 1966. 1363 pp. [English-Pilipino dictionary-thesaurus.] Roneoed: about 26000 entries.

Pilipino specialized dictionaries

716

Jose R. Sytangco: *Scientific dictionary, English-Pilipino*. Manila: Pamantasang Santo Tomas, 1977. 538 pp.

Flawed (see Richardson's fuller annotation [27]) by its use of newly invented or obscure terms instead of the current ones if these happen to be loanwords.

Pilipino idioms and phrases

717

Damiana L. Eugenio: *Philippine proverb lore*. Quezon City: Philippine Folklore Society, 1975. 191 pp.
(Reprint issue, 2.)

1592 proverbs from ten Philippine languages, with English translations, arranged alphabetically under English keywords. Introductory study, pp. 1-65.

Pilipino language

718

Paul Schachter, Fe T. Otanes: *Tagalog reference grammar*. Berkeley: University of California Press, 1972. 566 pp.
Under the auspices of the Philippine Center for Language Study.

An elaborate grammar with generous exemplification.

THAI

Thai dictionaries

719

Manit Manitcharoen: *Photchananukrom Thai*. Bangkok, 1971. 1600 pp.
Cover title in English: *The most up-to-date Thai dictionary.*

[Thai dictionary.] Third edition of a medium-sized monolingual dictionary, a work much indebted to the Royal Institute dictionary [721] but including many additional technical terms and foreign loanwords. Scientific Latin, and sometimes English, glosses are added in defining technical terms.

Second edition: 1964. 1571 pp. First edition: 1961.

720

Saranukrom Thai. Bangkok: Ratchabandit Sathan, 1956- .

[Thai encyclopaedia, edited by the Royal Institute.] A general encyclopaedia with some emphasis on Thailand. Entirely in Thai. I have seen nothing beyond vol. 17 (pp. 10505-11168), published 1981, about half way through the alphabet. Overtaken by:

Saranukrom watthanatam Phak Tai. Bangkok, 1986. 10 v. A modern, illustrated, alphabetical encyclopaedia in Thai.

Saranukrom Thai samrap yaowachon. Bangkok, 1973- . I have seen 14 volumes of this highly illustrated thematic encyclopaedia in Thai.

721

Photchananukrom chabap Ratchabandit Sathan. Bangkok, 1950. 1053 pp.

[Royal Institute dictionary.] A monolingual Thai dictionary compiled over the period 1932-1950. Aimed to *prescribe* a standard spelling (and the result is indeed generally accepted as the official standard) but to *describe* historical and existing usage as to pronunciation and meaning. Additionally, the pronunciation of each word is given in a phonologically normalized

Thai script. Includes scientific Latin glosses for botanical and zoological terms.

Frequently reprinted.

Thai bilingual dictionaries

722

So. Sethaputra: *New model Thai-English dictionary*. Bangkok, 1972. 2 v. (1072 pp.)

Notable (like its widely-distributed abridged relatives) for very clear discursive explanations of usage. About 12,000 entries, with many examples.

First edition: 1965.

723

George Bradley McFarland: *Thai-English dictionary*. Bangkok, 1941. 1019 + 39 pp.

About 20,000 entries, with examples. Published after its author's death and, no doubt for this reason, open to criticism for some inaccuracies. The glosses for Sankrit and Pali loanwords are said by Gedney in Sebeok [607] to be unreliable, while the phonetic transcriptions, given after each headword, are imperfect, as is indicated in the foreword to the Stanford reprints. Appendices (39 pp.): the thousand commonest Thai words; scientific Latin-Thai glossaries of names of birds, fishes, flora, shells, snakes.

Reprinted: Stanford: Stanford University Press, 1944; and later reprints.

Note also: Mary R. Haas: *Thai-English student's dictionary*. Stanford, 1964. 638 pp. Clear printing from typescript: about 12,000 entries, covering the modern spoken and written language. Adopts the spelling of the Royal Institute dictionary [721] and adds phonetic transcriptions. Includes place names and abbreviations. Preliminaries: alphabetical order, p. x; Brief description of Thai, pp. xi-xxii.

724

So. Sethaputra: *New model English-Thai dictionary*. 1961. 2 v. (1598 pp.)

Third edition. About 30,000 entries: a very comprehensive work, principally for Thai users, with many examples.

Second edition: 1952. First edition: 1940.

Note also: M. L. Manich Jumsai: *English-Thai dictionary*. Bangkok, 1953. 1568 pp.

725

D. J. B. Pallegoix: *Dictionarium linguae thai sive siamensis, interpretatione latina, gallica et anglica illustratum.* Paris: in Typographeo Imperatorio, 1854. 897 pp.

[Thai-Latin-French-English dictionary.] In five columns, the second giving romanized Thai with tone markings.

Reprint of the first edition: Farnborough: Gregg, 1972. 0-576-03340-5.

There was also a revised edition: D. J. B. Pallegoix: *Dictionnaire siamois français anglais = Siamese French English dictionary.* Bangkok: Catholic Mission, 1896. 1165 pp. [Thai-French-English dictionary.] Revised by J. L. Vey. This edition omitted the Latin column. About 33,000 entries; grammatical introduction, in French, English and Thai, on preliminary pages 1-69.

Note also: M. J. Cuaz: *Essai de dictionnaire français-siamois.* Bangkok: Mission Catholique, 1903. 1012 pp. [A preliminary French-Thai dictionary.]

Thai specialized dictionaries

726

Photchananukrom sap thahan Angkrit-Thai. Bangkok, 1970. 422 pp.

[English-Thai dictionary of military terms.] 2500 entries in English, with fairly discursive explanations in Thai. United States and international usage.

Thai language and script

727

Richard B. Noss: *Thai reference grammar.* Washington: Department of State, Foreign Service Institute, 1964. 254 pp.

A boldly original analysis, perhaps too much so to be fairly called a 'reference grammar'. In phonetic transcription (not Thai script).

728

Yu. Ya. Plam, L. N. Morev, M. F. Fomicheva: *Taiskii yazyk.* Moscow: Nauka, 1961. 150 pp.

[The Thai language.] A brief grammatical description in Russian with detailed attention to the writing system.

729

Phya Upakit Silpasarn: *Sayam waiyakon.* Bangkok, 1946-8. 4 v.

[Siamese grammar.] A detailed normative grammar of Thai on a traditional Pali basis, by a lecturer at Chulalongkorn University.

Vol. 1: *Akkharawitthi.* 4th edition, 1946. [Orthography]; vol. 2: *Wachiwiphak.* 5th edition, 1948. [Accidence]; vol. 3: *Wakkayasamphan.* 3rd edition, 1948. [Syntax]; vol. 4: *Chanthalak.* 1948. [Verse prosody.] Vol. 2 includes a survey of the royal language.

The traditional rules of prosody are also available in German in: Klaus Wenk: *Die Metrik in der thailändischen Dichtung.* Hamburg, 1961. 160 pp. [Metrics in Thai verse], a work suffering from numerous inaccuracies according to W. J. Gedney in Sebeok [607] p. 794.

730
Romanization guide for Thai script. Bangkok: Royal Institute, 1968. 26 pp.

A manual of the Royal Institute's widely-used 'general system'.

Note also: Nantana Danvithathana: *The Thai writing system.* Hamburg: Buske, 1987. 345 pp. 3-87118-753-4. History of the Thai writing system, pp. 18-121; Relationship between sounds and symbols of the modern system.

731
Anek Liangprasoet: *Wisamanayanam.* Bangkok, 1972. 2 v.

[Transliteration of names.] Tabular format, giving Thai transliterations for foreign proper names. Vol. 1 (499 pp.): Surnames; vol. 2 (869 pp.): Place names.

VIETNAMESE

Vietnamese dictionaries and encyclopaedias

732
Văn Tân: *Từ điển tiếng Việt.* Hanoi: Khoa Học Xã Hội, 1967. 1172 pp.

[Dictionary of Vietnamese.] Not seen: see the description by Cotter [30].

733
Lê Văn Đức, Lê Ngọc Trụ: *Việt-nam từ điển.* Saigon: Khai Trí, 1970. 2 v.

[Vietnamese dictionary.] A very useful work, though slightly complicated in its arrangement. Each volume contains three separately paginated sequences on different-coloured paper: general vocabulary, proverbs and idioms, places and persons.

734

Thanh-Nghị: *Việt-nam tân từ-điển minh-họa.* Saigon: Khai-Trí, 1965. 1538 pp.

[Big illustrated dictionary of Vietnamese.] Illustrated dictionary of the Larousse type. Essentially monolingual but includes one-word French translations. For a French-Vietnamese companion see **741**.

735

Đào Đăng Vỹ: *Việt-nam bách-khoa tự-điển = Dictionnaire encyclopédique viêtnamien = Vietnamese encyclopaedic dictionary.* Saigon, 1960. 3 v.

Terms are defined in Vietnamese, French and English: Chinese characters are also given. Not seen.

Vietnamese bilingual dictionaries

736

Bùi Phung: *Từ điển Việt-Anh = Vietnamese-English dictionary.* Hanoi: Hanoi University Press, 1986. 992 pp.

Second edition. Very poor paper. Claims to concentrate on contemporary Vietnamese, but also to include archaic words, foreign loan-words and slang.

First edition: 1977.

Note also: Nguyễn-Văn-Khôn: *Vietnamese English dictionary = Việt-Anh từ-điển.* Saigon: Khai-Trí, 1966. 1233 pp. This is still of value for its very generous exemplification.

737

Nguyễn Dình Hoà: *Vietnamese-English student dictionary.* Saigon, 1967. 675 pp.

A concise, practical dictionary, benefiting from the author's expertise in English. He was Professor at the University of Saigon and Cultural Counsellor at the Vietnamese Embassy in Washington.

Reprinted: Carbondale: Southern Illinois University Press; Amsterdam: Feffer and Simons, 1971. 0-8093-0476-7.

His earlier dictionary is slightly smaller: Nguyen-Dinh-Hoa: *Vietnamese-English dictionary.* Saigon, 1959. 568 pp. About 20,000 entries, with some guidance on usage. Includes pronunciation guide (International Phonetic

Alphabet) for north, central and south Vietnam. Formerly much used in the U.S. Armed Forces. Reprinted: Nguyen-Dinh-Hoa: *Hoa's Vietnamese-English dictionary.* Rutland: Tuttle, 1966. 0-8048-0618-7.

The author's first such work: Nguyen-Dinh-Hoa: *Vietnamese-English vocabulary.* Washington, 1955, was a typescript teaching glossary (9000 entries) compiled at Columbia University.

738

Từ điển Anh Việt. Hanoi: Khoa Học Xã Hội, 1975. 1959 pp.
Ủy Ban Khoa Học Xã Hội Việt Nam, Viện Ngôn Ngữ Học.

[English-Vietnamese dictionary.] A large scale dictionary of 65,000 headwords, including translations for many English phrases. The compilers being all Vietnamese, a serious defect is the inclusion of many practically unknown English words (e.g. 'defervescence') and the omission of many current and technical terms.

Unacknowledged reprint: Dang The Binh and others: *Từ điển Anh-Việt hiện đại = Modern English-Vietnamese dictionary.* Glendale, California: Dainamco, n.d.

739

Nguyễn Văn Khôn: *Anh-Việt từ-diển.* Paris: Viêt-Dang, 1955. 1741 pp.

[English-Vietnamese dictionary.] Useful because of its size, though there are quite a number of incorrect translations.

Also published: Saigon, 1956.

740

Eugène Gouin: *Dictionnaire vietnamien-chinois-français.* Saigon: Imprimerie d'Extrême-Orient, 1947.

[Vietnamese-Chinese-French dictionary.] A major work, in French rather than Vietnamese alphabetical order, arranged under morphemes with numbered subheadings for distinct meanings. These are followed by sub-entries for multisyllabic words and compounds, with references back to the numbered subheadings. A very comprehensive dictionary, but with only brief definitions and little exemplification. 'Chinese' is here only in the sense that nom characters are given for forms of Chinese origin: there is a 40-page index of Chinese characters but no French index.

Note also: Gustave Hue: *Từ điển Việt-Hoa-Pháp.* Saigon: Librairie Khai Trí, 1971. [Vietnamese-Chinese-French dictionary.]

741

Lê Khả Kế and others: *Từ điển Pháp-Việt = Dictionnaire français-vietnamien.* Hanoi: Agence de Coopération Culturelle et Technique, 1981. 1276 pp.
Comité des Sciences Sociales de la République Socialiste du Vietnam.

[French-Vietnamese dictionary.] A beautifully printed modern dictionary with a good selection of examples, synonyms, phrases and other semantic help. There were no French on the editorial committee; but for all that the vocabulary is fairly well-chosen and up-to-date.

Note also: Thanh Nghị: *Pháp-Việt tân từ điển minh họa.* Saigon: Khai Trí, 1967. 1613 pp. [New illustrated French-Vietnamese dictionary.] For a companion to this see **734**.

742

Đào Duy-Anh: *Pháp-Việt từ điển chú thêm chữ Hán = Dictionnaire français-vietnamien.* Saigon: Trường-Thi, 1957. 1958 pp.

[French-Vietnamese dictionary, with nom characters for Chinese terms.] Latest version of a big dictionary which retains its usefulness for older vocabulary: its strongest feature is the offering of precise Vietnamese renderings of French terms and phrases.

Second edition: Paris, 1950. First edition: 1936.

743

Nguyễn Luyện and others: *Bildwörterbuch Deutsch und Vietnamesisch = Từ điển bằng tranh Đức và Việt.* Leipzig: Verlag Enzyklopädie, 1981. 2 v.

[German and Vietnamese pictorial dictionary.] A work of the Duden kind. Vol. 1 pp. 1-290: bilingual list of numbered terms under 200 subject headings; pp. 297-370, German index; pp. 371-464, Vietnamese index. Vol. 2 consists of 200 full page line drawings, with numbered details, corresponding to the subject headings. Indispensable as a guide to technical terms in many fields.

744

Winfried Boscher, Phan trung Liên: *Wörterbuch Vietnamesisch-Deutsch.* Leipzig: Verlag Enzyklopädie, 1978. 738 pp.

[Vietnamese-German dictionary.]

Reprinted: Munich: Max Hueber, n.d.

Note also: Otto Karow: *Vietnamesisch-deutsches Wörterbuch = Từ-điển Việt-*

Đức. Wiesbaden: Harrassowitz, 1972. 1086 pp. [Vietnamese-German dictionary.] Adopts the old-fashioned 'etymological' arrangement. List of Chinese characters, pp. 955-983; list of nôm characters, pp. 987-1086.

745

Alexander de Rhodes: *Dictionarium annamiticum lusitanum et latinum.* Rome, 1651. 538 pp.
Ope Sacrae Congregationis de Propaganda Fide in luce editum.

[Vietnamese-Portuguese-Latin dictionary.] Latin index at end (88 pp.)

There is a biography of the author, by Claude Larre and Pham Dinh Khiem, in: Alexandre de Rhodes: *Catechismus in octo dies.* Saigon, 1961. Tercentenary republication (edited by André Marrillier) of the edition of Rome, 1651.

Note also: *Dictionnaire annamite-latin*; par un professeur. Hong Kong: Imprimerie de Nazareth, 1928. 361 pp. [Vietnamese-Latin dictionary.] Includes classified list of classical and Biblical proper names with Vietnamese renderings, pp. 345-351; Vietnamese-Latin glossary of place-names, pp. 351-361.

746

K. M. Alikanov, V. V. Ivanov, I. A. Mal'khanova: *Russko-V'etnamskii slovar'* = *Từ điển Nga-Việt.* Moscow: Russkii Yazyk, 1977. 2 v.

[Russian-Vietnamese dictionary.] One of the biggest bilingual dictionaries of Vietnamese. Generous with near-synonyms but short on exemplification.

Vietnamese specialized dictionaries

747

Diên-Hương: *Thành ngữ điển tích.* Saigon: Khai-Trí, 1969. 536 pp.
Cover title: *Từ-điển thành-ngữ điển-tích.*

[Classical literary Vietnamese.] Third edition. A dictionary-encyclopaedia, strong on phrases and idioms, with relevant literary examples. Also includes many proper names. Entries for poets include specimens of their work. Second edition: 1961. 503 pp. First edition: Saigon: Tác Gia, 1949. 2 v.

Note also: Trịnh Văn Thành: *Thành-ngữ điển-tích danh-nhân từ-điển.* Saigon: Tác Giả Giữ Bản Quyền, 1966. 2 v. [Dictionary of literary figures and literary terms.] Includes 10,000 terms and 5000 entries for literary allusions in addition to biographies. Entries vary greatly in length (up to 13 pp.).

748

Thuật ngữ my thuật Pháp-Việt Việt-Pháp có chú thêm tiếng Nga. Hanoi:

Khoa Học Xã Hội, 1970. 62 pp.
Ủy Ban Khoa Học Xã Hội Việtnam, Viện Ngôn Ngữ Học.

[French-Vietnamese and Vietnamese-French glossary of fine arts terminology, with a Russian index.]

Note also: *Thuật ngữ van học, my học: Nga-Pháp-Việt*. 1969. 55 pp. [Russian-French-Vietnamese glossary of criticism and aesthetics.] Tabular format: in Russian alphabetical order. No French or Vietnamese index.

749

Glossary of terms used in the Vietnamese press: reference aid. Arlington, Virginia: National Technical Information Service, 1985. 286 pp. Foreign Broadcast Information Service. (JPRS-SEA-85-004.)

'4th revision.' Tabular format. Appendices: Administrative subdivisions; Vietnamese rendition of foreign place names (omits Luân dôn 'London'); Weights and measures; Official correspondence and document terminology.

3rd revision: 1981.

750

Vũ-văn-Mẫu: *Từ-điển Pháp-Việt pháp-chính-kinh-tài xã-hội = Dictionnaire français-vietnamien des sciences juridiques, politiques, économiques, financières et sociologiques.* Saigon: Université Bouddhique Vạn-Hạnh, 1970. 895 pp.

[French-Vietnamese dictionary of juridical, political, economic, financial and sociological sciences.] A very comprehensive collection of phrases and expressions used in the social sciences. No Vietnamese index.

Note also: *Từ diễn thuật ngữ luật học Nga-Trung-Pháp-Việt.* Hanoi: Khoa Học Xã Hội, 1971. 336 pp. (Ủy Ban Khoa Học Xã Hội Việtnam, Viện Luật Học.) [Specialised law dictionary, Russian-Chinese-French-Vietnamese.]

Vũ-Văn-Mẫu and others: *Tiêu từ điển luật và kinh-tế.* Saigon: Tủ Sách Đại Học, 1973. 352 pp. A Vietnamese encyclopedia of jurisprudence. Terms are followed by a French equivalent, then a full discussion in Vietnamese.

Bùi-Quang-Khánh: *Từ-điển hành-chánh công-quyền Việt-Anh-Pháp = Dictionary of terms and idioms of public administration Vietnamese-English-French = Dictionnaire des termes et expressions de l'administration publique vietnamien-anglais-francais.* N.p., 1971. 361 pp. Tabular format in Vietnamese alphabetical order. Short on explanations, but an attempt is made to offer alternatives and near-synonyms. Reproduced from typescript.

Phạmxuân Thái: *Danhtừ triếthọc Việt-Pháp Anh-Việt. Phan Việt-Pháp = Vocabulaire philosophique vietnamien anglais francais vietnamien.* Partie vietnamienne-francaise = Philosophical lexicon Vietnamese English French English. N.p.: Tuhai, 1950. 112 pp. (Cover title: Danhtừ hiệnđại và triếthọc = Vocabulaire moderne et philosophique.) No English, in spite of the title. A list of terms in philosophy and some of the social sciences, in a curious non-standard Vietnamese orthography which leaves no spaces between syllables and therefore has to mark syllable-initial consonants in bold face. Tabular format: no explanations or examples.

For this author's linguistic preoccupations see: Phạmxuân Thái: *Reformed Vietnamese writing.* [Saigon? 1948.] Phạmxuân Thái: *Frater, the simplest international language ever constructed.* Saigon, 1957.

751

H. H. E. Loofs-Wissowa: *Vietnamese-English archaeological glossary with English index.* Canberra: The Australian National University, Faculty of Asian Studies, 1990. 103 pp.
With the assistance of Pham Van Minh and Nguyen M. Long.

1679 terms, generally followed by English equivalent. Some fuller explanations. *S.V.* marks words of Sino-Vietnamese origin. Intended to 'enable archaeologists to profit from Vietnamese archaeological reports with their specialized vocabulary'. Follows the newly official letter-by-letter alphabetical order.

752

Charles H. Reed: *Danh-từ giáo-dục Anh-Việt và Việt-Anh = Educational terms English-Vietnamese and Vietnamese-English.* Saigon, 1972. 345 pp.

Typescript. Gives equivalents and fairly extended explanations of terms in both English and Vietnamese: the explanations are repeated in each half of the work, swelling it considerably.

753

Từ điển thuật ngữ thư viện học Nga-Anh-Pháp-Việt. Hanoi: Khoa Học Xã Hội, 1972. 394 pp.
Ủy Ban Khoa Học Xã Hội Việtnam, Viện Ngôn Ngữ Học.

[Dictionary of librarianship and bibliography.] The main sequence is Russian-Vietnamese, followed by English, French and Vietnamese indexes.

754

Vũ-văn-Lê: *The military interpreter: English Vietnamese military handbook = Danh-từ quân-sự Anh-Việt.* Saigon: Khai-Trí [1967]. 248 pp.

Arranged by topic, with a detailed table of contents. The English is stiff and unnatural. Contents: Command and staff, Installations and centres, Office, Barracks, Training centres, Drill, Air Force, Navy, Artillery, Armoured corps, Transport, Engineers, Signals, Medical corps, Ordnance, Quartermaster corps, Psychology and intelligence, 'Struggle of politics', Defence, Guerrilla, Jungle warfare, Attack. Diagram of ranks and insignia, pp. 245-7.

755

Danh từ vật lý Nga-Anh-Việt = Russian-English-Vietnamese dictionary of physical terms. Hanoi: Khoa Hoc, 1964. 588 pp.
Ban Toán-Lý Thược Ủy Ban Khoa Học Nhà Nước.

A work of impressive size: 17200 terms in Russian alphabetical order. English index, pp. 429-581; list of foreign proper names used in Vietnamese terminology, especially eponyms, with the Vietnamese spelling (e.g. 'Bernoulli: Bec-nu-li. Bessel: Bet-xen'), pp. 582-5.

Note also: Hoàng-Xuân-Hãn: *Danh-từ khoa-học. Toán, lý, hoa, cơ, thiên-văn = Vocabulaire scientifique.* Saigon: Vinh-Bao, 1948. 191 pp. (Danh-từ khoa-học [1].) [Scientific vocabulary.] French-Vietnamese dictionary of physical sciences. Useful range of synonyms and of phrases. The introductory study of scientific terminology (pp. xi-xlix) includes a table of elements (scientific Latin, Vietnamese, French, English, German, Chinese, Japanese) and examples of the nomenclature of chemical compounds.

756

Lê-Khắc-Quyến: *Danh-từ y-học Pháp-Việt = Lexique des termes médicaux français-vietnamiens.* Saigon: Khai-Trí, 1971. 944 pp.

[French-Vietnamese dictionary of medical terms.] A very comprehensive vocabulary (25,000 terms). Supplementary glossary of English terms used in French medicine, pp. 903-916; of abbreviations, pp. 917-941 (including some chemical formulae); of symbols, p. 942.

Note also: Phạm-Khắc-Quảng, Lê-Khắc-Thiền: *Danh-từ y-học = Vocabulaire des termes techniques de medecine.* Paris: Minh-Tân, 1951. 256 pp. [French-Vietnamese dictionary of medical terminology.] About 12500 terms.

Vietnamese phrases and idioms

757

Nguyễn Văn Minh: *Việt-ngữ tinh-nghĩa từ-điển.* [Saigon:] Hoa Tiên, 1973. 2 v.

[Dictionary of Vietnamese synonyms.] Vol. 2 (193 pp.) forms a supplement, now first published, to vol. 1 which first appeared in 1952. Definitions with discussion of semantic points; also discusses changes of meanings occurring in compound words. Vol. 2 contains a cumulative index.

Note also: Trần Văn Điền: *Dictionary of synonyms and antonyms = Tự điển đồng nghĩa và phản nghĩa.* [Saigon:] Sống Mới [1970]. 581 pp. (Cover title: Tự điển Anh ngữ đồng nghĩa phản nghĩa.) A dictionary of English synonyms and antonyms with brief Vietnamese definitions.

758

Trần-Văn-Điền: *Tự-điển văn-phạm và cách dụng những tiếng thông dụng = Grammar of English words.* Saigon: Sống Mới, 1974. 1216 pp.

Dictionary, under English keywords, of English sentences with Vietnamese translations. Many errors in the English ('He was charged of robbery') but a very comprehensive list of Vietnamese expressions.

Note also: Phạm-Xuân-Thái: *Việt-Anh thong-thoại từ-điển = Vietnamese-English conversation dictionary.* Saigon, Hanoi: Tuqshaif [1948]. 218 pp. Under Vietnamese keywords this work lists common English expressions followed by phonetic transcription and Vietnamese translation. Not convenient for an English-speaking user, but an interesting collection of material. Pp. 199-211: List of European abbreviations with Vietnamese equivalents.

759

Lê Bá Kông: *Tu-diên đàm-thoại Việt-Anh = Vietnamese-English conversation dictionary.* Saigon: Ziên-Hông, 1966. 414 pp.

A useful alphabetical dictionary of phrases and conversational expressions.

Note also: P. J. B. Trương-Vĩnh-Ký: *Guide de la conversation annamite = Sách tập nói chuyện tiếng Annam và tiếng Langsa.* Saigon: Guilland et Martinon, 1882. 118 pp. [Guide to Vietnamese conversation.] Arranged by subjects, in dialogue style. No index. French sentence, Vietnamese sentence, literal French rendering of the Vietnamese words.

On this prolific author see the obituary by: Henri Cordier: 'Petrus Truong-Vinh-Ky: nécrologie' in *T'oung pao* n. s. vol. 1 (1900) pp. 261-8.

Vietnamese language and script

760

Nguyễn Dức Dân: *Dictionnaire de fréquence du vietnamien.* Paris: Universite de Paris VII, 1980. 325 pp. 2-85297-085-6.
Avec la collaboration de Lê Quang Thiem.

[Word frequency list for Vietnamese.] Detailed statistics in alphabetical order, pp. 20-140; List in descending order of frequency, pp. 142-204; Vietnamese-French dictionary of the resulting 'basic language', pp. 205-316. Based on an impressive selection of literary, dramatic, poetic and journalistic texts and children's literature. Differing frequencies in these various categories are recorded in the detailed statistics.

761

Trương Văn Chinh: *Structure de la langue vietnamienne*. Paris: Paul Geuthner, 1970. 478 pp.
(Publications du Centre Universitaire des Langues Orientales Vivantes, 6e serie, 10.)

[Structure of the Vietnamese language.] A systematic grammar, intended as a dispassionate description of the current language, aimed at readers with a knowledge of linguistics. Words and phrases, pp. 3-55; syntax of the sentence, pp. 59-185; Syntax of the grammatical 'molecule' or syntactic unit, pp. 189-431. Detailed index. French-Vietnamese-Chinese glossary of grammatical terminology, pp. 469-472.

A revised version of: Trương Văn Chinh, Nguyễn Hiến Lê: *Khao luan ve ngữ pháp Việt-nam*. Hue: Dai Hoc, 1963. 718 pp. [Vietnamese grammar.]

762

Laurence C. Thompson: *A Vietnamese grammar*. Seattle: University of Washington Press, 1965. 386 pp.

Contents: grammatical structure, compounds, derivatives; substantives, predicates, particles; sentence structure, register; personal names. Chapters preceding and following the formal grammar are noteworthy: Hanoi phonology, pp. 18-51; The writing system, pp. 52-77; Dialectal variations, pp. 78-104; Style, pp. 292-311; Lexical complexities, pp. 312-335. Glossary of difficult forms, pp. 336-359.

Note also: M. B. Emeneau: *Studies in Vietnamese (Annamese) grammar*. Berkeley: University of California Press, 1951.

763

Nguyễn Quí Hùng: *Văn-phạm Việt*. Saigon: Khai-Trí, 1965. 860 pp.

[Grammar of Vietnamese.] Strong on phonological and etymological links between Chinese and Vietnamese.

764

Nguyễn Quang Xỹ, Vũ Văn Kính: *Từ-điển chữ nôm*. Saigon: Bô Giáo-

Dục, Trung-Tâm Học-Liệu Xuất Bản, 1971.

[Nôm to quôc-ngu dictionary.] 10,000 terms. Contents: Index in character order (i.e. by number of strokes), pp. 3-102; alphabetical dictionary, including brief 'etymological' notes on nôm characters, pp. 105-860.

765

Đào Duy Anh: *Hiêu dinh-han man tu Hán Viêt tử điển*. Saigon: Trường Thị, 1957. 605 pp.

[Concise Sino-Vietnamese dictionary.] Latest printing of a specialized dictionary of the Chinese element in Vietnamese, giving Chinese characters, translations and explanations in everyday Vietnamese.

Third edition: Paris, 1951. Second edition: 1936. First edition: 1932.

MINORITY LANGUAGES OF LITERATURE

Achehnese

766

Hoesein Djajadiningrat: *Atjèhsch-Nederlandsch woordenboek met Nederlandsch-Atjèhsch register*. Batavia, 1934. 2 v.

[Achehnese-Dutch dictionary with Dutch-Achehnese index.] A very extensive encyclopaedic dictionary of what was once a ruling language of northern Sumatra. Based on published and manuscript literature (references given) and on oral sources: for earlier dictionaries see vol. 1 p. iv. In romanization. Substantial addenda, vol. 2 pp. 1289-1349. The Dutch-Achehnese index by G. W. J. Drewes, signalled in the title, did not (I think) appear.

Some copies are labelled as published at The Hague: Nijhoff.

Note also: A. J. W. Bikkers: *Malay, Achinese, French and English vocabulary alphabetically arranged under each of the four languages*. London: W. H. Allen, 1882. 352 pp.

767

Mark Durie: *A grammar of Acehnese on the basis of a dialect of north Aceh*. Dordrecht: Foris, 1985. 278 pp.
(Verhandelingen van het Koninklijk Instituut voor Taal-, Land- en Volkenkunde, 112.)

Closely printed. Sociolinguistic and historical introduction, pp. 1-8.

227

Balinese

768

J. Kersten: *Bahasa Bali*. Ende: Nusa Indah, 1984. 646 pp.

[The Balinese language.] The greater part of this work, pp. 133-646, is a Balinese-Bahasa Indonesia dictionary of modern colloquial Balinese. The first part is a grammar of Balinese in Indonesian, a revised translation of:

J. Kersten: *Balische grammatica*. The Hague, 1948. 102 pp. [Balinese grammar.]

Note also: *Kamus Indonesia-Bali*. Jakarta: Departemen Penelitian dan Kebudayaan, 1975. 221 pp. [Bahasa Indonesia-Balinese dictionary.] About 20,000 brief entries.

769

C. Clyde Barber: *A Balinese-English dictionary*. Aberdeen: Aberdeen University Library, 1979. 2 v. (809 pp.). 0-9505322-3-1.
Alternate title: *A dictionary of Balinese-English*.

About 32,000 brief entries: photocopied from typescript. A dictionary of the literary language, largely based on published material (e.g. van der Tuuk [770]) which it renders conveniently accessible. No precise definitions are given for flora and fauna: the author regrettably concluded that 'the taxonomy of the plants of the tropics is now being rewritten and long, obsolete Latin names would be worse than useless'. Balinese appears in romanization: 'I have used throughout a mechanical transliteration of the beautiful native script, not the modern roman orthography now often used in Bali.' The script, vol. 1 pp. vii-ix. Addenda, pp. 782-809.

Note also: C. Clyde Barber: *Grammar of the Balinese language*. Aberdeen: Aberdeen University Library, 1981. 437 pp. 0-9505322-4-X.

770

H. N. van der Tuuk: *Kawi-Balineesch-Nederlandsch woordenboek*. Batavia, 1897-1912. 4 v.

[Old Javanese and Balinese-Dutch dictionary.] About 40,000 entries, many very lengthy. Balinese script for headwords, followed by transliteration. A dictionary of the traditional bilingual Javanese-Balinese culture of Bali, and largely based on Balinese manuscripts of old and middle Javanese literary texts, to which references are given. A vast work of archipelagic erudition (published after the author's death), but considered to be seriously flawed as a tool for scholars of either language. Balinese words are glossed in Dutch. Javanese words are not: sometimes their traditional Balinese glosses are given, but these are not necessarily acceptable to students of Javanese.

See Zoetmulder and Robson [784] for further comment.

Batak

771
J. H. Neumann: *Karo-Bataks-Nederlands woordenboek*. Medan, 1951. 343 pp.

[Karo Batak-Dutch dictionary.] Dictionary of a language of northern Sumatra. Not seen.

Essentially a revision of: M. Joustra: *Karo-Bataksch woordenboek*. Leiden: Brill, 1907. 244 pp. [Karo Batak dictionary.] Batak script followed by romanization and Dutch gloss.

772
Joh. Warneck: *Toba-Batak-Deutsches Wörterbuch, mit einem Register Deutsch-Batak*. The Hague: Nijhoff, 1977. 332 pp. 90-247-2018-4.
With additions by Joh. Winkler; edited by R. Roolvink. The index is by K. A. Adelaar. Koninklijk Instituut voor Taal-, Land- en Volkenkunde.

[Toba Batak-German dictionary, with a German-Batak key.] Arranged under roots: in this language of complex affixation some forms may be difficult to find. In romanization. German-Batak section, pp. 291-332.

Note also: H. N. van der Tuuk: *Bataksch-Nederduitsch woordenboek*. Amsterdam: Muller, 1861. 551 pp.

[Toba Batak-Dutch dictionary.] Batak script is used for headwords and in examples throughout. With 30 beautiful colour plates illustrating technical terminology.

773
H. N. van der Tuuk: *A grammar of Toba Batak*. The Hague: Nijhoff, 1971. 405 pp.
Koninklijk Instituut voor Taal-, Land- en Volkenkunde. (Translation series, 13.)

Regarded as the author's greatest achievement. There is a foreword by A. Teeuw on van der Tuuk and his work. This English translation of the grammar makes very limited use of Batak script.

First published in Dutch: H. N. van der Tuuk: *Tobasche spraakkunst*. Amsterdam, 1864-7. 2 v. (431 pp.) [Toba Batak grammar.] Uses Batak script, accompanied by romanization, throughout.

Buginese and Makasarese

774

A. A. Cense, Abdoerrahim: *Makassaars-Nederlands woordenboek, met Nederlands-Makassaars register.* The Hague: Nijhoff, 1979. 989 pp. 90-247-2320-5.
Koninklijk Instituut voor Taal-, Land- en Volkenkunde.

[Makasarese-Dutch dictionary with Dutch-Makasarese key.] A historical and general dictionary with some notes on word origins. The Dutch-Makasarese section, pp. 917-989, is by J. Noorduyn.

775

B. F. Matthes: *Makassaarsch-Hollandsch woordenboek met Hollandsch-Makassaarsche woordenlijst.* The Hague: Nijhoff, 1885. 1170 pp.

[Makasarese-Dutch dictionary with Dutch-Makasarese glossary.] Revised edition. Both halves give Makasarese terms in both script and romanization. Additional notes on plant names, pp. 1108-1121. List of boat terms, pp. 1156-8.

First edition: Amsterdam: Muller, 1859. 943 pp. Separate indexes to plant names, pp. 855-877.

776

B. F. Matthes: *Boegineesch-Hollandsch woordenboek met Hollandsch-Boeginesche woordenlijst.* The Hague: Nijhoff, 1874. 1180 pp.

[Buginese-Dutch dictionary with Dutch-Buginese glossary.] A large scale historical dictionary: script followed by romanization in the main sequence. In the Dutch-Buginese section, pp. 914-1120, script only (not romanization) is given. List of boat terms, pp. 1159-1169.

777

Ü. Sirk: *The Buginese language.* Moscow: Nauka, 1983. 122 pp.
(Languages of Asia and Africa.)

A brief scientific grammar, using phonetic transcription only.

First published in Russian: Yu. Kh. Sirk: *Bugiiskii yazyk.* 1975.

There is also a French translation: J. Sirk: *La langue bugis.* Paris: Association Archipel, 1979. 196 pp. (Cahier d'Archipel, 10.)

778

B. F. Matthes: *Boeginesche spraakkunst.* The Hague: Nijhoff, 1875. 305

pp.

[Buginese grammar.] Uses Buginese script.

Note also: B. F. Matthes: *Makassaarsche spraakkunst*. Amsterdam: Muller, 1858. 135 pp. [Makasarese grammar.] A brief grammar in both script and romanization.

Cham

779

G. Moussay: *Dictionnaire cam-vietnamien-français = Từ-điển Cham-Việt-Pháp*. Phanrang: Centre Culturel Cam, 1971. 597 pp.

[Cham-Vietnamese-French dictionary.] A dictionary of the modern language of Phan-rang and neighbourhood (map of these and other Cham-speaking districts, p. vi). Tabular format: Cham terms appear in three forms: traditional Cham script, standard romanization of the script, transcription of modern pronunciation. Many text boxes giving technical terms. Script and phonology, pp. ix-xxiii; grammar, pp. xxiv-xxxix. List of Cham villages with Cham and Vietnamese names, pp. 477-491; kinship terms, pp. 493-8; French-Cham index, 43 pp.; Vietnamese-Cham index, 43 pp.; Latin-Cham index of zoological and botanical names, 2 pp.

780

Etienne Aymonier, Antoine Cabaton: *Dictionnaire cam-français*. Paris: Leroux, 1906. 587 pp.
(Publications de l'Ecole Française d'Extrême-Orient, 7.)

[Cham-French dictionary.] Essentially a dictionary of the medieval language recorded on inscriptions. Cham script (beautifully cast) and transliteration followed by French glosses. Many phrases. Complete French index, pp. 533-552; Cham index in romanized alphabetical order, pp. 553-587. Language and script, pp. vii-xxxiv.

Note also: Etienne Aymonier: *Grammaire de la langue chame*. Saigon: Imprimerie Coloniale, 1889. [Grammar of Cham.]

Javanese

781

S. Prawiro Atmodjo: *Bausastra Jawa*. Surabaya: Djojo Bojo, 1987. 471 pp.

[Javanese dictionary.] A concise monolingual dictionary of modern Javanese.

Supplement of modern loanwords, pp. 437-471.

782

Elinor Clark Horne: *Javanese-English dictionary*. New Haven: Yale University Press, 1974. 728 pp.

A substantial dictionary of the modern language, in roman script, with many brief examples. Sadly, many botanical terms are glossed with vague phrases such as 'a certain kind of flower'. Phonology, spelling, morphology, pp. x-xxvii; Social registers, pp. xxxi-xxxiii; Degree terms; Alphabetical lists of initial and final 'disguising elements', pp. xxxv-xxxix.

Note also: S. Prawiroatmodjo: *Bausastra Jawa-Indonesia*. Jakarta: Gunung Agung, 1981. 2 v. [Javanese-Bahasa Indonesia dictionary.] About 40,000 brief entries.

And: Th. Pigeaud: *Javaans-Nederlands handwoordenboek*. Groningen, 1938. 624 pp. [Concise Javanese-Dutch dictionary.]

An older work: J. F. C. Gericke, T. Roorda: *Javaansch-Nederlandsch handwoordenboek*. Amsterdam: Muller, 1901. 2 v. [Concise Javanese-Dutch dictionary.] This substantial work has headwords and examples in kawi script, and is useful for providing scientific Latin glosses for botanical and zoological terms. Addenda, vol. 2 pp. 807-872.

783

Th. Pigeaud: *Nederlands-Javaans handwoordenboek*. Groningen, 1948. 663 pp.

[Concise Dutch-Javanese dictionary.]

784

P. J. Zoetmulder, S. O. Robson: *Old Javanese-English dictionary*. The Hague: Nijhoff, 1982. 2 v. (2368 pp.)

A splendid work: 25,500 entries (entirely in romanization) with many subheadings for compounds. Of these entries over half are for words of Sanskrit derivation: for these, where necessary, semantic changes are noted on the basis of the *Sanskrit-English dictionary* of Monier Williams. List of source texts, pp. xviii-xxii: precise references, and contexts, appear in the entries. A long-needed replacement for van der Tuuk [770].

785

Th. Pigeaud: *Literature of Java*. The Hague: Nijhoff, 1967-70. 3 v.

Chiefly a catalogue of manuscripts in Leiden collections. Vol. 1, however, forms a systematic survey of Javanese literature.

786

A. S. Tesyolkin: *Yavanskii yazyk*. Moscow: Nauka, 1961.

[The Javanese language].

Note also: A. S. Tesyolkin: *Drevneyavanskii yazyk*. 1963. [The Old Javanese language.] These are brief scientific grammars in Russian in a standard format.

Madurese

787

Asis Safioedin: *Kamus bahasa Madura-Indonesia*. Jakarta: Departemen Penelitian dan Kebudayaan, 1977. 246 pp.

[Madurese-Bahasa Indonesia dictionary.] A short modern dictionary in roman script of the language of Madura, closely related to Javanese.

788

H. N. Kiliaan: *Madoereesch-Nederlandsch woordenboek*. Leiden: Brill, 1904-5. 2 v.

[Madurese-Dutch dictionary.] In this extensive work the headwords are in kawi followed by romanization. Etymologies are given as well as Dutch glosses.

Kiliaan also compiled a Dutch-Madurese dictionary.

Note also: P. Penninga, H. Hendriks: *Practisch Madoereesch-Hollandsch woordenboek*. Semarang: Van Dorp, n.d. 360 + 40 pp. [Handy Madurese-Dutch dictionary.] A concise dictionary in roman script, published around 1930.

789

H. N. Kiliaan: *Madoereesche spraakkunst*. Batavia, 1897. 2 v.

[Madurese grammar.]

Minangkabau

790

M. Thaib gl. St. Pamoentjak: *Kamoes bahasa Minangkabau-bahasa Melajoe-Riau*. Batavia: Balai Poestaka, 1935. 279 pp.

[Minangkabau-Malay dictionary.] A dictionary of about 12,000 entries, by a native speaker of this language of central Sumatra closely related to Malay. Roman script.

Note also: J. L. van der Toorn: *Minangkabausch-Maleisch-Nederlandsch woordenboek.* The Hague: Nijhoff, 1891. 392 pp. [Minangkabau-Malay-Dutch dictionary.] Headwords in Arabic script followed by romanization.

791

Gerard Moussay: *La langue minangkabau.* Paris: Association Archipel, 1981. 339 pp.

[The Minangkabau language.] A grammar: in roman script. Text reproduced from a messy typescript.

Note also: J. L. van der Toorn: *Minangkabausche spraakkunst.* The Hague, 1899. 227 pp. [Minangkabau grammar.] Roman script only.

Mon

792

H. L. Shorto: *A dictionary of modern spoken Mon.* London: Oxford University Press, 1962. 280 pp. 0-19-713524-2.
School of Oriental and African Studies.

An extensive Mon-English dictionary by an academic linguist (Professor at the School of Oriental and African Studies, London). The main dictionary is in romanization, followed by an index in Mon script, not complete but covering words encountered in literature.

Note also: Nai Tun Way; Lu Pe Win, editor: *Mun Myanma abidan.* Rangoon, 1977. Vol. 1. [Mon-Burmese dictionary.] An exhaustive dictionary of modern Mon in Mon and Burmese scripts; headwords are followed by phonetic transcriptions in IPA and in Burmese characters. Foreword in English. Phonology and script, preliminary pp. 23-49; some classified word lists (points of the compass, numerals, etc.) preliminary pp. 50-54. I have not seen subsequent volumes: the set was to be complete in five.

793

Robert Halliday: *A Mon-English dictionary.* Bangkok: Siam Society, 1922. 512 pp.

In Mon script, with romanization. Tabular format but allowing space for fairly full glosses and explanations. 15 pages of corrigenda after p. 512. Reprint: Rangoon: Ministry of Union Culture, Mon Cultural Section, 1955.

Note also: Edward O. Stevens: *A vocabulary English and Peguan to which are added a few pages of geographical names.* Rangoon: American Baptist Mission Press, 1896. 139 pp.

794

H. L. Shorto: *A dictionary of the Mon inscriptions from the sixth to the sixteenth centuries.* London: Oxford University Press, 1971. 406 pp. 0-19-713565-X.
(London Oriental series, 24.)

Incorporating materials collected by C. O. Blagden. Romanized text only: it is a remarkable fault (in a work of otherwise impressive scholarship) that not even a transliteration table is offered.

Shan

795

J. N. Cushing: *A Shan and English dictionary.* Rangoon: American Baptist Mission Press, 1914. 708 pp.
'Preface to the second edition' by H. W. Mix.

The only Shan-English dictionary. About 21,000 entries. 'The pronunciation common in the principalities of Laihka and Möngnai has been taken as standard.'

First edition: 1881.

Paired with: Mrs H. W. Mix, editor: *An English and Shan dictionary.* Rangoon: American Baptist Mission Press, 1920. 968 pp. This English-Shan dictionary is based on materials collected by J. N. Cushing, Maung Kham Mun, and Mrs Cushing. About 20,000 entries, with numerous phrases.

Note also: J. N. Cushing: *A grammar of the Shan language.* Rangoon: American Baptist Mission Press, 1887. 118 pp. Second edition.

First edition: 1871.

Sundanese

796

Kamus umum basa Sunda. Bandung: Tarate, 1975. 568 pp.

[Popular dictionary of Sundanese.] A monolingual dictionary of the main language of Sunda, closely related to Javanese. About 17,000 entries. The fourth printing, 1985, contains a 7-page addendum.

Note also: R. Satjadibrata: *Kamus basa Sunda.* Jakarta: Balai Pustaka, 1954. 479 pp. (BP, 1692.) [Sundanese dictionary.] Second edition.

First published as: R. Satjadibrata: *Kamoes basa Soenda*. 1948. 448 pp.

797

F. S. Eringa: *Soendaas-Nederlands woordenboek*. Dordrecht: Foris, 1984. 846 pp. 90-6765-056-0.
Koninklijk Instituut voor Taal-, Land- en Volkenkunde.

[Sundanese-Dutch dictionary.] Based on a manuscript by R. A. Kern, begun before 1950. Edited in collaboration with A. A. Fokker. About 24,000 entries. Roman script.

Note also: H. J. Oosting: *Soendasch-Nederduitsch woordenboek*. Batavia: Ogilvie, 1879. 874 pp. [Sundanese-Dutch dictionary.] Headwords and examples are in kawi throughout, with no transliteration.

There was also a supplement: Amsterdam: Muller, 1882. 206, xxi pp.

798

R. Satjadibrata: *Kamoes Soenda-Indonesia*. Jakarta: Balai Poestaka, 1950. 414 pp.
(BP, 1561.)

[Sundanese-Bahasa Indonesia dictionary.] Second edition.

First published as: R. Satjadibrata: *Kamoes Soenda-Melajoe*. 1944. 379 pp. [Sundanese-Malay dictionary.]

799

R. Momon Wirakusumah, I. Buldan Djajawiguna: *Tatabasa Sunda*. Bandung, 1957. 82 pp.

[Sundanese grammar.] In Bahasa Indonesia.

Note also: A. P. Pavlenko: *Sundanskii yazyk*. Moscow: Nauka, 1965. [The Sundanese language.] Brief grammar in Russian.

White Tai

800

Dieu Chinh Nhim, Jean Donaldson: *Pap san khham Pak Tay-Keo-Eng = Ngữ-vung Thai-Việt-Anh = Tai-Vietnamese-English dictionary*. Saigon: Bộ Giáo-Dục, 1970. 476 pp.

A dictionary of the White Tai dialect of Lai Chau. In roman (Vietnamese) script: table of three romanizations and the Chu Thai script, pp. ix-xv. Vietnamese index, pp. 393-427; English index, pp. 431-476.

Can be paired with: Lieutenant Minot: *Dictionnaire français-thay blanc.* Muong-Te, 1933. 92 pp. Glosses are in White Tai script only.

Note also: Lieutenant Minot: *Dialecte thay blanc.* Muong-Te, 1933. 101 pp. A grammatical sketch with some classified word lists.

The last two works were reprinted in one volume with a new title: Georges Minot: *Vocabulaire français-thai blanc et éléments de grammaire.* Hanoi, 1949. 101 + 92 pp. This includes, as an appendix, transliteration tables for White Tai and Black Tai scripts.

Tai Yuan

801

Udom Rungruangsi: *Photchananukrom Lanna-Thai.* Bangkok, 1991. 2 v. (1638 pp.)

[Tai Yuan-Thai dictionary.] Headwords and subheadings in Tai Yuan script, the best printed font of this complex script I have ever seen. Otherwise in Thai (but scientific Latin is added in glosses for flora and fauna).

802

Met Ratanaprasit: *Photchananukrom Thai Yuan-Thai-Angkrit.* 1965. 378 pp.

[Tai Yuan-Thai-English dictionary.] In three columns: the central column (Thai) is wider, with explanations and some examples. The Tai Yuan is in central Thai script. Thai index, pp. 266-310: no English index. Supplementary glossary of botanical names, Tai Yuan-Thai-scientific Latin, pp. 311-360; there are Thai and Latin indexes to this.

Note also: Herbert C. Purnell: *A short Northern Thai-English dictionary (Tai Yuan).* Chiangmai, 1963. 126 pp.

The Tai Yuan is here in phonetic script only.

803

L. N. Morev: *Yazyk ly.* Moscow: Nauka, 1978.

[The Lü language.] Grammar, in Russian, of the regional language of Xishuangbanna, differing little from the Khün of Kengtung and from Tai Yuan of northern Thailand.

Note also: Harald Hundius: *Phonologie und Schrift des Nordthai.* Stuttgart: Franz Steiner, 1990. 265 pp. (Abhandlungen für die Kunde des Morgenlandes, 48 iii.) [Phonology and script of Northern Thai.] Script and transliteration, pp. 119-247.

EXTERNAL LANGUAGES OF RELIGION AND POLITICS

Arabic

804

Abu Abdul Latif Al-Syeikh Ahmad bin Othman Bajunid: *Kamus pustaka Melayu-Arab*. Kuala Lumpur: Darulfikir, 1985. 998 pp.

[Literary Malay-Arabic dictionary.] Entirely in Arabic script except that Malay headwords of non-Arabic origin are accompanied by their roman forms.

805

Haji Dusuki Bin Haji Ahmad: *Kamus pengetahuan Islam*. Kuala Lumpur: Yayasan Dakwah Islamiah Malaysia, 1976. 425 pp.

Encyclopaedia of Islamic culture. In Bahasa Malaysia (headwords also in jawi script). Entries (about 3 per page) on religious and cultural concepts and on Islamic literary and historical figures. Historical maps, pp. 410-425.

Chinese, Pali, Sanskrit

806

Yen-Nguan Bhikkhu, Liang Sathirasut, Songvit Kaesri: *A dictionary of Buddhism, Thai-Pali-Chinese*. Bangkok: Wat Pho Maen Khunaram, 1978. 866 pp.

About 15,000 entries, in tabular format. Really a bilingual dictionary only, since the 'Thai' and 'Pali' are, I think in every case, the same word in Thai and roman scripts. Chinese index, pp. 745-866.

807

A dictionary of Buddhism, Chinese-Sanskrit-English-Thai. Bangkok: Wat Pho Maen Khunaram, 1976. 830 pp.
'Published by the Chinese Buddhist Order of Sangha in Thailand.'

An explanatory dictionary of Buddhist proper names and concepts. In tabular format. In Chinese character order: Sanskrit and Pali index (roman script) pp. 740-766; Thai index, pp. 767-819.

808

Prince Kitiyakara Krommaphra Chandaburinarünath: *Pali-Thai-English-Sanskrit dictionary*. Bangkok, 1970. 906 pp.

Based on the Prince's manuscript notes, made in the early 20th century, in a 1909 reprint of: Robert Caesar Childers: *A dictionary of the Pali language*. London, 1872. Useful as a guide to Thai Buddhist terminology. Pali headwords in both roman and Thai script: the Sanskrit terms offered are not necessarily translations but etymologies. Transliteration table of Thai as used in Pali and Sanskrit, p. 893.

809

Đoàn-Trung-Còn: *Phật-học từ-điển*. Saigon: Phật-Học Tòng Tho, 1966-8. 3 v.
(Phật-học, 23.)

[Encyclopaedia of Buddhism.] Each Vietnamese headword is followed by Chinese, romanized Pali or Sanskrit, and French version, then by a definition in Vietnamese. Encyclopaedic entries deal with both proper names and religious terminology. Indispensable. Text entirely in Vietnamese.

810

Tipitaka Pali-Myanma abidan. Rangoon.

[Pali-Burmese dictionary of the Tipitaka.] A very extensive work dealing exhaustively with the vocabulary of the Pali Buddhist scriptures. The work was nearing completion with vol. 15, published in 1982. Entirely in Burmese script.

811

A lexilogus of the English, Malay and Chinese languages, comprehending the vernacular idioms of the last in the Hokkeen and Canton dialects. Malacca: Anglo-Chinese College, 1841. 111 pp.
[By James Legge.]

Tabular format in five columns, the third giving Chinese characters.

English

812

Gregory R. Clark: *Words of the Vietnam War: the slang, jargon, abbreviations, acronyms, nomenclature, nicknames, pseudonyms, slogans, specs, euphemisms, double-talk, chants, and names and places of the era of United States involvement in Vietnam*. Jefferson, North Carolina: McFarland, 1990. 604 pp. 0-89950-465-5.

An alphabetical dictionary of English words, abbreviations, etc.; includes

Vietnamese terms and proper names found in English narratives of the war. Entires for people include brief biographical details. 10,000 entries (but many are cross-references). Amusing but difficult to read because of the heavy use of jargon in the definitions.

Note also: Linda Reinberg: *In the field: the language of the Vietnam War*. New York: Facts on File, 1991. 273 pp. 0-8160-2214-3. Simpler, more professional definitions: but less comprehensive.

813

Henry Yule, A. C. Burnell: *Hobson-Jobson: a glossary of colloquial Anglo-Indian words and phrases, and of kindred terms, etymological, historical, geographical and discursive*. London: Murray, 1903. 1021 pp.

New edition by William Crooke. Includes many terms and proper names originating in south east Asia, or forming part of the vocabulary of the English of the region.

Reprinted: London: Routledge & Kegan Paul, 1985. 0-7100-2886-5.

SOME LANGUAGES OF ORAL CULTURE

Akha

814

Paul Lewis: *Akha-English dictionary*. Ithaca: Cornell University, Department of Asian Studies, 1968. 363 pp.
Southeast Asia Program. (Data paper, 70. Linguistics series, 3.)

'I served as a missionary with the Burma Baptist Convention. I began learning the language while living in Pangwai, Kengtung State ... The Akha people live in southern Yunnan, China, Kengtung State, northwestern Laos, and northern Thailand.' About 6000 entries. Roman script, using diacritical marks for tones. 'Many [additional] specialized terms will be found in the notes I am writing for the Human Relations Area Files.'

Bahnar

815

Paul Guilleminet, R. P. Jules Alberty: *Dictionnaire bahnar-français*. Paris, 1959-63. Vols 1-2 (pp. 1-991).
(Publications de l'Ecole Française d'Extrême-Orient, 40.)

[Bahnar-French dictionary.] An ambitious work of which only the alphabetical section has appeared, in two volumes. It was to be followed by a classified list of classifiers, of onomatopoeias etc., of descriptive adjectives, and of pejoratives; then by an illustrated dictionary of technical terms in various fields.

Note also: P. X. Dourisboure: *Dictionnaire bahnar-français.* Hong Kong: Société des Missions-Etrangères, 1889. 363 pp. In tabular format.

Bare'e

816
N. Adriani: *Bare'e woordenboek met Nederlandsch-Bare'e register.* Leiden: Brill, 1928. 1074 pp.
Bataviaasch Genootschap van Kunsten en Wetenschappen.

[Bare'e-Dutch dictionary with Dutch-Bare'e key.] About 15,000 lengthy entries; some notes on cognates in related languages. Addenda, pp. 985-994; Dutch-Bare'e section, pp. 995-1074.

The same author compiled a very full grammar for this language of central Celebes: N. Adriani: *Spraakkunst der Bare'e-taal.* Bandung, 1931. 481 pp. (Verhandelingen van het Koninklijke Bataviaas Genootschap van Kunsten en Wetenschappen, Bandung, 70.)

Bikol

817
Malcolm Warren Mintz, José del Rosario Britanico: *Bikol-English dictionary = Diksionáriong Bíkol-Inglés.* Quezon City: New Day, 1985. 555 pp. 971-10-0212-4.

Indicates origin of loanwords from European and Chinese languages. Includes an English-Bikol section, pp. 57-212. Bikol dialects, p. 3; Sound system and grammar, pp. 4-46.

Earlier version: Honolulu: University of Hawaii Press, 1971. 1012 pp. 0-87022-528-6. (PALI language texts: Philippines.)

Note also: Malcolm W. Mintz: *Bikol grammar notes.* 1971. 279 pp. 0-87022-529-4. (PALI language texts: Philippines.)

Bima

818
J. C. G. Jonker: *Bimaneesch-Hollandsch woordenboek.* Bandung, 1896. (Verhandelingen van het Koninklijke Bataviaas Genootschap van Kunsten en Wetenschappen, Bandung, 48 i.)

[Bima-Dutch dictionary.] Dictionary of the language of eastern Sumbawa.

Accompanied by a grammar: J. C. G. Jonker: *Bimaneesche spraakkunst*. 1896. 487 pp. (Verhandelingen van het Koninklijke Bataviaas Genootschap van Kunsten en Wetenschappen, Bandung, 48 iii.)

Bola'ang Mongondou

819

W. Dunnebier: *Bolaang Mongondowsch-Nederlandsch woordenboek met Nederlandsch-Bolaang Mongondowsch register*. The Hague: Nijhoff, 1951. 635 pp.
Koninklijk Instituut voor Taal-, Land- en Volkenkunde.

[Bola'ang Mongondou-Dutch dictionary with Dutch index.] Dictionary of a language of northern Celebes.

The same author compiled a grammar: W. Dunnebier: 'Spraakkunst van het Bolaang-Mongondowsch' in *Bijdragen tot de taal-, land- en volkenkunde* vols 85-6 (1929-30). [Grammar of Bola'ang Mongondou.] List of contents, vol. 86 pp. 173-7.

Cebuano

820

John U. Wolff: *A dictionary of Cebuano Visayan*. Ithaca: Cornell University, Department of Asian Studies, 1972. 2 v. (1164 pp.)
Southeast Asia Program. (Data paper, 87. Linguistics series, 6.) Linguistic Society of the Philippines.

25000 entries (and 700 addenda) with many examples. 'Meant as a reference work for Cebuano speakers and as a tool for students.' Well printed in small but clear type, unusually for this series.

May be paired with: Rodolfo Cabonce: *An English-Cebuano Visayan dictionary*. Metro Manila: National Book Store, 1983. 1135 pp. 971-08-0052-3. A massive work by a local parish priest, with about 20,000 entries.

Gajo

821

G. A. J. Hazeu: *Gajôsch-Nederlandsch woordenboek met Nederlandsch-Gajôsch register*. Batavia, 1907. 1148 pp.

[Gajo-Dutch dictionary with Dutch-Gajo key.] An almost encyclopaedic dictionary of a language of northern Sumatra, indicating origins of loanwords, many of which come from Arabic. Dutch-Gajo section, pp. 1059-1129; addenda, pp. 1131-48. Brief grammatical introduction, pp. vii-xvii.

Galela

822
M. J. van Baarda: *Woordenlijst Galelareesch-Hollandsch, met ethnologische aantekeningen op de woorden die daartoe aanleiding gaven.* The Hague: Nijhoff, 1895. 536 pp.

[Galela-Dutch dictionary with ethnographical notes to relevant entries.] Galela is a language of the North Halmaheran family. No Dutch index. Not seen.

Note also: M. J. van Baarda: *Leiddraad bij het bestudeeren van 't Galela'sch dialekt op het eiland Halmaheira.* The Hague: Nijhoff, 1908. 168 pp. [Guide to the study of the Galela dialect of the island of Halmahera.] A grammar.

Galoli

823
Manuel Maria Alves da Silva: *Diccionario portuguez-galoli.* Macau: Typographia Mercantil, 1905. 387 pp.

[Portuguese-Galoli dictionary.] Dictionary of a language of east Timor.

Gorontalo

824
Mansoer Pateda: *Kamus bahasa Gorontalo-Indonesia.* Jakarta: Departemen Penelitian dan Kebudayaan, 1977. 338 pp.

[Gorontalo-Bahasa Indonesia dictionary.] Dictionary of a language of northern Celebes: one of the largest of a considerable series of dictionaries of minority languages published by the Indonesian Language and Literature Council.

Hiligaynon

825
Alonso Mentrida: *Diccionario de la lengua Bisaya Hiligeceina y Haraya de la Isla de Panay.* Manila: Tomas Oliva, 1841. 827 pp.

[Dictionary of Hiligaynon.] Revised edition, incorporating a Spanish-

Hiligaynon dictionary by Julian Martin (pp. 460-827).

Second edition: 1698. First published 1637.

Note also: Alonso Mentrida: *Arte de la lengua Bisaya-Hiligayna de la Isla de Panay*. Tambobong: Asilo de Huerfanos, 1894. 270 pp. Edited by José Aparicio. [Grammar of Hiligaynon.]

Previous edition: 1818. First published: Manila: 1618, but no copies of this edition are known. All bibliographical details in this entry come from Manuel [295] vol. 3 p. 385.

Hmong

826

Nguyễn Văn Chinh: *Từ điển Meo-Việt loai nho*. Hanoi: Khoa Học Xã Hội, 1971. 926 pp.

[Mieo-Vietnamese dictionary.] Not seen.

Note also: Lang Xiong, William J. Xiong, Nao Leng Xiong: *English-Mong-English dictionary = Phoo txais lug Aakiv-Moob-Aakiv*. Milwaukee: Xiong, 1983. 570 pp. Intended for migrants from Vietnam settled in the United States.

827

Ernest E. Heimbach: *White Meo-English dictionary*. Ithaca: Cornell University, Department of Asian Studies, 1969. 497 pp.
Southeast Asia Program. (Data paper, 75. Linguistics series, 4.)

Material gathered during 1954-63 in missionary work in northern Thailand, with visits to Laos. Roman script. Appendices: Patterns of tone change; Classifiers; Useful phrases; Proverbs, pp. 461-6; Farming calendar, p. 467; Post-verbal intensifiers; Classified vocabulary (a partial index) pp. 480-492; Kinship charts, pp. 492-7.

Note also: Yves Bertrais, R. P. Charrier: *Dictionnaire hmong (mèo blanc)-français*. Vientiane: Mission Catholique, 1964. Unnumbered pp. [White Meo-French dictionary.] Roneoed. A large scale work perhaps rather hastily reconstituted after the original data were lost.

Reprinted: Bangkok: Assumption Press, 1979 [not seen].

828

Thomas Amis Lyman: *Dictionary of Mong Njua, a Miao (Meo) language of Southeast Asia*. The Hague: Mouton, 1974. 403 pp.

The language is also known as Green Miao. Lyman worked with speakers in Nan province of Thailand. His work is a Hmong Neua-English dictionary employing a phonetic script. Explanations, pp. 15-40; correspondences with the Smalley-Heimbach orthography for White Miao (see **826**), pp. 65-6. Appendices (forming a partial English index) include: Body terms; Colours; Compass; Kinship terms; Minerals; Numerals; Opium etc.; Rice; Seasons; Sickness and medicine; Day, month and year names; Tools, instruments and weapons; Weaving. List of clans, p. 383.

Paired with: Thomas Amis Lymann [*sic*]: *English/Meo pocket dictionary*. Bangkok: Goethe-Institute, 1970. 131 pp. Tabular format at A4 size (requiring an unusually large pocket). Includes table 3, p. 130: The Meo tribes and their locations. Reprinted at reduced size, with the author's name respelt: 1973.

Note also: Thomas Amis Lyman: *Grammar of Mong Njua (Green Miao): a descriptive linguistic study*. Sattley, Calif.: Blue Oak Press, 1979. 100 pp.

Iban

829

Anthony Richards: *An Iban-English dictionary*. Oxford: Clarendon Press, 1981. 417 pp.

Very detailed dictionary begun in 1964 when the author retired from the Sarawak Civil Service; based both on oral work and on published literature. A proportion of the anthropological information embedded in entries is accessible through the very brief 'English-Iban guide to some of the longer entries', pp. xxvii-xxix. Iban was once better known as Sea Dayak, a fact never mentioned here.

Note also: *Kamus bahasa Iban-bahasa Malaysia*. Kuala Lumpur: Dewan Bahasa dan Pustaka, 1989. 425 pp. 983-62-0740-6. Edited by Hussain bin Jamil, Henry Gana Ngadi. An impressive modern dictionary, lacking the anthropological and botanical terminology of Richards'.

Superseded: N. C. Scott: *A dictionary of Sea Dayak*. London: School of Oriental and African Studies, 1956.

830

Asmah Hj. Omar: *The Iban language of Sarawak: a grammatical description*. Kuala Lumpur: Dewan Bahasa dan Pustaka, 1981. 285 pp.

A brief reference grammar.

Iloko

831

Morice Vanoverbergh: *Iloko-English dictionary. Rev. Andrés Caro's*

Vocabulario iloco-espanol translated, augmented and revised. [Baguio City, 1957.] 370 pp.

Substantial dictionary of a Philippine language in not quite perfect English.

Paired with: Morice Vanoverbergh: *English-Iloko thesaurus.* [Baguio City] n.d. 365 pp.

Note also: Morice Vanoverbergh: *Iloko grammar.* [Baguio City] 1955. 348 pp.

Kachin

832

O. Hanson: *A dictionary of the Kachin language.* Rangoon: Baptist Board of Publications, 1954.

'Revised edition' which I have not seen. The only available dictionary; in the standard roman script, which does not mark tones.

First edition: Rangoon: American Baptist Mission Press, 1906. 752 pp. About 15,000 entries.

This venerable work can now be paired with: Manam Hpang: *English Kachin Burmese dictionary = Inglik Jinghpaw Myen ga htai chyum.* Myitkyina, 1977. 644 pp. This includes appendices of technical terms: fruit, vegetables, diseases, animals, insects, reptiles, fishes, birds, trees and flowers, colours.

833

Ye. V. Puzitskii: *Kachinskii yazyk (yazyk chzhingpkho).* Moscow: Nauka, 1968.

[The Kachin (Chingpho) language.] A brief scientific grammar in Russian.

Note also: O. Hanson: *A grammar of the Kachin language.* Rangoon: American Baptist Mission Press, 1896. 231 pp. Appendices in this work: Names; Seasons, months, hours; Weights, measures, money; Terms of relationship, pp. 105-110.

Kadazan

834

A. Antonissen: *Kadazan-English and English-Kadazan dictionary.* Canberra: Government Printing Office, 1958. 274 pp.
Cover title: *Kadazan dictionary and grammar.*

Concise dictionary of a language of Sabah. Brief grammar, pp. 11-39.

Karen

835

Rev. J. Wade: *A dictionary of the Sgau Karen language*. Rangoon: American Baptist Mission Press, 1896. 1341 pp.
Assisted by Mrs S. K. Bennett; recompiled and revised by Rev. E. B. Cross.

Karen-English dictionary in Karen script. Revision of: Rev. J. Wade: *A vocabulary of the Sgau Karen language*. Tavoy: Karen Mission Press, 1849. 1024 pp.

Also to be consulted: Sau Kau-too, J. Wade: *Thesaurus of the Karen knowledge, comprising traditions, legends or fables, poetry, customs, superstitions, demonology, therapeutics etc., alphabetically arranged and forming a complete native Karen dictionary, with definitions and examples illustrating the usages of every word*. Tavoy, 1847-50. 4 v.

The Karen-English dictionary is paired with: Geo. E. Blackwell: *The Anglo-Karen dictionary*. Rangoon: Baptist Board of Publications, 1954. 543 pp.

Revision and abridgement of: J. Wade, Mrs J. P. Binney: *The Anglo-Karen dictionary*. Rangoon: American Baptist Mission Press, 1883. 781 pp.

Note also: Rev. J. Wade: *Karen vernacular grammar with English interspersed for the benefit of foreign students*. Rangoon, 1888. 256 pp. Second edition. First edition: Moulmein: American Mission Press, 1861.

Kayan

836

C. H. Southwell: *Kayan-English dictionary with appendices*. Baram, 1980. 380 pp.

A language of Sarawak. Photocopied from typescript. The appendices (9 pp. at end) are lists of flora and fauna.

Lahu

837

James A. Matisoff: *The dictionary of Lahu*. Berkeley: University of California Press, 1988. 1436 pp.
(University of California publications in linguistics.)

A Lahu-English dictionary with an introduction on the people and their culture. Not seen.

Note also: James A. Matisoff: *The grammar of Lahu*. 1982. 693 pp. Revised edition.

First edition: 1973. 673 pp. 0-520-09467-0. (University of California publications in linguistics, 75.) Reproduced from typescript. A highly technical work; good indexes.

Li'onese

838

P. Arndt: *Li'onesisch-Deutsches Wörterbuch*. Ende: Arnoldus-Druckerei, 1933. 555 pp.

[Li'onese-German dictionary.] A language of central Flores.

Maguindanaon

839

Robert E. Sullivan: *A Maguindanaon dictionary, Maguindanaon-English English-Maguindanaon*. Cotobato City: Notre Dame University, Institute of Cotobato Cultures, 1986. 545 pp. 971-129-000-6.

A southern Philippine language. Includes lists of numerals, weights and measures, months, colours; Male and female personal names, pp. 18-25; Verbal inflection, pp. 26-53. English-Maguindanaon section, pp. 360-545.

Manggarai

840

Jilis A. J. Verheijen: *Kamus Manggarai*. The Hague: Nijhoff, 1967-70. 2 v.
Koninklijk Instituut voor Taal-, Land- en Volkenkunde.

[Manggarai dictionary.] The language of the western part of Flores. A dictionary which is particularly informative on dialect variation and includes some etymological notes. Vol. 1 (772 pp.): Manggarai-Indonesian dictionary. Vol. 2 (269 pp.): Indonesian-Manggarai dictionary.

Ngadju

841

A. Hardeland: *Dajacksch-deutsches Wörterbuch*. Amsterdam: Muller, 1859. 638 pp.

[Dayak (i.e. Ngadju)-German dictionary.] In roman script.

The author had earlier published a grammar of this language of the Dayak group of southern Borneo: [A. Hardeland:] *Versuch einer Grammatik der Dajakschen Sprache.* 1858. 374 pp.

Palaung

842

Mrs Leslie Milne: *A dictionary of English-Palaung and Palaung-English.* Rangoon: Superintendent, Government Printing, 1931. 383 + 290 pp.

Based on the dialect of the Palaung speakers at Namhsan, capital of Tawngpeng (Northern Shan States). Appendices at end of first pagination: Kinship terms; Weights and measures; Glossaries of other dialects, pp. 355-383.

Rhadé

843

J. Davias-Baudrit: *Dictionnaire rhadé-français.* Dalat: Mission Catholique de Banmêthuôt, 1966.

'Substantial: extensive coverage of compounds and generous inclusion of sample sentences' (Tharp). Not seen.

Note also: James A. Tharp, Y-Bham Duôn-ya: *A Rhade-English dictionary with English-Rhade finderlist.* Canberra: Australian National University, Research School of Pacific Studies, Department of Linguistics, 1980. 271 pp. (Pacific linguistics, series C, 58.) Independent of Davias-Baudrit, and apparently based on a different dialect. In spite of the title, the two halves of the work are of similar size.

The series 'Pacific linguistics' contains many dictionaries and glossaries of minority south east Asian languages, generally rather less comprehensive than those listed here but in most cases forming the best available sources for the languages concerned. Full lists of the series appear at the end of each published volume.

Sengoi

844

Nathalie Means, Paul B. Means: *Sengoi-English English-Sengoi dictionary.* Toronto: Joint Center on Modern East Asia, 1986. 191 pp.

Dictionary of an Austroasiatic language spoken by 'the largest group of aboriginal people on the Malay Peninsula'. About 3500 entries in each half.

At each headword the standard Malay roman orthography is followed by a phonetic guide. Briefer than other dictionaries in this chapter, but included as the only representative of its language group.

Rotinese

845

J. C. G. Jonker: *Rottineesch-Hollandsch woordenboek*. Leiden: Brill, 1908. 806 pp.

[Rotinese-Dutch dictionary.] Dictionary of the language of Roti, south-west of Timor. Roman script.

Note also the enormous grammar by the same author: J. C. G. Jonker: *Rottineesche spraakkunst.* 1915. 714 pp. [Rotinese grammar.]

Sangir

846

K. G. F. Steller, W. E. Aebersold: *Sangirees-Nederlands woordenboek met Nederlands-Sangirees register*. The Hague: Nijhoff, 1959. 622 pp.

[Sangir Dutch dictionary with Dutch Sangir index.] Dictionary of a language of islands north of Celebes, based on the dialect of Manganitu (Pulau Sangihe) with additional information on others. The culmination of almost sixty years of research. Roman script.

Note also: N. Adriani: *Sangiresche spraakkunst*. Leiden: Nederlandsch Bijbelgenootschap, 1893. 284 pp. [Sangir grammar.]

Sasak

847

R. Goris: *Beknopt Sasaksch-Nederlandsch woordenboek*. Singaradja, 1938-9. 352 pp.
(Mededeelingen van de Kirtya Liefrinck-Van der Tuuk, 7-10.)

[Short Sasak-Dutch dictionary.] Sasak is the majority language of Lombok, closely related to neighbouring Balinese.

Srê

848

Jacques Dournes: *Dictionnaire srê (koho)-français*. Saigon, 1950.

[Srê (Koho)-French dictionary.] A Montagnard language of Vietnam.

Note also: S Drouin, K'Nai: *Dictionnaire français-montagnard (koho).* Fyan [1962?]. 4 v. [French-Koho dictionary.]

See: François Martini: 'De la transcription du srê (koho): à propos du dictionnaire du R. P. Jacques Dournes' in *Bulletin de la Société des Etudes Indochinoises* n.s. vol. 27 (1952) pp. 99-109. [The transcription of Srê (Koho): on Father Dournes' dictionary.]

Tetun

849

Cliff Morris: *Tetun-English dictionary.* Canberra: Australian National University, Research School of Pacific Studies, Department of Linguistics, 1984. 194 pp.
(Pacific linguistics, series C, 83.)

'The first substantial dictionary to English of any Timorese language. Tetun has for centuries been historically influential throughout the island, and a lingua franca in Portuguese East Timor.' The dictionary is based on Tetun-Los of the south coast, but includes information on other dialects. Grammatical notes, pp. xiv-xix.

Toradja

850

J. Tammu, H. van der Veen: *Kamus Toradja-Indonesia.* Rantepao: Jajasan Perguruan Kristen Toradja, 1972. 692 pp.

[Toradja-Bahasa Indonesia dictionary.] Dictionary of a language of Celebes. About 10,000 entries.

Based on: H. van der Veen: *Tae' (Zuid-Toradjasch)-Nederlandsch woordenboek met register Nederlandsch-Tae'.* The Hague, 1940. 930 pp.

[Tae' (South Toradja)-Dutch dictionary with Dutch-Tae' key.] Includes a short grammatical introduction.

Tobelo

851

A. Hueting: *Tobèloreesch-Hollandsch woordenboek met Hollandsch-Tobèloreesch inhoudsopgave.* The Hague: Nijhoff, 1908. 516 pp.

[Tobelo-Dutch dictionary with Dutch-Tobelo contents guide.] A North

Halmaheran language.

Tontemboan

852

J. Alb. T. Schwartz: *Tontemboansch-Nederlandsch woordenboek met Nederlandsch-Tontemboansch register.* The Hague, 1908. 690 pp.

[Tontemboan Dutch dictionary with Dutch index.] Dictionary of a language of northern Celebes.

Note also: N. Adriani, M. Adriani-Gunning: *Hoofdstukken uit de spraakkunst van het Tontemboansch.* The Hague, 1908. 259 pp. [Principles of Tontemboan grammar.]

Yao

853

Sylvia J. Lombard, Herbert C. Purnell Jr: *Yao-English dictionary.* Ithaca: Cornell University, Department of Asian Studies, 1968. 363 pp.
Southeast Asia Program. (Data paper, 69. Linguistics series, 2.)

Material gathered 1952-66 during residence in Yao villages in Chiengrai province and visits to refugee groups in Laos and South Vietnam. Roman script (see pp. x-xv) differing from the Vietnamese-based romanization used by Savina [620] (but that work is to be noted as providing a French-Yao dictionary). Appendices: Numbers, pp. 317-320; Kinship terms, pp. 321-7; Personal names; Proverbs and idioms, pp. 335-9; Classifiers. Substantial addenda, pp. 345-363.

Index

Aardrijkskundig en statistisch woordenboek 464
Abdoerrahim 774
Abhandlungen für die Kunde des Morgenlandes 803
Abhay, Thao Nhouy 121
About, Pierre-Edmond 423
Abu Abdul Latif Al-Syeikh Ahmad bin Othman Bajunid 804
Account of the areas of jurisdiction 476
Achehnese 766, 767
Achutegui, Pedro S. de 237
Adelaar, K. A. 772
Administrations et les services publics indochinois 97
Admiralty 93, 201, 480
Adriani, N. 816, 846, 852
Adriani-Gunning, M. 852
Advice and support 335
Advisory and combat assistance era 1954-1964 335
Advisory years to 1965 335
Aebersold, W. E. 846
Aéronautique Militaire de l'Indochine 94
Agard, A. 94
Agence Economique de l'Indochine 568
Agriculture: see under each country
Ahmad Bakeri bin Abu Bakar 178
Akha 814
Akha-English dictionary 814
Akkharanukrom phumisat Thai 418
Akkharawitthi 729
Alberty, R. P. Jules 815
Alexandre de Rhodes 745
Algué, José 384
Alikanov, K. M. 746
Aliyeva, N. F. 711
Alkema, B. 630
Allen, Betty Molesworth 583
Allen, J. de V. 354
Allison, Gordon H. 86

Almanach lao 129
Almanaque filipina i guía de forasteros 236
Alves da Silva, Manuel Maria 823
Alzon, Claude Hesse d' 321
Amatayakul, Tri 417
Amboinsch kruid-boek 557
Amended list of ancient monuments in Burma 406
American Ethnological Society 160
American Geographical Society of New York 634
American Institutes for Research, Kensington Office 622
American University 44, 108, 118, 133, 136, 137, 156, 165, 199, 220, 617, 623
Ampalavanar, Rajeswary 26
Amphibian fauna of Peninsular Malaysia 519
Anat Arbhabhirama 484
Ancheta, Herminia M. 291
Anek Liangprasoet 731
Angkor 112, 425, 433, 434
Anglo-Karen dictionary 835
Anglo-Chinese and Mohamedan calendar 358
Anh, Đào Duy- 742, 765
Anh, Nguyễn Huyền 270
Anh-Việt tù-điển 739
Annales de l'Académie des Sciences Coloniales 260
Annam 139, 444
Annam 139
Annam: études numismatiques 345
Annam central: Hué, tombes royales, Tourane, Mi-so'n 428
Annandale, Nelson 18
Annotated atlas of the Republic of Viet-Nam 135
Annotated bibliography of statistical publications 188
Annotated bibliography of bibliographies on Indonesia 24

Italicized entries are for titles. **Bold entries are subject guides**

Annotated statistical bibliography 81
Annuaire administratif, commercial et industriel 104
Annuaire administratif de l'Indochine 104
Annuaire administratif des services communs 104
Annuaire commercial du Tonkin 153
Annuaire commercial et administratif 104
Annuaire complet de l'Indochine 106
Annuaire de l'administration française en Indochine 104
Annuaire de l'Annam et du Tonkin 104
Annuaire de l'Indo-Chine Française 104
Annuaire de l'Indo-Chine 104
Annuaire de l'Indochine Française 104
Annuaire de l'Indochine complet 106
Annuaire de la Cochinchine Française 104
Annuaire des Etats-Associés: Cambodge, Laos, Vietnam 104
Annuaire diplomatique et consulaire 114
Annuaire du Cambodge 104
Annuaire général 104
Annuaire général de l'Indo-Chine 104
Annuaire général de l'Indo-Chine Française 104
Annuaire général du Vietnam 152
Annuaire illustré de la Cochinchine 154
Annuaire illustré du Cambodge 115
Annuaire industriel et commercial 152
Annuaire statistique de l'Indochine 102
Annuaire statistique du Cambodge 113
Annuaire statistique du Laos 126
Annuaire statistique du Viet-Nam 146
Annuaire statistique retrospectif du Cambodge 113
Annual bulletin of statistics 170, 171
Annual bulletin of statistics, Malaysia 169
Annual list of Government gazetted officers 66
Annual report of the Governor General 227
Annual report of the President of the Philippines 227
Annual report of the United States 227

Annual report on Sarawak 168
Annual report on Singapore 185
Annual report on the Federation of Malaya 168
Annual report on the Straits Settlements 168
Annual report on the social and economic progress 168
Annual report on the Malayan Union 168
Annual reports on the Federated Malay States 168
Annual reports on the states 168
Annual reports on the Unfederated Malay States 168
Annual statistical bulletin, Malaysia 169
Annual statistical bulletin Sarawak 171
Anthropology in Indonesia 629
Anthropometric data from Burma 58
Antonissen, A. 834
Apa & Siapa sejumlah orang Indonesia 1983-1984 283
Aparicio, José 825
Arabic 713, 804, 805
Arakan operations 303
Arakanese calendar 316
Arasaratnam, S. 350
Arbhabhirama, Anat 484
Archaeological Survey of Burma 314
Archéologie mône de Dvaravati 419
Archives des Affaires Etrangères 100
Archives des recherches agronomiques 593
Archivo del bibliófilo filipino 364
Area and country survey series 200
Area handbook for Burma 44
Area handbook for British Borneo 165
Area handbook for Cambodia 108
Area handbook for Indonesia 199
Area handbook for Laos 118
Area handbook for Malaysia 156
Area handbook for Malaysia and Singapore 156
Area handbook for North Vietnam 136
Area handbook for Singapore 181
Area handbook for South Vietnam 137

Italicized entries are for titles. **Bold entries are subject guides**

Area handbook for the Philippines 220
Area handbook for the Khmer Republic (Cambodia) 108
Area handbook for Thailand 71
Area handbook for Vietnam 133
Area handbook on British Borneo 165
Area handbook on Laos 122
Area handbook on the Philippines 221
Area handbook series 156, 181, 199, 220
Arief, Sritua 285, 287
Arifin, Winarsih 693
Army Medical Services campaigns: vol. 5, Burma 302
Arndt, P. 838
Art du Laos 435
Arte de la lengua Bisaya-Hiligayna de la Isla de Panay 825
Arthur D. Little Inc. 33
Arun Amatyakul 253
Aschmoneit, Walter 23
ASEAN who's who 273
Ashton, P. S. 573
Asia: reference works, a select annotated guide 19
Asia yearbook 12
Asian Development Bank 33
Asian historical dictionaries 329, 332, 348
Asie du Sud-Est 477
Asmah Haji Omar 625, 830
Association des Amis du Vieux Hué 139
Association of Southeast Asian Institutions 42
Association of the U.S. Army 335
Association of Vietnamese Engineers and Technicians 152
Atjèhsch-Nederlandsch woordenboek 766
Atlas archéologique de l'Indochine 429
Atlas colonial français 370
Atlas de Filipinas 384
Atlas de l'Indochine 372
Atlas de la ville de Louang-Phrabang 376
Atlas des colonies françaises 370, 375
Atlas des ressources physiques 366

Atlas [du Service Météorologique de l'Indochine] 103
Atlas ethno-linguistique 670
Atlas for marine policy in south east Asian seas 482
Atlas général de l'Indochine Française 374
Atlas Indonesia. Vol. 1: Umum 380
Atlas kebangsaan Malaysia 377
Atlas nasional 380
Atlas of physical, economic and social resources 366
Atlas of South-East Asia 367
Atlas of Southeast Asia 365
Atlas of the Philippines 382
Atlas of the Philippine Islands 384
Atlas tinjauan sumber daya lahan seluruh 379
Atlas van tropisch Nederland 381
Aubaret, G. 144
Aubréville, A. 526
Aung Khin, P. 402
Aung Thaw 401
Aung, Pearl 402
AUSA book 335
Australian Academy of the Humanities 605
Australian Development Assistance Bureau 512
Australian Museum 495
Australian National University 605, 628, 633, 689, 843, 849
Aymonier, Etienne 112, 780
Ayutthaya 417
Ayutthaya: the former Thai capital 417
B.R. 93, 201
Ba Han, Maung 646
Ba Thann Win 399
Ba Thaung, Bohmu 246
Backer, C. A. 555
Background notes: Kingdom of Laos 119
Background notes: Singapore 182
Baedeker's India 395
Baedeker, Karl 395
Bahasa Bali 768

Italicized entries are for titles. **Bold entries are subject guides**

Bahasa Indonesia / Bahasa Malaysia
   204, 486, 508, 528-530, 552, 572, 574,
   584, 586, 598, 637, 638, 678-713, 804,
   805, 811
Bahnar 815
Bajunid, Abu Abdul Latif Al-Syeikh
   Ahmad bin Othman 804
Bakhuizen van den Brink, R. C. 555,
   585
Bali 467
Bali 467
Bali & Lombok: a travel survival kit 467
Balinese 768-770
Balinese-English dictionary 769
Ban Nghiên Cứu Lịch Sử Đang 341
Ban Toán-Lý Thuộc Ủy Ban Khoa Học
   Nhà Nước 755
Bangkok 72, 414, 420
Bangkok: a city guide 414
Bangkok Chamber of Commerce directory
   89
Barber, C. Clyde 769
Bare'e woordenboek 816
Barraclough, Simon 697
Barthès, L. 107
Bartholomew 11
Barton, Thomas F. 365
Bartram, Edwin B. 562
Batak 771-773
Bataksch-Nederduitsch woordenboek 772
Bataviaasch Genootschap van Kunsten
   en Wetenschappen 816
Batraciens de l'Indochine 519
Baudenne, A. 436
Bausani, Alessandro 639
Bausastra Jawa 781
Bausastra Jawa-Indonesia 782
Bay of Bengal pilot 477
BBC 300
Beaufort, L. F. de 511
Beddome, R. H. 531
Beehler, Bruce M. 500
Bei, Ooi Jin 174
Béjaud, M. 569
Beknopt handboek der volkenkunde van

Nederlandsch Indie 630
Beknopt Sasaksch-Nederlandsch
   woordenboek 847
Beknopte encyclopaedie van
   Nederlandsch-Indie 204
Beknopte flora van Java 555
Beknopte grammatica van de Bahasa
   Indonesia 711
Beknopte Maleise grammatica 711
Belfield, H. Conway 161
Beltran-Gonzalez, Michaela 291
Bennison, J. J. 59
Beresford, Melanie 131
Bergen, John D. 335
Berger, Carl 335
Bernot, Denise 647
Berry, P. Y. 519
Bertrais, Yves 827
Berval, René de 121
Bezemer, T. J. 204, 630
Bhamo 405
Bhanoji Rao, V. V. 172
Bhargava, K. D. 303
Bibliografiya lingvisticheskikh rabot 3
Bibliographical series 24, 296, 629, 631
Bibliographic enumeration of Bornean
   plants 554
Bibliographie annamite 347
Bibliographie des voyages dans l'Indochine
   Française 261
Bibliographie du Laos 25
Bibliography and index of mainland
   Southeast Asian languages 2
Bibliography of official statistical yearbooks
   and bulletins 5
Bibliography of statistical sources on
   Southeast Asia 4
Bibliography of the Philippine Islands 27
Bibliotheca indosinica 242
Bích, Nguyễn Ngọc- 135
Bicol biographical encyclopedia 293
Bidalan Melayu 705
Biển, Viện Nghiên Cứu 507
Biểu, Nguyễn Trọng 580
Bijdragen tot de taal-, land- en

Italicized entries are for titles. **Bold entries are subject guides**

volkenkunde 819
Bikkers, A. J. W. 766
Bikol 293, 817
Bikol-English dictionary 817
Bikol grammar notes 817
*Bildwörterbuch Deutsch und
Vietnamesisch* 743
Bima 818
Bimaneesch-Hollandsch woordenboek 818
Bimaneesche spraakkunst 818
Binh, Dang The 738
Bính, Phan-Kě- 272
Binney, Mrs J. P. 835
Biografi penulis Brunei 274
Biografi penulis dan karya 280
*Biographical information on prominent
nationalist leaders* 258
**Biography 239-296; see also under
each country**
Biography of Malaysian writers 275
Biography series 295
Birds of Borneo 499
Birds of New Guinea 500
Birds of Singapore Island 497
Birds of the Malay peninsula 497
*Birds of the Malay peninsula, Singapore
and Penang* 497
Birds of the Philippines 501
Bird guide of Thailand 496
Birma: Land, Geschichte, Wirtschaft 46
Birmanie sous le régime britannique 49
Birmanskii yazyk 654
Bischoff 143
Bisheshwar Prasad 303
Blackwell, Geo. E. 835
Blagden, C. O. 77, 314, 429, 433, 626,
794
Blair, E. H. 364
Blanchard, Michel 422
Blanchard, Wendell 71, 73, 118
Blanco, Manuel 560
Blanford, W. T. 490
Blondel, F. 601
Blumentritt, Fernando 364
Board of Investment 89

Boegineesch-Hollandsch woordenboek 776
Boeginesche spraakkunst 778
Bois de l'Indochine 568
Bola'ang Mongondou 819
*Bolaang Mongondowsch-Nederlandsch
woordenboek* 819
Bollaert, Emile 257
Bonthonn, Khiou 103
Book of addresses of state functionaries
217
Booth, Anne 4
Borobudur 465
Boscher, Winfried 744
Botanical Survey of India 524
Botany bulletin 558, 589
Boulenger, George A. 515
Bourret, René 516, 519
*Bowker-Saur who's who in Asian and
Australasian politics* 14a
Bowman, John S. 333
Bowring, Sir John 78
BP 679, 710, 796, 798
Brébion, Antoine 260-262, 440
Brenier, H. 373
Brewster, Jennifer 4
*Briefing notes on the Royal Kingdom of
Laos* 119
Britanico, José del Rosario 817
British Association for Cemeteries in
South Asia 244
British Borneo, Singapore and Malaya
385
British Broadcasting Corporation 300
British Burma gazetteer 412
British Malaya 278
*British military administration in the Far
East 1943-1946* 302
British North Borneo 166, 170, 488
British North Borneo 166
British rule in Malaya 278
Brown, D. E. 194
Brown, Ian 26
Browne, F. G. 573
Bruce, Ginny 461
Bruk, S. I. 618

Italicized entries are for titles. **Bold entries are subject guides**

BRUNEI 165, 195, 196
  Agriculture 31, 378
  Biography 276
  Business 37, 40, 198
  Climate 174
  Culture 32
  Economy 378
  Ethnography 624
  Geography 31, 34, 365, 367, 378
  Government 39, 194, 301
  History 32, 36, 298, 302, 349
  Language 605, 606
  Literature 274
  Natural resources 36, 378, 492-494,
  502, 518, 529, 573, 590, 602
  Organizations 42
  Politics 38, 39
  Population 196, 197
  Statistics 39, 196, 197
  Transport 378
  Topography 385, 389-391, 446, 458,
  459
Brunei 21, 196
Brunei: the structure and history 194
Brunei forms of address 276
Brunei Shell 602
Brunei statistical yearbook 197
Bruzon, E. 103
Bucknill, Sir J. A. S. 497
Buddhism in Malaya 450
Buenaventura, Lee 471
Bugiiskii yazyk 777
Buginese 774-778
Buginese language 777
Bùi Phung 736
Bùi-Quang-Khánh 750
Bùi Quang Tung 346
Buku alamat pejabat negara R. I. 217
Buku panduan badan-badan perusahaan
  perniagaan Brunei 198
Buku saku statistik Indonesia 215
Buku tahunan perangkaan Malaysia 169
Buldan Djajawiguna, I. 799
Buletin perangkaan tahunan 169
Bulletin de l'Ecole Française

d'Extrême-Orient 314, 433
Bulletin économique de l'Indochine 594
Bunge, Frederica M. 44, 71, 156, 199,
  220
Bureau de la Presse et de l'Information
  257
Bureau for East Asia 366
Bureau of Forestry 575
Bureau of Government Laboratories
  561
Bureau of Public Affairs 182
Bureau of Public Affairs 119
Bureau of Special Research in Modern
  Languages 657
Bureau of the Census and Statistics
  229, 474
Bureau of Yards and Docks 564
Burkill, I. H. 486
BURMA 43-50, 52-56
  Agriculture 31, 46
  Biography 242-250, 308
  Business 37, 43, 61-64, 68, 70
  Calendar 299, 316, 609
  Chronology 315
  Climate 57, 58
  Culture 32, 311, 609
  Documents 300, 304-310, 313, 314,
  317
  Economy 46, 59, 172
  Ethnography 46, 48, 58, 611, 614,
  615
  Government 31, 34, 68, 365, 367
  History 32, 48, 49, 298, 302, 303,
  308, 309, 311, 312
  Languages 605, 606, 608, 609
  Literature 609, 638, 639
  Migration 59
  Monuments 314, 401, 406
  Natural resources 58, 483, 490, 492,
  493, 496, 502, 503, 516, 520, 524, 532-
  537, 565-566, 590, 591, 600
  Organizations 65, 250
  Politics 38, 39, 44-50
  Population 57-60
  Religion 242, 610

Italicized entries are for titles. **Bold entries are subject guides**

Statistics 39, 43-50, 52-60, 69
Transport 47, 400, 401
Topography 385, 386, 389-392, 395, 396-412
Burma 22, 44, 45, 385, 398, 407
Burma: administrative and social affairs 53
Burma: a country study 44
Burma: a handbook of practical information 48
Burma: a travel survival kit 396
Burma: information for travellers 403
Burma: its people and productions 483
Burma: Japanese military administration 313
Burma: national economy 53
Burma: postal history 312
Burma: preliminary edition 385
Burma: register of European deaths and burials 244
Burma: supplement to register of European deaths and burials 244
Burma: the struggle for independence 1944-1948 308
Burma business directory and national trade register 64
Burma gazetteer 408
Burma handbook 47
Burma handbook and directory 1895 68
Burma-Laos boundary 481
Burma Medical Research Institute 58
Burma Medical Research Council. Special report series 250
Burma parliamentary companion 67
Burma pocket almanac and directory 70
Burma Research Society fiftieth anniversary publication 534
Burma route book 411
Burma trade directory 64
Burma under British rule and before 49
Burma under British rule 49
Burma yearbook and directory 64
Burman: his life and notions 48
Burma's constitution and elections of 1974 310

Burmese 483, 535, 566, 637, 638, 640-655
Burmese and Arakanese calendars 316
Burmese calendar 316
Burmese-English dictionary 644, 645
Burmese personal names 245
Burmese proverbs 653
Burnell, A. C. 813
Burt Franklin bibliography & reference series 261
Business: see under each country
Business day's 1000 top corporations 231
Butler, J. 412
Butterflies in Thailand 521
Butterflies of India, Burmah and Ceylon 520
Butterflies of the Malay peninsula 522
Butterflies of the Australian region 523
Butterflies of West Malaysia and Singapore 522
Cá kinh tế vịnh bắc bộ 507
Cabaton, Antoine 112, 260, 780
Cabonce, Rodolfo 820
Cadière, L. 346
Cadogan guides 467
Calderón, Felipe G. 364
Calder, C. C. 524
Calendar: see under each country
Calendrier annamite-français de 1802 à 1916 340
Cambodge 112
Cambodge: fêtes civiles et religieuses 326
Cambodge, Laos, Vietnam 422
Cambodge-Laos-Viêt Nam 1/2 000 000 367
CAMBODIA 78, 93, 99-101, 108-112
  Agriculture 31, 367
  Biography 242
  Business 105-107, 115
  Calendar 299, 326, 609
  Chronology 322, 325, 328
  Climate 103, 366
  Culture 32, 99, 609
  Documents 300, 304, 323-324, 327

Italicized entries are for titles. **Bold entries are subject guides**

Economy 35, 94, 96, 366
Ethnography 611, 618, 619
Geography 31, 34, 93, 365-367
Government 39, 6, 97, 104, 108-111, 114, 301
History 32, 112, 298, 303, 321, 327
Languages 605-609, 618-620
Literature 609, 638, 639
Migration 95
Monuments 112, 256-263, 324, 427, 429, 433
Natural resources 366, 485, 492-493, 496, 502, 505, 516, 519, 522, 526, 540, 568-569, 580-581, 590
Politics 38, 39
Population 102, 113
Religion 242, 326, 610
Statistics 39, 93, 102-103, 113, 366
Transport 366
Topography 366, 385-386, 389-394, 421-433
Cambodia 110, 385
Cambodia: a country study 108
Cambodia: a travel survival kit 430
Cambodia: its people, its society, its culture 111
Cambodia-Laos boundary 481
Cambodian 526, 582, 594, 638, 656-667
Cambodian-English dictionary 657
Cambridge history of Southeast Asia 298
Cameron, Allan W. 337
Cameron, John 184
Campaigns in South-East Asia 303
Campaigns in the eastern theatre 303
Cantor, Theodore 510, 518
Caodaïsme (1926-1934) 343
Carey, Bertram S. 410
Carrapiett, W. J. S. 615
Carr, Jennifer L. 40
Carte ethnolinguistique de l'Indochine 618
Catalogue des produits de l'Indochine 485
Catalogue of Malayan fishes 510
Catalog of Annam coins 968-1955 345
Catechismus in octo dies 745

Catholic directory of the Philippines 237
Catholic Institute for Internationmal Relations 360
Cây-cỏ miền nam Việt-Nam 543
Cây cỏ thường thấy ở Việt Nam 545
Cebuano 820
Celebes 208
Cense, A. A. 631, 774
Census tables only 60
Center for Research in Social Systems 617
Center for Southeast Asian Studies 296, 353, 361
Centraal Kantoor voor de Statistiek 214, 216
Central Bureau of Statistics 214
Central Institute of English Language 616
Central Intelligence Agency 149, 263, 265, 266
Central Office of Information 322
Central Service of Statistics 81
Centrale Dienst voor Sibbekunde 241
Centre de Documentation sur l'Asie du Sud-Est 670
Centre for East Asian Cultural Studies 238, 239
Centre of Southeast Asian Studies monograph 478
Chabert, de 374
Chaffee, Frederic H. 220
Cham 779, 780
Chambre de Commerce et d'Agriculture du Cambodge 115
Chambre de Commerce de Saigon 154
Chan, Htoon 316
Chandaburinarünath, Prince Kitiyakara Krommaphra 808
Changing economy in Indonesia 216
Chánh phu cach mang lam thoi Cong Hoa 266
Chanthalak 729
Charrier (R. P.) 827
Chasen, F. N. 497
Cheam cheow heng 358

Italicized entries are for titles. **Bold entries are subject guides**

Checklist of government directories, lists and rosters 10
Checklist of the acquatic fauna of Siam 504
Check list for Bali, Nusa Tenggara and Timor 574
Chemin Dupontès, P. 124
Chen, Chingho A. 338
Ch'en Wei-lung 240
Chhibber, H. L. 600
Chi, Võ Văn 545
Chia Lin Sen 174
Chiang Mai 414
Chien, Nguyễn Văn 131
Childers, Robert Caesar 808
Chin Hills 60, 410
Chin Hills 410
Chin Wen 488
China-Laos boundary 481
China Sea directory 477
China Sea pilot 477
Chinese 620, 806, 807, 809, 811
Chinese Buddhist Order of Sangha in Thailand 807
Chinese minorities 200, 240, 279, 286, 622
Chinh, Nguyễn Văn 826
Chinh, Truong Van 761
Chit Ko Ko, U 535
Ch'ng Kin See 178
Chomsky, Noam 337
Chong-Yah, Lim 183
Chote Suvatti 539
Chronicle & directory for China 41
Chronologie des souverains de l'Annam 345
Chronology: see under each country
Chú, Phan Huy 347
Chulalongkorn 255
Chuyên, Vũ Văn 596
Cima, Ronald J. 130
Circonscriptions administratives 444
City of Yangon modernization record 63
Clarac, Achille 415
Clark, Gregory R. 812

Clavis Rumphiana botanica et zoologica 557
Clercq, F. S. A. de 552, 709
Clifton, Merritt 265a
Climate: see under each country
Climate of West Malaysia 174
Climatological data of Thailand 84
Climat du Cambodge 103
Coasts of Siam, Indo-China and south China 480
Coast and Geodetic Survey 384
Coast of Burma 480
Cochinchina 112, 130, 140, 142, 144, 154, 442, 547
Cockatoo's handbook: Philippines 232
Coedès, G. 112, 324
Coinage of Siam 320
Coins 309, 320, 345, 349
Coins and banknotes of Burma 309
Cole, Allan B. 323
Collection "Documents pour le Laos" 376
Collection de textes et de documents sur l'Indochine 324
Collection de textes et documents sur l'Indochine 433
Collection of chronicles 253
Collection of treaties and other documents 354
Collection UNESCO 269
Collier, H. J. 481
Collins field guide to the birds of south-east Asia 496
Collins, James T. 685
Colloque du XXIXe Congrès des Orientalistes 639
Colonial administration in the Far East 50
Colonie modèle 49
Colonisation de la Cochin-Chine 95
Colony of North Borneo annual report 168
Colony of Singapore annual report 185
Comber, Leon 357
Comité des Sciences Sociales de la République Socialiste 741

Italicized entries are for titles. **Bold entries are subject guides**

Comité du Plan 126
Comité Littéraire 668
Commaille, J. 432
*Commentary on Loureiro's Flora
  Cochinchinensis* 547
Commercial directory of Siam 90
Commercial directory for Siam 90
Commercial directory for Thailand 90
Commercial directory of Thailand 90
*Commercial marine fishes of the central
  Philippines* 514
Committee for Coordination of
  Investigations 366
Committee for Malay Studies 162
*Common snakes of south east Asia and
  Hong Kong* 516
Communist Party of Malaya 355
Compagnie Financière et Commerciale
  96
Complément à l'Inventaire descriptif 433
Completing a stewardship 278
Comrie, Bernard 637
Còn, Đoàn-Trung- 809
Concise Cambodian-English dictionary
  657
*Conflict in Indo-China and international
  repercussions* 323
Công-thương Việt-Nam 152
Congress of Southeast Asian Librarians
  239
Congrès d'Agriculture Coloniale, Paris,
  1918 582
Congrès des Orientalistes 639
Conklin, Harold C. 634
Connaissance du Viêt-Nam 134
Conrard, M. L. 569
*Contemporary English-Indonesian
  dictionary* 690
*Contemporary Indonesian-English
  dictionary* 685
*Continental shelf boundaries: Australia,
  Papua and Indonesia* 482
*Continental shelf boundaries: India,
  Indonesia, Thailand* 482
*Contribution à l'étude des plantes
  médicinales* 594
*Contribution à l'histoire des mouvements
  politiques* 343
Cook's guide to Burma 403
Cookson, John 199
*Cooperative societies in Singapore
  1925-1985* 351
Copeland, Edwin B. 563
Coquerel, A. 154
Corbet, A. Steven 522
Corbet, G. B. 492
Cordell, Helen 25
Cordier, Henri 242, 671, 759
Cornell University 73, 255, 814, 820,
  827, 853
Corner, E. J. H. 488, 549
Cotter, Michael 30
*Council of Ministers of the Socialist
  Republic of Vietnam* 266
Country survey series 73, 111, 165
Coup d'oeil général 207
Coverton, Mary 467
Cowan, C. D. 644
Craib, W. G. 525
Cranbrook, Earl of: see Medway, Lord
Crawfurd, John 36
Crévost, Charles 485, 582
Crew, F. A. E. 302
Critical survey of studies on Malay 712
*Critical survey of studies on the languages
  of Sumatra* 631
*Critical survey of studies on the languages
  of Sulawesi* 631
*Critical survey of studies on the languages
  of Java* 631
*Critical survey of studies on the languages
  of Borneo* 631
Crockett, Jeffery R. 706
Cronin, E. W. 496
Cronin, Richard P. 38
Crossroads 307
Crowther, Geoff 446
Cruickshank, Charles 302
Cuaz, M.-J. 672, 725
Cullinane, Michael 296

Italicized entries are for titles. **Bold entries are subject guides**

Cultural Information Analysis Center 617, 623

Culture: see under each country

Cummings, Joe 414, 421

Current trends in linguistics 607

Cushing, J. N. 795

Cushing, Mrs 795

Cyclopedia of South-East Asia 32

DA pam 44, 71, 108, 118, 136, 137, 156, 181, 199, 220, 617, 622, 623

D'Abrera, Bernard 523

Daftar alamat dan nomor telepon 217

Daftar buku terbitan Biro Pusat Statistik 214

Daftar istilah anatomi 702

Daftar istilah biologi 702

Daftar istilah geografi 700

Daftar istilah pertanian Indonesia-asing 584

Daftar nama dan alamat pejabat-pejabat 217

Đại-nam nhất-thống-chí 445

Đại Nam hóa tê dô lục 345

Dajacksch-deutsches Wörterbuch 841

Dalton, Bill 460

Dần, Nguyễn Đức 760

Đảng Lao Động Việt Nam, Ban Nghiên Cứu Lịch Sử Đang 341

Dang The Binh 738

Danh-từ dược-học Pháp-Việt có phần đối chiếu Việt-Pháp 595

Danhtừ hiệnđại và triếthọc 750

Danh-từ giáo-dục Anh-Việt và Việt-Anh 752

Danh-từ khoa-học 755

Danh-từ khoa-học. Toán, lý, hoa, cơ, thiên-văn 755

Danh-từ quân-sự Anh-Việt 754

Danh-từ thuc-vật-học Pháp-Việt 546

Danhtừ triếthọc 750

Danh từ vật lý Nga-Anh-Việt 755

Danh-từ y-học Pháp-Việt 756

Daniel, R. O. 351

Danvithathana, Nantana 730

Đào Đăng Vỹ 735

Đào Duy-Anh 742, 765

d'Aranjo, B. E. 456

Darby, H. C. 93, 201

da Silva, Manuel Maria Alves 823

Data paper 255, 814, 820, 827, 853

Data paper series 4

Dautremer, Joseph 49

Davias-Baudrit, J. 843

Davidson, Alan 502, 506

Davidson, J. A. 349

Davis, Gerald 312

Dawson, Thomas R. P. 281

Day, Francis 503

Dayrit, Marina G. 239

De la transcription du srê (koho) 848

De Marseille à Canton: guide du voyageur 428

De Saigon à Tourane 428

de Clercq, F. S. A. 552

Defense Advanced Research Projects Agency 117

Defense Mapping Agency 385

Degeorges, F. A. 521

De Haan, F. 288

De Hollander, J. J. 463

De Jong, L. 360a

Delacour, Jean 501

Deloustal, Raymond 340, 347

Delpy, E. 570

Delteil 440

Demetrio y Radaza, Francisco R. 363

Dennys, N. B. 164

Departemen Penerangan 217

Department of Agriculture and Natural Resources 599

Department of Agriculture, Industry and Commerce 203

Department of Agriculture 560

Department of Asian Studies: see Cornell University

Department of Civil Aviation 174

Department of Defense, Office of the Secretary of Defense 337

Department of General Statistics 81

Department of Health, Education and

Italicized entries are for titles. **Bold entries are subject guides**

Welfare 200

Department of Highways 418

Department of Information 168, 212, 359

Department of Linguistics 843, 849

Department of Local Administration 418

Department of Medical Research 250

Department of National Defense 383

Department of Railways 394

Department of State publication 182

Department of State, Bureau of Public Affairs 119, 182

Department of State, Division of Research for the Far East 342

Department of State, Interim Research and Intelligence Service 258

Department of State, Office of the Geographer 482

Department of State, Office of External Research 266

Department of Statistics 169, 187, 188

Department of Statistics Malaysia 170, 171

Department of Technical and Industrial Cooperation 80

Department of the Army 199, 335, 622, 623

Department of the Interior 385, 561, 575

Department of the Navy, Naval History Division 335

Description du Royaume Thai ou Siam 79

Description of habits and customs of the Muhsös 615

Descriptive dictionary of British Malaya 164

Descriptive dictionary of the Indian islands 36

Desraj, V. 565

Deuve, Jean 493, 516

De Wit, H. C. 557

Dhammarama, P. S. 664

Dialect-atlas van/of Lombok (Indonesia) 632

Dialecte thay blanc 800

Diccionario de la lengua Bisaya Hiligeceina y Haraya 825

Diccionario mitológico de Filipinas 364

Diccionario portuguez-galoli 823

Dickinson, Edward C. 496

Dictionarium annamiticum lusitanum et latinum 745

Dictionarium linguae thai 725

Dictionary and grammar of the Malayan language 691

Dictionary, Burmese and English 645

Dictionary, English and Burmese 645

Dictionary, English-Cambodian 658

Dictionary of Balinese-English 769

Dictionary of Buddhism 806, 807

Dictionary of Cebuano Visayan 820

Dictionary of colloquial Malay 686

Dictionary of current Burmese words 650

Dictionary of English-Palaung and Palaung-English 842

Dictionary of Lahu 837

Dictionary of Malaysian politics 697

Dictionary of Malayan medicine 598, 701

Dictionary of Malaysian Chinese 279

Dictionary of modern spoken Mon 792

Dictionary of Mong Njua 828

Dictionary of Philippine folk beliefs and customs 363

Dictionary of Philippine biography 295

Dictionary of Sea Dayak 829

Dictionary of synonyms and antonyms 757

Dictionary of terms and idioms of public administration 750

Dictionary of the Burman language 645

Dictionary of the economic products of the Malay peninsula 486

Dictionary of the Kachin language 832

Dictionary of the Mon inscriptions 794

Dictionary of the plant names of the Philippine Islands 561

Dictionary of the Pali language 808

Dictionary of the Sgau Karen language 835

Italicized entries are for titles. **Bold entries are subject guides**

Dictionary of the Vietnam war 333
Dictionnaire annamite-latin 745
Dictionnaire bahnar-français 815
Dictionnaire birman-français 647
Dictionnaire cam-vietnamien-français 779
Dictionnaire cam-français 780
Dictionnaire cambodgien-français 659, 661
Dictionnaire cambodgien 656
Dictionnaire des termes et expressions de l'administration 750
Dictionnaire de bio-bibliographie générale 260
Dictionnaire de fréquence du vietnamien 760
Dictionnaire encyclopédique viêtnamien 735
Dictionnaire français-cambodgien 661
Dictionnaire français-indonésien 693
Dictionnaire français-khmer 660
Dictionnaire français-thay blanc 800
Dictionnaire français-montagnard (koho) 848
Dictionnaire français-vietnamien des sciences juridiques 750
Dictionnaire français-malais 694
Dictionnaire français-vietnamien 741, 742
Dictionnaire général indonésien-français 692
Dictionnaire hmong (mèo blanc)-français 827
Dictionnaire khmer-russe 662
Dictionnaire laotien-français 670, 671
Dictionnaire laotien 17
Dictionnaire malais-français 694
Dictionnaire rhadé-français 843
Dictionnaire siamois français anglais 725
Dictionnaire srê (koho)-français 848
Dictionnaire vietnamien-chinois-français 740
Diên-Hương 747
Điền, Trần Văn 757, 758
Dieu Chinh Nhim 800
Diguet, E. 622
Diksionáriong Bíkol-Inglés 817

Diksyunaryo-tesauro Pilipino-Ingles 715
Dingley, E. Richard 488
Direction de la Statistique 126
Direction des Affaires Economiques 102
Direction des Affaires Politiques 343
Direction du Protocole 128, 264
Director of Survey (India) 386
Directorate General of Fisheries 512
Directorate of Foreign Information Services 212
Directorate of Intelligence 149, 263
Directorio oficial 230
Directory for Bangkok and Siam 91
Directory of Filipino writers 290
Directory of libraries in Malaysia 178
Directory of librarians in Southeast Asia 239
Directory of linguists and language education specialists 238
Directory of local administrative units 416
Directory of officials of Vietnam 149
Directory of scientific and technological institutions 92
Directory of selected scholars and researchers 239
Directory of Singapore manufacturers 191
Directory of social welfare agencies and organizations, Burma 65
Directory of TNCs in the Philippines 231
Directory of Viet-Nam, Laos and Cambodia 105
Discover Brunei 458
Discovering Thailand: a guidebook 415
District gazetteers of British India: a bibliography 408
Division of Commerce 203
Division of Research for the Far East 342
Divisions administratives et renseignements statistiques 444
Dix mille adresses 107
Dixon, Gale 478
Djajadiningrat, Hoesein 766

Italicized entries are for titles. **Bold entries are subject guides**

Djajawiguna, I. Buldan 799
Đoàn-Them 339
Đoàn-Trung-Còn 809
Documentos para la historia de Filipinas
    364
Documentos políticos de actualidad 364
Documents: see under each country
Documents graphiques de la conservation
    433
Documents illustrative of the Burmese war
    317
Documents on communism in Burma
    1945-1977 306
Doeppers, Daniel F. 296
Domschke, Eliane 8
Donaldson, Jean 800
Đồng-Dương Cộng-Sản Đảng 343
Dong Van Khuyen 336
Données ethnographiques 621
Donnison, F. S. V. 302
Dons de Nägsalad 588
Doudart de Lagrée 16
Douk Phana 594
Doumer, Paul 124
Dourisboure, P. X. 815
Dournes, Jacques 848
Draft of a short list of names 613
Drevneyavanskii yazyk 786
Drouin, S 848
du Bois, J. P. I. 289
Đức, Lê Văn 733
duc, Trang-hoï- 144
Duiker, William J. 332
Dumarçay, J. 433
Dumoutier, G. 597
Dunnebier, W. 819
Dunn, C. W. 644
Duôn-ya, Y-Bham 843
Dương Thị The 445
Dương, Nguyễn Văn 543, 595
Dupertuis, Sylvain 330
Dupontès, P. Chemin 124
duPont, John Eleuthere 501
Dupont, Pierre 419
Dupouy, Gaston 601

Durai Raja Singam, S. 449
Durand, Maurice M. 134, 269
Durie, Mark 767
Duroiselle, Charles 314, 404, 655
Dutch Borneo 208
Dutch New Guinea and the Molucca
    Islands 208
Dutch Timor and the lesser Sunda islands
    208
Eade, J. C. 299
Early years 1941-1960 335
Eastern Archipelago pilot 477
East Indies including Philippine Islands
    394
Eberhardt, Ph. 439
Echols, John M. 685, 690
Ecole Française d'Extrême-Orient 427,
    667
Ecole Supérieure de Pharmacie 597
Economic and social statistics, Singapore,
    1960-1982 188
Economic data book, Khmer Republic 113
Economic development in Burma 1951-60
    57
Economic handbook of the Pacific area 35
Economic Planning Unit, Statistics
    Section 197
Economy: see under each country
Education: see subheadings
    'Organizations' and 'Statistics'
    under each country
Educational terms English-Vietnamese and
    Vietnamese-English 752
Edwards, Norman 452
Eggan, Fred 221
Ei Shwe, U 649
Eliot, J. N. 522
Eliot, Joshua 389
Emanuels, H. W. 712
Embassy of the S R Vietnam, London
    151
Embree, Ainslie T. 14
Embree, J. 611
Emeneau, M. B. 762
Emigrants' Information Office 161

Italicized entries are for titles. **Bold entries are subject guides**

Eminent Filipinos 295
Eminent Indonesian Chinese 286
Empire d'Annam et le peuple annamite 139
Empire Khmèr: histoire et documents 327
Encyclopaedie van Nederlandsch-Indie 204
Encyclopaedie van Nederlandsch Oost-Indie 204
Encyclopedia of Asian history 14
Encyclopedia of the Philippines 222
Engineer Agency for Resources Inventories 366
English 812, 813
English, Leo James 714
English and Shan dictionary 795
English-Cebuano Visayan dictionary 820
English-Iloko thesaurus 831
English-Indonesian dictionary 690
English Kachin Burmese dictionary 832
English-Khmer dictionary 658
English-Lao Lao-English dictionary 669
English-Malay dictionary 689
English/Meo pocket dictionary 828
English-Mong-English dictionary 826
English-Tagalog dictionary 714
English-Thai dictionary 724
English Vietnamese military handbook 754
Enjoy, Paul d' 95
Enriquez, C. M. 614
Ensiklopedi Indonesia 681
Ensiklopedi nasional Indonesia 680
Ensiklopedia Indonesia 681
Enumeratio phanerogamarum bornearum 554
Enumeratio pteridophytarum bornearum 554
Enumeration of Philippine flowering plants 560
Epigraphia Birmanica 314
Erard, E. 97
Eringa, F. S. 797
Esche, Annemarie 648
Essai d'atlas statistique de l'Indochine Française 373
Essai de dictionnaire français-siamois 725
Essai sur la pharmacie annamite 597
Essences forestières du Cambodge 569
Esteves Felgas, Hélio Augusto 210
Etablissement du Protectorat Français au Cambodge 328
Etat actuel du Tunkin 100
Ethnic groups of French Indochina 619
Ethnic groups of insular Southeast Asia 624
Ethnic groups of mainland Southeast Asia 611
Ethnic groups of northern Southeast Asia 611
Ethnic map and gazetteer of northern Southeast Asia 611
Ethnobotany 576-599
Ethnographic atlas of Ifugao 634
Ethnographic study series 617, 623
Ethnographic Survey of India 58
Ethnographical and linguistic survey of Burma 615
Ethnographical data 621
Ethnographical Studies Service 622
Ethnographical survey of India: Burma 615
Ethnographical survey of Burma: questions 615
Ethnography 605-636; see also under each country
Etudes minéralogiques sur l'Indochine Française 601
Etudes vietnamiennes 132, 621
Eugenio, Damiana L. 717
Eveleth, F. H. 645
Exkursionsflora von Java 555
Export list of Myanmar 61
Exposé chronologique des relations du Cambodge avec le Siam 328
Exposé statistique du Tunkin 100
Exposition Coloniale Internationale 98, 102, 103, 139
Facts on foreign aid to Laos 119
Faculty of Fisheries and Marine

Italicized entries are for titles. **Bold entries are subject guides**

Science 509
Families of Burmese flowering plants 532
Far eastern economic review yearbook 12
Far East and Australasia 39
Faraut, Emile 115
Fasciculi Malayenses 18
Fauna 483-523
Fauna of British India 490
Fauna of India including Pakistan, Ceylon and Burma 490
Fauna of Thailand 491
Faure, F. 154
Favre, P. 694
Federal Research Division 130, 181
Federated Malay States civil service list 282
Federated Malay States 161
Federated Malay States year book 175
Federation of British Industries, Intelligence Department 600
Federation of Malaya: official year book 168
Federation of Malaya year book 175
Felgas, Hélio Augusto Esteves 210
Fenton, A. B. 411
Fern flora of the Philippines 563
Fêtes profanes et religieuses au Laos 331
Field guide to the birds of Java and Bali 498
Field guide to the birds of Borneo 498
Field guide to the butterflies of Thailand 521
Field guide to the mammals of Borneo 494
Field guide to the birds of South-East Asia 496
Field, Frederick V. 35
Filipino women in nation building 291
Filipino writers in English 290
Filliozat, J. 670
Final years 1965-1973 335
Financial and economic annual of Burma, July 1943 55
Finot, L. 612
Firmstone, H. W. 457

Fischer Länderkunde 31
Fischer, E. 381
Fish and fish dishes of Laos 506
Fisher, Charles A. 34
Fisheries 489, 502-514
Fisheries in Burma 503
Fisheries research bulletin 504
Fishes of India 503
Fishes of New Guinea 513
Fishes of Thailand 504
Fishes of the Indo-Australian archipelago 511
Fisk, E. K. 157
Flannery, Timothy 495
Fleet, J. F. 316
Fleischmann, Klaus 306
Fleming, W. A. 522
Fleurs de paroles 588
Flora 483-489, 524-575
Flora Burmanica 483
Flora Cochinchinensis 547
Flora de Filipinas 560
Flora Indiae Bataviae 530
Flora Indica 524
Flora Malesiana 529
Flora Malesiana bulletin 529
Flora of British India 524
Flora of India 524
Flora of Java 555
Flora of Thailand 525, 539
Flora of the Malay Peninsula 528
Flora van Nederlandsch Indie 530
Florae Indiae Batavae supplementum 553
Florae Siamensis enumeratio 525
Flore du Cambodge, du Laos et du Viêt-nam 526
Flore forestière de la Cochinchine 570
Flore générale de l'Indochine 526
Fodor's Southeast Asia 391
Fokker, A. A. 711
Fomicheva, M. F. 728
Food 58, 59, 184, 576-589
Fookien times Philippines yearbook 233
Forbes, W. Cameron 224
Forbes-Lindsay, C. H. 224

Italicized entries are for titles. **Bold entries are subject guides**

Forces Armées Royales Khmères 431
Foreign and Commonwealth Office 379
Foreign Area Studies 44, 108, 118, 133, 136, 137, 156, 165, 199, 220
Foreign Broadcast Information Service 749
Foreign Investment Commission 43
Foreign Office 208
Foreign Research Division 71, 108
Foresters' manual of dipterocarps 571
Forestry 489, 564-575
Forestry Research and Development Centre 574
Forests of the Philippines 575
Forest flora of British Burma 566
Forest trees of Sarawak and Brunei and their products 573
Francisco, Juan R. 635
Francis, Charles M. 494
Frater 750
French Indo-China 93
Friedberg, Claudine 587
Frodin, D. G. 1
Frontiers of Asia and Southeast Asia 481
Fund for Assistance to Private Education 382
Gage, A T. 528
Gainey, Jerry W. 616
Gajo 821
Gajôsch-Nederlandsch woordenboek 821
Galang, Zoilo M. 222
Galela 822
Galembert, J. de 97
Gale de Villa, Jill 471
Gallois, L. 374
Galoli 823
Gamble, J. S. 528
Gana Ngadi, Henry 829
Gang, C. Un 613
Garnier, Francis 16
Garros, G. 140
Gaspardone, Emile 347
Gazetteer of Burma 386, 412
Gazetteer of Indo-China 386

Gazetteer of Malaya 386
Gazetteer of Siam 386
Gazetteer of Sumatra and its outliers 386
Gazetteer of the District of Rangoon 412
Gazetteer of the Mergui District 412
Gazetteer of Upper Burma and the Shan States 409
Gazetteer of Vietnam 385
Gazetteers 385-486
Gazetteers 385
Gedney, W. J. 729
Gegenwärtiger Zustand von Tunkin 100
Geillustreerd handboek van Insulinde 206
Geillustreerde encyclopaedie van Nederlandsch-Indie 202
Gelb, Leslie 337
Genealogische bibliotheek 241
General directory of Vietnam 152
General Staff, Geographical Section 386
General Statistical Office 147
Generale Staf K. N. I. L. 360a
Geographical handbook series 93, 201
Geographical journal 48
Géographie physique, économique et historique 442
Geographische Handbücher 223
Geography: see under each country
Geography and discovery 261
Geography, archaeology, psychology, and literature 361
Geologic Survey Department 602
Geology and hydrocarbon resources of Negara Brunei Darussalam 602
Geology and mineral resources of the Philippine Islands 604
Geology of Indonesia 603
Gerard, P. N. 702
Gericke, J. F. C. 782
Gerini, G. E. 77
German, R. L. 161
German Agency for Technical Co-operation 512, 514
Gezaghebbers der Oost-Indische

Italicized entries are for titles. **Bold entries are subject guides**

Compagnie 241

Gheerbrandt, J.-L. 17

Gia Định thông chí 144

Giáp, Trần Văn 268

Gibbon, W. S. 354

Gids voor de Boroboedoer 465

Gilliard, E. Thomas 500

Gilliland, H. B. 527

Gimlette, John D. 598, 701

Ginsburg, Norton S. 122, 160, 165

Glenister, A. G. 497

Gloerfelt-Tarp, Thomas 512

Glosari istilah kesusasteran 696

Glosari perfileman 696

Glossary of terms used in the Vietnamese press 749

Golden Khersonese 305

Gonggryp, G. F. E. 202

Gonzalez, Andrew 238

Gorgoniyev, Yu. A. 662, 666

Goris, R. 847

Gorontalo 824

Gouin, Eugène 740

Gourdon, Henri 371

Gouvernement Général de l'Indochine 94, 96, 259, 343, 373

Government: see under each country

Government in the Union of Burma: GUB 1958 Nov.-1959 Feb. 54

Government of India 614

Government publications ... Government organization manuals 9

Goyer, Doreen S. 8

Graham, W. A. 77

Grammaire de la langue khmère (cambodgien) 667

Grammaire de la langue chame 780

Grammaire de la langue lao 676

Grammar of Acehnese on the basis of a dialect of north Aceh 767

Grammar of English words 758

Grammar of Lahu 837

Grammar of Mong Njua (Green Miao) 828

Grammar of the Balinese language 769

Grammar of the Burmese language 645

Grammar of the Kachin language 833

Grammar of the Shan language 795

Grammar of Toba Batak 773

Grandidier, Guillaume 370

Grand archipel d'Asie 477

Grant, Bartle 537

Grasses of Burma 536

Gray, Paul 413

Green Berets in Vietnam 1961-71 335

Griffin, A. P. C. 27

Groupes ethniques de l'Indochine Française 619

Guerrini, Dominique 123

Guesdon, J. 659

Guía de forasteros en Filipinas 236

Guía oficial de Filipinas 236

Guía oficial de las Islas Filipinas 236

Guibier, H. 568

Guide-annuaire illustré de la Cochinchine 154

Guide-annuaire de la ville de Pnom-Penh 115

Guide Arthaud 422

Guide aux ruines d'Angkor 432

Guide commercial 154

Guide des colonies françaises 423

Guide de l'Annam 439

Guide de la conversation annamite 759

Guide du français arrivant en Indochine 95

Guide du Tonkin du sud 428

Guide du voyageur à Saigon 440

Guide linguistique de l'Indochine Française 620

Guide touristique 438

Guide touristique générale de l'Indochine 423

Guide to Austroasiatic speakers and their languages 608

Guide to Bangkok with notes on Siam 420

Guide to Chiang Mai and northern Thailand 414

Guide to foreign investment in Myanmar

Italicized entries are for titles. **Bold entries are subject guides**

43

Guide to manuscripts and documents in the British Isles 15

Guide to Philippine flora and fauna 489

Guide to shrimps, prawns, lobsters and crabs 509

Guide to standard floras of the world 1

Guide to Thailand 415

Guide to the Mandalay Palace 404

Guide to the romanization of Burmese 655

Guide to the wats of Vientiane 434

Guide to Western manuscripts and documents 15

Guides Artou 422

Guides Madrolle 425

Guides Madrolle 426

Guignard, Théodore 671

Guilleminet, Paul 815

Gullick, J. M. 158

Gungwu, Wang 159, 184

Gunning, M. Adriani- 852

Gyi, Maung Maung 55

H.D. 480

H.O. 479

Haan, F. de 288

Haas, Mary R. 723

Hadi Podo 704

Hai muoi nam qua: việc từng ngày 1945-1964 339

Haji Dusuki Bin Haji Ahmad 805

Hall, D. G. E. 367, 644

Halliday, Robert 793

Hammond, L. P. 224

Hãn, Hoàng-Xuân- 755

Han, Maung Ba 646

Hancock, R. B. 655

Handboek voor Cultuur- en Handelsondernemingen 205

Handbook: Southeast Asian institutions of higher learning 42

Handbook and chart of South East Asian history 301

Handbook for travellers in India, Ceylon and Burma 403

Handbook for U. S. forces in Vietnam 138

Handbook of biological data on Burma 58

Handbook of national population censuses: Africa and Asia 8

Handbook of New Guinea birds 500

Handbook of Philippine language groups 635

Handbook of Sarawak 167

Handbook of the Federated Malay States 161

Handbook of the forest products of Burma 565

Handbook of the Netherlands East-Indies 203

Handbook on Burma 45

Handbook to British Malaya 161

Handbook to Singapore with map 456

Handbook to the birds of British Burmah 496

Handbook to the ferns of British India 531

Handbooks 93, 208

Handbooks for the Indian Army 614

Handleiding bij de beoefening der land- en volkenkunde 463

Hanson, O. 832, 833

Hảo, Lê Văn 621

Hardeland, A. 841

Hardiman, J. P. 409

Harimurti Kridalaksana 707

Harper, Peter 470

Harrison, Cuthbert Woodville 451

Harris, George L. 71, 133, 165

Hart, Donn V. 361

Harvey, Joan M. 6

Hasan, Ali Haji 378

Hattori, Shirô 605

Haughton, H. T. 457

Haut-Commissariat de la France pour l'Indochine 257

Haynes, H. S. 708

Hazeu, G. A. J. 821

Headley, Robert K. 657

Heimbach, Ernest E. 827

Henderson, John W. 441, 71, 156, 199

Henderson, M. R. 549

Italicized entries are for titles. **Bold entries are subject guides**

Hendriks, H. 788
Hendry, Robert S. 382
Henschel, Aug. Guil. Ed. Th. 557
Henty, E. E. 558
Hepburn, B. A. St J. 167
Herbarii amboinensis auctuarium 557
Herbarium amboinense 557
Herbert, Patricia M. 22, 638
Herklots, G. A. C. 583
Herre, Albert W. C. T. 510
Hesse d'Alzon, Claude 321
Heussler, Robert 278
Heyne, K. 586
Hickey, Gerald C. 122, 611
Hiển, Nguyễn Như 542
Hiêu dinh-han man tu Hán Việt tù điển 765
Highways and major bridges of Burma 399
Highways in Thailand 418
Hildebrand, F. H. 574
Hiligaynon 825
Hinduism in Singapore 454
Hishino, T. 674
Histoire budgétaire de l'Indochine 102
Histoire de la Mission du Tonkin 271
Histoire de la Mission de Cochinchine 271
Histoire de la Mission de Siam 253
Histoire et description de la Basse Cochinchine 144
Historic documents of the Lao Dong Party 341
Historical and cultural dictionary of Burma 311
Historical and cultural dictionaries of Asia 311, 318, 338, 362
Historical and cultural dictionary of Vietnam 338
Historical and cultural dictionary of Thailand 318
Historical and cultural dictionary of the Philippines 362
Historical atlas of Thailand 319
Historical dictionary of Vietnam 332

Historical dictionary of Singapore 348
Historical dictionary of Laos 329
Historical Section 208
Historical sites in Burma 401
History 297-364; see also under each country
History of services of gazetted and other officers in Burma 249
History of the "Ethnographical and linguistic survey" 615
History of the Second World War 302
History of U.S. decision-making process 337
History, sociology, mass media, and bibliography 361
Hla Pe 644, 653
Hmong 541, 826-828
Hồ, Phạm-Hoàng 543, 544
Hòa, Nguyễn Dình 269, 737
Hoàng-Xuân-Hãn 755
Hoàng-Hoc 665
Hoàng-Việt giáp tý niên biểu 344
Hoang Ngoc Lung 336
Hoa's Vietnamese-English dictionary 737
Hobday, J. R. 48
Hobson-Jobson 813
Hoc, Hoàng- 665
Hoefer, Hans Johannes 398, 437, 447, 471
Höfer, András 610
Hoke Sein, U 643
Holle lists 628
Holttum, R. E. 527, 529
Home Department 66
Hommes et destins: dictionnaire biographique d'Outre-Mer 256
Hongvivat, Nidda 417
Hoofdkwartier 360a
Hoofdstukken uit de spraakkunst van het Tontemboansch 852
Hooker, J. D. 524
Hooley, Richard 361
Horne, Elinor Clark 782
Horse Guards, Intelligence Division 163

Italicized entries are for titles. **Bold entries are subject guides**

Horton, A. V. M. 195
Hotels of French Indochina and Siam 424
Houel, L. 578
House Committee of Armed Services
 337
Houtman, Gustaaf 245
Hpang, Manam 832
Htar, Khin Thet 250
Htoon Chan 316
Htun, Maung Kyaw 642
Huân, Nguyễn Trần- 269
Huard, Pierre 134
Huber, E. 661
*Hudson's guide to Chiang Mai and the
 North* 414
Hudson, Roy 402, 414
Hue, Gustave 740
Hueting, A. 851
Huffman, Franklin E. 2, 658
Human Relations Area Files 73, 111,
 120, 122, 133, 160, 165, 200, 221, 624
Humbert, H. 526
Hundius, Harald 803
Hundley, H. G. 535
Hùng, Nguyễn Quí 763
Hương, Diên- 747
Hurrier, Paul 597
Husain, Safian 696
Hussain bin Jamil 829
Hydrographer of the Navy 477
Hydrographic Department 192, 480
Hydrographic Office 385, 479
Hyôjun marai-go daijiten 695
I.D. 201
Iban 499, 829, 830
Iban-English dictionary 829
Iban language of Sarawak 830
Ibrahim, Abdul Latif Haji 459
Ifugao 634
Illustrated cycle of Chinese festivities 350
Illustrated flora of South Vietnam 543
*Illustrated guide to the Federated Malay
 States* 451
Illustration 370
Ilmu alam ringkas Brunei 378

Iloko 831
Iloko-English dictionary 831
Iloko grammar 831
Im Proum 658
Images of Asia series 493
*Imperial gazetteer of India, Provincial
 series* 407
Imperial Japanese Government
 Railways 394
Importers and exporters directory for Siam
 90
*In the field: the language of the Vietnam
 War* 812
Index on AMS 1:50 000 maps of Thailand
 387
*Index to 'Materials for a flora of the
 Malay Peninsula'* 528
Index to map of Viet Nam 367
*Index to names on 1:50 000 maps of
 Vietnam* 387
*Index to names on Topocom 1:50 000
 maps of Laos* 387
India, Burma and Ceylon: information
 403
*India, Ceylon, Burma, Malaya, Siam and
 Java* 395
India Office and Burma Office list 249
Indian antiquary 316
Indian armed forces in World War II 303
Indian festivals in Malaya 350
Indigenous Languages of Thailand
 Research Project 616
Indisch verslag 213
Indo-China 93
Indochina 424
Indochina monographs 336
Indochine 98, 422
Indochine adresses 1938-39 106
*Indochine. Cochinchine, Annam, Tonkin,
 Cambodge, Laos* 423
*Indochine du nord: Tonkin, Annam, Laos,
 Yunnan* 425
Indochine du sud: de Marseille à Saigon
 426
Indochine Française: atlas indochinois 371

Italicized entries are for titles. **Bold entries are subject guides**

Indochine moderne: encyclopédie 96
Indochine, un empire colonial français 99
INDONESIA 199-208, 212-214, 680-681
   Agriculture 31, 379
   Biography 204, 217, 239, 240, 283-289
   Business 37, 40, 41, 219, 287
   Chronology 289, 360
   Climate 379-381
   Culture 32, 204
   Documents 300, 304, 357
   Economy 33, 35, 206, 216, 379-381
   Ethnography 463, 624, 629-630
   Geography 31, 34, 201, 204, 208, 214, 365, 367, 379-381, 464
   Government 39, 217-218, 285, 288-289, 301
   History 32, 36, 204, 288-289, 298, 360a
   Languages 204, 556, 585, 586, 605-607, 628, 631-633, 637, 709
   Literature 638, 639, 696, 785
   Migration 205, 211, 379
   Monuments 465
   Natural resources 33, 36, 379-381, 492-495, 498-500, 502, 511-513, 518, 523, 529-531, 552-559, 564, 574, 584-587, 589, 590, 603
   Organizations 239
   Politics 38, 39, 199-201, 204
   Population 214
   Statistics 39, 204, 212-216, 464
   Transport 33, 379
   Topography 202, 204, 211, 379-381, 385-386, 388-391, 393-395, 460-469
Indonesia 200, 385
Indonesia: an official handbook 212
Indonesia: a country study 199
Indonesia: a travel survival kit 461
Indonesia: dictionary of abbreviations 706
Indonesia: selected documents 359
Indonesia and Portuguese Timor 385
Indonesia facts and figures 214
Indonesia handbook 212, 460
Indonesia-Malaysia boundary 482

Indonesia pilot 477
Indonesia, Malaysia and Singapore handbook 389
Indonesia, Netherlands New Guinea 385
Indonesian-English dictionary 685
Indonesian Chamber of Commerce and Industry 219
Indonesian military leaders 285
Indonesian occupation of East Timor 360
Indonesian pilot 477
Indonesian ports: an atlas-gazetteer 478
Indonesian revolution 359
Indonesisch-Nederlands woordenboek 683
Indoneziiskii yazyk 711
Industrial and commercial directory 152
Information Division 185
Information for travellers landing at Manila 475
Information Malaysia: yearbook 175
Informe sobre el estado de las Islas Filipinas 224
Inglik Jinghpaw Myen ga htai chyum 832
Inhabitants of the Philippines 636
Inscriptions du Cambodge 324
Inscriptions of Burma 314
Insight guides 398, 447, 471
Institut Bouddhique 656
Institut d'Ethnologie 622
Institut National de la Statistique 113
Institute of Land Warfare 335
Institute of Pacific Relations 35
Institutions annamites en Basse-Cochinchine 142
Instrucciones sobre el régimen de las provincias y pueblos 364
Instructions nautiques 477
Ins and outs of Metro Manila 472
Intelligence 336
Intelligence Branch 411
Intelligence Department 201
Intelligence Division 163
Interim Research and Intelligence Service 258
International boundary study 481
International Congress on Natural

Italicized entries are for titles. **Bold entries are subject guides**

Products 592
Interpretation of Rumphius 557
Introduction à l'ethnobotanique du Cambodge 579
Introduction à la connaissance de la péninsule 609
Introduction à la littérature vietnamienne 269
Introduction aux littératures orientales 269
Introduction to Cambodian 666
Introduction to Chinese secret societies in Malaya 357
Inventaire descriptif des monuments Cams de l'Annam 441
Inventaire descriptif des monuments du Cambodge 433
Inventaire des inscriptions pâlies 314
Ira, Luning B. 473
Ireland, Alleyne 50
Irwin, A. M. B. 316
Irwin, Sir Alfred 316
Is trust vindicated? 54
Iskandar, Teuku 678
Islas Filipinas en 1882 224
Istilah biologi bahasa inggeris-bahasa Malaysia 702
Istilah drama dan teater 696
Istilah geologi 700
Istilah pendidekan melayu-inggeris-melayu 699
Istilah percetakan, penerbitan dan komunikasi 696
Istilah perdagungan, perusahaan dan ilmu akaun 698
Istilah pergigian 702
Istilah perhutanan bahasa inggeris-bahasa Malaysia 572
Istilah perikanan bahasa inggeris-bahasa Malaysia 508
Istilah perubatan 702
Istilah sains dan teknologi makanan 584
Istilah seni lukis inggeris-Malaysia-inggeris 696
Istilah tadbir rumahtangga 584

Itinéraires automobiles en Indochine 423
Ivanov, V. V. 746
Jaarboek van Nederlandsch-Indië 203
Jaarcijfers voor het Koninkrijk der Nederlanden 214
Jack-Hinton, Colin 356
Jacobson, G. 488
Jacob, Judith M. 657, 666
Jacquat, Christiane 576
James G. Furlong fund 655
James, D. M. D. 602
Jamieson, E. 615
Japan Academy 605
Japan Committee for the Republication and Relief 656
Java 36, 208, 288, 466, 785
Java and Madura 208
Java, geographisch, ethnologisch, historisch 466
Javaans-Nederlands handwoordenboek 782
Javaansch-Nederlandsch handwoordenboek 782
Javanese 781-786
Javanese-English dictionary 782
Jeffries, Bill 232
Jenkins, D. V. 488
Johnson, Anne 550
Joint U. S. Pacific Affairs Office 133
Joint Thai-U.S. Military Research and Development Center 418
Jones, Robert B. 255
Jonker, J. C. G. 818, 845
Journal of the Straits Branch of the Royal Asiatic Society 554
Joustra, M. 771
JPRS 619, 749
Judson's Burmese-English dictionary 645
Judson's English and Burmese dictionary 645
Judson Burmese-English dictionary 645
Judson, A. 645
Jumsai, M. L. Manich 724
Justices of the Supreme Court of the Philippines 292
Justice dans l'ancien Annam 347

Italicized entries are for titles. **Bold entries are subject guides**

Kachin 832, 833
Kachinskii yazyk (yazyk chzhingpkho)
    833
Kadazan 834
Kadazan-English and English-Kadazan
    dictionary 834
Kadazan dictionary and grammar 834
Kaesri, Songvit 806
Kailola, Patricia J. 512
Kalimantan 208
Kambodscha mit Angkor Wat, Birma, Laos
    392
Kamoes bahasa melajoe (Indonesia)-nippon
    695
Kamoes bahasa Minangkabau-bahasa
    Melajoe-Riau 790
Kamoes basa Soenda 796
Kamoes Soenda-Indonesia 798
Kamoes Soenda-Melajoe 798
Kampuchea: see Cambodia
Kampuchea 23
Kampuchea: politics, economics and society
    109
Kamus bahasa Gorontalo-Indonesia 824
Kamus bahasa Iban-bahasa Malaysia 829
Kamus bahasa Madura-Indonesia 787
Kamus bahasa Melayu 682
Kamus basa Sunda 796
Kamus besar bahasa Indonesia 679
Kamus Dewan 678
Kamus dwibahasa 689
Kamus fajar rumi-jawi 713
Kamus Indonesia-Bali 768
Kamus inggeris-melayu Dewan 689
Kamus Inggris-Indonesia 690
Kamus Manggarai 840
Kamus pengetahuan Islam 805
Kamus pustaka melayu-arab 804
Kamus singkatan2 dan akronama2 706
Kamus Toradja-Indonesia 850
Kamus umum bahasa Indonesia 679
Kamus umum basa Sunda 796
Kamus ungkapan Indonesia-inggris 704
Kapur, Basant K. 352
Karen 613, 835

Karen vernacular grammar 835
Karenni 60, 78
Karo-Bataks-Nederlands woordenboek 771
Karo-Bataksch woordenboek 771
Karow, Otto 744
Karta narodov Indokitaya 618
Kasatsart University 504
Kau-too, Sau 835
Kawi-Balineesch-Nederlandsch
    woordenboek 770
Kayan 836
Kayan-English dictionary with appendices
    836
Kế, Lê Khả 741
Keaughran, T. J. 190
Kelly, Francis J. 335
Kemp, Herman C. 24
Keng, H. 548, 551
Kepanduan bahari Indonesia 478
Kerr, A. F. G. 525
Kerr, Allen D. 669
Kersten, J. 768
Keys to the families and genera of higher
    plants in New Guinea 559
Keys, Peter 452
Kham Mun, Maung 795
Khana Rathaprasasanasat 252
Khánh, Bùi-Quang- 750
Khao luan ve ngũ pháp Việt-nam 761
Khin Maung Lwin, U 58
Khin Thet Htar 250
Khin, P. Aung 402
Khin, San 591
Khin, U 503
Khiou Bonthonn 103
Khit Pyin English English Burmese
    dictionary 646
Khmer 526, 582, 594, 638, 656-667
Khmer language 666
Khôn, Nguyễn-Văn- 736
Khỏn, Nguyễn Văn 739
Khrai pen khrai nai prathet Thai 252
Khuyen, Dong Van 336
Kiliaan, H. N. 788, 789
Kinabalu: summit of Borneo 488

Italicized entries are for titles. **Bold entries are subject guides**

King, Ben F. 496
King, G. 528
Kingdom and people of Siam 78
Kingdom of Laos 121
Kính, Vũ Văn 764
Kirby, S. W. 302
Kkhmerskii yazyk 666
Kkhmersko-russkii slovar' 662
Klein, W. C. 211
Klein, Wilhelm 398
Klinkert, H. C. 684
K'Nai 848
Ko, U Chit Ko 535
Koentjaraningrat 629
Kolb, Albert 223
Kolobkov, V. P. 649
Koloniaal verslag 213
Kompass buku merah 177
Kompass Malaysia 177
Kompass Philippines 231
Kompass Thailand 89
Kông, Lê Bá 759
Koninklijke Militaire Academie 463
Koninklijk Instituut voor Taal-, Land-
  en Volkenkunde 24, 629, 631, 683,
  712, 772-774, 797, 819, 840
Koninklijk Nederlandsch
  Aardrijkskundig Genootschap 381
*Koninkrijk der Nederlanden in de Tweede
  Wereldoorlog* 360a
Koorders, S. H. 555, 556
Kooyman, Mary 329
Korman, Richard I. 10
Kovin, R. 663
Kraemer, J. H. 564
Kratoska, Paul H. 448
Krausse, Gerald H. 21
Krausse, Sylvia C. Engelen 21
Kridalaksana, Harimurti 707
Kriegsgeschiedkundige Sectie 360a
Krommaphra Chandaburinarünath,
  Prince Kitiyakara 808
Kun, Thao 660
Kunstadter, Peter 611
Kuo Shou-hua 105

Kurz, S. 533, 566
Kwang, T. C. 705
Kyaw Htun, Maung 642
Labberton, D. van Hinloopen 206
la Bissachère, Pierre Jacques
  Lemonnier de 100
Labrousse, Pierre 692
Lace, J. H. 535
Lacroix, Désiré 345
Lafont, Pierre-Bernard 25, 120, 612,
  639
Lagrée, Doudart de 16
Lahu 837
Lajonquière, E. Lunet de 419, 429, 433
Lak phasa lao 677
Lâm, Trương-Bửu- 344
Land Resources Department NRI 379
Land resources of Indonesia 379
Lang Xiong 826
Language atlas of the Pacific area 605
Language map of Thailand handbook 616
**Languages 605-853; see also under
  each country**
Languages of Asia and Africa 666, 676,
  777
Languages of Irian Jaya 633
Langue bugis 777
Langue minangkabau 791
Lao 506, 525, 526, 541, 638, 668-677
Lao-English dictionary 669
Lao language 676
Lao personal names 265
Lao phrase book 674
Lao proverbs 675
LAOS 78, 93, 99-101, 116-125
  Agriculture 31, 366
  Biography 242, 256-262, 264-265
  Business 105-107, 127, 129
  Calendar 299, 330, 331, 609
  Chronology 322
  Climate 103, 126, 367
  Culture 32, 99, 121, 329, 609
  Documents 300, 304, 323
  Economy 33, 35, 94, 96, 119, 366
  Ethnography 611, 618, 619

Italicized entries are for titles. **Bold entries are subject guides**

Geography 31, 34, 93, 365-367
Government 39, 96, 97, 104, 123, 128, 292, 301
History 32, 292, 298, 303, 321, 329
Languages 605, 606, 608, 609, 612, 618-620
Literature 609, 638
Migration 95, 376
Monuments 427, 434, 435
Natural resources 33, 366, 485, 492, 493, 496, 506, 516, 519, 522, 526, 541, 568, 580, 590, 593, 601
Politics 38, 39, 116-125
Population 102, 126
Religion 242, 331, 434, 435, 610
Statistics 39, 93, 102, 103, 119, 126, 366
Transport 33, 366
Topography 366, 377, 385-387, 389-394, 421-428, 434-436
Laos 25, 124, 385
Laos: annual statistical report 126
Laos: a country study 118
Laos: beyond the revolution 116
Laos: its people, its society, its culture 120
Laos: politics, economics and society 116
Laos-Viet-Nam boundary 481
Laoskii yazyk 676
Laos-Thailand boundary 481
Larsen, K. 525
Latt, Tin Maung 63
Launay, Adrien 253, 271
Lê, Nguyễn Hiến 761
Lê, Vũ-văn- 754
Lê Bá Kông 759
Lê Khả Kế 741
Lê-Khắc-Quyến 756
Lê-Khắc-Thiền 756
Lê Ngọc Trụ 733
Lê Văn Đức 733
Lê Van Hảo 621
Lê-Văn-Thới 546
Lead and tin coins of Pegu and Tenasserim 309

Leaders of Malaya and who's who 277
Leading personalities in Cambodia 263
LeBar, Frank M. 120, 611, 624
Leclère, A. 326
Lecomte, Henri 526, 568
Lee Foundation 42
Lee, Oey Hong 300
Legge, James 811
Légumes indigènes susceptibles d'être consommés 578
Leiddraad bij het bestudeeren van 't Galela'sch dialekt 822
Lekagul, Boonsong 493, 496, 521
Leksikon Malaysia 707
Lemarié, Ch. 485
Le May, Reginald 320
Lemire, Charles 328
Lemoine, Jacques 541
Lent, John A. 353
LePoer, Barbara Leitch 71, 181
Letterature del mondo 639
Letterature del sud-est asiatico 639
Lévi, Sylvain 98
Lewis, Paul 814
Lewitz, S. 540
Lexilogus of the English, Malay and Chinese languages 811
Lexique des termes médicaux français-vietnamiens 756
Lexique français-laotien 672
Lexique français-cambodgien expliqué 664
Lexique franco-khmère 660
Lexique khmère-français 660
Liangprasoet, Anek 731
Liang Sathirasut 806
Libraries: see subheading 'organizations' under each country
Libraries in West Malaysia and Singapore: a short history 178
Library of Congress 71, 108, 130, 181
Lịch-triều hiến-chương loại-chí 347
Lich the ky 20, 1901-2000 340
Liễn, Ngô Vĩ 443
Liên, Phan trung 744
Ligne du Yun-nan 428

Italicized entries are for titles. **Bold entries are subject guides**

Lijst van de voornaamste aardrijkskundige namen 388
Lim Chong-Yah 183
Lim Huck Tee, Edward 178
Lim, Rodrigo C. 296
Limits in the seas series 482
Linguistic atlas of the Philippines 634
Linguistic Society of the Philippines 820
Linguistic survey of India 615
Linguistics in east Asia and south east Asia 607
Linguistics series 814, 820, 827, 853
Lintner, Bertil 243
Li'onese 838
Li'onesisch-Deutsches Wörterbuch 838
List of ancient monuments in Burma 406
List of geographical names 407
List of inscriptions found in Burma 314
List of objects of antiquarian and archaeological interest 406
List of pagodas at Pagan under the custody of Government 397
List of publications issued by Central Bureau 214
List of species and genera of Indian phanerogams 524
List of the Burmese names of trees and plants 566
List of trees, shrubs and principal climbers, etc. 535
List of trees, shrubs, herbs 535
Liste des membres du corps diplomatique 114
Liste des membres des missions diplomatiques 114
Liste des personnalités laos 264
Liste de khets (provinces) 431
Liste de mm. les membres du corps diplomatique et consulaire 128
Liste général de classement des monuments historiques 427
Listes générales des inscriptions et des monuments 324
Literature: see under each country

Literature of Java 785
Littératures contemporaines de l'Asie du Sud-Est 639
Livre d'or des négociants de Cochinchine 154
Livre d'or du Cambodge, de la Cochinchine et de l'Annam 262
Llamzon, Teodoro A. 635
Lloyd, Malcolm B. S. 412
Lo Man Yuk 449
Lombard, D. 639
Lombard, Sylvia J. 853
Lombok 467, 632
Lombok. Een dialectgeografische studie 632
London Oriental series 794
Lonergan, P. F. 458
Long Seama 662
Loofs-Wissowa, H. H. E. 751
Louis, Nicole 270
Loureiro, Joannes de 547
Lovett, Donald L. 509
Low, Hugh Brooke 627
Lowis, C. C. 615
Lozozki, Walter 345
Lu Pe Win 792
Luang-Phrabang 376
Luce, G. H. 314
Ludszuweit, Daniel 232
Lunet de Lajonquière, E. 419, 429, 433
Lung, Hoang Ngoc 336
Lược truyện các tác giả Việt-Nam 268
Lupaih, Pugguwon 634
Luping, Datin Margaret 488
Lwin, U Khin Maung 58
Ly Vou-Ong 660, 664
Lyman, Thomas Amis 828
McArthur, M. S. H. 195
McConnell, Fraiser 24
McDougall, Colin 450
McFarland, Curtis D. 634
McFarland, George Bradley 723
McGuire, R. E. 244
Machado, Kit G. 361
MacJohn's guide book for Singapore and

Italicized entries are for titles. **Bold entries are subject guides**

Johore 456
MacKinnon, John 498
McNeely, Jeffrey A. 493
McVey, Ruth T. 200
Madan, N. N. 303
Maday, Bela C. 156
Madoereesch-Nederlandsch woordenboek
788
Madoereesche spraakkunst 789
Madras Army 411
Madrolle guides 424
Madrolle, Claudius 424-426, 428
Madurese 787-789
Magic guide to Burma 402
Maguindanaon 839
Maguindanaon dictionary 839
Mahmud, Mahiddin 284
Mai's Auslandstaschenbücher 392
Major companies of the Far East 40
*Major companies of the Far East and
Australasia* 40
*Major languages of east and south-east
Asia* 637
Makasarese 774-778
Makassaars-Nederlands woordenboek 774
Makassaarsch-Hollandsch woordenboek
775
Makassaarsche spraakkunst 778
Makatuku Pemeke (na Nohi Pibni) 613
Makepeace, Walter 456
Malacca 184
*Malacca Strait and west coast of Sumatera
pilot* 477
**Malay 204, 486, 508, 528-530, 552, 572,
574, 584, 586, 598, 637, 638, 678-713,
804, 805, 811**
*Malay, Achinese, French and English
vocabulary* 766
Malay-English dictionary (romanised)
687
Malay-English dictionary 688
*Malay peoples of Malaysia and their
languages* 625
Malay poisons and charm cures 598
Malay proverbs 705

Malay States: see Malaysia
Malaya 160
*Malaya: a guide for businessmen and
visitors* 179
Malayan and Indonesian studies 686
Malayan civil list 282
Malayan ferns 531
*Malayan ferns and fern allies: supplement
1* 531
Malayan fern allies 531
Malayan forest records 571
Malayan fruits 583
Malayan statistics 169
Malayan wild flowers 549
Malayan year book 169, 175
MALAYSIA 156-168, 175, 184
  Agriculture 31, 377
  **Biography 241, 242, 273, 275, 277-
  282**
  Business 37, 40, 41, 175, 177, 179
  Calendar 350, 358
  Climate 174
  Culture 32, 353
  Documents 300, 304-305, 354, 355
  Economy 33, 35, 158, 159, 377
  Ethnography 184, 611, 624-627
  Geography 31, 34, 365, 367, 377, 488
  Government 39, 175, 176, 282, 301
  **History 32, 36, 298, 302-303, 353,
  356, 357**
  Languages 605, 606, 625
  **Literature 275, 280, 353, 638, 696,
  639**
  Migration 161
  Monuments 450
  **Natural resources 33, 36, 164, 166,
  167, 184, 486-488, 490, 492-494, 496-
  499, 502, 508-511, 515, 516, 518, 519,
  522, 524, 527-529, 548-550, 571-573,
  583, 584, 590, 598**
  Organizations 42, 175, 178, 281
  Politics 38, 39
  Population 169-171
  Religion 242, 450, 610, 805
  Statistics 39, 169-174

Italicized entries are for titles. **Bold entries are subject guides**

Transport 33
Topography 175, 377, 385-386, 389-391, 393-395, 445-451, 457
Malaysia 26, 158, 168, 447
Malaysia: a country study 156
Malaysia: a survey 159
Malaysia: economic expansion and national unity 158
Malaysia: official year book 168
Malaysia and Indo-China: information for visitors 393
Malaysia, Singapore and Brunei 385, 446
Malaysia yearbook 175
Malaysian Language and Literature Bureau 689
Malaysian studies 353
Mal'khanova, I. A. 746
Mallat, J. 225
Malleret, Louis 619
Maluku 468, 469
Mammals of Borneo 494
Mammals of New Guinea 495
Mammals of Southeast Asia 493
Mammals of Thailand 493
Mammals of the Indomalayan region 492
Mammifères du Laos 493
Manam Hpang 832
Mandalay 404, 405
Mandalay to Bhamo 405
Manggarai 840
Manich Jumsai, M. L. 724
Manila 235, 472, 473
Manit Manitcharoen 719
Mann, D. C. 458
Mansvelt, W. M. F. 216
Manual of Netherlands India 201
Manual of New Guinea legumes 589
Manual of statistics relating to the Federated Malay States 173
Manual of the dipterocarp trees of Brunei State 573
Manual of the grasses of New Guinea 558
Manual of the non-dipterocarp trees of Sarawak 573
Manuel, Corazon Avenir 363

Manuel, E. Arsenio 295
Manuel, Magdalena Avenir 295
Manuel du voyageur en Indochine du Sud 426
Manuel du voyageur en Indochine du Nord 425
Map of mainland Asia by treaty 481
Marai-go daijiten 695
Marcus, Russell 669, 675
Marine algae of South Vietnam 544
Maring, Ester G. 311, 362
Maring, Joel M. 311, 362
Maris, Yunus 713
Marrillier, André 745
Marsden, William 691
Marshall, G. F. L. 520
Marshall, H. B. 708
Martin, Denys 312
Martin, Julian 825
Martin, M. A. 579
Martini, François 848
Marxist regimes series 109, 116, 131
Mas Osman 274
Mas y Sans, Sinibaldo de 224
Masakazu, Taketomi 695
Masamune, G. 554
Mason, A. 467
Mason, Francis 483, 645
Maspero, Georges 99, 327, 346, 667
Massie, M. 17
Mat Tran Dan Toc Giai Phóng Mien Nam Việt Nam 337
Materia medica 590-599
Materials for a flora of the Malay Peninsula 528
Materials in languages of Indonesia 628
Mathieu, A. R. 121
Matière médicale cambodgienne 594
Matière médicale et pharmacopée sino-annamites 597
Matières alimentaires du Tonkin 582
Matisoff, James A. 837
Matocinos, Arlene 238
Matthes, B. F. 775, 776, 778
Matthews, N. 15

Italicized entries are for titles. **Bold entries are subject guides**

Mẫu, Vũ-văn- 750
Maung Maung Gyi 55
Maung Maung Nyunt 654
Maung Tin, U Pe 654
Maung Zaniya 311
Maxwell, W. G. 354
May Oung, Mg 315
Maybon, Charles B. 262
Mayr, Ernst 501
Means, Nathalie 844
Means, Paul B. 844
*Mededeelingen van de Kirtya
    Liefrinck-Van der Tuuk* 847
*Mededeelingen van het Centraal Kantoor
    voor de Statistiek* 216
*Medical services: campaigns in the eastern
    theatre* 303
Medicinal plants 592
Medicinal Plants Exhibition Committee
    592
Medicinal plants of the Philippines 599
*Medicinal plants of East and Southeast
    Asia* 590
Medina, Isagani R. 473
Medway, Lord 493, 494, 497, 499
Mella, Cesar T. 290
*Mémoires de l'Institut Océanographique
    de l'Indochine* 519
Mémoires de l'ORSTOM 516
*Memoir of the life and labours of the Rev.
    Adoniram Judson* 645
Menault, M. 594
Mentrida, Alonso 825
Mer de Chine 477
Merrill, Elmer D. 547, 554, 557, 560,
    561
Met Ratanaprasit 802
Metrik in der thailändischen Dichtung
    729
Metro Manila street directory 472
Metzger, Judith 590
Mialaret, Jean-Pierre 454
Migration: see under each country
Milburn, William 37
Military interpreter 754

*Million baht business information
    Thailand* 89
Milne (Mrs Leslie) 842
Milner, Anthony 638
Minangkabau 790, 791
*Minangkabausch-Maleisch-Nederlandsch
    woordenboek* 790
Minangkabausche spraakkunst 791
Mineral resources of Burma 600
Minh, Nguyễn Văn 757
Ministère des Affaires Etrangères 114,
    128, 264
Ministère du Plan 113
Ministerie van Oorlog 360a
Ministry of Agriculture 529
Ministry of Commerce and
    Communications 76
Ministry of Commerce 90
Ministry of Communications and
    Information 185, 186
Ministry of Culture 185, 186, 453
Ministry of Finance 81
Ministry of Health, Department of
    Medical Research 250
Ministry of Information 110
Ministry of National Development 80
Ministry of National Planning and
    Statistics 146
Ministry of Trade 61
Minorités ethniques du Vietnam 622
Minority groups in North Vietnam 622
*Minority groups in the Republic of
    Vietnam* 623
Minority groups in Thailand 617
Minot, Georges 800
Mintz, Malcolm Warren 817
Miquel, F. A. W. 530, 553
Missions diplomatiques et consulaires 114
Mission Pavie: exploration de l'Indo-Chine
    17
Mission Pavie: Indo-Chine 1879-1895 17
Mitteilungen des Instituts für Asienkunde
    306
Mix (Mrs) 795
Mix, H. W. 795

Italicized entries are for titles. **Bold entries are subject guides**

Miyatake, Seidô 695
Modern English-Vietnamese dictionary 738
Mogenet, Luc 376
Moluccas 468, 469
Momon Wirakusumah, R. 799
Mon 792-794
Mon-English dictionary 793
Monitoring Service of the British Broadcasting Corporation 300
Monographie des rues et monuments de Saigon 440
Monographie de la province de Biên-hoa 442
Monographs in international studies 195
Monographs of the Institute of Science and Technology 563
Monographs of the Malaysian Branch 494
Monograph of the Brunei Museum journal 194
Monograph series on Southeast Asia 353
Montagnards du Tonkin 622
Montyon, Antoine Jean-Baptiste Auget de 100
Monuments: see under each country
Monuments du Champa et du Cambodge 429
Moon, Brenda E. 15a
Moore, Frank J. 73
Morais, J. Victor 277
Morev, L. N. 673, 676, 728, 803
Morgan, J. R. 482
Morris, Cliff 849
Moscotti, Albert D. 310
Moskalyov, A. A. 676
Mosses of Singapore and Malaysia 550
Mosses of the Philippines 562
Most up-to-date Thai dictionary 719
Motor roads of Burma 400
Mots culturels khméro-français expliqués 663
Mountain regions and national minorities 621
Moussay, Gerard 779, 791
Moya y Jimenez, Francisco Javier de 224
Muller, Kal 468
Mulliner, Kent 348, 353
Mun Myanma abidan 792
Munro, I. S. R. 513
Munson, Frederick P. 108
Museum voor Economische Botanie te Buitenzorg 586
Musgrave, John K. 611
Mya-tu, M. 58
Myanaung U Tin 55
Myanma-hmu abidan 311
Myanma abidan akyin-gyok 640
Myanma swèzon kyan 641
Myanma thada 654
Myat, Tha 591
Myers, G. S. 510
N.P. 477, 480
Nai Tun Way 792
Nair, D. M. Nath 532, 534
Nam Hai di nhân liệt truyện 272
Nangle, M. C. 411
Nantana Danvithathana 730
Nao Leng Xiong 826
Nath, Dewan Mohinder 532, 534
National accounts of West Malaysia 1947-1971 172
National Census and Statistics Office 226, 228
National economic atlas 383
National Economic and Development Authority 226, 228
National Economy Department 146
National Historical Commission 295
National income of Burma 57
National Institute of Administration 150
National Institute of Statistics 146
National Library of Malaysia 178
National Research Council 92
National Statistical Coordination Board 228
National Statistical Office 81, 418
National University of Singapore 352
Native woods for construction purposes

Italicized entries are for titles. **Bold entries are subject guides**

564

*Natives of Sarawak and British North
  Borneo* 627

Natural History Museum publications
  492

Natural productions of Burmah 483

**Natural resources 483-604; see also
  under each country**

Natural resources atlas of Thailand 368

Natural Resources Board 487

Natural resources of Sarawak 487

Natural resources of South-East Asia 484

Nature 48, 49

Naval Intelligence Division 93, 201

Naval Staff 201

Navdocks 564

Navigation guides 477-480

Navy Department 564

Neal, D. G. 567

*NEDA statistical yearbook of the
  Philippines* 228

Nederlands-Indië contra Japan 360a

Nederlands-Javaans handwoordenboek 783

Nederlandsche oudheden in de Molukken
  469

Neher, Clark D. 73

Népote, Jacques 422

Netherlands East Indies 201

Neuf mars 1945--neuf mars 1948 257

Neumann, J. H. 771

New Guinea: Irian Jaya 468

New Guinea: journey into the stone age
  468

*New list of missionaries in China, Korea
  and Siam* 254

New Malaysian who's who 273

New model English-Thai dictionary 724

New model Thai-English dictionary 722

New Straits times directory (buku merah)
  177

Ng, F. S. P. 571

Ngadi, Henry Gana 829

Ngadja 841

Nghị, Thanh- 734, 741

Nghiên Cứu Biển, Viện 507

Nginn, Pierre Somchine 331

Ngo Quang Truong 336

Ngô Vĩ Liễn 443

Ngữ-vung Thai-Việt-Anh 800

Nguyễn Bá Trác 344

Nguyễn Đình Hòa 269, 737

Nguyễn Đức Dẫn 760

Nguyễn Hiến Lê 761

Nguyễn Huyên Anh 270

Nguyễn Luyện 743

Nguyễn Năng Vinh 580

Nguyễn Ngọc-Bích 135

Nguyễn Như Hiền 542

Nguyễn Quang Xỹ 764

Nguyễn Quí Hùng 763

Nguyễn Trần-Huân 269

Nguyễn Trọng Biểu 580

Nguyễn Văn Chien 131

Nguyễn Văn Chinh 826

Nguyễn Văn Dương 543, 595

Nguyễn-Văn-Khôn 736, 739

Nguyễn Văn Minh 757

Ngwe Daung Byu 650

Nha Khi Tuong 340

Nhà Văn-Hóa 155

Nhim, Dieu Chinh 800

Nhouy Abhay, Thao 121

Nicéville, Lionel de 520

Nidda Hongvivat 417

Niên giám thống kê 146

Niên-giám thống-kê Việt-Nam 146

Niên-giám van-nghê-si và hiêp-hôi
  van-hóa 155

Nieuw Guinea 211

Nieuw maleisch-nederlandsch woordenboek
  684

*Nieuw plantkundig woordenboek voor
  Nederlandsch Indie* 552

1907 handbook to Singapore 456

1972 national economic atlas 383

Nisbet, John 49

Nomenclature des communes du Tonkin
  443

*Nomenclature des principales essences
  forestières* 570

Italicized entries are for titles. **Bold entries are subject guides**

Noorduyn, J. 631
Nores, Georges 423
North Borneo, Brunei, Sarawak 165
North Viet Nam Affairs Division 133
Northern Illinois University 353, 361
Northern Vietnam 385
Noss, Richard B. 727
*Note on the Palaungs of Hsipaw and
    Tawngpeng* 615
Notes and statistics, Burma 69
Notes and statistics in four parts 69
*Notes on a visit to the rivers Belait and
    Tutong* 195
Notice sur la province de Hung-hoa 443
Notice sur la province de Sontay 443
Notice sur la province de Ninh-binh 443
Notice sur la province de Hung-yen 443
Notice sur le Laos français 125
*Notices sommaires sur les territoires
    militaires* 443
Novak, John A. 345
Novikov, N. N. 649
NP 477
Nugroho 214
Numismatique annamite 345
Nunn, G. Raymond 19, 20
Nuttige planten van Nederlandsch-Indie
    586
Nyunt, Maung Maung 654
O. I. R. report 342
Oates, Eugene W. 412, 490, 496
Oceanic linguistics special publications
    608, 635
Ochse, Jacob Jonas 585
Oey Hong Lee 300
Office of Air Force History 335
Office of Armed Forces Information
    and Education 138
Office of Education 200
Office of External Research 266
Office of Intelligence Research 342
Office of Media Services 119
Office of Public Communication 182
Office of State Universities 616
Office of the Board of Investment 89

Office of the Geographer 385, 482
Office of the National Research
    Council 92
Office of the Secretary of Defense 337
*Official directory of the Republic of the
    Philippines* 230
*Official guide to Ayutthaya and Bang
    Pa-in* 417
Official guide to eastern Asia 394
Official history of the Indian armed forces
    303
Official roster of officers and employees
    230
Oil fields of Burma 600
Okell, John 654, 655
Old Javanese-English dictionary 784
Olson, James S. 333
Omar, Asmah Hj. 625, 830
*On the geography of Burma and its
    tributary states* 51
Ooi Jin Bei 174
Oosting, H. J. 797
*Orchids of Burma (including the
    Andaman Islands) described* 537
Order of battle 334
*Orders and families of Malayan seed
    plants* 548
Organisation administrative au Laos 123
*Organisation of the Government of
    Malaysia* 176
Organizational directory of Thailand 85
*Organizational directory of the
    Government of Thailand* 85
Organizations: see under each country
Oriental commerce 37
OSD Task Force 337
Osman-Rani, H. 157
Otanes, Fe T. 718
Oung, Mg May 315
Our tropical possessions in Malayan India
    184
Overseas Development Administration
    379
Oxford in Asia historical reprints 36, 78,
    691

Italicized entries are for titles. **Bold entries are subject guides**

Oxford in Asia university readings 174
Pacific linguistics 605, 628, 633, 843, 849
Pagan 397
Pagan: art and architecture of old Burma 397
Pagan races of the Malay peninsula 626
Pakinnaka-dipani kyan 642
Palaung 842
Palawan 588
Pali 806, 808-810
PALI language texts: Philippines 817
Pali-Thai-English-Sanskrit dictionary 808
Palic, Vladimir M. 9
Pallegoix, Jean-Baptiste 79, 725
Pamoentjak, M. Thaib gl. St. 790
Pandai Berbahasa Inggris 704
Panduan perpustakaan di Malaysia 178
Panganiban, José Villa 715
Pap san khham Pak Tay-Keo-Eng 800
Papers in international studies 7
Papers on Malay subjects 162
Papua New Guinea 24
Pardo de Tavera, T. H. 27, 599
Parkes, Carl 391
Parkin, Robert 608
Parmentier, Henri 324, 433, 435, 441
Parti Communiste Indochinois (1925-1933) 343
Parti National Annamite au Tonkin 1927-1932 343
Parti National Annamite des émigrés en Chine 343
Parti Révolutionnaire du Jeune Annam 343
Pascoe, Edwin Hall 600
Pateda, Mansoer 824
Pathet Lao: leadership and organization 117
Pauer, Gyula 365
Paulus, J. 204
Pavie 17
Pavie, Auguste 17
Pavlenko, A. P. 799
Payne, Junaidi 494

Pe, Hla 644, 653
Pe Maung Tin 654, 314
Pearl of the East: a guide to Burma and its people 402
Pearson, J. D. 15
Pelet, P. 375
Pemeke (na Nohi Pibni), Makatuku 613
Penang 180, 184, 190, 448
Penang almanac and directory 190
Penang guide 448
Penang, Singapore and Malacca almanac and directory 190
Penders, Chr. L. M. 359
Pendlebury, H. M. 522
Penninga, P. 788
Pentagon papers 337
Penzer, N. M. 600
Peplow, Evelyn 470
Percheron, Maurice 96
Permar, Bernard J. 345
Perry, Lily M. 590
Personalia van staatkundige eenheden 217
Personnalités du Cambodge 263
Personnel of the Philippine puppet government 230
Pételot, Alfred 593
Peters, Jens 470
Pétillot, Loys 505
Petit dictionnaire des principaux mots étrangers 709
Petit dictionnaire français khmer 660
Petit dictionnaire français-cambodgien 660
Petit dictionnaire français-khmer 660
Phaen thi tanon nai prathet Thai 369
Phạm Bình Quyến 542
Phạm-Hoàng Hộ 543, 544
Phạm-Khắc-Quảng 756
Phạm Thị Thoa 445
Phan-Văn-Tây 581
Phạmxuân Thái 750, 758
Phan Huy Chú 347
Phan-Kế-Bính 272
Phan trung Liên 744

Italicized entries are for titles. **Bold entries are subject guides**

Phana, Douk 594
Pháp-Việt tân từ điển minh họa 741
Pháp-Việt từ điển chú thêm chữ Hán 742
Phật-học 809
Phật-học từ-điển 809
Phetsarath, Tiao Maha Upahat 121
Phia Sing 506
Philippine almanac and handbook of facts 234
Philippine atlas 382
Philippine birds 501
Philippine Center for Language Study 718
Philippine Coast and Geodetic Survey 383
Philippine coast pilot 479
Philippine company profile 231
Philippine economic atlas 383
Philippine Folklore Society 717
Philippine geographical names 474
Philippine Islands: preliminary edition 385
Philippine Islands 224
Philippine Islands 1493-1898 364
Philippine Islands pilot 477
Philippine journal of linguistics. Special monograph issue 635
Philippine minor languages 635
Philippine palaeography 635
Philippine proverb lore 717
Philippine statistical yearbook 228
Philippine statistics yearbook 228
Philippine statistics, 1903-1959 229
Philippine studies 361
Philippine Studies Program 221
Philippine vacations and explorations 471
Philippine yearbook 226, 233
Philippinen 223
Philippinen: Reise-Handbuch 470
PHILIPPINES 220,221, 223-227
   Agriculture 31, 223, 382, 383
   Biography 222, 239, 290-296
   Business 37, 40, 41, 231, 233-236
   Calendar 237, 472
   Chronology 232, 234

Climate 382, 383
Culture 32, 222, 361-363
Documents 300, 304, 364
Economy 33, 35, 229, 382, 383
Ethnography 363, 634-636
Geography 31, 34, 223, 365, 367, 382-384
Government 39, 230
History 32, 36, 224, 298, 361, 362
Languages 560, 561, 599, 605, 606, 635, 715, 717
Literature 290, 361
Migration 232, 236
Natural resources 33, 36, 382, 383, 489, 492, 493, 501, 502, 514, 560-563, 575, 588, 590, 599, 604
Organizations 232, 237-239, 382
Politics 38, 39, 220-221, 223-225, 364
Population 228
Religion 237, 364
Statistics 39, 226-229, 234, 382, 383
Transport 33, 382-384
Topography 232, 382-385, 389-391, 394, 470-476
Philippines 27, 225, 471
Philippines: a country study 220
Philippines: a travel survival kit 470
Philippines best 1000 corporations 231
Philippines handbook 470
Philippines under Spanish and American rules 224
Philippines who's who 294
Philosophical lexicon 750
Phinney (Miss) 645
Phnom Penh 115
Phonetic transliteration 655
Phonologie und Schrift des Nordthai 803
Phoo txais lug Aakiv-Moob-Aakiv 826
Photchananukrom chabap Ratchabandit Sathan 721
Photchananukrom Lanna-Thai 801
Photchananukrom sap thahan Angkrit-Thai 726
Photchananukrom Thai 719
Photchananukrom Thai

Italicized entries are for titles. **Bold entries are subject guides**

Yuan-Thai-Angkrit 802
Phung, Bùi 736
Physical fitness of the Burmese 58
Pierce, John R. 501
Pierre, L. 570
Pigeaud, Th. 782, 783, 785
Pil, Teresita Veloso 363
Pilipino 637, 638, 714-718
Pinratana, Amnuai 521
Pinther, Miklos 634
Plam, Yu. Ya. 3, 676, 728
Place names 63, 449, 457, 473
Plantas medicinales de Filipinas 599
Plantes et fleurs comestibles de l'Indochine 578
Plantes médicinales du Cambodge, du Laos et du Viêtnam 593
Plants from the markets of Thailand 576
Pluvier, Jan M. 301
Pocket guide to Vietnam 138
Podo, Hadi 704
Poerwadarminta, W. J. S. 679, 683
Political alignments of Vietnamese nationalists 342
Political economy of Malaysia 157
Political science, economics, and linguistics 361
Political, social and economic terminology 650
Politics: see under each country
Pollacchi, P. 370
Ponglux, Dhavadee 592
Population: see under each country
Port of Singapore Authority 192
Port Weld to Kuantan 449
Porter, Gareth 337
Portuguese Timor 208
Postguide 471
Posthumus, O. 555
Post-war occupation forces 303
Potential tree species for Negara Brunei Darussalam 573
Pouchat, J. 578
Powell, J. H. G. 405
Power struggle in South-East Asia 300

Prachum phongsawadan 253
Practisch Madoereesch-Hollandsch woordenboek 788
Prasad, Bisheshwar 303
Prasad, S. N. 303
Prathet Thai Shell 369
Pratt, Thane K. 500
Prawiro Atmodjo, S. 781, 782
Preap-Sokh 658
Précis of information concerning the Straits Settlements 163
Preliminary report on the forest and other vegetation of Pegu 566
Prescott, D. F. 481
Prescott, J. R. V. 481
Présence du royaume lao 121
Présence militaire française en Indochine 1940-1945 321
Priangan: de Prianger-Regentschappen 288
Princess Chulabhorn Science Congress 592
Prince of Wales' Island register and directory 180
Prodromus florae Sumatranae 553
Proum, Im 658
Province de Nam-dinh 444
Province de Thanh-hoa 444
Province of Burma 50
Provincia de Agustinos Calzados de Filipinas 560
Public Administrative Division 85
Publications de l'Académie des Sciences d'Outre-Mer 256
Publications de l'Ecole Française d'Extrême-Orient 242, 345, 429, 433, 435, 780, 815
Publications de l'Ecole Française d'Extrême-Orient 25
Publications de l'Institut de Recherches Historiques 344
Publications du Centre Universitaire des Langues 761
Publications in the languages of Asia 657, 669

Italicized entries are for titles. **Bold entries are subject guides**

Publications of the American Ethnological Society 160
Publications of the Institute of Historical Research 344
Purnell, Herbert C. 802, 853
Pusat Pembinaan dan Pengembangan Bahasa 679
Puteh, Mansor 696
Puzitskii, Ye. V. 833
Quah, Jon S. T. 28
Quah, Stella R. 28
Quán, Quốc Sử 346
Quảng, Phạm-Khắc- 756
Quarterly civil list for Burma 66
Quartermaster-General of the Madras Army 411
Quartermaster-General's Department 411
Quisumbing, Eduardo 599
Quốc Sử Quán 346
Quyến, Lê-Khắc- 756
Quyến, Phạm Bình 542
R & A 258
Races of Burma 614
Radaza, Francisco R. Demetrio y 363
Rainey, B. L. 303
Rainfall statistics of the British Borneo Territories 174
Rajendra Singh 303
Ramsden, H. A. 320
Rand, Austin L. 500
Rangoon 62, 63
Rangoon guide book 63
Rao, V. V. Bhanoji 172
Rapport au Conseil de Gouvernement 101
Rapport sur l'exercice du protectorat 101
Rapport sur la situation administrative 101
Raquez, A. 327
Ratanaprasit, Met 802
Ratchabandit Sathan 416, 418, 720, 721
Rathenberg, Erhard 392
Rau, Anke 514
Rau, Norbert 514
Ravenstock's Manila city directory 235

Ray, Sidney H. 631
Reconquest of Burma 303
Records of the Botanical Survey of India 524
Recueil des principales ordonnances royales 347
Recueil de statistiques 102
Reed, Charles H. 752
Reference grammar of colloquial Burmese 654
Reformed Vietnamese writing 750
Refugee Studies Programme 360
Refugees 119
Regeerings-almanak voor Nederlandsch-Indie 218
Regional Institute of Higher Education and Development 239
Régions montagneuses et minorités nationales en RDV 621
Register of industry and commerce of Thailand 89
Registry of industry and commerce 231
Reid, Anthony 468
Reid, Helen 468
Reid, Lawrence A. 361, 635
Reinach, Lucien de 124
Reinberg, Linda 812
Reinhorn, Marc 670, 676
Reith, G. M. 456
Reitinger, Frank F. 516
Reitsma, S. A. 462
Relación de las encomiendas 476
Relation sur le Tonkin et la Cochinchine 100
Religion: see under each country
Religionen der Menschheit 610
Religionen Südostasiens 610
Report of an enquiry into the standard and cost of living 59
Report on Brunei in 1904 195
Report on North Borneo 168
Report on Singapore 185
Report on the administration of Burma 56
Report to the people by the Government of the Union of Burma 52

Italicized entries are for titles. **Bold entries are subject guides**

Report to the Pyithu Hluttaw 52
Republic of the Philippines official directory 230
Research Analysis Branch 258
Research and Documentation Division 150
Research institutes and researchers 239
Research institutes and researchers of Asian studies 238
Research notes and discussion series 310
Research Registration Division 92
Research School of Pacific Studies 605, 628, 633, 843, 849
Ressources économiques et financières de l'état 347
Retana, W. E. 364
Retizos, Isidro L. 294
Retreat from Burma 303
Revel, Nicole 588
Revised flora of Malaya 527
Revolution and its aftermath in Kampuchea 325
Rhadé 843
Rhade-English dictionary 843
Rhind, D. 536
Rhodes, Alexander de 745
Richard, Emilien 570
Richards, Anthony 829
Richardson, Jim 27
Riches of the wild: land mammals of Southeast Asia 493
Richesse du Cambodge: la pêche et les poissons 505
Richesses du Tong-kin 143
Ricklefs, M. C. 36
Ridley, H. N. 528, 551
Ridout, Lucy 413
Roberts, Chester F. 160
Roberts, T. D. 44, 118
Robertson, J. A. 364
Robinson, Daniel 421
Robinson, H. C. 497, 515
Robinson, Herbert C. 18
Robinson, Michael 309
Robson, S. O. 784

Rodger, Alex. 535, 565
Roe, F. W. 487
Roeder, O. G. 284
Roland-Cabaton, M.-A. 242
Rollet, B. 540
Romanization guide for Thai script 730
Romanized spelling of provinces, districts 416
Romein, J. E. 380
Rong biển Việtnam 544
Roolvink, R. 772
Roorda, T. 782
Roper, Geoffrey 15b
Rosell, Anna-Brita 434
Rosenstock's press reference library 296
Rosiny, Tonny 392
Rossington, Maurice H. 244
Ross, Russell R. 108
Rotary Club, Saigon 438
Roth, Henry Ling 627
Rotinese 845
Rottineesch-Hollandsch woordenboek 845
Rottineesche spraakkunst 845
Routes by land and water in British Burma 412
Routes in Upper Burma 411
Rowland, Ian 209
Royal Institute: see Ratchabandit Sathan
Royal orders of Burma, AD 1598-1885 307
Royal Survey Department 319, 368
Royaume du Laos 123
Ruang chotmaihet khong khana Bat luang Farangset 253
Rumphius, G. E. 557
Rumphius memorial volume 557
Russian-English-Vietnamese dictionary of physical terms 755
Russier, Edouard 371
Russier, Henri 371
Russko-laosskii uchebnyi slovar' 673
Russko-birmanskii slovar' 649
Russko-V'etnamskii slovar' 746
Russko-v'etnamskii slovar' biologicheskikh

Italicized entries are for titles. **Bold entries are subject guides**

nazvanii 542
Russko-v'etnamskii slovar' po pishchevoi promyshlennosti 580
Rutter, Owen 166
RVNAF 336
RVNAF and US operational cooperation 336
RVNAF logistics 336
Sabah 166, 170, 488
Sabah Society 488
Sabah Society monograph 488
Sách tập nói chuyện tiếng Annam và tiếng Langsa 759
Sacks, I. Milton 342
Sacra Congregatio de Propaganda Fide 745
Safioedin, Asis 787
Sahsodawmya atthappatti 246
Saigon 440
Sailing directions for Strait of Malacca 479
Sailing directions for the north-east coast of Borneo 479
Sailing directions for the western shores 479
Sailing directions for New Guinea 479
Sailing directions for the Philippine Islands 479
Sailing directions for Celebes 479
Sailing directions for Soenda Strait 479
St. John, R. F. St. Andrew 645
Salim, Peter 690
Salons 615
Salzner, Richard 606
Sam-Thang 660
Sandstrom, George 501
Sangir 846
Sangirees-Nederlands woordenboek 846
Sangiresche spraakkunst 846
Sans, Sinibaldo de Mas y 224
Sanskrit 807-809
Santiruk, T. 577
San Khin 591
Saranukrom Thai 720
Saranukrom Thai samrap yaowachon 720

Saranukrom watthanatam Phak Tai 720
Saran Singh 349
Sarawak 167, 171, 487
Sasak 847
Sastri, K. N. V. 303
Sathirasut, Liang 806
Satjadibrata, R. 796, 798
Sau Kau-too 835
Savigny 143
Savina, F. M. 620
Savoir botanique des Bunaq 587
Sawyer, Frederic H. 636
Sayam waiyakon 729
Schachter, Paul 718
Schmidgall-Tellings, A. E. 685
Scholberg, Henry 408
School of Oriental and African Studies 644, 657, 792
Schreiner, Alfred 142
Schriften des Instituts für Asienkunde 46
Schrock, Joann L. 617, 623
Schrock, Joan L. 622
Schroeder, Albert 582
Schroeder, Albert 345
Schroeder, Karl 582
Schwartz, J. Alb. T. 852
Scientific and technical terms, A-Z 652
Scientific dictionary, English-Pilipino 716
Scott, James George 48, 49, 409
Scott, N. C. 829
Seafood of south-east Asia 502
Seama, Long 662
Seaports 33, 37, 477-480, 203, 218
Sebeok, Thomas A. 607
See, Ch'ng Kin 178
Seidenfaden, Erik 420
Sein, U Hoke 643
Sen, Chia Lin 174
Senator Gravel edition 337
Sengoi-English English-Sengoi dictionary 844
Seng, You Poh 183
Sengoi 844
Seri Cd 584, 700
Seri pata dasar 707

Italicized entries are for titles. **Bold entries are subject guides**

Série Hanoi 582
Serpents de l'Indochine 516
Serpents du Laos 516
Service de la Statistique du Laos 126
Service de la Statistique Générale 102
Service Géographique 372, 431
Service Hydrographique de la Marine 477
Service Météorologique 103
Service National de la Statistique 126
Sethaputra, So. 722, 724
Setting of the stage to 1959 335
Seventy-five years' Mohamedan-English calendar 358
Sevilla, Victor J. 292
Shadily, Hassan 681, 685, 690
Shan 525, 534, 795
Shan and English dictionary 795
Shan of Burma 243
Shan State 51, 60, 243, 409, 534
Sharp, Lauriston 73
Shaw, Lewis A. 309
Shelford, R. 518
Shipping guide of Singapore 192
Shorto, H. L. 792, 794
Short Northern Thai-English dictionary 802
Shou-hua, Kuo 105
Shway Yoe: see Scott, James George
Siam 77, 424
Siam: a handbook 77
Siam: basic handbook 75
Siam: general and medical 76
Siam: nature and industry 76
Siam and its productions, arts and manufactures 77
Siam directory 88, 91
Siam Society 525
Siamese coins and tokens 320
Siamese French English dictionary 725
Siamese plant names 538
Siamese porcelain and other tokens 320
Siaran perangkaan tahunan Malaysia 169
Siaran perangkaan tahunan 170, 171
Sigler, David Burns 333

Sila Viravong, Maha 668, 677
Silpasarn, Phya Upakit 729
Silvestre, J. 139
Simple key to one hundred common trees of Burma 565
Sing, Phia 506
Singam, S. Durai Raja 449
SINGAPORE 156, 159, 162-164, 168, 181-186
  Agriculture 31
  Biography 240, 277
  Business 37, 40, 41, 190-193
  Calendar 350, 358
  Climate 174
  Culture 32, 352
  Documents 304
  Economy 33, 35, 159, 183
  Ethnography 181
  Geography 31, 34, 365, 367
  Government 39, 189
  History 32, 36, 298, 302, 303, 348, 349, 351, 356
  Literature 352
  Migration 161
  Monuments 452, 454
  Natural resources 33, 36, 164, 486, 492, 493, 496, 502, 508-511, 515, 516, 519, 522, 527-529, 550, 551, 583, 590
  Organizations 189, 190
  Politics 38, 39, 181-185
  Population 187, 188
  Religion 350, 454
  Statistics 39, 183, 185-188
  Transport 33
  Topography 385, 386, 389-391, 393-395, 445, 452-457
Singapore 28, 185
Singapore: a country study 181
Singapore: a guide to buildings 452
Singapore: twenty-five years of development 183
Singapore almanac and directory 190
Singapore and Malayan directory 190
Singapore and Straits directory 190
Singapore and Straits bazaar book 193

Italicized entries are for titles. **Bold entries are subject guides**

Singapore directory for the Straits Settlements 190
Singapore economy 183
Singapore facts and pictures 186
Singapore facts and figures 186
Singapore Government directory 189
Singapore guide and street directory 453
Singapore Indian Chamber of Commerce trade directory 191
Singapore Manufacturers' Association 191
Singapore studies 352
Singapore tide tables and port facilities 192
Singapore year book 185
Singh,Rajendra 303
Singh, Saran 349
Siri istilah DBP 699
Sirk, Yu. Kh. 777
Situation de l'Indochine 101
Sixteen tables of Thai alphabets current in Siam 612
Skeat, Walter William 626
Sketch map history of Malaya 356
Smales, C. B. 565
Smarnond, Auratai 86
Smirnova, S. V. 542
Smith, Harold E. 318
Smith, Harvey H. 71, 136, 137
Smith, Roger M. 304
Smith, W. D. 604
Smithies, Michael 415
Smitinand, Tem 525, 538, 577
Smythies, Bertram E. 499
Snakes of Malaya 516
Snelleman, Joh. F. 204
Sơ liệu thống kê 147
Sơ liệu thống kê, 1930-1984 147
Société des Arts et des Sciences de Batavia 709
Société des Missions-Etrangères 271
SOE in the Far East 302
Soemargono, Farida 693
Soendaas-Nederlands woordenboek 797
Soendasch-Nederduitsch woordenboek 797

Somchine Nginn, Pierre 331
Some commercial timbers of Thailand 567
Some common Burmese timbers 565
Some medicinal and useful plants, both indigenous and exotic 591
Songvit Kaesri 806
Soon, Tan Kee 457
Soriano, D. H. 294
Sorokina, A. I. 580
Sources of the economic history of Southeast Asia 4
South China Morning Post Ltd 471
South-East Asia: a social, economic and political geography 34
South east Asia: documents 304
South East Asia Documentation Group 355
South east Asia handbook 391
South east Asia in maps 365
South East Asia Library Group 638
South-East Asia languages and literatures 638
South-East Asia on a shoestring 390
South east Asia Program 73, 255, 814, 820, 827, 853
South east Asia series 7
South east Asia Studies 200
South east Asian affairs 1991 38
South east Asian ephemeris 299
South east Asian history and historiography 644
South east Asian institutions of higher learning 42
South east Asian periodicals: an international union list 20
South east Asian references 7
South east Asian regional transport survey 33
South east Asian tribes, minorities and nations 611
South Seas Society 240
South Sulawesi 468
South Vietnam 385
South Viet Nam National Front for Liberation: documents 337

Italicized entries are for titles. **Bold entries are subject guides**

Southeast Asia: filed above at South east Asia
Southern Vietnam and the South China Sea 385
Southwell, C. H. 836
Souverains et notabilités d'Indochine 259
Souvignet, E. 141
Spearman, H. E. 412
Special Burma studies issue 307
Special report series 58
Special warfare 199
Spice islands: exotic eastern Indonesia 468
Spice islands: the Moluccas 468
Spoor, S. H. 360a
Sprachenatlas des indopazifischen Raums 606
Sre 848
Sritua Arief Associates 285, 287
Srivisar, Phya 74
Standard catalogue of Malaysia-Singapore-Brunei 349
Standard trade and industry directory of Indonesia 219
Standard trade directory of Indonesia 219
Stanton, Shelby L. 334
State of Brunei annual report 196
State Secretariat 196, 197
Statistical abstract 214
Statistical annual for the Netherlands 214
Statistical bibliography 81
Statistical data of the Socialist Republic 147
Statistical description of the forests of Thailand 567
Statistical pocket book of Indonesia 215
Statistical yearbook, Thailand 81
Statistical yearbook for Asia and the Pacific 13
Statistical yearbook of the Kingdom of Siam 81
Statistical yearbook of Indonesia 214
Statistical yearbook 146
Statistical yearbook for Asia and the Far East 13

Statistical year book 57
Statistics: see under each country
Statistics Asia and Australasia 6
Statistics Department 169
Statistik Indonesia 214
Statistisch jaaroverzicht van Nederlandsch-Indie 214
Statistisch zakboekje voor Nederlandsch Indie 215
Steinberg, David J. 111
Steller, K. G. F. 846
Sternstein, Larry 72, 319
Stevens, Alan M. 685
Stevens, E. A. 645
Stevens, Edward O. 645, 793
Stevenson, Robert C. 645
Stewart, J. A. 644
Stibbe, D. G. 204
Stockwell, A. J. 354
Stokhof, W. A. L. 628
Story of a working man's life 483
Storz, Hans-Ulrich 46
Strachan, Paul 397
Straits calendar and directory 190
Straits Settlements civil service list 282
Straits Settlements 162
Straits Settlements directory 190
Straits times directory of Singapore and Malaysia 190
Straits times directory of Singapore 190
Straits times directory of Malaysia 190
Straits times directory of Singapore and Malaya 190
Stranger's guide 456
Streets of Manila 473
Structure de la langue vietnamienne 761
Stuart-Fox, Martin 116, 329
Studies in Vietnamese (Annamese) grammar 762
Study and preservation of historic cities 397
Stutterheim, W. F. 465
Suddard, Adrienne 120
Südostasien 31
Südostasien, austral-pazifischer Raum 31

Italicized entries are for titles. **Bold entries are subject guides**

Sulawesi 208, 468
Sullivan, Joseph J. 704
Sullivan, R. E. 839
Sumatra 208
Sumatra 208
Sumatra: seine Pflanzenwelt und deren Erzeugnisse 553
Sumatra: zijne plantenwereld 553
Summary of world broadcasts. The Far East 300
Summers, Harry G. 333
Sun Htoo editorial staff 646
Sundanese 796-799
Sundanskii yazyk 799
Supasit buran 675
Supreme Command Headquarters 368
Survey Department 455
Survey of economic conditions in the Philippine Islands 224
Survey of library resources 15a
Survey of world cultures 73, 111, 120
Suryadinata, Leo 286, 707
Sutisna, U. 574
Suvarnasuddhi, K. 567
Suvatti, Chote 491, 504, 539
Symington, C. F. 571
Symons, Gifford N. 358
Sytangco, Jose R. 716
Tables for the transliteration of Shan names into English 409
Tables synoptiques de chronologie vietnamienne 346
Tabouillot, L. 154
Tae' (Zuid-Toradjasch)-Nederlandsch woordenboek 850
Tagalog 637, 638, 714-718
Tagalog-English dictionary 714
Tagalog reference grammar 718
Tai languages 525, 637, 800-803
Tai-Vietnamese-English dictionary 800
Taiskii yazyk 728
Taketomi Masakazu 695
Tammu, J. 850
Tan, Steven 349
Tan Kee Soon 457

Tân-Việt Cách-Mệnh Đảng 343
Tandart, S. 661
Tantra, I. G. M. 574
Tarling, Nicholas 298
Tata bahasa baku bahasa Indonesia 710
Tatabasa Sunda 799
Tavera, T. H. Pardo de 27, 599
Tây, Phan-Văn- 581
Taylor, Edward H. 517
Taylor, John G. 360
Taylor, L. F. 615
Tee, Edward Lim Huck 178
Teeuw, A. 632, 683, 712, 773
Teixeira, Manuel 260
Tellings, A. E. Schmidgall- 685
Temminck, Coenraad Jacob 207
Temple, R. C. 626
Tên làng xã Việt Nam đần thế kỷ XIX 445
Ten years of socio-economic development 126
Tenasserim 483
Tennessee Valley Authority 366
Tep Yok 660
Terreur Rouge en Annam (1930-1931) 343
Territorial forces 336
Tesauro diksiyunaryo ingles-pilipino 715
Tesaurus umum bahasa Melayu 703
Test for technology 335
Teston, Eugène 96
Tesyolkin, A. S. 711, 786
Tettoni, Luca Invernizzi 414
Tetun 849
Tetun-English dictionary 849
Text-Book Committee 407
Tha Myat 591
Thai 504, 525, 576, 637, 638, 719-731
Thái, Phạm-Xuân- 750, 758
Thai Chamber of Commerce business directory 89
Thai-English dictionary 723
Thai-English student's dictionary 723
Thai plant names: botanical name, vernacular name 538

Italicized entries are for titles. **Bold entries are subject guides**

Thai reference grammar 727
Thai titles and ranks 255
Thai writing system 730
Thaib gl. St. Pamoentjak, M. 790
Thaik, Eugene 243
THAILAND 71-80, 720
   Agriculture 31, 366, 368
   Biography 75, 239, 241, 242, 251-255
   Business 37, 40, 41, 87-91
   Calendar 299, 609
   Climate 81, 84, 368
   Culture 32, 318, 609
   Documents 300, 304
   Economy 33, 35, 72, 368
   Ethnography 611, 616, 617
   Geography 31, 34, 365-368
   Government 39, 85-88, 90-91, 301
   History 32, 298, 318-320
   Languages 605-609, 612, 616
   Literature 609, 638, 639
   Monuments 112, 419
   Natural resources 33, 368, 484, 491-
   493, 496, 502, 504, 516-517, 521, 525,
   538, 539, 567, 576, 577, 590
   Organizations 42, 74, 92, 239
   Politics 38, 39, 71-79
   Population 81
   Religion 79, 242, 253, 254, 610
   Statistics 39, 71, 72, 74, 76, 77, 80-
   84, 368
   Transport 33, 368, 369
   Topography 82, 368, 369, 385-387,
   389-391, 393-395, 413-420
Thailand 29, 73, 385
Thailand: a country study 71
*Thailand: a handbook of historical
   statistics* 83
Thailand: a travel survival kit 414
Thailand: its people, its society, its culture
   73
Thailand: national resources atlas 368
Thailand: natural resources profile 484
*Thailand: the environment of
   modernisation* 72
Thailand: the rough guide 413

Thailand Army Mapping Department
   368
Thailand Development Research
   Institute 484
Thailand facts and figures 80
Thailand in figures 82
Thailand, Indochina and Burma handbook
   389
Thailand investment July 1987 89
Thailand official yearbook 1964 74
Thailand yearbook 87
Thailand's government 86
Thammasat Mahavitthalayai 252
Thamniap thong thi 416
Than Tun 307, 397
Thành, Trịnh Văn 747
Thanh Nghị 734, 741
Thành-ngữ điển-tích danh-nhân từ-điển
   747
Thành ngữ điển tích 747
Thành tich tám năm hoạt dộng cúa
   chánh phú 1 145
Thao Kun 660
Tharp, James A. 843
Thaung, Bohmu Ba 246
Thaw, Aung 401
The, Dương Thị 445
The-Mulliner, Lian 348
Them, Đoàn- 339
Theobald, W. 412, 483
Theraphan L. Thongkum 616
Thesaurus of the Karen knowledge 835
Thiemmedh, J. 504
Thien, Le-Khac- 756
Thion, Serge 325
Thoa, Phạm Thị 445
Thối, Lê-Văn- 546
Thomas Cook 403, 475
Thomas, Jerome B. 599
Thomas, W. L. 611
Thompson, Laurence C. 762
Thomson, Thomas 524
Thongkum, Theraphan L. 616
Thornton, Thomas 37
Those who were there 265a

Italicized entries are for titles. **Bold entries are subject guides**

Thu-tei-thana abidan-mya hmat-su 651
Thuật ngữ my thuật 748
Thuật ngữ van học, my học:
 Nga-Pháp-Việt 748
Tiêu-từ-điển nhân-vật lịch-sử Việt-Nam
 270
Tiêu từ điển luật và kinh-tế 750
Tim Penyusun Kamus 679
Times atlas of the world 11
Times business directory of Singapore 190
Times comparative dictionary of
 Malay-Indonesian synonyms 707
Timor 208-210, 360
Timor 209
Timor português 210
Tin Maung Latt 63
Tin, Myanaung U 55
Tin, Pe Maung 654, 314
Tinker, Hugh 308
Tipitaka Pali-Myanma abidan 810
To Angkor 424
Toba-Batak-Deutsches Wörterbuch 772
Tobasche spraakkunst 773
Tobelo 851
Tobèloreesch-Hollandsch woordenboek 851
Tóm tắt đặc điểm các họ cây thuốc 596
Tổng niên giám Việt-Nam 152
Tongking 141, 143, 153, 443, 444
Tonkin du Sud, Hanoï 428
Tontemboan 852
Tontemboansch-Nederlandsch woordenboek
 852
Top-1000 231
Topografische Dienst in
 Nederlandsch-Indië 381
Topography 365-482; see also under
 each country
Toradja 850
Tournier 125
Town and Country Planning
 Department 573
Trác, Nguyễn Bá 344
Tradelink 1987/88 SMA directory 191
Trade directory of the Socialist Republic of
 Vietnam 151

Trade directory of Myanmar 61
Traditional recipes of Laos 506
Traditions of royal lineage in Siam 255
Trager, Frank N. 313
Trần Văn Điền 757, 758
Trần Văn Giáp 268
Trang-hoï-duc 144
Transactions of the American
 Philosophical Society 547
Translation series 773
Transport: see under each country
Traveller's handbook to French Indochina
 and Siam 424
Travellers world guides 389
Trawled fishes of southern Indonesia 512
Treasury Department 384
Treaties and engagements affecting the
 Malay States and Borneo 354
Treaties and engagements 354
Tree flora of Indonesia 574
Tree flora of Malaya 571
Tri Amatayakul 417
Tribes of Burma 615
Trịnh Văn Thành 747
Trồng cây ăn trái 581
Tropische groenten 585
Trụ, Lê Ngọc 733
Truong, Ngo Quang 336
Trương-Bửu-Lâm 344
Trương Văn Chinh 761
Trương-Vĩnh-Ký, P. J. B. 759
Từ điển Anh-Việt hiện đại 738
Từ điển Anh ngữ đồng nghĩa phản nghĩa
 757
Từ điển Anh Việt 738
Từ điển bằng tranh Đức và Việt 743
Từ-điển Cham-Việt-Pháp 779
Từ-điển chữ nôm 764
Từ điển công nghiệp thực phẩm Nga-Việt
 580
Từ-điển đàm-thoại Việt-Anh 759
Tự điển đồng nghĩa và phản nghĩa 757
Tự-điển hành-chánh công-quyền
 Việt-Anh-Pháp 750
Từ điển Meo-Việt loại nho 826

Italicized entries are for titles. **Bold entries are subject guides**

Từ điển Nga-Việt 746
Từ điển Pháp-Việt 741
Từ-điển Pháp-Việt pháp-chính-kinh-tài xã-hội 750
Từ điển tên sinh vật Nga-Việt 542
Từ-điển thành-ngữ điển-tích 747
Từ điển thuật ngữ luật học Nga-Trung-Pháp-Việt 750
Từ điển thuật ngữ thư viện học Nga-Anh-Pháp-Việt 753
Từ điển tiếng Việt 732
Tự-điển văn-phạm và cách dụng những tiếng thông dụng 758
Từ-điển Việt-Đức 744
Từ điển Việt-Hoa-Pháp 740
Từ điển Việt-Anh 736
Tủ Sách Hội Dược Học Việt-Nam 596
Tủ sách Viên Khao Cô 344
Tuck, H. N. 410
Tun, Than 307, 397
Tung, Bùi Quang 346
Tung-nan-ya hua-ch'iao wen-jen chuan-lüeh 240
Tuong, Nha Khi 340
Tweedie, M. W. F. 516
Twenty-five years of economic and financial statistics 229
Tylor, E. B. 48
Tzang Yawnghwe, Chao 243
U Tin, Myanaung 55
Uhlenbeck, E. M. 631
Uhlig, Harald 31
Ulack, Richard 365
Umali, Ricardo M. 489
Un Gang, C. 613
Unabridged Malay-English dictionary 686
UNESCO 269, 635
Unger, Leonard 116
Union catalogue of Philippine biographical 296
Union Indochinoise Française ou Indochine Orientale 94
United Nations Economic Committee for Asia 366

United States-Vietnam relations 1945-1967 337
United States Agency for International Development 119, 126, 366
United States Air Force in Southeast Asia 335
United States Army 108
United States Army in Vietnam 335
United States Army, Center of Military History 335
United States Board on Geographic Names 385
United States Embassy in Vientiane 119
United States Mission in Viet Nam 133
United States Navy and the Vietnam conflict 335
United States Operations Mission 85, 418
Universal Burmese-English-Pali dictionary 643
Université de Paris 597
University English-Burmese dictionary 646
University of California publications in linguistics 837
University of Chicago 160
University of Chicago, Philippine Studies Program 221
University of Oxford, Refugee Studies Programme 360
University of Rangoon 644
University of the Philippines Library 239
University of Wisconsin 296
Upahat Phetsarath, Tiao Maha 121
Upakit Silpasarn, Phya 729
Usages de Cochinchine 140
US Army and allied ground forces in Vietnam 334
US Army Special Forces 1961-1971 335
US Marines in Vietnam 335
US Operations Mission: see United States Operations Mission

Italicized entries are for titles. **Bold entries are subject guides**

USAHA Advertising Corporation 192
USAID: see United States Agency for
International Development
USIS 119
Uy Ban Khoa Hoc Xa Hôi Viêtnam
738, 748, 753
Vacananukom phasa law 668
Vacananukrama Khmera 656
Vade mecum commercial 154
Vademecum voor Ned.-Nieuw-Guinea 211
Vajiranana National Library 612
Valencia, M. R. 482
Valeros, Florentino B. 290
Valeros-Gruenberg, Estrellita 290
van Alderwerelt van Rosenburgh, C. R.
W. K. 531
van Alphen, H. 463
van Baarda, M. J. 822
van Bemmelen, Reinout Willem 603
van den Brink, R. C. B. 555, 585
van der Lith, P. A. 204
van der Toorn, J. L. 790, 791
van der Tuuk, H. N. 770, 772, 773
van der Veen, H. 850
van de Wall, V. I. 469
van Hinloopen Labberton, D. 206
Văn hóa tùng thư 445
Văn kien Đảng 341
Văn kien lịch sử Đảng 341
Vanoverbergh, Morice 831
Văn-phạm Việt 763
van Resandt, W. Wijnaendts 241
van Rosenburgh, C. R. W. K. van
Alderwerelt 531
van Royen, P. 559
van Steenis-Kruseman, M. J. 529
van Steenis, C. G. G. J. 529
*Van Stockum's travellers' handbook for
the Dutch East Indies* 462
Văn Tân 732
Varenflora voor Java 555
Variétés tonkinoises 141
Vegetables in south-east Asia 583
Vegetables of the Dutch East Indies 585
Velder, Christian 392

Vella, Walter F. 73
Veloso Pil, Teresita 363
Vercourt, Bernard 589
*Verhandelingen van het Koninklijke
Bataviaas Genootschap* 816, 818
*Verhandelingen van het Koninklijk
Instituut* 632, 767
Verheijen, Jilis A. J. 840
*Verslag eener botanische dienstreis door de
Minahasa* 556
Verslag van bestuur en staat 213
*Versuch einer Grammatik der Dajakschen
Sprache* 841
Vertebrate fauna of the Malay Peninsula
515
Veth, P. J. 463, 466
Vey, J. L. 725
Vickery, Michael 109, 255
Vidal, Jules 541
Việc từng ngày 339
Việc từng ngày 1945-1964 339
Viện Nghiên Cứu Biển 507
Viện Nghiên Cứu Hán Nôm 445
Viện Ngôn Ngữ Học 738, 748, 753
Vientiane 127, 434
Vientiane guide 1991 127
Vies des Gouverneurs Généraux 289
Việt-Anh thong-thoại từ-điển 758
Việt-Anh từ-điển 736
Viet Nam: filed below at Vietnam
Việt-ngữ tinh-nghĩa từ-điển 757
Việt sử thông giám cương mục 346
VIETNAM 93, 99-101, 130-145, 733
 Agriculture 31, 366
 **Biography 130, 155, 241, 242, 256-
 262, 265a-272**
 Business 37, 41, 105-107, 151-154
 Calendar 299, 340, 346, 609
 Chronology 322, 339, 344
 Climate 103, 366
 Culture 32, 99, 132, 134, 338, 609
 **Documents 300, 304, 323, 324, 337,
 341, 343**
 Economy 33, 35, 94, 96, 143, 366
 Ethnography 611, 618, 619, 621-623

Italicized entries are for titles. **Bold entries are subject guides**

Geography 31, 34, 93, 144, 365-367, 370-375, 442

Government 39, 96, 97, 104, 149, 150, 301

History 32, 298, 303, 321, 332-336, 338, 342, 345, 347

Languages 605-609, 620

Literature 155, 268, 269, 638, 639, 747

Migration 95

Monuments 112, 324, 427, 429, 437, 440, 441

Natural resources 33, 366, 485, 492, 493, 496, 502, 507, 516, 519, 526, 542-547, 568, 570, 578, 580-582, 590, 593, 595-597, 601

Organizations 155

Politics 38, 39, 130-144, 342

Population 102, 146, 147

Religion 242, 271, 610, 622

Statistics 39, 93, 102, 103, 135, 146, 147, 366, 373

Transport 33, 366

Topography 366, 370-375, 385-387, 389-391, 393, 394, 421-429, 437-445

Vietnam 437

Vietnam: a country study 130

Vietnam: a guide to reference sources 30

Vietnam: a history in documents 337

Vietnam. Pagoden und Tempel im Reisfeld 437

Vietnam: politics, economics and society 131

Vietnam: the definitive documentation 337

Việtnam bách-khoa tự-điển 735

Vietnam battle chronology 333

VietNam, Cambodia, Laos, and Thailand 1:1,900,800 367

VietNam crisis: a documentary history 1940-1956 337

ViệtNam danh-nhân tự-điển 270

VietNam "demarcation line" 481

VietNam documents and research notes 133, 150

VietNam government organization manual, 1957/58 150

Vietnam, Laos and Cambodia: chronology of events, 1945-68 322

Vietnam, Laos and Cambodia 421

ViệtNam niên-giám thống-kê 146

Vietnam order of battle 334

Việtnam Quốc-Dân Đảng 343

VietNam statistical yearbook 146

Vietnam studies 335

Việtnam tân tự-điển minh-họa 734

Việtnam tự điển 733

Vietnam War: an almanac 333

Vietnam War almanac 333

Vietnamese 526, 542, 570, 582, 593, 595-597, 637, 638, 732-765

Vietnamese encyclopaedic dictionary 735

Vietnamese-English student dictionary 737

Vietnamese-English vocabulary 737

Vietnamese-English conversation dictionary 758, 759

Vietnamese-English archaeological glossary 751

Vietnamese-English dictionary 736, 737

Vietnamese grammar 762

Vietnamese studies 132, 621

Vietnamesisch-deutsches Wörterbuch 744

Villa, Jill Gale de 471

Vinh, Nguyen Nang 580

Viravong, Maha Sila 668, 677

Võ Văn Chi 545

Vocabulaire des termes techniques de medecine 756

Vocabulaire français-thai blanc 800

Vocabulaire moderne et philosophique 750

Vocabulaire philosophique 750

Vocabulaire scientifique 755

Vocabularies in languages of Indonesia 628

Vocabulary English and Peguan 793

Vocabulary of Malay medical terms 702

Vocabulary of the Sgau Karen language 835

Voorhoeve, C. L. 633

Italicized entries are for titles. **Bold entries are subject guides**

Voorhoeve, P. 631
Vouong, Ly 660, 664
Voyage d'exploration en Indo-Chine 16
Vreeland, Herbert H. 111
Vreeland, Nena 181, 199, 220
Vũ Văn Chuyên 596
Vũ Văn Kính 764
Vũ-văn-Lê 754
Vũ-văn-Mẫu 750
VWP-DRV leadership, 1960 to 1973 150
Vỹ, Đào Đăng 735
Wachiwiphak 729
Wade, J. 835
Wainwright, M. D. 15
Wakkayasamphan 729
Walinsky, Louis J. 57
Wang Gungwu 159, 184
War against Japan 302
War Office, Horse Guards, Intelligence
    Division 163
Warneck, Joh. 772
Wat Pho Maen Khunaram 806
Watts, Michael 29
Wau Ecology Institute handbook 500
Way, Nai Tun 792
Wayland, Francis 645
Wayside trees of Malaya 549
Weber, M. 511
Weissblatt, Franz J. 296
Wells, David R. 497
Wenk, Klaus 729
Wernstedt, Frederick L. 361
West Irian 208, 211, 468, 633
Westfall, Gloria 5
Wheatley, Paul 305
Wheeler, Tony 390, 396, 430, 446, 467
Whitaker, Donald P. 108, 118
White Meo-English dictionary 827
Whitfield, Danny J. 338
Whitford, H. N. 575
Whitmore, T. C. 571, 574
Who is who in Indonesian military 285
*Who's who in Asian and Australasian
    politics* 14a
Who's who in Burma 248

Who's who in Burma 1961 247
Who's who in Cambodia: a reference aid
    263
Who's who in Indonesian business 287
Who's who in Indonesia 284
Who's who in Malaya 277
Who's who in Malaysia and Singapore
    277
*Who's who in Malaysia, Singapore and
    Brunei* 277
Who's who in medicine in Burma 250
Who's who in North Vietnam 266
*Who's who in sports in Malaysia and
    Singapore* 281
Who's who in Thailand 251
Who's who in the Philippines 296
Who's who in Vietnam? 267
*Who's who of the Republic of South
    Vietnam* 266
Wijnaendts van Resandt, W. 241
*Wild mammals of Malaya and offshore
    islands* 493
*Wild mammals of Malaya (Peninsular
    Malaysia) and Singapore* 493
Wilkinson, R. J. 687, 688
Willdenow, Carolus Ludovicus 547
Willer, Thomas F. 7
Willis's Singapore guide 455
Willis, A. C. 455
Wilson, Constance M. 83
Wilson, Horace Hayman 317
Win, Ba Thann 399
Win, Lu Pe 792
Winant, Thomas T. 313
Winkler, Joh. 772
Winstedt, R. O. 162, 682, 686, 705
Wirakusumah, R. Momon 799
Wisamanayanam 731
Wolff, John U. 685, 820
Wolters, O. W. 644
Women's International Group 127
Won Zoon Yoon 313
Wong, C. S. 350
Woordenlijst Galelareesch-Hollandsch 822
Words of the Vietnam War 812

Italicized entries are for titles. **Bold entries are subject guides**

Working aid for collectors of Annamese coins 345
World bibliographical series 21, 22, 24-29, 209
World survey of Islamic manuscripts 15b
World's major languages 637
Wörterbuch Burmesisch-Deutsch 648
Wörterbuch Vietnamesisch-Deutsch 744
Wright, I. R. 354
Wulf, Annaliese 437
Wurm, Stephen A. 605
Wyatt, David K. 78
Xiong, Lang 826
Xiong, Nao Leng 826
Xiong, William J. 826
Xmirnop, X. V. 542
Xôrôkin, A. I. 580
Xỹ, Nguyễn Quang 764
Y-Bham Duôn-ya 843
Yale linguistic series 658
Yale University, Southeast Asia Studies 200
Yambot, Efren 234
Yangon 62, 63
Yangon City Development Committee 62
Yangon directory 92-93 62
Yao 853
Yao-English dictionary 853
Yavanskii yazyk 786
Yayasan Indonesia Hijau 498
Yazyk ly 803
Yearbook of Philippine statistics 228
Yearbook of statistics, Singapore 187
Yearbook of statistics, Malaysia 169
Yearbook of the Netherlands East Indies 203
Yen-Nguan Bhikkhu 806
Yi Yi, Daw 651
Yok, Tep 660
Yoon, Won Zoon 313
You Poh Seng 183
Yuk, Lo Man 449
Yule, Henry 51, 813
Yusuf, P. M. 276

Zaidi, Ilias 280
Zaniya, Maung 311
Zasloff, Joseph T. 116, 117
Zeemansgids voor Indonesië 478
Zimmermann, Dale 500
Zimmermann, E. A. W. von 100
Zinn, Howard 337
Zoetmulder, P. J. 784
Zoon Yoon, Won 313

Italicized entries are for titles. **Bold entries are subject guides**